# DUAL CITY
## RESTRUCTURING NEW YORK

# DUAL CITY

## RESTRUCTURING NEW YORK

EDITED BY

John Hull Mollenkopf AND Manuel Castells

RUSSELL SAGE FOUNDATION　　　　　　　NEW YORK

# The Russell Sage Foundation

The Russell Sage Foundation, one of the oldest of America's general purpose foundations, was established in 1907 by Mrs. Margaret Olivia Sage for "the improvement of social and living conditions in the United States." The foundation seeks to fulfill this mandate by fostering the development and dissemination of knowledge about the political, social, and economic problems of America.

The Board of Trustees is responsible for oversight and the general policies of the Foundation, while administrative direction of the program and staff is vested in the President, assisted by the officers and staff. The President bears final responsibility for the decision to publish a manuscript as a Russell Sage Foundation book. In reaching a judgment on the competence, accuracy, and objectivity of each study, the President is advised by the staff and selected expert readers. The conclusions and interpretations in Russell Sage Foundation publications are those of the authors and not of the Foundation, its Trustees, or its staff. Publication by the Foundation, therefore, does not imply endorsement of the contents of the study.

**Library of Congress Cataloging-in-Publication Data**

Dual city: restructuring New York / edited by John Hull Mollenkopf and Manuel Castells
    p.    cm.
  Includes bibliographical references and index.
  ISBN 0-87154-606-X
  ISBN 0-87154-608-6 (pbk)
    1. New York (N.Y.)—Economic conditions.  2. New York (N.Y.)—Social conditions.  I. Mollenkopf, John H., 1946–   .  II. Castells, Manuel.
HC108.N7D83  1991      90-46448
307.76'09747'1—dc20

First Paperback Edition 1992

The paper used in this publication meets the minimum requirements of American National Standard for Information Sciences—Permanence of Paper for Printed Library Materials, ANSI Z39.48-1984.

10 9 8 7 6 5 4 3 2 1

## The City in the Twenty-First Century

THE ROBERT F. WAGNER, SR. INSTITUTE OF URBAN PUBLIC POLICY

THE GRADUATE SCHOOL OF THE CITY UNIVERSITY OF NEW YORK

The Robert F. Wagner, Sr. Institute of Urban Public Policy supports the development of volumes on the City in the Twenty-First Century. The books seek to stimulate dialogue between policymakers and the research community and to provide a broad perspective on issues facing the modern city. Joseph S. Murphy, University Professor of Political Science and Chancellor of the City University of New York from 1982 to 1990, serves as general editor of the series. Asher Arian, Director of the Wagner Institute, is editor.

The Robert F. Wagner, Sr. Institute of Urban Public Policy was established at the Graduate School and University Center of The City University of New York in 1987. It uses the resources of the academic community to understand and address the pressing social problems facing New York City and other large urban areas. Its agenda includes the analysis of the social, legislative, and political legacy associated with Senator Robert F. Wagner, Sr., a key architect of the American welfare state during and after the New Deal.

The preparation of this volume was sponsored by the Committee on New York City of the Social Science Research Council.

**John Mollenkopf, Chair**
The Graduate Center, City University of New York

**Manuel Castells**
University of California-Berkeley and
Universidad Autonoma de Madrid

**Michael P. Conzen**
University of Chicago

**Kenneth T. Jackson**
Columbia University

**Ira Katznelson**
New School for Social Research

**Ann R. Markusen**
Rutgers University

**Olivier Zunz**
University of Virginia

**David L. Szanton, Staff**
Social Science Research Council

# Contributors

**Thomas Bailey,** Conservation of Human Resources Project, Columbia University

**Charles Brecher,** Wagner School of Public Service, New York University

**Steven Brint,** Department of Sociology, Yale University

**Manuel Castells,** Department of City and Regional Planning, University of California-Berkeley and Instituto Universitario de Sociologia de Nuevas Tecnologias, Universidad Autonoma de Madrid

**Frank DeGiovanni,** Community Development Research Center, New School for Social Research

**Matthew Drennan,** Graduate School of Public Administration, New York University

**Stephen Duncombe,** Sociology Program, City University of New York Graduate Center

**Cynthia Fuchs Epstein,** Sociology Program, City University of New York Graduate Center

**Norman Fainstein,** Dean of Liberal Arts and Sciences, Baruch College, City University of New York

**Susan Fainstein,** Department of Urban Planning and Policy Development, Rutgers University

**Ian Gordon,** Department of Geography, University of Reading

**Michael Harloe,** Department of Sociology, University of Essex

**Richard Harris,** Department of Geography, York University

**Raymond Horton,** Graduate School of Business, Columbia University

**Sarah Ludwig,** Urban Research Center, New York University

**Lorraine Minnite,** CUNY Data Service, City University of New York Graduate Center

**John Mollenkopf,** Political Science Program, City University of New York Graduate Center

**Mitchell Moss,** Urban Research Center and Wagner School of Public Service, New York University

**Saskia Sassen,** Department of Urban Planning, Columbia University Graduate School of Architecture Planning and Preservation

**Edward Soja,** Department of Urban Planning, University of California–Los Angeles

**Mercer Sullivan,** Community Development Research Center, New School for Social Research

**Ida Susser,** Health Sciences Division, Hunter College, City University of New York

**Roger Waldinger,** Department of Sociology, City College, City University of New York

# Contents

# Preface and Acknowledgments

This volume is the second of four projected works sponsored by the Research Committee on New York City of the Social Science Research Council. The committee began its work by asking how economic, cultural, and political forces have interacted historically during the mercantile, industrial, and postindustrial phases of New York City's development. This effort produced a first volume, published by the Russell Sage Foundation, entitled *Power, Culture, and Place: Essays on New York City.* Our subsequent work took three paths. The present volume explores the economic, cultural, and political aspects of the postindustrial transformation of New York City, focusing on how economic restructuring and the emergence of a new racial, ethnic, and gender division of labor have influenced such basic processes as class formation, mothering, mass communications, crime, neighborhood change, and political mobilization.

The Committee is supporting two additional projects. *Capital of the American Century*, edited by Martin Shefter, analyzes whether and how New York City succeeded in its efforts to dominate the continental system of cities in the domains of economics, politics, and culture, despite constantly losing competitive advantage. It explores such topics as the relationships between the New York, Tokyo, and London capital markets, the impact of New York elites on U.S. foreign policy, and New York's role in high culture. A final volume, *The Landscape of Modernity*, edited by Olivier Zunz and David Ward, will contain essays on the economic, political, and cultural forces that shaped the origins, development, and uses of New York's highrise corporate office district.

The impetus for founding the New York City Committee in May 1985 came from Kenneth Prewitt, then president of SSRC and now executive vice president of the Rockefeller Foundation, David L. Szanton of the SSRC staff, and Ira Katznelson, then dean of the Graduate Faculty at the New School. Szanton has been a prime force in the Committee's development and achievements, while David Featherman, the current SSRC president, has enabled us to grow in new directions. Dozens of others, including Karen Brody and Marilyn Stevens of the SSRC and Wagner Institute staffs, have also sustained the Committee's work. Especially important have been the Committee's members and the participants in its substantive working groups. The Russell Sage Foundation provided initial funding for the Committee's work and its president, Eric Wanner, and former vice president, Peter De Janosi, have provided sound advice along the way. The Robert F. Wagner, Sr. Institute of Urban Public Policy at the CUNY Graduate Center, under the able direction of Asher Arian, generously funded the Dual City working group which produced this volume. The Spencer Foundation, under the direction of the late Lawrence Cremin, also supported the Committee.

Lisa Nachtigall, publications director at Russell Sage, has ensured that this volume has attained the Foundation's customary level of excellence in production, while Charlotte Shelby has been an indefatigable and always supportive managing editor. Our authors always rallied when called upon to improve their chapters, and the results speak for themselves. It has been a pleasure for us to work with them.

# PART I

# Introduction

# Introduction

## John Mollenkopf / Manuel Castells

Our good city of New York has already arrived at the state of society
to be found in the large cities of Europe; overwhelmed with population,
and where the two extremes of costly luxury in living,
expensive establishments and improvident wastes are presented
in daily and hourly contrast with squalid mixing and hapless destruction.[1]

Philip Hone, 1843

## New York City
## as the Social Laboratory for the New Society

Just as Philip Hone, Richard Henry Dana, and Charles Dickens contrasted
such "dark, filthy, violent, and degraded" places as the "Five Points"
with the bright achievements of Broadway a century and a half ago, observers are again depicting New York as 'two cities," one rich and one
poor.[2] Despite the economic slowdown since the stock market crash of
October 1987, New York incontestably remains a capital for capital, re-
splendent with luxury consumption and high society, as *Town and Country* proclaimed in a cover story on the "empire city." But New York also
symbolizes urban decay, the scourges of crack, AIDS, and homelessness,
and the rise of a new underclass. Wall Street may make New York one of
the nerve centers of the global capitalist system, but this dominant position has a dark side in the ghettos and barrios where a growing population of poor people lives.

These trends have prompted the literary imagination to embrace the
"dual city" metaphor, as in Tom Wolfe's best-selling *Bonfire of the Vani-
ties*. In it, Sherman McCoy, a Wall Street "master of the universe," is
brought low by his contact with the mean streets and political byways of
the South Bronx.[3] Nor is the appeal of the "dual city" metaphor merely

3

journalistic or literary: *New York Ascendant,* the report of the City's Commission on the Year 2000, expressed a similar view. Noting that "New York's poverty is not new," it found that "today's poor live in neighborhoods segregated by class with few connections to jobs. . .a city that was accustomed to viewing poverty as a phase in assimilation to the larger society now sees a seemingly rigid cycle of poverty and a permanent underclass divorced from the rest of society."[4]

The brutal attack by a band of black teenagers, out "wilding" in Central Park, on a young woman investment banker brought home the clash between two subcultures distinguished by race, class, and place that nonetheless uneasily share public spaces. This assault punctuated a series of interracial attacks that began with white youths chasing a black man to his death on a busy highway in Howard Beach, Queens, and continued, shortly before the 1989 Democratic mayoral primary election, with the murder of another black youth who had come to the Italian neighborhood of Bensonhurst to look at a used car.[5]

These events, together with the post-stock market crash economic slowdown, provided the backdrop to a pivotal moment in the city's political development, the defeat of Mayor Edward I. Koch and the election of David N. Dinkins as New York City's first African–American mayor. A coalition centered in the white middle class neighborhoods of Brooklyn, Queens, and Staten Island had twice reelected Mayor Koch, and he saw himself as a strong proponent of middle class values and interests. Rightly or wrongly, others perceived the Koch administration's rhetoric and policies as having worsened the racial and class tensions afoot in New York City during the 1980s.[6]

Growing disaffection from Mayor Koch, reaction against the racial attacks, and coalition-building on behalf of David Dinkins revitalized a liberal electoral alignment that had been dormant since the 1969 reelection of John Lindsay. In the September 1989 Democratic primary blacks combined with both Latinos and a substantial number of white liberals to defeat Mayor Koch and nominate David Dinkins for mayor. In the November general election, the Republican candidate, Rudolph Giuliani, recreated the core of the Koch coalition, but Dinkins was able to retain enough white support (approximately 28 percent of the white voters) to win a narrow victory. The desire among excluded groups for a more responsive government fused with white liberal dismay at emerging divisions within the city to constitute a new, if fragile, majority.

There can be little doubt that New York City's trajectory towards greater racial and income polarization helped bring the Dinkins administration to power and will severely test its ability to govern. This trajectory poses critical questions not only for the city's people and their political leaders, but also for social scientists. These questions require careful analysis, not merely journalistic, literary, or even political recognition.

This volume presents a rigorous examination of emerging patterns of inequality in the postindustrial city and their causes and consequences. It seeks to translate the popular conception of a city divided between rich and poor, white and black, into more subtle research questions about how class, race, ethnicity, and gender divisions have intersected with the city's economic transformation to form complicated new patterns.

We use New York City as a laboratory because, as Saul Bellow wrote, "what is barely hinted in other cities is condensed and enlarged in New York," and because the New York experience illuminates not just one great city, or indeed all large cities, but the forces affecting most of the globe. Just as Chicago was central to nineteenth century urban industrialization, and the founders of modern social science studied it to understand these processes, New York can be viewed as central to understanding the late twentieth century postindustrial transformation.

We begin this exploration by describing how New York City's economic structure has been changing. Next, we relate these structural changes to the formation of a new ethnic, racial, and gender division of labor that provides upward mobility for some groups while isolating others in contracting sectors. We elaborate this analysis by examining the growth of an informal economy, the changing shape of the public sector, and changing spatial patterns of work and residence. With this context, we turn to two occupational strata that characterize the postindustrial city: upper professionals and women clerical workers. We also examine how the tendencies toward polarization may be seen in the spheres of child-rearing and family disorganization, street crime, the mass media, and patterns of neighborhood change. We then analyze how broader economic and cultural trends influence patterns of community organization and electoral participation. The volume concludes by turning outward, comparing New York to Los Angeles and London.

These essays do not present an exhaustive analysis of the transformation of New York. Many other social strata, ranging from white ethnic, blue collar workers to the wealthy and powerful, deserve further study, as does the controversial question of whether an underclass exists in New York. Essays on patterns of inequality in education, income distribution, or race relations would also help provide a more complete picture. We do not argue that New York's experience was the only possible form that the postindustrial transformation could take, or even that the particular form it took was necessary. The following chapters nevertheless do illuminate how global economic restructuring influenced the weaving of the social, cultural, and political fabric in one profoundly revealing case, New York City.

## An Overview of the Postindustrial Transformation

What is the nature of the current restructuring that is creating a postindustrial city? Some reject the term *postindustrial*, arguing that while manufacturing employment has fallen, manufacturing output still constitutes a large portion of the GNP and remains central to the nation's competitive position.[7] Others object to the implication in Daniel Bell's original formulation that knowledge has somehow replaced capital as the organizing principal of the economy. These observations are well taken: our use of *postindustrial* implies neither that industrial production has become economically irrelevant nor that control over knowledge has replaced return on investment as the organizing principal of the world capitalist economy. But the term does capture a crucial aspect of how large cities are being transformed: employment has shifted massively away from manufacturing (and handling goods more generally) toward corporate, public, and nonprofit services; occupations have similarly shifted from manual workers to managers, professionals, secretaries, and service workers.

The enormity and richness of the postindustrial transformation can be compared only to the nineteenth century industrial revolution. Basic changes in global capitalism drove both. Global economic competition, a major technological revolution, the formation of a new international division of labor, the growing power of finance relative to production, the spatial concentration of global financial markets, the growth of global telecommunications networks, and migration from Third World industrializing nations to the core cities of the first world are among the forces at work.[8]

New York is central to these processes, whether one looks at international trade, financial markets, shifting patterns of global investment in manufacturing, or telecommunications technologies. At its core is the Manhattan central business district, where 2 million people work in 600 million square feet of office space. The surrounding 30-county region contains another 8 million jobs, producing a gross city product of $150 billion and gross regional product of $425 billion in 1985.[9] Half of the gross city product, in turn, originates from its advanced corporate service firms. Although the 1987 stock market crash has slowed their growth, over the long term they will continue to drive the city's economic transformation.

New York's share of foreign deposits in U.S. banks[10] and U.S. offices of foreign banks[11] are steadily increasing, while its share of U.S. banking assets has held steady at one-third over the last decade.[12] In 1970, 47 foreign banks in New York City had assets of $10 billion. By 1985, 191 banks with assets of $238 billion had New York offices employing 27,000 people. More importantly, New York City-based firms held a quarter of the assets of the world's 130 largest institutional investors.[13] A quarter of all U.S. securities firms with more than 50 employees were located in New York.[14] The tremendous growth in investment banking between 1977 and 1987 was reversed by the aftermath of the 1987 market crash and the deflation of the 1980s financial boom. But a period of consolidation may well make this industry more competitive in the long term; even now, despite the decline in securities employment, other advanced corporate service sectors continue to grow.

Six of the "big eight" accounting firms and 19 of the world's 30 largest advertising agencies are headquartered in New York City.[15] A third of all U.S. law firms with more than 100 members are located in New York; only one-fifth of all such firms have foreign offices, but half are located in New York City.[16] New York City accounts for 20 percent of national employment in "information intensive industries" and has a higher ratio of such employment than any other city except Washington and Boston.[17] No other city has done more to propagate the forces of global economic change and none has felt their impact more strongly.[18]

As service activities boomed over the last several decades, disinvestment decimated manufacturing in New York City, especially during the crisis of the mid 1970s. Manufacturing remains important to the region, but New York can no longer claim to be an industrial city. Since 1965, the number of *Fortune* 500 industrial firms headquartered in Manhattan fell from 128 to 48, while manufacturing employment dropped from 865,000 (almost a quarter of the total) to 355,000 (under 10 percent of the total).[19] Related sectors like trucking, warehousing, and wholesale trade experienced a similar collapse.

The shift toward corporate, nonprofit, and public services produced important changes in the occupational mix and the nature of the city's labor market at a time when racial succession and immigration were simultaneously reshaping the city's population and labor force. These demographic shifts intersected with economic change to produce a new racial/ethnic/gender division of labor and, as wealth and poverty both grew, new forms of inequality.[20] In the mid 1950s, blue collar white ethnics were the single largest social stratum. Turn-of-the-century immigrants and their children still made up an industrial working class of considerable proportions. Today, their numbers are vastly diminished; those who remain are increasingly elderly.

In their place, three new groups have become predominant: mostly white male professionals and managers; more typically female and black or Latino clerical and service workers; and Latino and Asian manufacturing workers. In the decade of rapid economic growth after 1977, real incomes rose strongly for many groups in the city. But despite the decade of economic expansion, poverty increased from 15 percent in 1975 (about 20 percent over the national average) to 23 percent in 1987 (almost twice the national average).[21]

The increase of female-headed households, low labor force participation rates for virtually all subgroups of the population, and the decline of the real value of transfer payments contributed to the growth of poverty.[22] Moreover, blacks and Latinos have been largely excluded from the most rapidly growing and remunerative occupations in the postindustrial economy.[23] New York has thus been transformed from a relatively well-off, white blue collar city into a more economically divided, multiracial, white collar city.[24]

These transformations had a strong impact on space and place. The magnificence of the Manhattan central business and shopping district and the resurgence of luxury residential areas may be juxtaposed to the massive decay of the city's public facilities and poor neighborhoods. Uses and places associated with the industrial city were abandoned. During the 1970s, the housing market collapsed in large parts of the Bronx, northern Manhattan, the Lower East Side, and Central Brooklyn, all concentrations of poor black and Latino populations, erasing all but a few lingering signs of the white working class cultures that once flourished in these neighborhoods. The South Bronx became a worldwide symbol of urban decay, while major city highways and bridges had to be closed because they were caving in.

Reinforced by the "new immigration" from the Caribbean, the growing black and Latino populations spread outward from the collapsing ghettos into former white working class neighborhoods like East Flatbush, prompting the remaining white ethnics to create defended enclaves on the city's periphery.[25] Meanwhile, the boom in central business office construction, the expansion of nonprofit institutions like hospitals and universities, and gentrification reshaped areas linked to the postindustrial economy. The expanding professional class created new demand for housing, leading to the construction of luxury condominiums, the conversion of manufacturing loft space in Manhattan, and gentrification of late nineteenth century, upper middle class brownstone neighborhoods.

New forms of social inequality thus interacted with the processes of neighborhood formation and group segregation to produce a paradoxical mix of splendor and decay. Between 1969 and 1975, decay and decline provided the predominant motif, especially in disinvested industrial areas, former white working class neighborhoods, and poor black and Latino ghettos. During the 1977–1987 boom, the white middle and upper middle class professional and managerial strata experienced a considerable growth in income. They fashioned their spaces not only in old upper class areas, but fueled the creation of new residential and consumption zones in former industrial areas like SoHo and in townhouse areas like the Upper West Side, Chelsea, Brooklyn Heights, and Park Slope.

The waning white ethnic, middle and lower middle class retreated to enclaves on the city's periphery, while the rising new immigrant lower middle class took their place. Immigrants have flowed into New York from parts of the world being penetrated by the forces of rapid change, ranging from the Caribbean and Latin America to China and other parts of Asia. Meanwhile, the increasing number of poor households, often single mothers and their children, lost market power relative to other groups and became increasingly restricted to the poorest quality housing.

These economic, social, and spatial changes embody the postindustrial transformation as it has occurred in one particular case. Inevitably, these changes have altered the calculus of political interests in New York City. They strengthened the economic and social ecologies of some interests. Core economic institutions like commercial banks, investment banks, corporate law firms, and real estate developers, for example, had the incentive, the means, and the structural and political position to gain government support for their development goals. The economic and fiscal crisis of the mid-1970s clearly made the political environment more receptive to their interests. But they were not the only rising constituency: the increasingly kaleidoscopic racial, ethnic, and gender division of labor also created many other less well organized constituencies.

Others interests were undermined. Most importantly, the descendants of the Irish, German, Italian, and Jewish immigrant workers of the latter half of the nineteenth century waned in number and became more conservative in the face of racial succession. Though Fiorello La Guardia broke ground for both groups in 1933, Italians and Jews did not rise to the top positions within the Democratic party until the 1950s; indeed, the first Jewish mayor was not elected until 1973.[26] But by the 1980s, however, white flight, the growth of the black and Latino populations, and the strength of the new immigration had already made non-Latino whites a minority in the population, if not yet among registered voters. Organizations ranging from the unions that had represented Jewish garment workers or Italian stevedores to the regular Democratic political clubs faced declining membership and weakening power.

The postindustrial transformation thus altered the raw ingredients

**Figure I.1  Map of Places Cited**

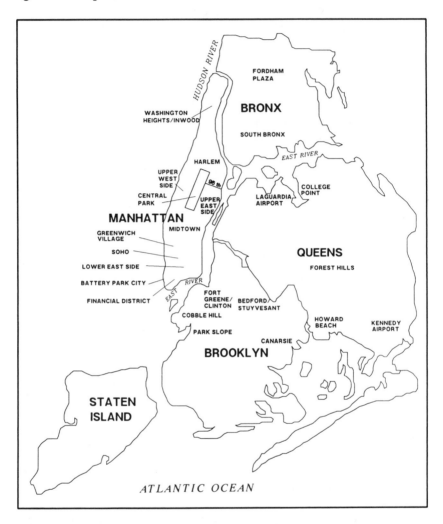

from which political power is fabricated in New York City. In the short run, the Koch administration was able to forge a political coalition based on the declining white electoral constituencies and the rising economic interests that endured for more than a decade. But tensions partly engendered by the policies of this coalition undermined it and opened the way to an alternative coalition based on rising electoral constituencies that ranged from native-born blacks and Puerto Ricans to Caribbean and Latino immigrants to liberal elements of the new white professional strata.

# Dimensions of Polarization

Have the last two decades actually produced a New York composed of two separate and unequal cities, as the popular image would have it? If one could answer this question by looking at trends in income inequality and poverty, the answer would clearly be yes. But the dual city metaphor which the city's income polarization suggests to observers is gravely flawed as an analytic approach. The "two cities" of New York are not separate and distinct, but rather deeply intertwined products of the same underlying processes. Moreover, the complexity of inequality in New York defies simple distinctions between white and black, yuppies and the underclass, Manhattan and the other boroughs. Growing inequality is not the product, for example, of a widening gap between white and black incomes. But even if the dual city metaphor can be scientifically misleading and often rhetorical or ideological, it nevertheless challenges us to explore the dimensions of growing inequality and explain the sources of the tendencies toward polarization.

## Income Inequality and Poverty

The 1977–1987 boom in New York City generated substantial gains in real income and wealth for many of its residents. Despite the halt to the growth in employment after 1987, earnings continued to rise. But Figure I.2 shows that the distribution of these income gains was highly unequal across the different population deciles between 1977 and 1986.

For the bottom 20 percent of the city's households, conditions worsened in absolute as well as relative terms, while the top 10 percent of the population experienced a real income gain of over 20 percent. Although the national income distribution also became more unequal, New York City's trend was worse.[27] The ratio of total income received by the top tenth to that received by the bottom tenth increased from 14.5 to 19.5.[28] Put another way, the top tenth of the population gained almost a third of all income gains and the top 20 percent of the population gained half. Meanwhile, the bottom 20 percent lost not only relative to better-off people, but absolutely compared to what they had a decade earlier.

If prosperity for the upper fifth was one major reason for this growing inequality, the growth of poverty was the other. The total number of persons officially classified as poor climbed from 1.1 million in 1975 to 1.7 million in 1984 and remained at this level in 1987. The number of persons with incomes of less than 75 percent of the poverty level climbed even more steeply, from 560,000 to 1,100,000.[29]

At least four mutually reinforcing factors contributed to this growth in

**Figure I.2    Rates of Growth of Real Incomes, by Income Decile, New York City: 1977–1986 (1986 dollars) (percent change)**

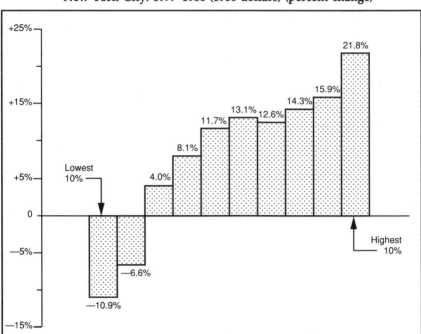

poverty: (1) the number of female-headed households with children grew about 15 percent over this period to almost 400,000 (accounting for 1,350,000 people); (2) the percentage of these households receiving public assistance and the real value of the basic welfare grant fell; (3) labor force participation rates for blacks and Latinos declined slightly during the 1980s, particularly for women; and (4) Latino families fared worse than other groups, and they became a larger proportion of the population.[30] Labor force participation rates are lower for all groups of workers in New York compared to other central cities and the nation, but the gaps are biggest for women, Latinos, and teenagers.[31]

The growth of persistent, extreme, and concentrated poverty has led some social scientists as well as more popular interpreters to embrace the idea of an "underclass" in New York City.[32] Erol Ricketts and his colleagues have defined census tracts having large percentages of female-headed households, welfare families, high school dropouts, and adult men not in the labor force as underclass areas. They found that with less than 3 percent of the national population, New York City accounted for 19 percent of the census tracts so defined.[33]

## The Limitations of the Dual City Metaphor:
## Cross-cutting Distinctions

But can this pattern of growing inequality and worsening poverty be explained, or even illuminated, by the simple metaphor of a dual city or an underclass segregated from the opportunities enjoyed by an overclass? We think not. The mechanisms generating inequality are simply too complex, and the resulting fragmentation too great, to be captured by any simple dichotomy. As Sharpe and Wallock write,

> Besides lacking historical specificity, the two-cities metaphor is deceptively simplistic. [It] limits our comprehension not only of the social processes of advanced capitalism, but of its structural characteristics. The class, ethnic, and racial map of contemporary New York is vastly more complex than the metaphor allows.[34]

We can fully understand the causes of contemporary urban inequality only by examining the social fabric in all its richness. We must explore how economic, cultural, and political forces intersect and interact to shape inequality. Mercer Sullivan's chapter on the economic functions of crime in poor neighborhoods and Saskia Sassen's discussion of the informal economy should warn us away from the idea that so-called underclass areas are isolated from the larger economy.

It is clear that such lines of social division as race, class, ethnicity, gender, and geography do not simply overlap and reinforce each other. As Bailey and Waldinger's chapter shows, income inequality cannot be summarized in a simple dichotomy between prospering white Manhattan corporate service professionals and a black and Latino underclass in the surrounding boroughs. Granted, the economic core is made up of mostly white, mostly male, owners, managers, and professionals, as Steven Brint's chapter shows. But subordinate or peripheral groups take on a kaleidoscopic variety, distinguished by labor force status, occupation, economic sector, race, national origin, gender, household form, community formation, and relation to the welfare state. Different groups face different constraints and opportunities, with different resources, and follow different strategies. Their situations are often ambiguous; their actions produce distinctly postindustrial cleavages.

The inadequacy of simple dichotomous distinctions can be demonstrated easily. For example, differences between whites and blacks do not explain growing income inequality. As Figure I.3 shows, though black median income fell slightly relative to whites' between 1977 and 1980, it recovered by 1986. Instead of lagging uniformly behind whites, many

14

**Figure I.3  Real Median Household Income,
by Racial and Ethnic Group:
New York City: 1977–1986
(1986 dollars)**

**Figure I.4  Real Median Household Income
as Proportion of White
Median Household Income,
by Racial and Ethnic Group:
New York City: 1977–1986
(1986 dollars)**

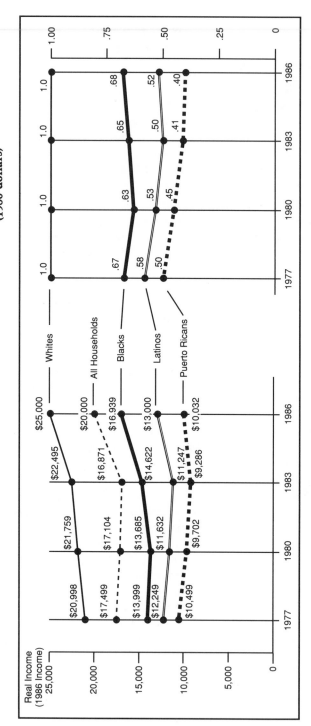

*Source:* For Figures I.1–I.4, Philip Weitzman, *Worlds Apart* (New York: Community Service Society, 1989), Figures 2, 3, and 6.

blacks gained ground. The inequality among blacks thus became greater. On the other hand, Latinos, particularly Puerto Ricans, lagged behind whites and blacks. Puerto Rican median real income fell fully one-fifth relative to whites over the decade, despite falling unemployment rates for Latinos. The chapter by Waldinger and Bailey suggests some of the specific mechanisms that may lie behind these patterns. Blacks were able to expand their access to jobs in government, social services, and a few corporate services, expanding the black middle class. Public service in particular provided a path for upward mobility in income and occupation. Latinos, by contrast, were concentrated in sectors like durable manufacturing that have declined most rapidly in recent decades.

Just as race intersects with income inequality in complex ways, so does ethnicity. The terms *minority, black,* and *Latino* have become misleading abstractions. The so-called new immigration has overwhelmed these categories, dividing them by ethnicity and nativity.[35] Waldinger's work indicates that the foreign-born segment of the black population, some 15 percent of the total, seem to be doing better on average than their native-born counterparts.[36] West Indian, Latin American, and Asian immigration have created vibrant new neighborhoods in Brooklyn, Queens, and the Bronx—a fact incompatible with the notion that class, race, and space intersect only in the form of white prosperity and underclass ghettos. Mitchell Moss and Sarah Ludwig show how this complexity is reflected in the resurgence of immigrant newspapers.

Gender also crosscuts the categories of race and class. On the one hand, as Epstein and Duncombe show in their chapter, the postindustrial labor force is becoming more feminized and women's labor force participation has been rising. On the other, Susser's chapter suggests that traditional mothering is declining. Yet the number of female-headed households has risen and constitutes a major source of poverty and inequality; the low rate of female labor force participation in New York relative to other cities is noteworthy. On issues of work and family, divisions have emerged not only between men and women, with the latter gaining slowly on the former, but among women.

Economic sector also complicates patterns of inequality. The divergence between growing sectors, like investment banking and the social services, and declining sectors, like apparel manufacturing, is clearly delineated in Drennan's opening chapter. Those associated with the former have benefited: those with the latter have suffered. Brecher and Horton's chapter on the public sector shows that this growing sector has its own patterns of development which have simultaneously reinforced market trends while providing benefits to the city's employees and contractors. Even the declining sectors are complex. Sassen shows how informal activities have arisen within declining sectors as more formal and legitimate firms fail. Sullivan also shows how some people have profited by decline. Relations between growing and declining sectors of the economy, while competitive and sometimes antagonistic, have symbiotic aspects. The flight of workers with other choices out of declining sectors has been so rapid as to create opportunities for those, like Latino immigrants, with few choices.

Nor can the differences between "winners" and "losers" in New York City's economy be explained, as Kasarda and others have suggested, by a growing disparity between the education levels required by the jobs in growing sectors of New York's economy and the educational attainments of its black population.[37] The growth of the services has continued demand for low-skilled, low-education labor. Moreover, as Bailey and Waldinger show, many blacks have upgraded their occupational status. Meanwhile, blacks remain underrepresented in certain growing sectors, such as investment banking, and indeed are restricted to lower paid parts of sectors where their share is rising, despite the substantial rise of black educational attainment rates since 1970. These patterns cannot be explained by the mismatch hypothesis, but instead suggest continuing racial discrimination.[38]

## From the Dual City to a More Complex Social Dynamic

Spurred by global restructuring, the postindustrial transformation of New York City has had complicated effects on that city which notions like the dual city or the underclass not only do not capture, but obscure. But despite these flaws, the dual city metaphor has the virtue of directing our attention to the new inequalities that define the postindustrial city, just as depictions of "How the Other Half Lives" defined the emerging industrial city a century ago. The popular embrace of the dual city image urges us to give this phenomenon analytic, as well as political, attention. If simple dichotomies fail to capture the complexity of inequality or the sources of tendencies toward polarization, and if they lead us away from the processes that bind both ends of the polarization together, then how can this complexity best be synthesized? The following chapters provide an interesting theoretical lead about how we might understand the complexity and subtlety of this interaction in New York City.

Many of the chapters suggest that economic restructuring and the new racial/ethnic/gender division of labor have enabled the upper professionals of the corporate sector to form an organizational nucleus for a wider network of middle class managers and professionals which spreads from the economy's corporate sector into its nonprofit and public services. This largely white, disproportionately male stratum has benefited directly and disproportionately from the development of New York City's corporate economy. Certainly, the economic boom between 1977 and 1987 gave great impetus to this group which, until 1989, provided the core constituency for the dominant electoral coalition. Much of what happens in arenas ranging from politics and the housing market to patterns of child rearing and even crime reflects the interests, values, and lifestyles of this stratum.

But economic restructuring and the new racial/ethnic/gender division of labor have placed the remaining social strata in increasingly diverse positions with a multiplicity of interests and values, divided by race, ethnicity, nativity, and gender. Local society is thus increasingly fragmented, hindering potential alliances among these groups and providing ample latitude for the political establishment to capitalize upon differences among them. As a result, cultural, economic, and economic polarization in New York takes the form of a contrast between the organized core of professionals and managers and a disorganized periphery that ranges from Chinese or Dominican women garment workers or restaurant workers through native-born black male civil service professionals to West Indian building tradesmen, and even to white women clerical workers in the central business district.

The chapters in this volume illustrate ways that this differential capacity for social organization is expressed and reinforced in the cultural, spatial, and political structure of New York. In short, the forces that are transforming New York favor the coherent organization of the economic core and tend to disorganize groups outside this core. As with any social construction, this pattern has developed its own contradictions, which came to a head in the mayoral elections of the fall of 1989. The visible social brutality expressed in the image of the dual city, and the cynicism with which former Mayor Edward I. Koch and other leaders appeared to sanction it, generated a crisis of political legitimacy. His governing coalition was based on an alliance between beneficiaries of the boom in real estate and the financial services and the organized public sector producer interests, particularly the regular Democratic party leadership. The collapse of this electoral coalition in the 1989 Democratic primary and Republican Rudolph Giuliani's narrow failure to regroup the economically and socially dominant interests mark the limits of producer-interest politics as an instrument for managing the social tensions of such a dynamic and complex city. The future course of the restructuring of New York will depend significantly on whether Mayor David N. Dinkins can construct a governing coalition able and willing to overcome, rather than embrace, these divisive tendencies.

## Notes

1. Hone, Philip, *Diary 1828–1851*, Tuckerman, Bayard, ed. (New York: Dodd, Mead, 1899), vol. 2, pp. 293–294, as cited in Buckley, Peter G., "Culture, Class, and Place in Antebellum New York," in Mollenkopf, J., ed., *Power, Culture, and Place: Essays on New York City* (New York: Russell Sage Foundation, 1988), p. 30.

2. Lucid, Robert F., ed., *The Journal of Richard Henry Dana, Jr.* (Cambridge: Belknap Press, 1968), vol. 1, p. 119, as cited in Buckley, "Culture, Class, and Place," p. 28; Lindstrom, Diane, "Economic Structure, Demographic Change, and Income Inequality in Antebellum New York," in Mollenkopf, *Power, Culture, and Place*, shows clearly that then, as now, rapid economic growth was accompanied by rising income inequality in New York.

3. Sharpe, William, and Leonard Wallock, "Tales of Two Cities: Gentrification and Displacement in Contemporary New York," in Campbell, Mary B., and Mark Rollins, eds., *Begetting Images: Studies in the Art and Science of Symbol Production* (New York: Peter Lang, 1989), pp. 169–199, trace this theme in contemporary fiction set in New York.

4. *New York Ascendant*, The Report of the Commission on the Year 2000 (New York: Harper & Row, 1988), pp. 51, 53.

5. Stone, Michael, "What Really Happened in Central Park: The Night of the Jogger-and the Crisis of New York," *New York* (August 14, 1989): 30–43, calls the event a "psychic turning point" for the city. For background on the Howard Beach and Bensonhurst attacks, see Kornblum, William, and James Beshers, "White Ethnicity: Ecological Dimensions," in Mollenkopf, *Power, Culture, and Place*, pp. 201–221.

6. Despite a decade of rising real incomes and economic growth, a WNBC/*New York Times* poll of city residents on June 11–16, 1989, reported that 48 percent felt that conditions were getting worse in the city compared to five years earlier, 24 percent felt they were the same; only 22 percent thought conditions had improved. Some 37 percent said race relations had worsened in the last year; only 12 percent saw improvement.

7. Two quite different statements of the view that manufacturing remains central to the long-term prospects of the economy are Cohen, Stephen S., and John Zysman, *Manufacturing Matters: The Myth of the Post-industrial Economy* (New York : Basic Books, 1987); and Hicks, Donald A., *Advanced Industrial Development* (Boston: Oelgeschlager, Gunn, and Hain, 1985). Hicks is more sympathetic to the concept of postindustrialism than are Cohen and Zysman.

8. See Sassen, Saskia, *The Mobility of Labor and Capital* (Cambridge: Cambridge University Press, 1988).

9. Regional Plan Association, "New York in the Global Economy: Studying the Facts and the Issues." Presented to World Association of Major Metropolises meeting, Mexico City, April 1987, p. 1.

10. Drennan, Matthew, "Local Economy and Local Revenues," in Brecher, Charles, and Raymond D. Horton, eds., *Setting Municipal Priorities, 1988* (New York: New York University Press, 1987), p. 28.

11. Noyelle, Thierry, "The Future of New York as a Financial Center." Paper prepared for conference on future shocks to New York, Citizen's Budget Commission, January 24, 1989, Table 6. See also Noyelle, Thierry, ed., *New York's Financial Markets* (Boulder: Westview Press, 1989).

12. Noyelle, "Future," Table 5.

13. Noyelle, "Future," Table 1.

14. Drennan, "Local Economy," pp. 33–34.

15. Ibid. See also Noyelle, Thierry, and Anna Dutka, *International Trade in Business Services: Accounting, Advertising, Law and Management Consulting* (Cambridge: Ballinger, 1988). Recent mergers have reduced the "big eight" to the "big six," but have not changed New York's dominance.

16. Mollenkopf, John, "The Corporate Legal Services Industry," *New York Affairs* 9,2 (1985): 34–49.

17. Drennan, Matthew, "Information Intensive Industries in Metropolitan Areas of the United States," *Environment and Planning A* 21 (1989), Tables 6 and 7.

18. Regional Plan Association, "New York in the Global Economy". More generally, see Glickman, Norman, "International Trade, Capital Mobility, and Economic Growth: Some Implications for American Cities and Regions in the 1980s," in Hicks, Donald, and Norman Glickman, eds., *Transition to the 21st Century* (Greenwich, CT: JAI Press, 1983), 205–240; Noyelle, Thierry, and Tom Stanback, *The Economic Transformation of American Cities* (Totowa, NJ: Rowman & Allanheld, 1983); and Vogel, David, "New York, London, and Tokyo: The Future of New York as a Global and National Financial Center," in Shefter, Martin, ed., *Capital of the American Century?* (forthcoming).

19. Noyelle and Peace, "Information Industries," pp. 10–11; Conservation of Human Resources, *The Corporate Headquarter Complex in New York City* (New York: Conservation of Human Resources, 1977); New York State Department of Labor, "A Quarter Century of Changes in Employment Levels and Industrial Mix" (Bureau of Labor Market Information, 1984), p. 38; New York State Department of Labor, New York City Office, *Annual Labor Area Report*, Fiscal Year 1989 (July 1989), p. 2. Less than half the remaining manufacturing jobs are actually production workers; the rest are front office personnel in manufacturing firms.

20. See Waldinger, Roger, "Changing Ladders and Musical Chairs: Ethnicity and Opportunity in Post-industrial New York," *Politics and Society* 15,4

(1986–87): 369–402, and the chapter by Bailey and Waldinger in this book for discussions of the new ethnic division of labor.

21. City of New York, Human Resources Administration, Office of Policy and Program Development, *Dependency*, Vol. 5 (October 1989), Table 3. See also Tobier, Emanuel, *The Changing Face of Poverty: Trends in New York City's Population in Poverty 1960–1990* (New York: Community Service Society of New York, 1984).

22. City of New York, Human Resources Administration, Office of Policy and Program Development, *Dependency* (June 1988); U.S. Department of Labor, Bureau of Labor Statistics, New York Regional Office, "The Current Population Survey as an Economic Indicator for New York City," Table 6.

23. See Stafford, Walter, *Closed Labor Markets* (New York: Community Service Society, 1987).

24. For a discussion of these trends, see Mollenkopf, "The Postindustrial Transformation of the Political Order in New York City," in Mollenkopf, *Power, Culture, and Place*.

25. For a discussion of this process in Queens, see Kornblum and Beshers, "White Ethnicity."

26. La Guardia's mother was Jewish and he spoke Yiddish, but his identity was more Italian than Jewish. La Guardia was a Republican fusion candidate. Vincent Impellitteri was the first Italian Democrat to be elected, in 1950. Mayor Abraham Beame, a product of the Jewish ascendancy in Democratic party politics, became mayor of New York in 1973.

27. For example, between 1975 and 1987, the percentage of aggregate income received by New York City families in the lowest fifth of the income distribution fell from 5.1 to 3.0 percent, while that of the top fifth rose from 43.8 to 49.2 percent. Only the top fifth gained share. In the U.S., the bottom fifth fell less, from 5.5 to 4.6 percent, and the top fifth gained less, from 40.6 to 42.9 percent, and both the top two fifths gained share. Thus, the family income distribution in New York City worsened considerably more than in the U.S. as a whole. See City of New York, Human Resources Administration, Office of Policy and Program Development, *Dependency*, Vol. 5 (October 1989), Table 2, p. 8. New York's poor also lost more ground in absolute as well as relative terms. In contrast to New York, U.S. House of Representatives, Committee on Ways and Means, "Background Material and Data on Programs within the Jurisdiction of the Committee on Ways and Means," 1988 edition (Washington, DC: U.S. Government Printing Office, March 24, 1988), pp. 740–744, shows that the income of the bottom 20 percent of families and individuals in the U.S. declined only 1 percent in real terms between 1978 and 1986, while that of the top 20 percent climbed 12 percent. See also Harrison, Bennett, and Barry Bluestone, *The Great U-Turn: Corporate Restructuring and the Polarizing of America* (New York: Basic Books, 1988).

28. Weitzman, Philip, *Worlds Apart* (New York: Community Service Society, 1989), Chap. 2, Fig. 5.

29. City of New York, HRA, *Dependency* (1989), Table 11A, 11C.

30. City of New York, HRA, *Dependency* (1989), Table 9A gives the percentage of female-headed households and their rate of public assistance; New York State Department of Labor, New York City Office, *Annual Labor Area Report,* Fiscal Year 1985, Table 7, and Fiscal Year 1989, Table 8, give labor force participation rates for 1975 through 1987. Rosenberg, Terry J., *Poverty in New York 1985-1988: The Crisis Continues* (New York: Community Services Society, 1989), analyzes labor force participation rates by group for the 1980s.

31. Bureau of Labor Statistics, "Current Population Survey," Table 10.

32. For a journalistic account of New York, see Auletta, Ken, *The Underclass* (New York: Random House, 1982). The academic study of the underclass has expanded rapidly in the wake of Wilson, William J., *The Truly Disadvantaged* (Chicago: University of Chicago Press, 1987).

33. Ricketts, Erol, and Isabel Sawhill, "Defining and Measuring the Underclass," *Journal of Policy Analysis and Management* 7,2 (1988): 316–325; Ricketts, Erol, and Ronald Mincy, "Growth of the Underclass 1970–1980" (unpublished paper, The Urban Institute, February 1988).

34. Sharpe and Wallock, "Tales of Two Cities." See also Marcuse, Peter, " 'Dual City': A Muddy Metaphor for a Quartered City" International Journal of Urban and Regional Research 13,4 (December 1989): 697–708; and Steinberg, Stephen, "The Underclass: A Case of Color Blindness," *New Politics* (Fall 1989). "The reality," Marcuse writes, "is neither one of duality or of arbitrary plurality; there are definable, structural differences, along definable lines of cleavage, with definable interrelationships, among groups and the individuals that belong to them. The task of defining these differences is hardly an easy one. The 'dual city' metaphor hinders the task."

35. Waldinger, Roger, "Race and Ethnicity," in Brecher, Charles, and Raymond D. Horton, eds., *Setting Municipal Priorities, 1990* (New York: New York University Press, 1989), pp. 50–79.

36. Waldinger, Roger, "Changing Ladders and Musical Chairs"; Farley, Reynolds, and Walter Allen, *The Color Line and the Quality of Life in America* (New York: Russell Sage Foundation, 1987) Chapter 12, "Race, Ancestry, and Socioeconomic Status: Are West Indian Blacks More Successful?" argues that, controlling for labor force status and experience, occupation, and education, immigrant blacks earned about what native-born blacks did. However, these controls remove a number of important differences between the two groups.

37. For a recent statement, see Kasarda, John D., "Urban Industrial Transition and the Underclass," *The Annals of the American Academy of Political and Social Science* 501 (January 1989): 26–47.

38. Bailey, Thomas, "Black Employment Opportunities," in Brecher and Horton, eds., *Setting Municipal Priorities, 1990,* pp. 80–109. Bailey shows that the discriminatory gap in earnings, controlling for education, did not decrease for black men and increased substantially for black women. See also Stafford, Walter, *Closed Labor Markets: Underrepresentation of Blacks, Hispanics, and*

*Women in New York City's Core Industries* (New York: Community Service Society, 1985); Stafford, Walter W., with Edwin Dei, *Employment Segmentation in New York City Municipal Agencies* (New York: Community Service Society, 1989); and Fainstein, Norman I., "The Underclass/Mismatch Hypothesis as an Explanation for Black Economic Deprivation," *Politics & Society* 15,4 (1986–1987): 403–451.

PART **II**

# The Forces
# of Transformation

# 1

# The Decline and Rise
# of the New York Economy

## Matthew P. Drennan

## Introduction

Little can be understood about the New York City economy without reference to the wider metropolitan area, other metropolitan economies, the national economy, and the international economy. For at least 50 years the central city, artificially bounded in the distant past, has not been a sufficient unit for analysis of the urbanized or metropolitan economy.

The appropriate geographic unit of analysis for the urbanized economy centered in Manhattan south of 60th Street is the New York–Northern New Jersey–Long Island Consolidated Metropolitan Statistical Area (CMSA). It includes 24 contiguous counties in 3 states, of which 11 are in New York (the 5 counties of New York City plus 6 suburban New York counties), 12 are in northern New Jersey, and 1 is in Connecticut.[1] Although the 7.2 million residents of New York City represent only two-fifths of the region's population, the central significance of the city in the region's economy cannot be denied. The non–New York City part of the region (and indeed the non-Manhattan part of the city) still depends strongly on the Manhattan central business district. In 1988, earnings of all people who work in Manhattan were $105 billion. Of that total, $65 billion, or not quite two-thirds, was a net outflow to individuals who reside outside Manhattan; i.e., in the other 4 boroughs ($27 billion) and in the suburbs ($33 billion).[2]

Just as a city is not a sufficient unit of analysis of an urban economy, neither is a nation. From the sixteenth century onward, a focus on national performance has clouded our vision of the national and international economic linkages among cities. Historians of antiquity have focused upon the economic linkages between Athens and its colonial cities throughout the Mediterranean; historians and economists covering the Middle Ages have focused upon the economic and political power exercised by Venice over Constantinople, Dubrovnik, and Bruges. But in the modern era little is known about the economic linkages between London and the colonial capital cities, pre- and postindependence. Little is known about the economic linkages between New York and the cities of the Confederacy, which developed or altered during Reconstruction after the Civil War, and how that might have affected the economic character of those southern cities up to the present time.

This chapter presents a paradox about the New York City economy and then attempts to explain it. The explanation rests upon factors outside the city and forces common to other large cities within large urban areas. The paradox is that at the same time that New York City has become a smaller, poorer, and in some respects less economically important part of the region and nation, it has also remained dominant in some booming economic activities often linked to the international economy. Its recent economic history has thus been one of simultaneous decay and growth.

The urban experts who produced the New York Metropolitan Region Study almost three decades ago did not foresee this paradox. They projected that the city would become smaller within the region, but their population forecasts for the region overshot the mark by almost 7 million and for the city by 0.5 million.[3] They had assumed that fertility rates of the 1950s would continue when, in fact, U.S. fertility peaked in the late 1950s and then went down sharply until the 1980s.[4] Regional employment was overestimated by 1.8 million and city employment by 0.9 million. The employment forecast was closer to the mark: it assumed that the employment to population ratio would decline slightly (from 0.41 to 0.40) when, in fact, it rose to 0.45.[5] Understandably (given their fertility assumptions), they had not anticipated the remarkable rise in female labor force participation over the past three decades. The *Metropolis 1985* forecast also did not anticipate the most central feature of the region's economic transformation over the past 30 years—the decline in manufacturing. The region was expected to add 0.8 million manufacturing jobs from 1956 to 1985, but it lost 0.6 million. The best minds of the late 1950s did not expect New York to become smaller, poorer, and deindustrialized. What can hindsight tell us that they did not see?

# The Decline of New York City

## Becoming Smaller and Poorer

New York City's population of 7.8 million was 52 percent of the region's population in 1955. Fourteen years later, in 1969, the city's population had not changed while the region's population was up to 17.9 million, so the city accounted for only 44 percent of the region's population.[6] By 1988, New York City's population had dropped to 7.3 million and the region's population was up to 18.0 million. The city now accounts for only 41 percent of the region's population, but it has at least held this share in the 1980s.[7] Thus, New York City is smaller absolutely and relatively than it was 30 years ago.

The same is true for almost all large cities in the United States, which collectively showed a peak in population in the 1970 census. There were 26 cities with populations over 500,000 in 1970, up from 21 in 1960, and their aggregate population was 31.8 million, a rise of 3.2 million over 1960. In 1970 those 26 cities accounted for about half the population of their collective metropolitan areas. By 1980, only 22 cities had more than one-half million residents, and their aggregate population had fallen 10 percent since 1970 to 28.4 million. As with New York, there has been some recovery since 1980. In 1986, the population in those largest cities had risen to 30.0 million, but their share of their metropolitan areas' population has continued to diminish to 46 percent.[8]

As in other cities, New York's population has also become more black, Hispanic and Asian. Table 1.1 presents the black and Hispanic origin share of families in large cities. From 1969 to 1979, the share of black families rose markedly, and the share of white families dropped. From 1979 to 1987, although the black and white shares showed little change, the Hispanic share (which includes white and black) jumped up, as did the share of "other," which is mostly Asian.

Over the past two decades, New York City has become poorer relative to the nation, the state, and the region of which it is a part. In 1969, the city's per capita personal income was 24 percent higher than the nation, 5 percent higher than New York State, and 3 percent lower than the region. By 1988, per capita personal income of the city was only 17 percent higher than the nation, the same as the state, and 13 percent lower than the region.[9]

But the region includes the city, and so the extreme income differences within the region are muted. Table 1.2 shows per capita personal income for Manhattan, the other four boroughs, and New York suburbs. In 1979,

Table 1.1   Families in Central Cities of Large Metropolitan Areas (over 1 million), Percent Distribution, by Race and Hispanic Origin

|  | 1969 | 1979 | 1987 |
|---|---|---|---|
| All Families (thousands) | 7,472 | 7,826 | 10,449 |
| White | 75.8% | 69.2% | 67.8% |
| Black | 22.7% | 27.5% | 26.4% |
| Hispanic | N.A. | 11.7% | 16.5% |
| Other | 1.5% | 3.3% | 5.8% |

Sources: Data for 1987 from U. S. Bureau of the Census, Current Population Reports, Series P-60, No. 162, "Money Income of Households, Families, and Persons in the United States: 1987," (1989). Data for 1979 and 1969 from same series, No. 129 (1981) and No. 75 (1970).

Table 1.2   Per Capita Personal Income, Manhattan, Other Four Boroughs, and New York Suburbs: 1979 and 1988

|  | 1979 | 1988 | Percent Change, 1979–1988 |
|---|---|---|---|
| Manhattan | $16,040 | $32,049 | 99.8 |
| Other Four Boroughs[a] | 8,407 | 15,919 | 89.4 |
| Northern Suburbs[b] | 12,537 | 27,490 | 119.3 |
| Long Island[c] | 10,995 | 23,948 | 117.8 |
| Other Four Boroughs as Percentage of |  |  |  |
| Manhattan | 52.4% | 49.7% |  |
| Northern Suburbs | 67.1 | 57.9 |  |
| Long Island | 76.5 | 66.5 |  |

Source: U. S. Department of Commerce, Bureau of Economic Analysis, "County and Metropolitan Area Personal Income," Survey of Current Business (April 1990).

[a]Brooklyn, Queens, Bronx, and Staten Island.
[b]Westchester, Rockland, and Putnam Counties.
[c]Nassau and Suffolk Counties.

per capita income of the four outer boroughs was only 52 percent of the per capita income of Manhattan, 67 percent of the northern suburbs, and 77 percent of the Long Island suburbs. From 1979 to 1987, per capita income growth of the three affluent areas outstripped growth in the other four boroughs so that their relative position became even worse.

But New York's relative income decline is also part of a national pattern. The level of median family income is linked to residential patterns within metropolitan areas and to race. Both white and black families in large metropolitan areas have higher median incomes than nonmetropolitan families (see Table 1.3). That accords with the long held perception of greater affluence in urbanized areas. But large metropolitan areas show a sharp $9000 divergence between central city and suburban median family incomes in 1987. That huge difference prevails for both white and black families. Not only are central city families much less affluent than suburban families regardless of race, but the relative standing of central city families deteriorated from 1969 to 1979. After 1979, white central city's families maintained their relative standing, but black families continued to lose ground. Also, the poverty rate among black families in central cities is almost three times higher than for white families in central cities (31 percent versus 11 percent).

Given that the median black family income is lower than that of whites, that the central city poverty rate among black families is three times greater than that of white families, and that the black population's concentration in large cities has increased while the white concentration has decreased, it is hardly surprising that *all* large cities, not just New York, are becoming poorer relative to their suburban areas.

### Crumbling Pillars of the Economic Base

In 1969, New York City's total employment of 3.8 million was not much different than it had been in the mid 1950s. But then it went into a relentless 8-year decline, bottoming out at 3.2 million in 1977. The subsequent recovery brought employment back to 3.6 million in 1988, still 200,000 below the 1969 peak.[10] Table 1.4, which utilizes a different employment data series, which includes the self-employed, shows that the non–New York City parts of the region had moderate employment growth from 1969 to 1977, but this was not sufficient to offset the massive employment decline in the city. In the post-1977 recovery, the non-city parts of the CMSA had stronger employment growth than the city. Thus by 1989, the CMSA had 2.0 million more jobs than in 1969, while the city had 0.1 million fewer jobs.

The employment losses in New York City since 1969 have been concentrated in producing and moving goods and the headquarters of manufacturing firms, as seen in Table 1.5. Each of the five categories showed huge losses in the city from 1969 to 1988. The region outside the city had gains in three out of five of the categories, but only in one (wholesale trade) was the gain large enough to offset the city's loss. The net result is that the entire region had employment losses in four of the five categories (all but wholesale trade) amounting to one-half million jobs. In the largest category, manufacturing, suburban losses (–133,000) combined with a hemorrhaging of manufacturing jobs in the city (–465,000) resulted in a

Table 1.3    Median Family Income, by Race and Residence:
1969, 1979, and 1987

| | Percentage of Families Below Poverty Level, 1987[b] | 1969 | 1979 | 1987 |
|---|---|---|---|---|
| White Families | | | | |
| United States | 8.2 | $ 9,794 | $20,502 | $32,274 |
| Large metropolitan areas[a] | 7.3 | 11,300 | 23,486 | 37,861 |
| Central cities | 10.7 | 10,073 | 19,731 | 31,773 |
| Suburbs | 5.5 | 11,918 | 25,135 | 40,807 |
| Nonmetropolitan areas | 11.0 | 8,313 | 17,551 | 25,736 |
| Central cities/suburbs | | 84.5% | 78.5% | 77.9% |
| | | | | |
| Black Families | | | | |
| United States | 29.9 | $ 5,999 | $11,644 | $18,098 |
| Large metropolitan areas[a] | 27.8 | 7,275 | 12,975 | 20,659 |
| Central cities | 30.7 | 7,045 | 11,861 | 18,255 |
| Suburbs | 21.2 | 8,235 | 16,505 | 27,090 |
| Nonmetropolitan areas | 40.0 | 3,970 | 9,267 | 12,861 |
| Central cities/suburbs | | 85.5% | 71.9% | 67.4% |

*Sources:* Income data for 1987 from U. S. Bureau of the Census, Current Population Reports, Series P-60, No. 162, "Money Income of Households, Families, and Persons in the United States: 1987" (1989). Data for 1979 and 1969 from same series, No. 129 (1981) and No. 75 (1970). Poverty data for 1987 from same series, No. 163, "Poverty in the United States 1987" (1989).

[a]Population of one million or more.
[b]Poverty rates are for all metropolitan areas, not just the large ones.

net regional loss of 0.6 million jobs. (The count of manufacturing jobs includes jobs in headquarters of industrial corporations.)

But once again, neither the city nor the region are unique in this respect. In the past two decades, the metropolitan areas of the Northeast and North Central states—the manufacturing belt of the nation—have collectively lost substantial numbers of their manufacturing jobs.[11] And the central cities of those metropolitan areas, as New York City, have lost more heavily.[12]

**Table 1.4    Total Employment Trends, by Residence: 1969–1989 (thousands)**

| Area | 1969 | 1977 | 1989 | Average Percent 1969–1977 | Annual Change 1977–1989 |
|---|---|---|---|---|---|
| Manhattan | 2,781 | 2,344 | 2,693 | −2.1 | 1.2 |
| New York City | 4,275 | 3,659 | 4,160 | −1.9 | 1.1 |
| New York Suburbs and Fairfield | 1,763 | 1,990 | 2,874 | 1.5 | 3.1 |
| Northeastern New Jersey | 2,311 | 2,498 | 3,351 | 1.0 | 2.5 |
| Total CMSA | 8,349 | 8,147 | 10,385 | −0.3 | 2.0 |

*Notes:*    New York Suburbs and Fairfield includes Nassau and Suffolk counties on Long Island plus Westchester, Rockland, Putnam, and Orange counties in New York, and Fairfield County in Connecticut.

Northeastern New Jersey includes twelve counties: Essex, Morris, Sussex, Union, Bergen, Passaic, Hudson, Middlesex, Somerset, Hunterdon, Monmouth, and Ocean.

CMSA is the Consolidated Metropolitan Statistical Area, and it includes all of the above areas: namely, New York City (5 counties); New York Suburbs (6 counties) and Fairfield County in Connecticut, and Northeastern New Jersey (12 counties), for a total of 24 counties.

The departure of *Fortune* 500 headquarters has contributed to this crumbling economic base. No other event so alarms the city's business groups. In 1965 there were 128 *Fortune* 500 headquarters in New York City; by 1988, the number was down to 48. But this is not new. In 1917, before there was a *Fortune* 500 list, data compiled from *Moody's Industrials* and annual reports indicate that 150 of the 500 largest industrial corporations were headquartered in New York City.[13] Because of all the churning in the list, the net changes do not represent just moveouts. An analysis of the changes from 1965, when the New York count was 128, to 1975, when the New York count was 90, indicated that the 66 losses were due to moves to suburbs (25), moves out of region (13), acquisition by other corporations (21), and changes in size or reclassification (7). Move-ins (6) and additions to the list because of size or reclassification (22) produced gains of 28.[14]

But the New York City experience is not unique. Data for the ten largest, old metropolitan areas of the Northeast and North Central states indicate that they collectively had 302 of the *Fortune* 500 headquarters in 1957, down just slightly from their 1917 total of 316. But thereafter the headquarters became more footloose. By 1974 they were down to 237 headquarters, with seven of the ten places having losses.[15]

**Table 1.5   Goods Production and Distribution Employment, by Industry: 1969 and 1989 (thousands)**

| Industry | Region | City | Region ex City |
|---|---|---|---|
| **1969** | | | |
| Manufacturing | 1,767 | 826 | 941 |
|   Mfg. Administrative Offices | N.A. | 86 | N.A. |
| Wholesale Trade | 478 | 309 | 169 |
| Water Transportation | 65 | 49 | 16 |
| Trucking and Warehousing | 102 | 41 | 61 |
| Railroads | 25 | 13 | 12 |
| Total | 2,437 | 1,238 | 1,199 |
| **1989** | | | |
| Manufacturing | 1,169 | 361 | 808 |
|   Mfg. Administrative Offices | N.A. | 33 | N.A. |
| Wholesale Trade | 587 | 229 | 358 |
| Water Transportation | 30 | 12 | 18 |
| Trucking and Warehousing | 84 | 26 | 58 |
| Railroads | 11 | 3 | 8 |
| Total | 1,881 | 631 | 1,250 |
| **Employment Change, 1969–1989** | | | |
| Manufacturing | −598 | −465 | −133 |
|   Mfg. Administrative Offices | N.A. | − 53 | N.A. |
| Wholesale Trade | +109 | − 80 | +189 |
| Water Transportation | − 35 | − 37 | + 2 |
| Trucking and Warehousing | − 18 | − 15 | − 3 |
| Railroads | − 14 | − 10 | − 4 |
| Total | −556 | −607 | + 51 |

*Sources:* U. S. Department of Labor, Bureau of Labor Statistics. Nonagricultural establishment employment, unpublished data.

Just as the decline of New York's relative affluence may be explained in the familiar terms of an increased concentration of lower income minorities in central cities and the increased concentration of higher income whites in the suburbs, New York City's crumbling manufacturing base has resulted from trends influencing all large, old central cities. Modern manufacturing operations tend to be in one-story buildings with loading docks and parking facilities on acres of land near interstate highways. It is usually not cost-efficient to build such facilities in old central cities. The rationale for factories in central cities a half century or more ago (a huge labor force with access to public transportation, a huge market, electric power, and rail links) is now irrelevant.

The interstate highway system accelerated the long-run decline in intercity transport costs for goods and people and contributed to shifting manufacturing, wholesale trade, and trucking outside of central cities. Rising central city operating costs and the falling relative costs of moving goods into cities made it clear that firms could serve large city markets without being located in the city. Before the interstate highway system was completed, it was said that eastern Pennsylvania was overnight from New York's garment center. Now, North Carolina is overnight by truck, and jet air freight makes Taiwan and Hong Kong practically overnight from New York. Much the same can be said about the decline of the port and the movement of *Fortune* 500 firms to suburban locations with good airport access.

## The Rise of New York

### Corporate Service Firms

Although technological progress has pulled apart New York City's manufacturing and goods distribution base, the same technological forces have paradoxically fueled the strong rise of the corporate service firms that have led the city's economic recovery since 1977. For example, while jet air travel made headquarters more footloose, it also extended the competitive reach of New York's corporate service firms (law, investment banking, advertising, business consulting, and other business services) deep into other metropolitan markets both in the United States and abroad. Interviews with executives of corporations that had departed New York City for the suburbs or distant locations revealed that all of them continued to use the same New York law firms, investment banks, commercial banks (except for payrolls), and accounting firms as they had when they were in the city.[16] Computer and telecommunications technology, which eliminated thousands of clerical jobs and freed backoffice functions from city locations, also extended the competitive reach of New York City financial institutions, transforming them into national and international operations.

Corporate services clearly drive New York's export activities. Of New York's 53 detailed industry sectors, 21 have been identified through location quotients as export industries over a 20-year time span. Table 1.6 presents their employment grouped by function for 1977 and 1988. As noted, the goods production and distribution group has been declining for decades. Even in the growth period between 1977 and 1989, it fell by 112,000 jobs.

The producer services or corporate services group is comprised of twelve industries, five of which are financial. Corporate services are specialized activities required by corporations, governments, and nonprofit institutions. Those services include telecommunication, air transportation and transportation services, commercial and investment banking, legal services, advertising, computer services, accounting, and business consulting. The producer services group is by far the largest part of the city's export base. It led the recovery of the city since 1977, adding 271,000 jobs.

The consumer services group includes three large industries: private health, private education, and private social services. It has added 165,000 jobs since 1977, and in 1989, with 527,000 jobs, it exceeded the goods production and distribution group. Identifying export industries for the more relevant geographic unit of analysis, the region, reveals very few differences. Private social services, an export industry of the city, is not an export industry of the region. Two additional manufacturing industries— chemicals (which includes pharmaceuticals and cosmetics manufacturing) and instruments—are export industries of the region but not of the city.

The strong expansion in producer and consumer services since 1977 has led to their increased dominance of New York City's export base. By 1989, they represented 78 percent of the city's export industries' employment, up from 68 percent in 1977. So goods production and distribution now account for only 22 percent of export industry employment in New York City.

In the Stanback-Noyelle taxonomy of urban places, areas that specialize in producer and consumer services are classified as "nodal," providing services to a hinterland. They classify four places (New York, Los Angeles, Chicago, and San Francisco) as "national nodal" because their hinterland is the entire nation.[17] In the transformation of the U.S. economy since 1969, nodal places have fared well while those that specialized in goods production have suffered relative and absolute economic decline. Manufacturing places were concentrated in the Northeast and North Central states while the Sunbelt had more nodal places. Snowbelt/Sunbelt is

Table 1.6    Employment in Export Industries of New York City: 1977 and 1989 (thousands)

| Industry | 1977 | 1989 |
|---|---|---|
| Production and Distribution of Goods | | |
| Apparel | 153 | 100 |
| Printing and Publishing | 90 | 89 |
| Leather Goods | 15 | 6 |
| Miscellaneous Manufacturing | 46 | 27 |
| Water Transportation | 23 | 12 |
| Wholesale Trade | 248 | 229 |
| Subtotal | 575 | 463 |
| Producer Services | | |
| Air Transportation | 50 | 51 |
| Transportation Services | 24 | 25 |
| Communication | 76 | 65 |
| Banking | 134 | 169 |
| Security Brokers | 70 | 146 |
| Insurance Carriers | 79 | 64 |
| Insurance Agents | 24 | 28 |
| Real Estate and Miscellaneous Financial | 94 | 114 |
| Business Services | 195 | 297 |
| Motion Pictures | 20 | 22 |
| Legal Services | 39 | 76 |
| Miscellaneous Services | 55 | 74 |
| Subtotal | 860 | 1,131 |
| Consumer Services | | |
| Health Services | 185 | 250 |
| Educational Services | 66 | 99 |
| Social Services and Nonprofit Organizations | 111 | 178 |
| Subtotal | 362 | 527 |
| Total Export Industry Employment | 1,797 | 2,121 |

*Source:* New York State Department of Labor, unpublished data.

a false dichotomy because such Snowbelt places as New York, Boston, Baltimore, and Columbus have had growing, even booming, metropolitan economies over the past decade. They are all nodal places. Manufacturing cities like Detroit, Pittsburgh, Cleveland, Milwaukee, St. Louis, Birmingham, and New Orleans, some Snowbelt and some Sunbelt places, have had weak or declining economies.

Producer services firms have expanded in New York City and other national nodal cities because the benefits of agglomeration are far more important to producer service firms than to manufacturing and headquarters. Producer service firms are information-intensive; information is complex, nonroutine, and not internal to the firm. Mergers and acquisitions require teams of highly specialized lawyers, investment bankers, and consultants. Media campaigns require teams of advertising executives, artists, and media specialists. A "spatial bias" thus favors places that developed a critical mass of firms serving local headquarters before technology enabled them to disperse widely. As Pred says, "The costs of not having a location in a large metropolitan complex favored by spatial biases in the availability and accessibility of information are ordinarily regarded as prohibitive, especially since numerous office and business-service personnel spend 20 hours or more per week exchanging information."[18] Manhattan is the world's largest shopping center for producer services.

### Internationalization

As the major commercial and financial center in the world's largest national economy, New York City has also been well positioned to benefit from the increased global interdependence evident in the expansion of foreign trade, the growth of U.S. assets abroad and of foreign assets in the United States, the growth of international banking, the expansion of foreign capital invested in U.S. securities and credit markets, and the increased volume of international air travel and phone calls from the United States. All have had long-term growth rates well above the rate of growth in the GNP.[19]

The decline in *Fortune* 500 headquarters would suggest that New York's role in managing production has diminished significantly. In 1972, Stephen Hymer theorized that a few world cities would emerge where the management and control of worldwide production would be centralized.[20] He was partly wrong because he did not see that New York could become less important in the management of domestic production even while it became more important in international production, as evidenced by New York City's and region's commanding position as the site for the headquarters of the *Forbes* list of the 100 largest U.S. multinational corporations (see Table 1.7).

Of the 100 largest multinational corporations in the United States (ranked by foreign revenues), 24 had their headquarters in New York City and 16 in the New York suburbs. Those located in New York City are

Table 1.7    Total and Foreign Revenues of U.S. Multinational Corporations: 1986 (dollars in billions)

| Headquarters Location | Number of Firms | Foreign Revenues | Total Revenues | Foreign Revenues as Percentage of Total |
|---|---|---|---|---|
| Greater New York Area | 40 | $212 | $ 515 | 41.2 |
| New York City | 24 | $137 | $ 293 | 46.8 |
| New York City Suburbs | 16 | $ 75 | $ 222 | 33.8 |
| Elsewhere U.S. | 60 | $172 | $ 704 | 24.4 |
| Total | 100 | $384 | $1,219 | 31.5 |

Source: "Global Business Survey," Forbes (July 7, 1987): 152–156.

particularly international. Almost one-half their revenues were from their foreign operations, compared to one-third for the suburban 16. In contrast, the remaining 60 multinationals headquartered elsewhere in the United States received less than one-quarter of their revenues from foreign operations. With foreign revenues of $137 billion in 1986, the New York City 24 accounted for 36 percent of the foreign revenues of the 100 largest American multinational corporations. If the suburban headquarters are added in, the region's share becomes 55 percent.

New York City's corporate service firms were well positioned to capture the benefits from the increasing international interdependence of the U.S. economy. Indeed, the multinational corporations and corporate service firms in New York, London, Tokyo, and other major centers may, in fact, have been the prime creators of this increased global interdependence. They did not just react to it, they helped make it happen.

The focus on the nation-state in the collection of economic data prevents us from knowing the dollar value of New York City corporate service firms' foreign sales. It is probably a larger number than the dollar value of U.S. exports of wheat and soybeans, which are known (by country as well as the total, $7.6 billion). So, to demonstrate the increased international character of corporate service firms in New York City requires indirect evidence.[21]

Foreign deposits at the nation's ten largest banks totaled $195 billion in 1986. Six of the ten are New York City banks and together they had 85% of those foreign deposits, up from their 1976 share of 69%. Foreign-owned banks are an increasing force in New York City. In 1970, 47 foreign banks had assets of $10 billion. In 1985, 191 banks with assets of

$238 billion employed 27,000 in New York City. This is a clear example of how growth impulses are transmitted from one urban center to another.[22]

Of the 251 largest law firms in the United States (firms with more than 100 members), 56 have 1 or more foreign branches, and 28 of those are based in New York City.[23] Six of the "Big 8" accounting firms are head-quartered in New York City, and they are even more internationally oriented than the big law firms. Their 1983 worldwide fees were $8.4 billion, of which $3.7 billion was from foreign work (equivalent to the value of U.S. soybean exports). The "Big 8" firms have twice as many branch offices abroad than they have in North America.

Seven of the ten largest management consulting firms in the United States have their head offices in New York City. They have 73 foreign branch offices. Of the 30 largest advertising agencies in the world, 23 of them are U.S. firms, and 19 are located in New York City. The New York firms had gross income of $3.7 billion in 1983, of which $1.3 billion was from foreign sales.

The bottom line is that of the $98 billion in private sector real gross city product (1982 dollars) generated in New York City in 1988, one-half ($48 billion) originates with the corporate service firms.[24] One can only guess what part of that is derived from foreign business, but that share has undoubtedly gone up.

### Is the Rise of New York Now Ended?
### A Post-Crash Appraisal

The stock market crash of October 1987 ended the palmy days of Wall Street expansion in employment and earnings, the office building boom in Manhattan and the suburbs, and the breathtaking upward spiral of residential property values. Although stock prices recovered their losses by the spring of 1990, the volume of trading is still low by 1987 standards. Other key Wall Street business activities have also turned sour, namely, mergers and acquisitions and junk-bond financing. Many of the heroes of the 1980s are now either in financial difficulties, in jail, or indicted (Trump, Boesky, Milken, and Helmsley).

From the end of 1987 to the spring of 1990, jobs in securities and banking fell by 33,000, construction jobs are down by 8,000, and all private sector employment in the city is 50,000 lower, a 1.6 percent drop. But producer services other than finance have gained 22,000 jobs since the crash, and consumer services are up 97,000. A steady rise in local government employment of 31,000, despite looming state and local budget difficulties, has somewhat offset the private sector loss (see Table 1.8). Cur-

**Table 1.8   Post-Stock Market Crash Employment, by Industry in New York City (thousands)**

|  | 1987 4th Quarter | 1990 2nd Quarter | Change '87–4 to '90–2 |
|---|---|---|---|
| Securities and Banking | 338 | 305 | −33 |
| Real Estate and Other Financial | 216 | 216 | 0 |
| All Other Producer Services | 602 | 624 | +22 |
| Total Producer Services | 1,156 | 1,145 | −11 |
| Consumer Services | 447 | 544 | +97 |
| Construction | 123 | 115 | −8 |
| All Private Sector | 3,055 | 3,005 | −50 |
| Government | 584 | 615 | +31 |
| Total Employment | 3,639 | 3,620 | −19 |

*Source:* New York State Department of Labor, unpublished data.

rent shortfalls in city tax revenue collections may lead, however, to city government layoffs, and certainly to service cuts and tax increases.

There is no doubt that the city's economy is in a crash–induced recession, which has been exacerbated by a slowdown in national economic growth in 1990. But it is only that—a recession, not the beginning of another long economic decline similar to the one that took place between 1969 and 1977. The rise of New York is not over; it is only temporarily stalled. The strongly international producer services sector (both financial and nonfinancial) that has driven the restructuring of the New York economy over the last decade will serve the city well in the 1990s. Post–1992 Western European integration and the opening up of Eastern Europe will stimulate demand for the services which New York exports. Just as Los Angeles, the U.S. gateway city to the Far East, has benefited from economic expansion of the Pacific Rim, so too will New York benefit as the U.S. gateway city to Europe. A European boom will accrue to the benefit of New York's producer service economy and its resident labor force.

## Conclusion

The decline of New York and the rise of New York are not neatly contained in separate sequential time frames—they are concurrent phenomena with some common technological causes. The paradox stated at the beginning of this chapter is resolved in perceiving two cities in one space. The one city, based upon producing and moving goods and upon industrial headquarters, has been in decline for decades. The other city, based upon producer services marketed worldwide, has been mostly on the rise over the same decades. Simultaneous with those opposite economic tides, the city's population became relatively poorer and increasingly minority in its composition. We know that the rising relative poverty is not simply the result of the shrinking manufacturing city and a job mismatch (see Chapter 2 in this book). We know we cannot optimistically hope that the expanding producer services city will reverse the relative poverty. But we do not yet understand how the shrinking economy, the expanding economy, and the rising relative poverty in New York and other cities are all interrelated.

## Notes

1. U.S. Department of Commerce, Bureau of the Census, *Statistical Abstract of the United States: 1987* (Washington, DC: U.S. Government Printing Office, 1986), p. 888.

2. U.S. Department of Commerce, Bureau of Economic Analysis, unpublished computer printouts, "Local Area Personal Income by Major Source," April 1990. See also U.S. Department of Commerce, Bureau of Economic Analysis, unpublished computer printouts, "Local Area Personal Income by Major Source, 1969–1987," April 1989.

3. Vernon, Raymond, *Metropolis 1985* (Cambridge: Harvard University Press, 1960), Appendix Tables A-2 to A-7.

4. U.S. Department of Commerce, Bureau of the Census, *Statistical Abstract, 1987*, Table No. 81, p. 58.

5. Council of Economic Advisors, *Economic Report of the President 1988* (Washington, DC: U.S. Government Printing Office, 1988), pp. 283 and 286.

6. U.S. Department of Commerce, Bureau of the Census, *Statistical Abstract, 1987*.

7. U.S. Department of Commerce, Bureau of Economic Analysis, "County and Metropolitan Area Personal Income," *Survey of Current Business* (April 1990): 34–58.

8. U.S. Department of Commerce, Bureau of the Census, *Statistical Abstract, 1988* (Washington, DC: U.S. Government Printing Office, 1987), Tables Nos. 34 and 37.

9. See Note 7.

10. New York State Department of Labor, unpublished computer tables, "Employees on Nonagricultural Payrolls" (1990).

11. U.S. Department of Labor, Bureau of Labor Statistics, *Employment, Hours, and Earnings, States and Areas, 1939–82* (Washington, DC: U.S. Government Printing Office, 1984).

12. Mieszkowski, Peter, "Recent Trends in Urban and Regional Development," in Mieszkowski, Peter, and Mahlon Straszheim, eds., *Current Issues in Urban Economics* (Baltimore: Johns Hopkins University Press, 1979), p. 10.

13. The 1976 and 1987 count are from Drennan, Matthew P., "Local Economy and Local Revenues," in Brecher, Charles, and Raymond D. Horton, eds., *Setting Municipal Priorities, 1988* (New York: New York University Press, 1987), p. 25. Data for earlier years are from Conservation of Human Resources, *The Corporate Headquarters Complex in New York City* (Montclair, NJ: Allanheld Osmun, 1977), pp. 38–40.

14. Conservation of Human Resources, *Corporate Headquarters Complex*, p. 40.

15. Ibid., p. 38.

16. Ibid., p. 65.

17. Noyelle, Thierry, and Thomas M. Stanback, Jr., *The Economic Transformation of American Cities* (Totowa, NJ: Rowman & Allanheld, 1984), p. 260.

18. Pred, Allan, *City Systems in Advanced Economies* (New York: Wiley, 1977), p. 24.

19. Drennan, Matthew P., "Information Intensive Industries in Metropolitan Areas of the United States," *Environment and Planning A* 21, 1989.

20. Hymer, Stephen, "The Multinational Corporation and the Law of Uneven Development," in Bhagwati, J., ed., *Economics and World Order from the 1970s to the 1990s* (New York: Macmillan, 1972), pp. 113–140.

21. Data in the next three paragraphs are from Drennan, "Information Intensive Industries," pp. 27–35, and Noyelle, Thierry, and Anna Dutka, *International Trade in Business Services: Accounting, Advertising, Law and Management Consulting* (Cambridge: Ballinger, 1988), Tables 2.1, 3.3, 3.4, and 3.6.

22. Pred, *City Systems*, p. 24.

23. Mollenkopf, John, "The Corporate Legal Services Industry," *New York Affairs* 9,2 (1985): 34–49.

24. The estimates of real gross city product are from the author's econometric model and data base for the city and region (GOTHAM). For an explanation of how the estimates are derived, see Drennan, Matthew P., "An Econometric Model of New York City and Region: What It Is and What It Can Do," *Economic Development Quarterly* 3, 4 (November 1989).

# 2

# The Changing Ethnic/Racial Division of Labor

Thomas Bailey / Roger Waldinger

## Economic Change and the Employment of Minorities

The impact of the postindustrial transformation of the nation's cities on their minority populations is a central issue in urban research. The general consensus holds that the shift from goods to services has undermined the historic role that cities have played as staging grounds for the integration of unskilled, newcomer groups. But just why the service economy has this effect remains a matter of considerable debate. One view contends that the root problem is a skills mismatch; that the flight of manufacturing has left low-skill minorities stranded, shut out of the burgeoning service sector because they lack the educational proficiencies that this new growth pole demands. The alternative view emphasizes instead the polarization of the urban economy. Here the argument is that the replacement of manufacturing by services has actually increased the number of low-level jobs in which minority workers are employed while also generating jobs at the top. From this perspective, the problem is that job loss is concentrated in the middle tier of the job hierarchy, leaving more low-paid jobs at the bottom and fewer opportunities to get ahead.

New York represents an extreme case of the changes that have altered urban economies in the United States. In New York the rise of services took place earlier and the shift away from goods production was more far-reaching than elsewhere in the country. On the demographic side, New York is not quite as dominated by its minority population as are some other major cities. Nonetheless, the 1980s have probably seen New York become a "majority minority" city; the latest estimates suggest that together, blacks, Hispanics, and Asians may well comprise the majority of the city's population.

As we shall show, both the mismatch and polarization views are inadequate guides to the economic changes that native minorities and immigrants have undergone in New York. This chapter will attempt to develop an alternative interpretation of the impact of the urban postindustrial transformation on minorities, in the light of the New York experience. Our analysis builds on our previous efforts to address this issue; we now bring new data to bear on the question and also take the story up to date. After examining the mismatch and polarization hypotheses, we present the outlines of an alternative framework and then some general demographic, industrial, and occupational trends in the city over the last 20 years that bear on the controversy. Next, we analyze the employment, occupational, and income trends for native black and foreign-born Hispanics and Asians. We conclude by using our framework to develop predictions about the future of the three groups in question.

Our analysis is based primarily on two sources of data. For our analysis of developments during the 1970s, we use the Public Use Samples from the 1970 and 1980 Censuses of Population. For trends in the 1980s we use published data from the Current Population Survey and from the New York State Department of Labor's Covered Employment series.

## The Changing Urban Economy: Mismatch or Polarization

In general terms, the mismatch hypothesis suggests that the increase in the educational and skill demands of the urban economy have outstripped the skills of an increasingly large segment of the urban population. Thus, minority populations that have traditionally relied on low-skilled employment will no longer have this access to the urban job market.

In the policy discussion within which the mismatch thesis is debated, the story is essentially about black men and how they have been harmed by manufacturing's decline. As Frank Levy notes in his recent volume on income inequality in the 1980 Census Monograph series:

> Between 1950 and 1960 New York. . .had sustained its population through high birthrates and significant in-migration from rural areas. Many of the in-migrants were black, and over the decade the proportion of blacks in the city's population rose from 10 to 15 percent. The in-migrants were coming in search of higher incomes, and in these early postwar years the cities could accommodate them. Cities had both cheap housing and, most impor-

tant, manufacturing jobs. . . .Because of these jobs, cities could still serve as a place for rural migrants to get a start.[1]

What was true in New York as of the late 1950s rapidly changed. As manufacturing declined, the city lost its historic function as a staging ground for unskilled newcomers. Whereas manufacturing jobs had long permitted "immigrants access in to the mainstream economy (albeit to the bottom rungs of the socioeconomic ladder)," the growth of employment in services—whether consisting of high-level jobs or low-skilled jobs in traditionally female occupations—had negative implications, especially for black males.[2] As Levy notes, writing of the postindustrial shift, "for poorly educated black men from rural areas, things were getting worse."[3] The problems of the fathers have since been passed on, in aggravated fashion, to their sons. The population of young blacks has increased disproportionately, and as William Wilson, another proponent of the mismatch, argues, "much of what has gone awry in the inner city is due in part to the sheer increase in the number of young people, especially young minorities."[4] This greatly expanded cohort of young black workers must now enter a labor market in which skill requirements have been greatly increased. To quote Bureau of Labor Statistics Commissioner Samuel Ehrenhalt:

> Projections issued recently by the New York State Department of Labor on average annual openings for New York City over the next several years indicate that over 70 percent of the 286,000 annual job openings in the city will be white collar with 30 percent in professional and managerial occupations characterized by substantial knowledge requirements. Such jobs place a premium on the ability to deal with information, computer and communications skills rather than manual skills and tools. With the knowledge content of jobs increasingly significant, how does this match with New York City's labor supply? While New York City has a large and well-qualified labor force, significant elements find themselves increasingly disadvantaged in functioning in New York City's emerging white collar, communications, and computer oriented knowledge using economy.[5]

The alternative interpretation of industrial restructuring and its impact on minority well-being puts matters in reverse: in this version, it is not the poor who are left out, but rather the middle.[6] Phrased this way, the story about the polarization of urban economies is linked to broader controversies about changes in inequality in the United States. Proponents of the polarization view take a different view of the decline of manufacturing than do advocates of the mismatch hypothesis. If the mismatch view is based on a conception of manufacturing as a locus of entry-level jobs available for the unschooled, the polarization thesis conceptualizes manufacturing as a locus of unionized, primary sector jobs attached to well-developed internal labor markets, which are in turn available to workers of low- or middle-level skills. Thus, Bennett Harrison, in his review of the history of the restructuring of the New England economy, concludes from a comparison of declining manufacturing industries and growing high-tech manufacturing and service industries that "the region's industry mix is becoming increasingly characterized by growing industries which provide relatively unstable and low-wage jobs." Moreover, New England's service/high-tech economy appeared to impose new barriers to upward mobility: displaced manufacturing workers were generally unsuccessful in obtaining high-paid jobs in growth sectors and those who started out at the bottom in the services did not succeed in moving into better-paying jobs. More recent analysis conducted by Harrison and Bluestone confirm the same trend for the U.S. economy as a whole in recent years:

> When we studied to what extent inequality might be due to a shift in employment from the generally high-paying, durable-goods manufacturing sector to the lower-paying service sector, we found. . .about a fifth of the increase in the overall inequality of wages since 1978 is attributable to this shift. Jobs in the durable manufacturing sector pay much more equitably than jobs in the service sector.[7]

The implications of polarization for minorities is generally a muted subtheme in the overall debate.[8] Levy notes that in contrast to the case of white males, the incomes of black males are increasingly polarized, with the split particularly noticeable between 25–34-year-old black males with at least some college and those who never finished high school.[9] Whereas Levy's finding draws our attention to polarization within minority populations, most advocates of the polarization view contend that the shift away from manufacturing produces disproportionate displacement among minorities and thereby widens the split between minorities and whites.[10]

But the emphasis on displacement obscures one of the crucial contentions of the polarization theory, namely, that because the shift to services actually generates jobs for people with relatively low skills, it might also have created the demand for workers willing to work at low-status, low-paying jobs. Indeed this is the position developed by Sassen who argues that "The expansion in the supply of low-wage jobs, particularly pronounced in major cities, can then be seen as creating employment opportunities for immigrants even as middle-income blue and white collar native workers are experiencing high unemployment because their jobs are being either downgraded or expelled from the production process."[11] Such low-wage jobs are increasingly found in the advanced services which "are characterized by a much higher incidence of jobs at the high and low paying ends than was the case in what were once the major growth industries, notably manufacturing."[12] The proliferation of very high-paid workers further adds to the demands for immigrants who are needed to attend to the household needs and elaborate consumption wants of these high-income gentrifiers.[13]

While data can be marshalled to support both displacement and polarization stories, our own research over the last 5 years has developed a more complicated picture of the interaction between the city's structural changes and the fortunes of the various nonwhite ethnic groups that make up a growing part of New York's population. Economic distress among blacks or youth, we have shown, has had little to do with the decline of manufacturing since neither group was particularly dependent on manufacturing before the onset of either the city's economic crisis or its revival. The shift to services, however, has affected the two groups quite differently: youth found their opportunities dwindle because technological changes led to job losses in the city's growth sectors.[14] By contrast, the occupational profile of employed blacks improved over the course of the 1970s, with the result that they were well-positioned to take advantage of the positions that opened up during the rapid growth years of the 1980s.[15] Immigrant employment has burgeoned, precisely in those industries that have declined since the onset of the city's crisis almost 20 years ago. Although this might be grist for the polarization mill, the evidence indicates that despite problems with English-language facility and inadequate educational training, immigrants have made considerable economic progress, through mobility associated with entrepreneurship as well as through movement into growth sectors.[16]

In our view, both the mismatch and the polarization hypotheses share two fundamental weaknesses. First, they put almost exclusive emphasis on the demand side, arguing that changes in the employment opportunities of urban ethnic groups can for the most part be explained by understanding how the structure of the economy has changed. Second, they fail to recognize the tremendous heterogeneity among the minority populations, even among groups with generally low levels of education, in urban centers.[17] These two flaws are integrally related. Once the low-skilled and minority populations are disaggregated, it becomes clear that some groups experience much greater economic and occupational mobility than others. And once these disparities are put into relief, a demand-side explanation begs the question of how to account for different outcomes among groups that all face the same labor market.

Like the alternative theories, our framework recognizes that the structural changes on the demand side are fundamental influences on urban employment. Indeed we concur with mismatch proponents that skill demands in urban economies are clearly rising. But our framework emphasizes two related sets of interactions that both the mismatch and polarization views ignore—the interaction among separate minority/immigrant groups and the differential interactions between those groups and the changing structure of the economy. In the case of New York City, this focus leads us to emphasize three factors:

1. Changes in the relative labor supply of the various ethnic groups, in particular the dramatic drop in the population of native whites after 1970.
2. The tendency for minority groups to be concentrated in particular occupations or industries.
3. The interactions between economic change and group characteristics, which allow groups to become less dependent on those concentrations and to shift to an employment pattern more similar to the labor force as a whole.

The economic changes of the 1970s in New York City were accompanied by dramatic changes in the composition of the labor force. The white non-Hispanic population of the city fell by 2 million—any analysis of the employment trends for the city's minorities that fails to take account of that compositional shift will be misleading. Since whites tend to have the best jobs, their exit expands the job opportunities for all other groups and often allows nonwhites to move up the job hierarchy.

Although this compositional change creates opportunities for minorities in both entry-level and higher-level positions, it does not determine the allocation of the vacancies among the various minority groups. Differences in group characteristics, such as predispositions, skills, and other endowments and societal reactions, in particular, discrimination, interact with the changing economic structure to create initial industrial and occupational specializations. Given the way in which ethnic networks channel the flow of information and job finding assistance, recruitment into positions opened up by the departure of whites tends to build on these original specializations. Indeed, each of the groups we shall analyze has a marked concentration in one or two industries. And since access to ethnic networks is based on particularistic criteria, and job information and assistance comprise scarce resources, the creation of these specializations involves a process of boundary creation and maintenance, restricting members of other groups from jobs or occupations within the niche.

These specializations or niches are sources of employment and opportunities for minorities as long as economic and demographic factors allow those niches to grow. As we shall see, in manufacturing in New York City, ethnic niches could expand in an eroding sector, since the outflow of native-born whites was great enough to offset the effects of sectoral decline. However, the long-term implications of specialization for stable integration into the economy and upward mobility are more complicated. Broadening the economic base is imperative unless a group is small or, if large, has an area of specialization which is large and growing—in either case the employment needs of the group can be satisfied within the niche. Under certain conditions the resources or skills developed within a particular niche can be used to move backward or forward into related economic sectors. Specializations based either in entrepreneurship or in government lend themselves to this type of niche-expansion strategy; by contrast, replacement labor in low-level, declining industries may not provide the type of resources needed to build on the niche developed at the time of initial entry into the labor market. Thus, the employment opportunities of particular groups are determined not only by the process that sorts them into niches, but also by how they use or fail to use those areas of specialization to integrate into the general economy.

## Economic and Demographic Trends in New York City

The outlines of the change in the city's economy are well known and are discussed in detail the previous chapter. Manufacturing employment, which has been falling gradually ever since it had peaked in the late 1940s, took a nosedive in 1969 and eroded severely for the next 6 years, after which time the pace of decline leveled off. Manufacturing was by no means the only sector to do poorly: severe losses were also sustained among private employers in construction; transportation, communications, and utilities (TCU); trade; and personal services. Total employment in the public sector also declined during the mid-1970s though, as Table 2.1 shows, it rebounded by the end of the decade. Only professional services generated substantial numbers of new jobs, though the finance, insurance, and real estate (FIRE) sector, and the business service sector grew substantially in percentage terms.

Although the city's economy has expanded steadily throughout the 1980s, the broad industrial and occupational trends established during the 1980s have continued (see Table 2.2). In contrast to the 1970s, construction has experienced a boom. Manufacturing, whose fortunes seemed to brighten briefly in the late 1970s, has resumed its rapid down-

**Table 2.1  Employment of New York City Residents, by Industry: 1970, 1980**

| Industry | 1970 | | 1980 | | Change | Percent Change % |
|---|---|---|---|---|---|---|
| | Employment | Distribution % | Employment | Distribution % | | |
| Construction | 88,800 | 3.6 | 61,720 | 2.7 | (27,080) | -30.5 |
| Manufacturing | 527,200 | 21.5 | 409,620 | 17.6 | (117,580) | -22.3 |
| TCU | 204,400 | 8.3 | 169,880 | 7.3 | (34,520) | -16.9 |
| Wholesale | 124,100 | 5.1 | 108,060 | 4.6 | (16,040) | -12.9 |
| Retail | 306,800 | 12.5 | 261,740 | 11.2 | (45,060) | -14.7 |
| FIRE | 222,600 | 9.1 | 246,940 | 10.6 | 24,340 | 10.9 |
| Business Services | 128,200 | 5.2 | 144,800 | 6.2 | 16,600 | 12.9 |
| Personal Services | 112,900 | 4.6 | 79,080 | 3.4 | (33,820) | -30.0 |
| Professional Services | 279,200 | 11.4 | 353,300 | 15.2 | 74,100 | 26.5 |
| Miscellaneous | 36,600 | 1.5 | 40,260 | 1.7 | 3,660 | 10.0 |
| Public | 425,600 | 17.3 | 452,060 | 19.4 | 26,460 | 6.2 |
| Total | 2,456,400 | 100.0 | 2,327,460 | 100.0 | (128,940) | -5.2 |

*Sources:* U.S. Census of Population, 1970, 1980, Public Use Sample, by residence.

*Note:* All tables are for New York City.

Table 2.2    Change in Employment, by Industry in New York City: 1980–1987

|              | 1980   | 1987   | Change | Percent Change |
|--------------|--------|--------|--------|----------------|
| Construction | 76.8   | 118.7  | 41.9   | 54.6           |
| Manufacturing| 495.7  | 378.8  | −116.9 | −23.6          |
| TCU          | 257.0  | 214.4  | −42.6  | −16.6          |
| Wholesale    | 246.0  | 236.2  | −9.8   | −4.0           |
| Retail       | 366.8  | 400.8  | 34     | 9.3            |
| FIRE         | 448.1  | 548.9  | 100.8  | 22.5           |
| Services     | 894.4  | 1107.8 | 213.4  | 23.9           |
| Public       | 516.8  | 579.5  | 62.7   | 12.1           |
| Total        | 3301.6 | 3585.1 | 283.5  | 8.6            |

*Source:* New York State Department of Labor, Covered Employment Series, by place of work.

ward slide. Meanwhile, growth has been concentrated in the FIRE, business, and professional services, and public sectors.

These trends in the industrial distribution are not in dispute, but their implications for the distribution of income and the growth or decline of jobs at the bottom of the employment hierarchy are hotly contested. Though employment of 25–64-year-olds declined by 6 percent during the decade, a few occupations expanded, as can be seen from Table 2.3. The number of professionals increased by 16.6 percent, managers were up 27.7 percent, and service workers gained an additional 5.8 percent. All of the blue collar occupations shrank. Industrial change alone did not account for the magnitude of these shifts: within every sector the mix of occupations underwent considerable change as well. The overall trend was toward occupational upgrading, not polarization: the proportion of workers employed in all blue collar occupations (craft, operative, laborer, and service) substantially declined in every sector except professional services; in FIRE and business and repair services blue collar decline occurred despite growing employment in the sector; and in all other sectors, the fall-off in blue collar employment was greater than the proportional decline of the sector.[18]

Due to changes in occupational categories made by the Census Bureau, consistent time series data for occupations for the 1980s are not available; consequently, we display data organized along the new occupational categories for just 4 years, 1983–1986 (Table 2.4). These data show considerable fit with the industrial growth data displayed in Tables 2.2 and 2.3. Professional and managerial jobs grew by almost 24 percent during those

Table 2.3    Employment of New York City Residents, by Occupation: 1970, 1980

| All Employed | 1970 | 1980 | Change | Percent Change |
|---|---|---|---|---|
| Managers | 215,300 | 274,960 | 59,660 | 27.7 |
| Professionals | 392,100 | 457,380 | 65,280 | 16.6 |
| Sales | 168,500 | 131,520 | (36,980) | −21.9 |
| Clericals | 604,000 | 566,460 | (37,540) | −6.2 |
| Craft | 272,400 | 200,340 | (72,060) | −26.5 |
| Semiskilled | 290,200 | 210,180 | (80,020) | −27.6 |
| Transport | 105,300 | 76,520 | (28,780) | −27.3 |
| Laborers | 79,900 | 56,320 | (23,580) | −29.5 |
| Service Workers | 311,000 | 329,180 | 18,180 | 5.8 |
| Private Household | 31,500 | 20,140 | (11,360) | −36.1 |
| Farm | 1,300 | 740 | (560) | −43.1 |
| Total | 2,471,500 | 2,323,740 | (147,760) | −6.0 |

Sources: 1970, 1980 Census of Population, Public Use Samples (tabulations for all employed 25–64 years old).

3 years. Craft jobs grew by over 10 percent while operator jobs continued to decline, falling by 8 percent over the decade. Even within the white collar sector, the lower level jobs grew much more slowly: sales, clerical, and even service occupations followed a pattern of growth that resembled the trajectory of manufacturing more than the finance or business services sectors. Thus, despite a much better overall employment picture in the 1980s, the transformation of the city toward a service- and a professional- and managerial-oriented economy continued.

Although occupational trends are consistent with the characterization of the economy advanced by mismatch proponents, income data reveal a more complex picture. As Table 2.5 shows, earnings inequality among the employed widened between 1970 and 1980. The key indicator is the ratio of mean earnings between workers in the top and bottom quintiles, which grew from 8.34 in 1970 to 9.43 in 1980. Examination of other ratios, however, indicate that growth in earnings inequality was principally confined to very low-wage, male earners, whose median earnings barely increased by a third over the course of the decade. By contrast, earnings in other quintiles suffered marginal erosion; moreover, the female to male disparity narrowed in every quintile. Finally, the earnings data suggest not so much a growth of low-level jobs, but rather a depression of earnings in the remaining low-skilled positions, which is indeed what one would ex-

**Table 2.4    Employment of New York City Residents, by Occupation: 1983–1986**

| | 1983 % | 1983 Number | 1986 % | 1986 Number | Percent Growth |
|---|---|---|---|---|---|
| Executive, Administrative and | | | | | |
| Managerial | 11.7 | 319 | 13.3 | 395 | 23.8 |
| Professional Specialty | 13.9 | 379 | 15.8 | 470 | 23.7 |
| Technicians and Related | | | | | |
| Support | 2.1 | 57 | 2.2 | 65 | 14.0 |
| Sales | 10.3 | 281 | 9.9 | 294 | 4.6 |
| Administrative Support, | | | | | |
| Including Clerical | 23.1 | 631 | 21.8 | 648 | 2.7 |
| Service | 16.6 | 453 | 15.7 | 467 | 3.0 |
| Precision Production, Craft, | | | | | |
| and Repair | 8.3 | 227 | 8.5 | 253 | 11.5 |
| Machine operators, | | | | | |
| Assemblers, and Inspectors | 7.0 | 191 | 5.9 | 175 | −8.2 |
| Transportation and Material | | | | | |
| Moving | 3.5 | 96 | 3.6 | 107 | 12.0 |
| Handlers, Equipment | | | | | |
| Cleaners, Helpers, and | | | | | |
| Laborers | 3.1 | 85 | 2.9 | 86 | 1.8 |
| Other | 0.4 | 11 | 0.4 | 12 | 8.9 |
| Total | 100.0 | 2,730 | 100.0 | 2,972 | 8.9 |

*Sources:* U.S. Department of Labor, Bureau of Labor Statistics, "Geographic Profile of Employment and Unemployment, 1983 and 1986. Bulletins # 2216 and 2279, October 1984 and May 1987.

pect given the severe competitive pressures with which New York's manufacturing sector has been beset.

The polarization view falls short in its empirical claims about changing job structure, yet it does at least venture an answer for the puzzle of why so many immigrants have been moving to New York. Over the course of the 1970s, New York received about 80,000 immigrants each year, the vast bulk of whom came from the Caribbean, Latin America, and Asia. Immigration data for the 1980s indicate little change in national composition, but do suggest that the flows have moved a notch higher, with the number of legal immigrants arriving in New York or adjusting status in New York averaging about 90,000 per year. Although intercensal estimates of New York's ethnic population vary—with some surveys placing the white population at below the 50 percent level and others just above it—all sources confirm a continuing decline in the proportion of white,

**Table 2.5  Mean Earnings, by Quintile, Men and Women: 1970, 1980**

| | Men and Women | | Women | | Men | |
|---|---|---|---|---|---|---|
| | 1970 | 1980 | 1970 | 1980 | 1970 | 1980 |
| Bottom Fifth | $1,979 | $3,229 | $1,073 | $2,432 | $3,300 | $4,373 |
| Second Fifth | $4,934 | $8,202 | $3,421 | $6,200 | $6,200 | $10,036 |
| Third Fifth | $6,854 | $12,018 | $5,009 | $9,903 | $8,200 | $14,464 |
| Fourth Fifth | $9,049 | $16,919 | $6,683 | $13,424 | $10,400 | $19,684 |
| Top Fifth | $16,470 | $30,458 | $10,726 | $22,314 | $19,100 | $35,607 |
| | | | | | | |
| Top Fifth/Bottom Fifth | 8.34 | 9.43 | 10.00 | 9.18 | 5.79 | 8.14 |
| Top Fifth/Second Fifth | 3.34 | 3.71 | 3.14 | 3.48 | 3.08 | 3.55 |
| Top Fifth/Middle Fifth | 2.40 | 2.53 | 2.14 | 2.25 | 2.33 | 2.46 |
| Top Fifth/Fourth Fifth | 1.82 | 1.80 | 1.60 | 1.66 | 1.84 | 1.81 |

| | 1970 | 1970 |
|---|---|---|
| Women: Men | | |
| Bottom Fifth | 0.33 | 0.56 |
| Second Fifth | 0.55 | 0.64 |
| Third Fifth | 0.61 | 0.68 |
| Fourth Fifth | 0.64 | 0.68 |
| Top Fifth | 0.56 | 0.63 |

*Sources:* 1970, 1980 Census of Population, Public Use Samples.

non-Hispanic New Yorkers. Blacks appear to comprise the single largest group of "minority" New Yorkers, but the various estimates also suggest that the number of blacks has grown modestly during the 1980s and that the spurt in minority numbers has mainly been due to large increases among Hispanics, and secondarily among Asians.

If traditional immigrant jobs are disappearing so rapidly, as the mismatch hypothesis suggests, and low-level jobs are not proliferating, contrary to polarization claims, what is the source of opportunity for the immigrants who have been arriving in ever greater numbers? The key to the answer lies in changes in the size of the white population. The 1970s saw severe declines in the numbers of non-Hispanic whites living in New York: as a result of suburbanization and flight to the Sunbelt there were two million fewer whites living in New York in 1980 than a decade before. White losses in the labor market were also disproportionate, with the most severe declines occurring in sectors like manufacturing and retailing, which contained sizeable concentrations of older white workers.

Although the decline in the white population appears to have abated during the past several years, the most recent estimates point to continued erosion in the white population base. Moreover, the white workers who were still employed in low-level manufacturing, service, or retailing jobs in 1980 were nearing the end of their working careers; their likely exits from the labor force may well have opened new vacancies for immigrants. Thus, the changing composition of the work force may have offset the impact of occupational upgrading, producing more, not fewer, low-level job openings for immigrants and minorities.

Compositional effects clearly explain part of the story, but they cannot account for the contrast in various immigrant and minority group employment experiences. In the next sections we will try to explain some of that variation by analyzing the employment trends for three minority groups—native-born blacks, foreign-born Asians, and Hispanics.

## The Employment of Foreign-Born Hispanics and Asians and Native-Born Blacks in New York City: 1970–1986

In this section, we build on our previous work by examining the experience of three groups: native blacks, foreign Hispanics, and foreign Asians. We examine data from the 1970–1980 period, with particular attention to changes in occupations and earnings and the place of New York's heterogeneous ethnic populations in the occupational and earning hierarchies. We also attempt to extend this analysis to the 1980–1987 period. This latter treatment is admittedly speculative—since it involves adjustments from two different data bases—but it provides a reasonable technique for estimating the impact of industrial change on the groups in question. We will fill the reader in on the details of the data bases and manipulations as we move on.

### Native Blacks

The economic position of New York's native black population has been transformed by the bust-and-boom cycles of the city's economy and the simultaneous shifts in its occupational and industrial structure. In net terms, native blacks were among the losers during the downturn of the 1970s; in this respect they differed from Hispanics, Asians, and even immigrant blacks, who actually gained jobs—often in very significant numbers—during this period, as can be seen from the data displayed in Table 2.6. (See Tables 2.10 and 2.14 for comparable data on Asians and Hispanics.) Of course, the native black population gains were much smaller than those other groups', but after taking population size into account, the employment to population rates for black native males fell from 80.9 percent in 1970 to 66.9 percent in 1980, a level which left them below all other ethnic groups. Mitigating these negative developments was the fact that the 1970–1980 employment decline for native blacks was considerably less than the fall-off in the overall economy. The black occupational structure was also overhauled, moving black workers, as a group, to higher-level and in many ways preferable jobs.

The relative deterioration in the black employment–population ratio was not a direct result of the pattern of industrial employment, and it had little to do with the fortunes of manufacturing. In 1970, 15 percent of New York's blacks were manufacturing workers, in contrast to more than a fifth of all employed New Yorkers (see Table 2.6). Overall, native blacks suffered no more from the pattern of industrial decline during the 1970s than did the city's labor force as a whole. Blacks' greatest single industrial liability was their concentration in personal services, where total employment declined by 30 percent during the 1970s. The most striking aspect of the black industrial distribution in 1970—their extreme concentration in public sector employment—proved to be a source of shelter against the ravages of the decade, since government employment grew while private employment declined.

By the end of the decade, employed blacks had experienced a general improvement in their pattern of industry specialization. Fewer blacks were employed in personal services and retail and they had found more jobs in the FIRE, particularly in the professional services sectors. But the

**Table 2.6   Native Black Industrial Employment: 1970, 1980**

| Industry | 1970 Employment | 1970 Distribution % | 1980 Employment | 1980 Distribution % | Change | Percent Change |
|---|---|---|---|---|---|---|
| Construction | 11,100 | 3.0 | 6,900 | 1.9 | (4,200) | −37.8 |
| Manufacturing | 56,200 | 15.0 | 43,580 | 12.0 | (12,620) | −22.5 |
| TCU | 34,400 | 9.2 | 28,880 | 7.9 | (5,520) | −16.0 |
| Wholesale | 10,700 | 2.9 | 10,860 | 3.0 | 160 | 1.5 |
| Retail | 38,400 | 10.3 | 28,080 | 7.7 | (10,320) | −26.9 |
| FIRE | 20,600 | 5.5 | 27,060 | 7.4 | 6,460 | 31.4 |
| Business Services | 18,500 | 4.9 | 20,060 | 5.5 | 1,560 | 8.4 |
| Personal Services | 34,400 | 9.2 | 16,660 | 4.6 | (17,740) | −51.6 |
| Professional Services | 36,900 | 9.9 | 47,500 | 13.0 | 10,600 | 28.7 |
| Miscellaneous | 5,400 | 1.4 | 3,160 | 0.9 | (2,240) | −41.5 |
| Public Sector | 107,200 | 28.7 | 131,540 | 36.1 | 24,340 | 22.7 |
| Total | 373,800 | 100.0 | 364,280 | 100.0 | (9,520) | −2.5 |

*Sources:* 1970, 1980 U.S. Census of Population, Public Use Samples.

most significant development during the decade was the 22.7 percent increase in the proportion of native blacks employed by government—at a time when public employment among prime-age adults increased by just over 6 percent.

The story on the occupation side is more complicated, in part because the occupational shifts reflect both industrial restructuring and changes in the type of jobs that people did *within* industries. Table 2.7, which presents occupational data from 1970–1980, illustrates the impact of native blacks' 1970 dependence on low-skill jobs *outside* of the manufacturing sector: these positions involved precisely those activities that were either spun off to other areas or discontinued during the years of economic contraction. While jobs were lost at the low end, native blacks scored sizeable gains in white collar employment, including significant numbers of professional and managerial jobs. And as shown by the data in the last column of Table 2.6, which measures the change in "share" after controlling for occupational change and relative change in group size, white collar and blue collar changes moved in the opposite direction in every case.[19] Whereas blacks gained in share in professional, managerial, sales, and clerical jobs (which in the former two categories means that their gains were disproportionate to the increases generated in these two growing categories), their losses in all the blue collar categories exceeded the downward impact of economic decline and occupational contraction.

Because the data sources for the intercensal years are inadequate due to small sample size and infrequent collection of nativity data, it is impossible to trace out the post-1980 changes in the employment of the groups with which we are interested. Nonetheless, we have attempted to project employment changes, using 1980 census data as a base, and multiplying group employment in each industry by the proportional 1980–1987 gain or loss displayed in Table 2.2 for that industry for the total New York City economy. What these data show is that by 1980 employed native blacks were well positioned to undergo the radical economic shifts that have transpired in the course of the last several years. Overall, our estimates suggest that if group employment change in each industry was proportional to industry gains or losses, native blacks should have gained a disproportionate share of the jobs generated during that period, despite the continuing decline of New York's low-skill sectors (see Table 2.8). Several factors account for this forecast: blacks' heavy overrepresentation in government, a sector that grew vigorously during this period; their strong, if still slightly underrepresented, concentrations in the burgeoning FIRE and service sectors; and their underrepresentation in the constantly eroding manufacturing sector.

Thus, the overall pattern is one of exit from low-end industries and

**Table 2.7  Native-Born Black Occupational Employment: 1970–1980**

| | 1970 | 1980 | Change | Group Size | Interaction | Shift |
|---|---|---|---|---|---|---|
| Managers | 12,000 | 23,520 | 11,520 | 1,031 | 4,356 | 7,164 |
| Professionals | 34,600 | 49,780 | 15,180 | 2,972 | 8,733 | 6,447 |
| Sales | 10,600 | 10,020 | (580) | 911 | (1,416) | 836 |
| Clericals | 89,300 | 113,560 | 24,260 | 7,671 | 2,121 | 22,139 |
| Craft | 37,400 | 24,760 | (12,640) | 3,213 | (6,681) | (5,959) |
| Semiskilled | 47,600 | 28,540 | (19,060) | 4,089 | (9,036) | (10,024) |
| Transport | 28,100 | 18,140 | (9,960) | 2,214 | (5,266) | (4,694) |
| Laborers | 18,600 | 11,880 | (6,720) | 1,598 | (3,891) | (2,829) |
| Service Workers | 77,700 | 76,640 | (1,060) | 6,674 | 11,217 | (12,277) |
| Private Household | 17,400 | 7,000 | (10,400) | 1,495 | (4,780) | (5,620) |
| Farm | 500 | 60 | (440) | 43 | (172) | (268) |
| Total | 373,800 | 363,900 | (9,900) | 32,109 | (8,143) | (1,757) |

*Sources:* 1970, 1980 Census of Population, Public Use Samples.

*Note:* Tabulations for all employed 25–64 years old.

59

**Table 2.8    Estimated Change in Native-Born Black Employment: 1980–1987**

| Industry | Number | Percent Change |
|---|---|---|
| Construction | 3,764 | 54.6 |
| Manufacturing | (10,277) | −23.6 |
| TCU | (4,787) | −16.6 |
| Wholesale | (433) | −4.0 |
| Retail | 2,603 | 9.3 |
| FIRE | 6,087 | 22.5 |
| Services | 20,848 | 23.9 |
| Public Sector | 15,959 | 12.1 |
| Total | 33,765 | 9.3 |

Source: New York State Department of Labor, Covered Employment Series.

Note: Percent change for all employed New Yorkers (Table 2.2) applied to 1980 industrial employment for group.

occupations, gains in white collar jobs, and continued extreme concentrations in the public sector. What was the net effect of these changes on the labor market position of *employed* native blacks? To answer this question, we first calculated separate earnings quintiles for all employed males and females for 1970 and 1980 and then calculated the proportion of native black males and females that fell within each quintile for the total population of each sex. Those data, displayed in Table 2.9, show a modest gain for native blacks. The basic trend was that the distribution of earnings for men and women alike evened out, with the proportion in the bottom 40 percent declining and the proportion in the top 40 percent expanding. Because these improvements in black distribution occurred at a time of widening earnings disparities among quintiles, however, the fact that half of employed black males were in the bottom two quintiles in 1980 indicates that native blacks have made only limited progress in advancing beyond the ranks of the working poor.

DISCUSSION    Three trends stand out from this review of the changing labor market position of native black New Yorkers: their growing concentration in public sector employment, which employed fully one-third of native blacks in 1980; their extensive transition from blue collar to white collar occupations; and the detachment of a growing proportion of male adults from economic activity. Neither the mismatch nor polarization view would have predicted the two trends among the employed; and while the last development can be read as an instance of polarization, it

**Table 2.9    Income Distribution for Native-Born Blacks: 1970, 1980**

| Quintiles | Men | | Women | |
|---|---|---|---|---|
| | 1970 % | 1980 % | 1970 % | 1980 % |
| Bottom Fifth | 29.62 | 24.00 | 21.41 | 18.82 |
| Second Fifth | 30.87 | 25.80 | 23.14 | 18.75 |
| Third Fifth | 22.02 | 22.60 | 23.49 | 25.36 |
| Fourth Fifth | 11.97 | 19.10 | 20.81 | 21.74 |
| Top Fifth | 5.53 | 8.50 | 11.15 | 15.32 |
| Bottom 40 Percent | 60.49 | 49.80 | 44.55 | 37.57 |
| Top 40 Percent | 17.50 | 27.60 | 31.96 | 37.06 |

Sources: 1970, 1980 Census of Population, Public Use Samples.

Note: This table indicates the percent of the employed members of each group that falls into each quintile for the total population of each sex.

involves a very different kind of differentiation than that implied by the theory.

Although black overrepresentation in government is widely noted, its relationship to the life chances of blacks, as well as its linkages to overall job opportunities, are rarely explored. Our review of the 1970–1980 period suggests that government employment is a niche that cushions blacks heavily against the impact of adverse economic changes—whether cyclical or structural. The analysis of the 1980s reinforces this conclusion: starting the decade with one-third of workers employed in the public sector and the rest dispersed among both growing and declining sectors, blacks should have been sheltered from the winds of change blowing through the private sector. While we must await results of the 1990 census to know for sure, our analysis suggests that changes in any one private sector industry should not have had a major effect on the overall employment picture for native blacks.

Consequently, we conclude that, largely due to their gains in public sector employment, the period since 1970 has been one of improvement in the labor market position of employed native black New Yorkers. To be sure, progress has been limited; the confinement of half of all employed black males to the bottom two earnings quintiles underlines the barriers to continued economic mobility. However, the most troublesome sign among native blacks is not to be found among the employed; rather it is the rising number of blacks who are excluded from the labor force and whose fortunes, it may be argued, increasingly diverge from those blacks who are employed. From this standpoint, polarization may be an apt characterization of the changing situation of New York's native black population. But the emphasis on the contrast between employed and unemployed brings us quite a distance from the arguments of Harrison and Bluestone or Sassen. Polarization now refers to the growing internal stratification between employed and unemployed blacks (and other groups as well); and the debate no longer revolves around the (spurious) issue of whether growth in services multiplies the number of bad jobs, but rather concerns the questions of which jobs, especially entry-level jobs, are allocated to which groups and how.

*Foreign-Born Hispanics*

The experience of immigrant Hispanics stands in sharp contrast to the story we have just told for native blacks. The major trend, of course, is the phenomenal increase in Latino migration to New York that actually began in the early 1960s, but which has continued without stop or slowdown to the present day. So extensive was this migration that the single largest group of 1965–1980 immigrants residing in New York at the time of the 1980 census was 98,000 Dominican newcomers; Ecuadorians and Colombians ranked alongside Dominicans among the ten most populous 1965–1980 immigrant groups as of 1980.

The puzzle of this large migration wave is the question of what drew Latino migrants to New York. A look at the 1970 industrial distribution would suggest that immigrant Hispanics were poised for disaster, heavily overrepresented in many of the industries that would suffer the most devastation during the following decade. Nonetheless, the 1970s saw their employment increase by over 50 percent. And while the proportion of immigrant Hispanics who were employed dropped between 1970 and 1980, the decline was no greater than the fall-off experienced by native whites and thus compared favorably with the fortunes of native blacks.

Table 2.10 presents the industrial employment of foreign-born Hispanics in 1970 and 1980. In 1970, just over a third of these immigrants was employed in manufacturing; by contrast only a fifth of city residents was similarly employed. Personal services, which was to shrink by over 30 percent during the next 10 years, and retail, another sector slated for severe erosion, were the other chief concentrations of Hispanic immigrant employment. The 1980 figures show that the industrial distribution of immigrant Hispanics had actually gotten worse. Although the city's manufacturing sector had eroded severely, and the large increase in immigrant Hispanics should have produced some spillover outside goods production, foreign-born Hispanics were even more concentrated in manufacturing as of 1980 than they had been 10 years before. And what appeared to

**Table 2.10  Foreign-Born Hispanic Industrial Employment: 1970, 1980**

| Industry | 1970 Employment | 1970 Distribution % | 1980 Employment | 1980 Distribution % | Change | Percent Change |
|---|---|---|---|---|---|---|
| Construction | 3,600 | 3.3 | 3,420 | 2.0 | (180) | −5.0 |
| Manufacturing | 37,700 | 34.2 | 60,140 | 35.2 | 22,440 | 59.5 |
| TCU | 5,900 | 5.4 | 9,420 | 5.5 | 3,520 | 59.7 |
| Wholesale | 4,900 | 4.5 | 7,000 | 4.1 | 2,100 | 42.9 |
| Retail | 15,100 | 13.7 | 22,500 | 13.2 | 7,400 | 49.0 |
| FIRE | 9,200 | 8.4 | 15,300 | 8.9 | 6,100 | 66.3 |
| Business Services | 5,300 | 4.8 | 10,560 | 6.2 | 5,260 | 99.2 |
| Personal Services | 7,300 | 6.6 | 11,620 | 6.8 | 4,320 | 59.2 |
| Professional Services | 14,600 | 13.3 | 15,420 | 9.0 | 820 | 5.6 |
| Miscellaneous | 400 | 0.4 | 1,980 | 1.2 | 1,580 | 395.0 |
| Public Sector | 6,100 | 5.5 | 13,700 | 8.0 | 7,600 | 124.6 |
| Total | 110,100 | 100.0 | 171,060 | 100.0 | 60,960 | 55.4 |

*Sources:* 1970, 1980 Census of Population, Public Use Samples.

63

Table 2.11   Estimated Change in Foreign-Born Hispanic Employment: 1980–1987

| Industry | Number | Percent |
|---|---|---|
| Construction | 1,866 | 54.6 |
| Manufacturing | (14,183) | −23.6 |
| TCU | (1,561) | −16.6 |
| Wholesale | (279) | −4.0 |
| Retail | 2,086 | 9.3 |
| FIRE | 3,442 | 22.5 |
| Service | 9,444 | 23.9 |
| Public | 1,662 | 12.1 |
| Total | 2,476 | 1.4 |

*Source:* New York State Department of Labor, Covered Employment Series.

*Note:* Percent change for all employed New Yorkers (Table 2.2) applied to 1980 industrial employment for group.

be a silver lining in the 1970 patterns—a slight overrepresentation in professional services, which grew handsomely in the following 10 years—proved to be of hardly any benefit. By 1980, 9 percent of employed immigrant Hispanics were working in professional services, in contrast to 15 percent of all New Yorkers.

Just how exposed this position left immigrant Hispanics in face of the continuing structural changes of the 1980s can be seen by looking at the employment projections for 1987 (Table 2.11). These estimates are derived by multiplying the group employment in the industry in 1980 by the overall growth of that industry in the city between 1980 and 1987. What they suggest—assuming that the group's share of each industry remained stable—is that immigrant Hispanic employment should have barely risen over a 7-year period while overall employment climbed by 8.6 percent. That this estimate may not be plausible is of little matter; indeed, application of a similar technique for the 1970–1980 period would have also predicted a decline, even though the group's employment jumped by 50 percent. The import of the projection is otherwise: to remind us of how disadvantaged immigrant Hispanics were relative to the changing structure of the economy; and to suggest that factors quite separate from structural change were responsible for the growing employment of this group.

Data on occupational distributions are entirely consistent with what we have seen from the industry side. Because of their tremendous growth, foreign Hispanics gained in every occupation (see Table 2.12). Nevertheless, the strongest growth took place among operatives, where immigrant

**Table 2.12   Foreign-Born Hispanic Occupational Distribution: 1970–1980**

| | 1970 | 1980 | Change | Occupational Change | Group Size | Interaction | Shift |
|---|---|---|---|---|---|---|---|
| Managers | 5,500 | 11,800 | 6,300 | 1,524 | 4,003 | 5,527 | 773 |
| Professionals | 10,700 | 13,620 | 2,920 | 1,781 | 7,787 | 9,569 | (6,649) |
| Sales | 3,700 | 5,520 | 1,820 | (812) | 2,693 | 1,881 | (61) |
| Clerical | 20,800 | 26,820 | 6,020 | (1,293) | 15,138 | 13,845 | (7,825) |
| Craft | 13,200 | 18,600 | 5,400 | (3,492) | 9,607 | 6,115 | (715) |
| Semiskilled | 28,300 | 46,400 | 18,100 | (7,803) | 20,597 | 12,793 | 5,307 |
| Transport | 1,900 | 5,900 | 4,000 | (519) | 1,383 | 864 | 3,136 |
| Laborers | 2,700 | 4,760 | 2,060 | (797) | 1,965 | 1,168 | 892 |
| Service Workers | 21,100 | 34,280 | 13,280 | 1,233 | 15,357 | 16,590 | (3,310) |
| Private Household | 2,200 | 2,800 | 600 | (793) | 1,601 | 808 | (208) |
| Farm | 0 | 40 | 40 | 0 | 0 | 0 | 40 |
| Total | 110,100 | 170,640 | 60,540 | (10,971) | 80,131 | 69,160 | (8,620) |

*Sources*: 1970, 1980 Census of Population, Public Use Samples.

*Note*: Tabulations for all employed 25–64 years old.

65

**Table 2.13     Income Distribution for Foreign-Born Hispanics: 1970, 1980**

|  | Men | | Women | |
|---|---|---|---|---|
| Quintiles | 1970<br>Percent | 1980<br>Percent | 1970<br>Percent | 1980<br>Percent |
| Bottom Fifth | 38.87 | 31.44 | 21.75 | 28.65 |
| Second Fifth | 28.06 | 31.02 | 34.75 | 34.63 |
| Third Fifth | 15.83 | 20.26 | 22.17 | 18.61 |
| Fourth Fifth | 9.56 | 10.37 | 14.07 | 11.50 |
| Top Fifth | 7.68 | 6.91 | 7.25 | 6.61 |
| Bottom 40 Percent | 66.93 | 62.46 | 56.50 | 63.28 |
| Top 40 Percent | 17.24 | 17.28 | 21.32 | 18.11 |

*Sources:* 1970, 1980 Census of Population, Public Use Samples.

*Note:* This table indicates the percentage of the employed members of each group that falls in each quintile for the total population of each sex.

Hispanics recorded a *gain in share* despite the decline registered by the occupation as a whole. And the same pattern of growing shares in declining, blue collar occupations held true for transport operatives, laborers, and craft workers as well. By contrast, the Hispanic immigrant share of employment in service occupations remained essentially unchanged between 1970 and 1980, thus suggesting little connection between the rise of services and the labor market position of this group. Looking at the top of the occupational hierarchy, the data for professional and clerical jobs show that the immigrant Hispanic share actually *fell* when other factors—economic contraction, occupational change, and group change—are controlled.

The gloomy impression is reinforced by data on the income distribution presented in Table 2.13. For men, there was a slight movement from the bottom to the second fifth of the distribution. There was a substantial growth of the middle quintile, but this was at the expense of the number of Hispanic immigrants in the top fifth. The trends for women were even worse. Here, there was a large increase in the women in the bottom fifth and decreases in all the other quintiles, with the largest drops coming at the top. The picture is dampened even further by the fact that the earnings of workers in these bottom-level quintiles failed to keep pace with the gains posted by workers at the top.

DISCUSSION   Despite the profound changes in the city's economy that have taken place over the last 20 years, the employment patterns of Hispanic immigrants have remained remarkably stable. Their dependence on manufacturing and blue collar employment has actually grown, but they do not seem to have experienced a significant relative decline in their employment status. What factors account for this experience? First, some portion of the low-level employment reflects the characteristics of the recent arrivals. Thus a deterioration of the income distribution may have resulted from the arrival of low-skilled recent immigrants rather than a deterioration of resident incomes. Second, the massive exodus of whites from manufacturing actually opened more jobs in manufacturing for other ethnic groups than were lost as a result of the sector's overall decline. The garment industry is a good case in point: during the 1970s whites dropped out of the effective labor supply; and as the numbers of white workers plummeted, immigrant Hispanics, who were already concentrated in garments, were well positioned to take up the slack.[20] Moreover, the small immigrant businesses that account for an important part of Hispanic immigrant manufacturing employment do provide some mobility opportunities for Hispanic immigrants; the continuation of this stream of immigration provides the low-cost labor supply on which those small businesses and the opportunities they represent depend.[21]

## Foreign-Born Asians

Asians were the greatest beneficiaries of the 1965 amendments to the country's immigration laws, and the influx of new Asian immigrants into New York quickly made itself felt in the labor market. The growth among foreign-born Asian workers was even more dramatic than the increase among immigrant Hispanics: numbering only 31,000 in 1970, immigrant Asian workers had tripled by the end of the decade. Retailing was the principal Asian concentration in 1970, which left them extraordinarily dependent on an industry whose fortunes would deteriorate severely over the next 10 years. To make matters worse, Asians were also overrepresented in manufacturing, which accounted for almost one-quarter of their 1970 jobs. Thus, more than one-half of the Asian immigrants in the city in 1970 were employed in two sectors that were to fare much worse than the city as a whole during the subsequent 10 years.

But no disaster occurred. Between 1970 and 1980, when the economically active population in New York was declining, the employment–population ratios for Asian immigrants—both men and women— grew by more than 10 percentage points. The unemployment rates grew slightly, but joblessness among both men and women did not go above 4 percent in 1980, a figure well below the city's average. The 1970 to 1980 years also saw some important shifts in Asians' distribution among industries (see Table 2.14). Although the Asian share of manufacturing jobs remained constant, they grew less dependent on retail trade. Unlike native blacks and foreign Hispanics, Asians were able to benefit from the growth of the FIRE sector. These gains in FIRE were of a piece with an overall pattern of gradual diversification out of the 1970 concentrations.

Nonetheless, Asians entered the 1980s poorly positioned to deflect the blows of structural change. Our projections for 1980 to 1987 show that Asian employment should have increased by only 5.2 percent, assuming, of course, that gains or losses in the industries in which they were employed in 1980 account for all of the employment change (see Table 2.15). As with the case of foreign Hispanics, this estimate cannot be reconciled with other information that we have about the rapidly growing Asian economic base in New York City. In this instance, our assumption about stability in industrial distribution might be a bit faulty, since the influx of highly educated Asians as well as the successful school performance of Asian immigrant children suggest that the overall skill endowment of the group may be rising. But these changes are likely operate at the margins; nobody, to our knowledge, has noticed a sudden disappearance of Chinese restaurants and garment factories or a wave of failure among Korean grocery stores. Hence, the basic point remains: that industrial change has a limited impact on the economic fortunes of New York's immigrant groups; and other explanations must be found to account for the successful integration and adaptation of the newcomers who have arrived in the city over the past twenty years.

Some clues toward such an explanation can be found by reviewing the data on the occupational side, presented in Table 2.16. Immigrant Asians increased their employment in *every* occupation—gains that are not so surprising if one considers the overall increase of the group itself. Nonetheless, occupational shares, adjusted for population and occupational changes, grew in all of the white collar occupations, in sharp contrast to the situation among immigrant Hispanics. Particularly strong gains in share were registered among managers, supporting the arguments we have made elsewhere about the growth of immigrant economies and their positive impact on immigrants' opportunities for upward mobility. Strong increases in share registered among sales and clerical workers also point to the importance of the immigrant-economy connection. While professionals comprise the one exception to the pattern of sizeable gains in white collar shares, absolute levels of employment nonetheless registered impressive growth. Changes on the blue collar side are of equal interest. While Asians made large gains in craft employment, their adjusted shares in the lower-level blue collar occupations of operative and service worker dropped, in clear contrast to the Hispanic case.

Thus, not only did the industrial position of immigrant Asians provide

**Table 2.14  Foreign-Born Asian Industrial Employment: 1970, 1980**

| Industry | 1970 Employment | 1970 Distribution % | 1980 Employment | 1980 Distribution % | Change | Percent Change |
|---|---|---|---|---|---|---|
| Construction | 100 | 0.4 | 1,100 | 1.2 | 1,000 | 1000.0 |
| Manufacturing | 6,200 | 22.6 | 21,960 | 23.1 | 15,760 | 254.2 |
| TCU | 700 | 2.6 | 4,120 | 4.3 | 3,420 | 488.6 |
| Wholesale | 1,200 | 4.4 | 5,440 | 5.7 | 4,240 | 353.3 |
| Retail | 8,100 | 29.6 | 22,960 | 24.2 | 14,860 | 183.5 |
| FIRE | 600 | 2.2 | 7,640 | 8.0 | 7,040 | 1173.3 |
| Business Services | 1,000 | 3.6 | 3,340 | 3.5 | 2,340 | 234.0 |
| Personal Services | 3,100 | 11.3 | 3,800 | 4.0 | 700 | 22.6 |
| Professional Services | 3,800 | 13.9 | 15,500 | 16.3 | 11,700 | 307.9 |
| Miscellaneous | 400 | 1.5 | 580 | 0.6 | 180 | 45.0 |
| Public Sector | 2,200 | 8.0 | 8,600 | 9.0 | 6,400 | 290.9 |
| Total | 27,400 | 100.0 | 95,040 | 100.0 | 67,640 | 246.9 |

*Sources:* 1970, 1980 Census of Population, Public Use Samples.

**Table 2.15    Estimated Change in Foreign-Born Asian Employment: 1980–1987**

| Industry | Number | Percent |
|---|---|---|
| Construction | 600 | 54.6 |
| Manufacturing | (5,179) | −23.6 |
| TCU | (683) | −16.6 |
| Wholesale | (217) | −4.0 |
| Retail | 2,128 | 9.3 |
| FIRE | 1,719 | 22.5 |
| Service | 5,540 | 23.9 |
| Public | 1,043 | 12.1 |
| Total | 4,952 | 5.2 |

*Source:* New York State Department of Labor, Covered Employment Series.

*Note:* Percent change for all employed New Yorkers (Table 2.2) applied to 1980 industrial employment for group.

them with a secure foothold in the economy, it also provided outlets for movement into higher-level occupations. This conclusion is consistent with the data on earnings distribution (Table 2.17). Overall, the proportion of Asians in the bottom income quintiles dropped substantially, with gains occurring in the other quintiles. This pattern, however, obscures important differences between men and women. Whereas the disparity between the earnings of Asian and other men diminished between 1970 and 1980, it increased among women. This change cannot accurately be interpreted as evidence of polarization, since it is likely that other factors—in particular, the large number of entrants, many of whom lacked English-language ability and previous work experience—contributed more powerfully to the growth of very low-paid female workers.

DISCUSSION    Like immigrant Hispanics, foreign Asians have been the inheritors of positions vacated by whites. As we have noted, the white labor force declined disproportionately during the 1970s; and within the sectors in which immigrant Asians were concentrated, the white declines were even more severe. Thus, opportunities for ethnic succession allowed Asians to increase their employment in declining sectors like manufacturing and retail. But the pattern of Asian gain within declining industries differed in one important respect from the Hispanic experience. Because retailing and manufacturing industries—in particular, garments, restaurants, and food retailing—are strongholds of Asian business, the expansion of the Asian niche added jobs at all levels of the job hierarchy, not

**Table 2.16   Foreign-Born Asian Occupational Distribution: 1970–1980**

| | 1970 | 1980 | Change | Occupational Change | Group Size | Interaction | Shift |
|---|---|---|---|---|---|---|---|
| Managers | 2,900 | 11,560 | 8,660 | 804 | 6,689 | 7,493 | 1,167 |
| Professional | 6,800 | 23,860 | 17,060 | 1,132 | 15,686 | 16,818 | 242 |
| Sales | 200 | 4,360 | 4,160 | (44) | 461 | 417 | 3,743 |
| Clericals | 3,200 | 14,540 | 11,340 | (199) | 7,381 | 7,183 | 4,157 |
| Crafts | 500 | 4,100 | 3,600 | (132) | 1,153 | 1,021 | 2,579 |
| Semiskilled | 6,800 | 17,160 | 10,360 | (1,875) | 15,686 | 13,811 | (3,451) |
| Transport | 100 | 1,000 | 900 | (27) | 231 | 203 | 697 |
| Laborers | 100 | 980 | 880 | (30) | 231 | 201 | 679 |
| Service Workers | 6,700 | 16,500 | 9,800 | 392 | 15,455 | 15,847 | (6,047) |
| Private Household | 100 | 800 | 700 | (36) | 231 | 195 | 505 |
| Farm | 0 | 20 | 20 | 0 | 0 | 0 | 20 |
| Total | 27,400 | 94,880 | 67,480 | (16) | 63,204 | 63,188 | 4,292 |

*Sources*: 1970, 1980 Census of Population, Public Use Samples.

*Note*: Tabulations for all employed 25–64 years old.

**Table 2.17   Income Distribution for Foreign-Born Asians: 1970 and 1980**

|  | Men | | Women | |
|---|---|---|---|---|
| Quintiles | 1970 % | 1980 % | 1970 % | 1980 % |
| Bottom Fifth | 47.46 | 35.40 | 28.00 | 27.93 |
| Second Fifth | 19.77 | 22.21 | 22.00 | 23.94 |
| Third Fifth | 11.30 | 16.58 | 20.00 | 14.60 |
| Fourth Fifth | 10.17 | 11.14 | 16.00 | 14.11 |
| Top Fifth | 11.30 | 14.67 | 14.00 | 19.42 |
| Bottom 40 Percent | 67.23 | 57.61 | 50.00 | 51.87 |
| Top 40 Percent | 21.47 | 25.81 | 30.00 | 33.53 |

*Sources:* 1970, 1980 Census of Population, Public Use Samples.

*Note:* This table indicates the percentage of the employed members of each group that falls into each quintile for the total population of each sex.

disproportional gains at low levels, as was the case among Hispanics. Moreover, the economic position of Asians has been strengthened as a result of movement out of the traditional sectors of the ethnic economy. To some extent, gains in FIRE and professional services may actually reflect a diversification of the ethnic economy itself; in fact, enclaves like Chinatown and Flushing are important centers of professional and business services for the Asian community. But it also appears likely that gains in the services have taken place outside the ethnic economy, reflecting the integration of Asians into the broader economy.

# Developments in the Future

The framework in this chapter has emphasized three factors: changes in the relative labor supply of the various ethnic groups; the tendency for minority groups to be concentrated in particular occupations or industries; and the interactions between economic change and group characteristics which differentially allow groups to shift to an employment pattern more similar to the labor force as a whole. This analysis suggests a number of predictions about the prospects of the three ethnic groups that we have studied in this chapter.

## Native Blacks

As we have argued, the black vulnerability in 1970 did not result from their concentration in manufacturing, but rather from their overrepresentation in personal service and low-level occupations outside of manufacturing. The exodus of whites opened some higher-level white collar occupations; consequently, blacks as a group moved into these jobs and out of personal services and low-skilled blue collar work. Of course, the main locus of concentration—the public sector—held up relatively well. Indeed, much of blacks' occupational progress and the benefit they derived from the fall in the white population took place among the ranks of government employees.

But overall, we conclude with a pessimistic note on black employment prospects for the 1990s. Our pessimism stems from the conclusion that the sources of strength in the recent past—most notably, black public sector gains—may not prove adequate in the future. Governments are unlikely to generate enough jobs or enough better jobs to provide continuing mobility and employment opportunities. And, so far, the native black community has failed to reduce its dependence on the public sector and benefit from gains made in the city's most dynamic sectors, the advanced corporate services. Indeed this pessimism seems to be borne out by the occupational data from the 1980s and the continued low levels of native black labor force participation.

## Foreign-Born Hispanics

The decline of the white population and the developed Hispanic networks and businesses in the manufacturing and blue collar industries allowed this group of immigrants to more-or-less hold their own despite heavy concentration in the declining sectors. But the drawbacks of this particular employment pattern are more likely to emerge in the future. The 1980s have seen manufacturing jobs hemorrhage at 1970 rates. And the impact of compositional changes is unlikely to be as great as in the past: although whites may continue to flee manufacturing more rapidly than the sector itself declines, the proportion of whites left in manufacturing is already low. In addition, the 1986 reform of the immigration law to impose employer sanctions may succeed in reducing illegal immigration and thereby weaken the viability of small immigrant business, in turn restricting the associated opportunities for upward mobility. This development, along with growing competition in manufacturing from Asian workers and businesses, may reduce their ability to take a disproportionate advantage of the blue collar jobs that do remain. If these developments do take place, then foreign-born Hispanics will either have to shift to a very different pattern of employment or face serious labor market problems. And so far there has been no indication of a reduction in the reliance on their traditional industrial and occupational niches.

*Foreign-Born Asians*

Asians, like the Hispanics, were able to counteract much of the adversity of the 1970s based on their strength in two niches—manufacturing and retail—which allowed them to take advantage of opportunities opened by the drop in the white population. Although their industrial distribution still was concentrated among weak sectors in 1980, two factors position them well for the future. First, they have begun to reduce their dependence on these two niches; and second, they have been able to make important occupational advances within those traditional areas of concentration.

## Conclusion

Our review of the experience of native blacks and immigrant Asians and Hispanics demonstrates the weaknesses of both the mismatch and the polarization theories in explaining the changes that these groups have undergone. If the mismatch thesis is understood as a statement about the declining opportunities for those with low levels of education, there is certainly evidence from the New York case to support it. But as a theory making predictions about the impact of structural change on employment opportunities, the mismatch perspective gets little support. Groups that are concentrated in declining industries do not always suffer most from industrial decline. Moreover, the specifics of the mismatch predictions are inappropriate. As we emphasized throughout this discussion, the mismatch hypothesis has been primarily framed to relate the continued employment problems of blacks to the decline of manufacturing; as such, it is of little use in explaining the experience of black New Yorkers.

The polarization view has the great advantage of addressing a question that the mismatch hypothesis cannot even consider: why New York and other like cities have received so many low-skilled immigrants at a time when employers are reputed to hire none but the highly educated. But the polarization view suffers from serious problems. First, whereas the decline of steel, auto, and other heavy industries has indeed eliminated well-paying, desirable jobs, the same cannot be said for the demise of New York's manufacturing industries, which have been a concentration of low-paying jobs ever since World War II. Second, the occupational data show little evidence of polarization *among the employed*: the growth has been concentrated in managerial and professional positions which have increased much more substantially than either service occupations or other blue collar occupations in the service sector. Third, our data on the earnings distribution, while indicating a trend toward greater inequality, do not suggest that immigrants have become increasingly concentrated at the bottom part of the earnings distribution. Fourth, the services-immigration nexus receives no support at all: shares of service jobs virtually remained unchanged among Hispanics and declined very substantially among Asians. Finally, that version of polarization linking immigration to services is an incomplete account of the impact of the shift from manufacturing to services on minorities in general, since it says nothing about the employment trends of native-born blacks.

Profound economic change causes serious problems for many groups of workers, and New York's experience with the structural transformation of its economy and labor markets has been no exception. Indeed large numbers of New Yorkers lost jobs or saw employment opportunities eliminated or restricted over the last two decades. Certainly, the prospects of illiterate residents of the city or those with low levels of educational attainment have deteriorated during this period. Theories such as the mismatch and the polarization perspectives make an important contribution to the understanding of inequality and employment in the United States by emphasizing the importance of the demand side of the labor market and the limitations and inequalities that are inherent in the structure of the economy. But the impact of economic transformation is not simple or straightforward. There are opportunities in the apparently most devastated industries, and a foothold in the ascendant sectors is no guarantee against misfortune. Our study of economic change in New York highlights the importance of two factors: the opportunities and risks created by the growth and decline of possibly competing groups, and the group and social resources that must also be brought to bear in order to confront the changing opportunities available in the labor market.

# Notes

1. Levy, Frank, *Dollars and Dreams: The Changing American Income Distribution* (New York: Russell Sage Foundation, 1987), p. 112.
2. Kasarda, John D., "Entry-level Jobs, Mobility, and Urban Minority Employment," *Urban Affairs Quarterly* 19,1 (1983): 22.
3. Levy, *Dollars and Dreams*, p. 113.

4. Wilson, William J., "The Urban Underclass in Advanced Industrial Societies," in Peterson, Paul E., ed., *The New Urban Reality* (Washington, DC: The Brookings Institution, 1985), p. 150.

5. Ehrenhalt, Samuel, "The Outlook for the New York City Labor Market." Speech delivered to the Fifteenth Annual Institute on the Challenges of the Changing Economy of New York City (April 28, 1982), pp. 22–25.

6. Harrison, Bennett, "Rationalization, Restructuring, and Industrial Reorganization in Older Regions: The Economic Transformation of New England Since World War II" (Cambridge: Joint Center for Urban Studies of MIT and Harvard University, 1982), Working Paper No. 72, p. 81. Though in theory the mismatch and polarization views offer alternative explanations of the impact of urban change on minorities, in practice both explanations are advanced at the same time. Wacquant and Wilson include, among the "spatial and industrial changes. . .that have converged to undermine the material foundations of the. . .ghetto": "the decentralization of industrial plants. . .the flight of manufacturing jobs. . .the general deconcentration of metropolitan economies and the turn toward service industries and occupations. . .; *and the emergence of post-Taylorist, so-called flexible forms of organizations. . .which has (sic) intensified job competition and triggered an explosion of low-pay, part-time work* [emphasis added]." In Wacquant, L.J., and W.J. Wilson, "The Cost of Racial and Class Exclusion in the Inner City," *The Annals of the American Academy of Political and Social Science* 501 (January 1988): 11.

7. Harrison, Bennett, and Barry Bluestone, *The Great U-Turn: Corporate Restructuring and the Polarizing of America* (New York: Basic Books, 1988), p. 120.

8. As an indicator of how peripheral minority issues are to the overall debate on inequality, the index of Harrison and Bluestone's recent *The Great U-Turn* lists only three pages in which the impact of structural changes on minorities is discussed.

9. Levy, *Dollars and Dreams*, p. x. Harrison and Bluestone, *Great U-Turn*, p. 120, concur with Levy in this respect.

10. See for example, Wacquant, L. J., and W. J. Wilson, "Beyond Welfare Reform: Poverty, Joblessness, and the Social Transformation of the Inner City." Paper presented at the Rockefeller Foundation Conference on Welfare Reform, February 1988, pp. 15–16.

11. Sassen-Koob, Saskia, "The New Labor Demand in World Cities," in Smith, Michael P., ed., *Cities in Transformation: Capital, Class, and Urban Structure* (Beverly Hills: Sage, 1984), p. 257. See also Sassen, Saskia, *The Mobility of Labor and Capital* (New York: Cambridge University Press, 1988), Chapter 5.

12. Sassen-Koob, "New Labor Demand," p. 257.

13. Sassen further contends that there has been an "expansion of low-wage jobs in the manufacturing sector," which has further amplified the demand for immigrant labor; many of these jobs are to be found in a growing "informal sector that contains a large number of sweatshops." See Sassen, *The Mobility of Labor and Capital*, p. 145. However, while relative wages in manufacturing

have clearly suffered considerable decline, many of the manufacturing jobs that have recruited immigrants already ranked low on the pay scale before the massive erosion of goods production jobs began. Whereas the proportion of low-wage jobs within the manufacturing sector may have increased somewhat, there is no manufacturing industry that has escaped the severe downward trend. Thus, the absolute number of low-wage manufacturing jobs and the number of such jobs relative to all jobs has declined. It is possible that some manufacturing jobs do not get counted in the normal statistical series, falling into the underground economy, as Sassen contends in Chapter 3 in this volume. But the possibility that the underground economy may have grown offers no explanation for the issue at hand; namely, how to account for the very observable and measurable increase in immigrant population and employment.

14. Waldinger, Roger, and Thomas Bailey, "The Youth Employment Problem in the World City," *Social Policy* 16,1 (1985): 55–59.

15. Waldinger, Roger, "Changing Ladders and Musical Chairs: Ethnicity and Opportunity in Post-Industrial New York," *Politics & Society* 15,4 (1986–7): 369–402.

16. Waldinger, Roger, *Through the Eye of the Needle: Immigrants and Enterprise in New York's Garment Trades* (New York: New York University Press, 1986); Waldinger, "Changing Ladders"; Bailey, Thomas, *Immigrant and Native Workers: Contrasts and Competition* (Boulder, CO: Westview Press, 1987).

17. In his most recent writing, John Kasarda has acknowledged the anomaly of high levels of immigration and immigrant employment in precisely those cities that have experienced the most severe manufacturing declines. Kasarda then switches to a supply-side explanation, arguing that in contrast to blacks, Asian and Hispanic can mobilize informal ethnic and kinship resources that spur a high business start-up rate. See Kasarda, John D., "Urban Industrial Transition and the Underclass," *The Annals of the American Academy of Political and Social Science* 501 (January 1988): 42–45. While differences in group resources undoubtedly help to explain some of the native black/new immigrant disparities, predispositions toward entrepreneurship are a necessary, but not sufficient, condition of business development. In the absence of an environment conducive to small businesses and opportunities for small business owners, immigrant firms are unlikely to grow. In New York, as in other immigrant-receiving cities, the processes of compositional change and ethnic occupational succession have been the chief sources of opportunities for new immigrant firms. For elaborations of this argument see Waldinger, *Eye of the Needle*, esp. Chapter 5, and Waldinger, Roger, Howard Aldrich, and Robin Ward, eds., *Immigrants and Enterprise: Ethnic Business in Europe and the United States* (Beverly Hills: Sage, 1990).

18. See Waldinger, Roger, "The Problems and Prospects of Manufacturing Workers in the New York City Labor Market." Report prepared for the CUNY Worker Literacy Project, February 1988.

19. The tables on occupational change utilize a technique known as "shift-share" analysis. The virtue of the procedure is that it decomposes the effects attributable to the factors of particular interest here: composition (or "group size"), occupational change, and "share," a residual term that reflects the shifts in the ethnic division of labor. The column for "group size" shows calculations made on the assumption that change in an occupation reflects changes in a group's relative size (after adjustments have been made for the impact of the local economy's decline). The column for "occupational change" shows calculations made on the assumption that groups gained or lost jobs because the occupations on which they had been dependent in 1970 waxed or waned over the course of the decade. The column labeled "interactive" adds group size and occupational change effects, thus indicating whether the two factors worked in opposite or reinforcing directions. Finally, the column for "share" shows whether a group's employment in an occupation increased or decreased, net of "group size" and "occupational change." For further details on the procedure, see Waldinger, "Changing Ladders," p. 378.

20. Waldinger, *Eye of the Needle.*

21. Bailey, *Immigrant and Native Workers.*

# 3

# The Informal Economy

## Saskia Sassen

The main theories of economic development generally do not foresee the possibility that an informal economy might arise in postindustrial societies. This controversial possibility demands not only empirical documentation but also a theoretical defense. As used here, the informal economy concept describes income-generating activities that take place outside the framework of public regulation, where similar activities are regulated.[1] Although particular instances of informal work in highly developed countries may resemble those of an earlier period, against the backdrop of decades of growing regulation that reduced and in many sectors virtually eliminated unregulated income-generating activity, they are actually a new development. Informal work is dissonant with the dominant economic theories, whether neoclassical or Marxist, that posit the disappearance and absorption of unregulated activities.[2]

To theorize the growth of an informal economy, we must rethink the propositions about advanced economies which explicitly or implicitly preclude such a development. Such a rethinking is under way for the case of manufacturing.[3] Most of this retheorizing has focused on industrial organization, particularly trends toward vertical disintegration and decentralization.[4] More generally, analysis has centered on what has come to be referred to as the decline of the Fordist model of production and the rise of new regimes of accumulation.[5] This has led to an examination of how such trends have affected the overall organization of work and economic activity in what were once areas dominated by large-scale vertically integrated firms.[6]

A parallel examination of how such trends are playing themselves out

**79**

in major cities is now beginning to take place.[7] Earlier works that go beyond a mere description of occupational and sectoral shifts only begin to
analyze how the rise of services has reshaped urban economies.[8] The
present study of the informal economy asks whether decentralization and
vertical disintegration have also occurred in the urban economic structure
and whether they propel informalization. This would ground informalization within the basic properties of advanced urban economies. Such an
explanation diverges from the common notion that the growth of an informal economy in cities like New York and Los Angeles results from the
survival strategies of Third World immigrants.

To identify the links between informalization and advanced capitalism,
this chapter will examine changes in types of jobs, types of firms, and
subcontracting that could induce informalization. There is no precise
measure of the informal economy and there is no exhaustive evidence.
The economic restructuring that has contributed to a decline of the manu-
facturing-dominated industrial complex of the postwar era and the rise of
a new, service-dominated industrial complex provides the context within
which informalization must be analyzed.

## The Informal Economy: An Analytical Specification

The informal economy can be analyzed only in relation to the formal
economy and the institutional framework whereby the state explicitly reg-
ulates the process and outcomes of income-generating activities according
to a set of enforceable legal rules. Without such an institutional framework, there can be no informal economy. In other words, while today's
sweatshops may look similar to sweatshops of one hundred years ago, the
subsequent implementation of various health and labor code regulations
gives the sweatshops of today a different form and meaning than when
the vast majority of manufacturing took place in an unregulated environment. The implementation, however imperfect, makes informalization a
distinct process today.

Although certain activities lend themselves to informalization, it is not
their intrinsic characteristics but rather the boundaries of state regulation
that determine informalization. As these boundaries vary, so will the definition of what is informal.[9] The informal economy is not a clearly defined
sector or set of sectors with a common position in the work process. It is,
rather, a highly opportunistic process with changing boundaries. The key
to an analysis of the informal economy is, then, an understanding of the
basic dynamics that induce informalization, notwithstanding the regulatory intent of the state and institutional arrangements, such as unions

and governmental enforcement agencies, which act as barriers to informalization.

Castells and Portes point out that the absence of institutional regulations may rest in different elements of the work process: the status of labor, the conditions of work, the form of management.[10] But it is not intrinsic to any of these. Informality does not necessarily reside in the characteristics of the workers. In principle, an undocumented immigrant may be employed in a fully regulated job in the formal economy in full compliance while a citizen may be employed in an informal shop.[11] It is true that a large number of undocumented immigrants in the U.S. work in the informal economy,[12] but it is also true that many of the illegal homeworkers in the Netherlands are Dutch citizens,[13] and many of the workers in the unregulated factories of Emilia-Romagna in Italy are Italian citizens.[14] The expansion of informalization does not depend in principle on the existence of an immigrant labor force. Secondly, informal work produces legal products at home when such work is banned, or done in factories which violate various codes, thereby becoming illegal. Finally, when a factory or a shop operates in violation of health, fire, labor, tax, zoning, or other such regulations, or when a taxi is not licensed as required, they are part of the informal economy even if all the workers are properly documented.

An issue on which there is little agreement concerns the place of criminal activities. "Underground economy" is an umbrella term that has been used for several kinds of irregular economic activity. According to some, the underground and the informal economy are the same. This chapter takes the contrary position, which differentiates these activities in order to understand their specific dynamics and effects. We can begin by distinguishing at least three different components of the underground economy: (1) Criminal activities which by their very nature could not be carried out above ground. (2) Tax evasion on licit forms of income, something all states seem to confront. In the United States, the available information shows a large jump in unreported income. Tax evasion is now considered a severe problem, which it was not in the 1950s, 1960s, and early 1970s. (3) The informal economy which consists of the production and distribution of licit goods and services taking place in violation of the regulatory framework. While criminal activities have to be underground, work carried out in the informal economy could in principle take place in the formal economy. The interesting question is why it does not.

How, then, does informalization as we have defined it fit in the advanced economy of New York City? The existing literature on the "informal sector" has tended to focus on Third World countries and has, wittingly or not, assumed that such sectors will not occur in advanced industrialized countries. Criminal activities and underreporting of income, unlike the informal economy, are recognized to be present in advanced industrialized economies. Their occurrence is not inconsistent with central propositions in the main theories of economic development. Indeed, income underreporting is clearly a response to the implementation of a taxation system regulated by the state. We will not therefore explore these phenomena.

Is the informal economy a marginal sphere that provides cheap labor to marginal firms? Or are components of the informal economy connected to the major growth sectors? Since much of the expansion of the informal economy in U.S. cities has been located in immigrant communities, some see its expansion as being due to the large influx of Third World immigrants. Cheap immigrant workers keep backward sectors of the economy alive, in this view. We should not assume that Third World immigration causes informalization. Immigrants may be in a favorable position to seize the opportunities represented by informalization. But the opportunities are not necessarily created by immigrants. They may well result from basic trends in the advanced industrialized economies. Similarly, what are perceived as backward sectors of the economy may not be remnants from an earlier phase of industrialization but may well represent a downgrading of work involving growing sectors of the economy. The organizing question must thus be whether informalization is part of the overall economic dynamic and how it helps constitute a "dual" city.

## Conditions for Informalization in Advanced Economies

Several interrelated economic and spatial processes must be considered if we are to establish the theoretical and empirical plausibility of informalization in advanced economies. One is the labor market impact of the sectoral and occupational transformation in advanced economies over the last two decades, including the increased earnings dispersion and the growth of high- and low-income jobs. Another is the decline of Fordism, which entails a change as mass production, unions, and the "social contract" they forged lose their economic and political force. A third process involves the spatial transformation of the economy.

Post–World War II economic growth contributed to a vast expansion of the middle class while deterring and reducing informalization. Suburban-led growth was capital-intensive and promoted the consumption of standardized products. These developments facilitated unionization and other forms of workers' empowerment that can be derived from the centrality of mass production and mass consumption to national economic growth. The incorporation of workers into formal labor market relations reached its highest level in the late 1960s and early 1970s. The economy transmitted the benefits accruing to the core manufacturing industries on to more peripheral sectors of the economy. The benefits of price and market stability and increases in productivity could be transferred to secondary firms, including suppliers and subcontractors but also to unrelated industries. Although a vast array of firms and workers still did not benefit from this shadow effect, their number was probably at a minimum in the postwar period.[15] By the early 1980s the wage-setting power of leading industries and this shadow effect had eroded significantly.

The growth of small production runs, smaller scale enterprises, high product differentiation, and rapid changes in output have also transformed the organization of manufacturing production, promoting subcontracting and more flexible ways of organizing production.[16] These trends have helped to feed the decline of unions in manufacturing, the loss of various contractual protections, and the increase of involuntary part-time and temporary work or other forms of contingent labor. An extreme indication of this downgrading is the growth of sweatshops and industrial homework.[17] The consolidation of a downgraded manufacturing sector through piecework and industrial homework has arisen not only within industries with organized plants and reasonably well-paid jobs but also in new activities associated with the growing sectors of the economy and society.[18]

In addition, the growth industries of the 1980s—finance, insurance, real estate, retail trade, business services—show low average pay, greater earnings dispersion, weak (if any) unions, and a higher incidence of part-time and of female workers compared to the leading manufacturing industries of the 1950s and 1960s. Nationally, Blumberg has calculated that real earnings in these industries declined after the early 1970s.[19] A study of 1980 census data by Sheets, Nord, and Phelps found that producer services and retail trade employment in major metropolitan areas were particularly strongly associated with the prevalence of low-wage jobs.[20] Harrison and Bluestone, the OECD, and Bell and Freeman found growing wage dispersion within industries and a tendency for industries with low average wages to suffer additional declines in wages and for those with high average wages to experience additional increases.[21] A growing body of research has shown that loose labor markets contribute to the declining economic position of urban minority groups.[22]

The impact of these trends on wages and incomes can be seen by comparing data from the 1950s and 1960s with those of the 1970s and 1980s. Inflation-adjusted average weekly wages peaked in 1973, stagnated over the next few years, and fell in the decade of the 1980s.[23] Furthermore, up to 1963, inequality in the distribution of earnings declined. Since 1975, the opposite has been occurring. Harrison and Bluestone used CPS data to show that the index of inequality grew 18 percent from 1975 to 1986. Other studies find the same trend.[24] The national data show a clear increase in low-wage, full-time, year-round jobs since the late 1970s and a less pronounced increase in high-income jobs. In contrast to the decade from 1963 to 1973, when 9 out of 10 new jobs were in the middle earnings group and high-paying jobs actually lost share, only one in two new jobs was in the middle earnings category after 1973.[25] The rising numbers of low-paid workers who are not employed full-time and year-round reinforce this trend.[26] By 1986, they were a third of the labor force.[27]

What matters for the purpose of this analysis is that the broader social compact between labor and employers in the leading industries has eroded. This compact rested on growing mass consumption fueled by the rising wages of unionized workers. In the case of industries that are growing most rapidly in New York, analyzed above by Drennan, such a compact is unlikely. Moreover, the national trend toward wage and income inequality has also taken its toll on the organization of work and family in New York City.

## The Case of New York City

Several of the leading service industries are far more heavily concentrated in New York City than in the country as a whole. In 1985, over 26 percent of the city's employment was in FIRE (SIC 60–69), the communications group (SIC 48), business services (SIC 73) and legal services (SIC 81), compared to 15 percent for the nation. The incidence of these industries is also higher than in Los Angeles or Chicago, where it reached 17.8 percent and 20.3 percent. Producer services broadly defined accounted for 32 percent of all employment in the city in 1985, up from 25 percent in 1970, with a total employment of almost one million, accounting for 35 percent of the city's payroll in 1985. (They accounted for almost 40 percent of employment and 45 percent of payroll in Manhattan.)[28]

Sheets, Nord, and Phelps have shown that these sectors have the strongest impact nationally on the increase in the proportion of low-wage jobs in major metropolitan areas.[29] From 1970 to 1980, service industries had a significant effect on the growth of employment paying below poverty-level wages. In retail industries, such as eating and drinking establishments, a 1 percent increase in employment resulted in a 0.88 percent increase in such jobs. Even in "corporate services" (FIRE, business services, legal services, membership organizations, and professional services), a 1 percent employment increase generated a 0.37 percent increase in full-time, year-round, low-wage jobs.

While the growth of these industries in New York City, and especially in Manhattan, has probably been much stronger in higher-paid occupations than elsewhere in the country, the evidence suggests that they have also increased the number of low-wage jobs. Data from the New York State Department of Labor show that two sectors have had above average increases in the 1980s: financial services, up 10.3 percent from 1986 to 1987 and services generally up 8.4 percent. Financial services was the highest-paying sector, with annual average pay in New York City of $43,964 in 1987 compared to an average of $28,735 for all jobs in the city.[30] The next highest paid major industry group, transportation and public utilities, was far below this level. At the same time, unpublished data from the New York State Department of Labor based on occupational surveys in 1984, 1985, and 1986, show that even in financial services, 49.4 percent of the workers are clerical and another 13 percent are service, production, and maintenance workers.[31] These figures suggest considerable earnings dispersion even within the city's flagship industry.

Data on earnings by occupation and industry for different boroughs of the city point to significant earnings differences between manufacturing and nonmanufacturing, between the corporate services and other service industries, and between Manhattan and the other boroughs. Surveys from the Bureau of Labor Statistics for the New York metropolitan area show that a majority of the 35 clerical occupational categories and the 21 office technical categories show a clear pattern of higher average weekly or hourly earnings in manufacturing than in nonmanufacturing industries.[32] County business pattern data on average weekly earnings also show that jobs located in Manhattan pay significantly higher wages than do jobs in the same industry in the other boroughs. For example, average weekly earnings in the financial services ranged from $732 in Manhattan to $344 in the Bronx; in the case of business services, from $501 in Manhattan to $242 in Staten Island.

The New York State Department of Labor estimates that over half of the new jobs created and about half of all new openings in 1988–1989 will be low- to medium-low wage jobs and the other half, higher-income jobs. Of 666,249 total expected openings, only 56,739 will be newly created jobs, about 300,000 will be separations, and another 300,000 occupational transfers. With over 200,000, clerical groups will have the largest number of openings, followed by the services groups with over 170,000. Professional and technical occupations will have 92,000 openings. Cleaning and food service will have the largest number of openings in the service industries. Private household openings are expected to number almost 17,000. Over 18,000 of the *new* jobs will be professional and technical jobs, 6,000 will be managerial, 18,000 will be clerical, and another 18,000 will be service jobs.

The growth of industries with concentrations of high- and low-income jobs has influenced the organization of work, the types of jobs being created, and patterns of consumption. The expansion of high-income strata and the related gentrification of housing and retail markets rests, in the last analysis, on the availability of a large supply of low-wage workers. The typical middle class suburb rests on large capital investments in suburban land, road and highway construction, private automobiles, and rail transit.[33] High-income central city gentrification replaces much of this capital with low-wage labor.

Any city as dense as New York City naturally creates demand for small, full-service retail outlets located close to consumers. But the simultaneous growth of high-income and low-income households reinforces this trend. Instead of suburban self-service supermarkets and department stores, New Yorkers patronize delicatessens and specialty boutiques that operate in different ways and sell different things than do their suburban counterparts. High-income gentrifiers prefer goods and services that often cannot be mass-produced or sold through mass outlets. Customized production, small runs, specialty items, and fine food dishes are generally produced through labor-intensive methods and sold through small, full-service outlets. Part of this production can be subcontracted to low-cost operations, sweatshops, or households. Besides reducing labor costs, this enables production to take place in cheap space, a considerable advantage in a time of strong demand for centrally located land.

The growing low-income population also contributes to the proliferation of small operations and the move away from large, standardized factories and large chain stores for low-price goods. Small establishments relying on family labor, often falling below minimum safety and health standards, typically meet the consumption needs of the low-income population. Cheap, locally produced sweatshop garments, for example, can compete with low-cost Asian imports. Products and services ranging from low-cost furniture made in basements to "gypsy cabs" and family daycare meet the demand arising from the low-income population. The low cost of entry into such operations creates intense competition and marginal returns.

Under such conditions, low-cost labor and the ability to organize production flexibly are crucial. The next section will provide greater detail about such activities as the creation of jitney lines servicing only the financial district; the increase of gypsy cabs in low-income neighborhoods not served by regular cabs; the increase in custom woodwork for gentrified areas; low-cost rehabilitation in poor neighborhoods; and the increase of homeworkers and sweatshops making either expensive designer items for boutiques or very cheap products. Susser's chapter provides additional evidence on household and childcare services.

We may thus derive operating hypotheses about the trends encouraging informalization in the economies of major cities: (a) expanding high-income populations increase demand for high-priced, customized services and products; (b) expanding low-income populations increase demand for low-cost services and products; (c) small firms able to produce customized services and goods in limited runs arise either as final producers or subcontractors to meet these demands; d) given relatively low capital costs of entry, these firms operate at narrow profit margins in a highly competitive environment where success depends on the ability to mobilize low-wage labor and reduce operating costs; e) these conditions in turn encourage noncompliance with regulations regarding wages and working conditions and induce informalization in a broad range of economic activities.

### Informalization Trends In New York City

The author's research has combined (a) secondary analysis of employment data; (b) ethnographic research in select communities and workplaces; (c) interviews with local planning officials, union officials, community members, and government inspectors; and (d) examination of data on occupational safety and health violators and overtime or minimum wage legislation violators. On the basis of these data, industries were targeted for in-depth study of their informal component. Fieldwork was undertaken where community boards and local development corporation officials identified a large informal sector or many immigrant workers.[34] Zoning maps and data from the Department of Buildings were used to obtain more detailed information on these sites. Field visits were made to construction, garment, footwear, furniture, retail, and electronics firms in four of the five boroughs of New York City to determine the extent and kinds of informal activities and the possible need for new modes of regulation.[35]

These efforts suggest the following profile of the informal economy in New York City: (a) informal work is present in a rather wide range of industrial sectors including apparel, accessories, construction contractors, special trade contractors, footwear, toys and sporting goods, furniture and woodwork, electronic components, packaging, transportation; (b) informal work also took place to a lesser extent in packaging notions, making lampshades, artificial flowers, jewelry, distribution activities, photoengraving, manufacturing explosives, etc.; (c) such operations tended to be located in densely populated immigrant areas; (d) residential or commercial gentrification has begun to displace some "traditional" sweatshop activity (notably garments); and (e) in these areas, new forms of unregistered work catering to a new clientele have begun to emerge.[36]

CONSTRUCTION    New York City had 10,305 registered construction firms in 1988, up from 7,636 in 1980 and 8,718 in 1970.[37] Two-thirds were special trade contractors (SIC 17). They employed 116,618 workers, up from 75,135 in 1980 and 106,688 in 1970. Firms averaged 11 workers, and almost 80 percent of all firms employed fewer than 10. This is a labor-intensive industry, especially in the additions and alterations segments.[38] Major changes in the industry in New York City include a decline in the share of unionized work, the growth of subcontracting, and a "parallel industry" of residential rehab jobs undertaken by immigrant workers. The number of Hispanics in the industry overall has increased significantly over the last decade, much of it accounted for by subcontracting work.[39]

The incidence of informal work varies considerably according to scale of the job. While the construction of new commercial buildings in Manhattan is still unionized and highly regulated, a great deal of commercial and residential alterations and renovations is done without the required permits and is likely not to meet various codes. Residential construction has long had the highest incidence of nonunion work. Nonunion contractors in New York make heaviest use of immigrants in their labor force. In a 4-block survey undertaken in Manhattan done by the Department of Buildings in 1981, 90 percent of all interiors had been done without a building permit.[40] Other citywide surveys of "illegal" construction work confirm this finding.[41] On the other hand, there is little informal work in large public works projects. Until recently, this was also the case with large private sector projects, but these contractors are also increasingly resorting to nonunion subcontractors, including unlicensed operators, resulting in a rise in the violations recorded by the Department of Buildings and OSHA. The Union of Construction Contractors estimates that 33 percent of the $4 billion private construction industry is now nonunion and that a growing share of the latter is unregistered.[42] Informal work is rising in foundation excavations and trenching, mostly in outlying areas. Finally, there is a high incidence of informal work in such specialized crafts as stonecutting, masonry, and plastering (SIC 174), where unregistered immigrants have filled a vacuum in domestic skills (SIC 174).

APPAREL    In 1988, 4,751 apparel firms (SIC 23) were registered in New York City. According to the official count these firms employed a total of

99,912 workers at an average of 21 workers per firm. Forty percent of all registered firms had fewer than 10 workers while half had between 10 and 49 workers. These firms are increasingly located outside Manhattan in the outer boroughs, especially Queens and Brooklyn, and in the metropolitan area counties in New Jersey.[43] Home production of highly specialized and high-fashion work, including knitwear, has also increased.[44]

Informal work seems to have grown since the early 1970s. Department of Labor violations, raids by the Immigration and Naturalization Service, union organizers, interviews with homeworkers, and other sources all point to an increase of production workers in unregistered work situations, notably sweatshops and industrial homework. The International Ladies Garment Workers Union found fewer than 200 sweatshops in New York City in the early 1970s; the union's research department estimated that there were 3,000 such shops by the 1980s, often in areas of the city where they had never been previously, employing 50,000 workers in sweatshops and 10,000 homeworkers.[45] Other studies support the finding that sweatshops are increasing and spreading to new locations.[46] According to the New Jersey Department of Labor, the use of New Jersey homeworkers to make goods for New York City firms has also risen rapidly over the last few years.[47]

The incidence of informal work is most prevalent in women's and children's wear and probably least common in men's wear. Sweatshops and homework are growing in knitwear, furs, embroidery, stuffed toys, and clothing for toys. Interviews with homeworkers confirmed that hourly or piece rate wages are very low. However, we also found an upgraded version of homework.[48] Some freelance or independent designers had immigrant workers come into their homes (typically large converted lofts in lower Manhattan) and work off-the-books. Some middle class women also took in expensive cloth and clothes to do finishing work at home or did knitting on special machines purchased by the workers themselves; these cases all involved Chinese or Korean households in middle class residential neighborhoods in the city. In other words, a dynamic and growing high-price market has incorporated production from sweatshops and the home (of poor and middle class immigrants and of designers). New Hispanic immigrants, especially Dominicans and Colombians, have replaced Puerto Ricans as the leading group of owners in the Latino population; the Chinese have increased their number of shops over the last 10 years; and the Koreans are emerging as the newest ethnic group to set up sweatshops and homework arrangements.

ELECTRONICS    According to the official count, 388 electric and electronic equipment manufacturing firms (SIC 36) employing 17,666 workers registered in New York City in 1988.[49] The average firm size in 1988 was 45 workers, but most firms employed fewer than 10. In other words, employment is concentrated in larger firms, but smaller firms are the most numerous. Electronics manufacturing and the broader category covered by SIC 36 have not received much study over the last decade in the New York area. The available evidence suggests that the number of firms and jobs are declining rapidly.

Several patterns relating to the informal economy may be identified.[50] First, the aggregate declines veil the growth of some segments of this industry. Older branches, largely traditional electrical machinery firms characterized by large size and unionized labor, are indeed declining. But alongside this decline, a new subsector of small firms has arisen. It has almost no unionized labor and relies on a network of subcontractors for greater efficiency, quality, and speed. Interviewees described such subcontractors as "garage-fronts," "basement shops," and "neighbors."

Homework typically involved work taken home by technical personnel or owners, often engineers. Several of the firms interviewed had started as garage fronts or basement shops, informal operations located in residential, middle class neighborhoods. This contrasts with that of the garment industry, where most homework and sweatshops are located in low-income neighborhoods. Electronics homework also tended to be carried out as "extra work" by workers already employed by the firm.[51] Informal work is less clearly linked to reducing wage costs than in the garment industry; it may represent a way of lowering the entry costs and enabling entrepreneurs to explore production and market conditions.

FURNITURE AND FIXTURES   In 1988, New York City had 398 registered firms in this industry (SIC 25) employing 8,288 workers, a decline from 10,176 in 1980 and 16,568 in 1970. With an average size of 20 workers per firm, almost half of all firms employed fewer than 10 workers. Major changes over the last decade include a massive decline in larger, standardized firms, many of which left for the South, and an increase in more highly craft-based furniture making and woodwork. A precise count is not possible because many of the latter firms are unregistered and located largely in residential areas.

The emergence of informal work in this industry may be a recent event. Almost all earlier production was formal, whether mass production or high-priced customized work. Industry specialists and our fieldwork suggest that informal work has grown up to provide the customized work and products demanded by commercial and residential gentrification. The newly founded International Design Center in Queens has also generated demand for new production. While the industry lost 20 percent of its registered labor force over the last decade, new furniture-making shops have been set up in Queens and Brooklyn. These shops employ highly skilled immigrants to produce high-cost, crafted woodwork for higher-income residents. Most are not in sites zoned for manufacturing. Many are located on second floors, which command lower rents. We heard of low-cost furniture-manufacturing shops catering to low-income communities, mostly immigrant communities, and were able to identify two such shops in basements in Manhattan. Both are informal operations serving the local immigrant community. They make simple, basic furniture: tables, chairs, shelves, cabinets.

OTHER SECTORS    The footwear industry has experienced massive losses in its registered work force, losing 21 percent of its workers in the last five years alone. But unregistered production both of low-cost standardized and highly crafted footwear (e.g., sandals and moccasins) nonetheless has been increasing. One estimate from industry sources is that at least 10 percent of all footwear production is informal. Furthermore, subcontracting and use of homework have increased even in unionized shops, according to the union that represents most footwear workers (Amalgamated Clothing and Textile Workers Union, or ACTWU).

The most notable development of informal work in transportation is the increase in so-called gypsy cabs and unregistered vans operating in the city. There are now twice as many gypsy cabs and so-called liveries as there are licensed taxicabs. The Commissioner of Transportation cites 21,000 such cars.[52] In addition, an as yet unidentified number of vans function as an informal mass transportation system serving specific employers or jitney routes. Gypsy cabs serve areas not well served by the formal transportation system or by the licensed cabs, often low-income immigrant or minority communities. In areas that entail transfers or two and even three fares in the formal system, a single-fare, one-ride informal van becomes attractive to low-income commuters. A variant is jitneys following established public transportation routes picking up people before or after the bus.

Retail sales are rife with informal operations. Records at the Department of Finance and Taxation show increased violations both in unlicensed street vending and flea markets and high-priced jewelry and fur shops that use fictitious out-of-state addresses to avoid sales taxes. Hundreds of auto-repair "shops" can be seen on the streets of immigrant neighborhoods.[53] The evidence is too fragmentary on these sectors to warrant a detailed presentation.

## Discussion

The evidence points to several distinctions that have implications for theory and policy. The first concerns the origin of demand for informally produced or distributed goods and services. It can result from demand in the formal economy, from both final consumers and firms. Most of the informal work in the garment, furniture, construction, packaging, and electronics industries is of this type. It can also arise in the immigrant communities where such activities are performed.

Second, a variety of different market contexts can promote informalization. Pressure to reduce labor costs in the garment industry has been exerted by massive competition from low-wage countries. In this instance, informal work represents an acute example of exploitation. The rapid increase in the volume of residential renovations associated with the transformation of low-income, dilapidated neighborhoods into higher-income commercial and residential areas has also given rise to informalization. The volume of work, its small scale, labor intensity, high skill content, and short-term nature are all conducive to informal work. Informal work can also arise from inadequate formally produced services and goods, which may be too highly priced, inaccessible, or simply not provided in low-income areas. Examples of informal production to fill these gaps include gypsy cabs, informal neighborhood childcare centers, low-cost furniture manufacturing shops, informal auto repair, and a whole range of other activities. Clusters of informal shops can eventually generate agglomeration economies that attract additional entrepreneurs. This is illustrated by the emergence of auto repair "districts," vendors' "districts," or clusters of both regulated and informal factories in areas not zoned for manufacturing. These may signal to employers the existence of an informal "hiring hall."

Third, enterprises in the informal economy face different kinds of locational constraints. For some firms, access to cheap labor induces them to locate in New York City, though typically in combination with access to the city's final or intermediate markets. Access to low-wage immigrant workers allows these firms to compete with Third World factories or to provide rapid production turnover times. The expansion of the Hispanic population in New Jersey has brought about a rapid growth of garment sweatshops and homework in several New Jersey counties. In contrast, shops engaged in customized production or operating on subcontracts evince locational dependencies on New York City. These firms are bound to specific clients or customers, require specialized design services, require brief turnover between design and production, demand a critical volume of spending capability on the part of buyers, or utilize immigrant enclaves. Leaving New York for a lower-cost location may not be an option for such firms, leading them to bid up space and reduce the supply of low-cost space.

Fourth, we can distinguish among the types of jobs in the informal economy. Many are unskilled, with no training opportunities, involving repetitive tasks. But others demand high skills or acquisition of a skill. The growth of informalization in the construction and furniture industries can be seen as having brought about a re-skilling of the labor force. Some jobs pay extremely low wages, others pay average wages, and still others were found to pay above-average wages. Typically, however, there seems to be a saving involved for the employers or contractors compared with what would have to be paid in the formal market.

Fifth, we can identify different locations in the spatial organization of the informal economy. Immigrant communities are a key location for informal activities, meeting both internal and external demand for goods and services. Gentrifying areas are a second important location, containing such informal activities as renovation, alteration, small-scale new construction, woodwork, and installations. Other locations in low-rent loft areas may house informal manufacturing and industrial service areas serving a citywide market. Finally, areas like 14th Street provide markets to street vendors.

A theme common to many of these variations is that the city's larger formal economy creates and/or promotes the informal production of goods and services. It generates demand for specific kinds of products and services, such as those associated with residential or commercial gentrification, that are suited to low-cost, small-scale production. This suggests that the informal sector does not result simply from immigrant survival strategies but is rather integral to the structural transformation of the New York City economy. Workers and firms respond to the opportunities this transformation presents. However, this response is conditioned by the position in which workers and firms find themselves. Immigrant communities occupy what might be called a "favored" structural location to seize both the entrepreneurial opportunities and the less desirable jobs being generated by informalization.

## Conclusion

This discussion sought to underscore two points. First, the economic development of New York City cannot be understood in isolation from the fundamental changes in the organization of advanced economies. The economic, political, and technical forces that have undermined the central role of mass production also weakened the regulatory framework that shaped employment relations. The service industries that have driven large urban economies during the 1980s show greater dispersion or inequality in occupations and earnings, a proliferation of jobs in the lower-paying echelons, and weak or absent unions. Only against this backdrop does the prevalence of informalization in advanced economies make sense.

The institutional and regulatory framework that shapes contemporary employment relations differs greatly from the earlier one. This framework has influenced the sphere of social reproduction and consumption which, in turn, feeds back into the organization of work and the distribution of earnings. Whereas this feedback bolstered the growth of a suburban middle class in the earlier period, it currently fosters a growing dispersion of earnings and labor market casualization.

The second basic point is that these structural trends have produced increased economic polarization. Although the middle strata still constitute the majority, the conditions that contributed to their expansion and politicoeconomic power—the centrality of mass production and mass consumption—have been displaced by new sources of growth. This is not simply a quantitative transformation, but provides the elements for a new economic regime.[54] This tendency towards polarization may be seen in the spatial organization of economic activity, the structures of social reproduction, and the organization of the labor process. In sum, the growth of the informal economy in New York City represents not a regression from or an anomaly in an otherwise advanced capitalist economy, but a fundamental aspect of the postindustrial city.

# Notes

The author wishes to thank the Revson Foundation, the Flora Hewlitt Foundation through the Institute for Latin American and Iberian Studies of Columbia University, the Department of Urban Planning at Columbia for supporting the research described here, as well as the Robert Wagner Institute of Urban Public Policy of the City University. I am grateful to Wendy Grover, Robert Smith, and Gail Satler for outstanding fieldwork, and to the members of the Committee on New York City and the Dual City working group for their invaluable criticisms and suggestions.

1. Castells, Manuel, and Alejandro Portes, "World Underneath: The Origins, Dynamics, and Effects of the Informal Economy," in Portes, A., M. Castells,

and L. Benton, eds., *The Informal Economy* (Baltimore and London: The Johns Hopkins University Press, 1989).

2. Landes, D. S., *The Unbound Prometheus* (Cambridge: Cambridge University Press 1969); Braverman, H., *Labor and Monopoly Capital* (New York: Monthly Review Press, 1974).

3. Piore, Michael, and Charles Sabel, *The Second Industrial Divide* (New York: Basic Books, 1984); Scott, Allen J., and Michael Storper, eds., *Production, Work, Territory: The Geographical Anatomy of Industrial Capitalism* (Boston: Allen & Unwin, 1986); Taylor, M. J., and N. J. Thrift, "Industrial Linkage and the Segmented Economy: I. Some Theoretical Proposals," *Environment and Planning A,* 14,12 (1982), pp. 1601–1613; Holmes, John, "The Organization and Locational Structure of Production Subcontracting," in Scott and Storper, *Production, Work, Territory,* pp. 80–106; Berger, S., and M. J. Piore, *Dualism and Discontinuity in Industrial Societies* (Cambridge: Cambridge University Press, 1980).

4. Piore and Sabel, *The Second Industrial Divide*; Scott and Storper, *Production, Work, Territory.*

5. Aglietta, Michael, *A Theory of Capitalist Regulation: The U.S. Experince* (Norfolk, UK: Lowe and Brybone, 1979); Lipietz, Alan, "New Tendencies in the International Division of Labor: Regimes, Accumulation, and Modes of Regulations," in Scott and Storper, *Production, Work, and Territory.*

6. Massey, Doreen, *Spatial Divisions of Labor* (London: MacMillan, 1984); Hill, Richard Child, "Comparing Traditional Production Systems: The Case of the Automobile Industry in the United States and Japan," *International Journal of Urban and Regional Research* 13,3 (September 1989): 462–480; Capecchi, Vittorio, "The Informal Economy and the Development of Flexible Specialization in Emilia-Romagna," in Portes, Castells, and Benton, *The Informal Economy.*

7. Castells, Manuel, *The Informational City* (London: Basil Blackwell, 1989); Sassen, Saskia, *The Global City: New York, London, Tokyo* (Princeton, NJ: Princeton University Press, forthcoming).

8. Stanback, T. M., Jr., and T. J. Noyelle, *Cities in Transition: Changing Job Structures in Atlanta, Denver, Buffalo, Phoenix, Columbus (Ohio), Nashville, Charlotte* (Totowa, NJ: Allanheld, Osmun, 1982); Sassen-Koob, Saskia, "The New Labor Demand in World Cities," in Smith, Michael P., ed., *Cities in Transformation: Capital, Class, and Urban Structure* (Beverly Hills: Sage Publications, 1984).

9. Fernández-Kelly, M. P., and Saskia Sassen, "Collaborative Study on Hispanic Women in the Garment and Electronic Industries in New York and California." Final Report submitted to the Revson, Ford, and Tinker foundations (1990).

10. Castells and Portes, "World Underneath," in Portes, Castells, and Benton, eds., *The Informal Economy.*

11. The passing of sanctions against employers for knowingly hiring undocumented workers alters this proposition in those cases where the employer knowingly hires such a worker. The informality then resides in the form of management.

12. Sassen, Saskia, "New York City's Informal Economy"; Stepick, Alex, "Miami's Two Informal Sectors," and Fernández-Kelly, M. Patricia, and Anna M. García, "Informalization at the Core: Hispanic Women, Homework, and the Advanced Capitalist State," in Portes, Castells, and Benton, *The Informal Economy*.

13. Renooy, P. H., *Twilight Economy: A Survey of the Informal Economy in the Netherlands* (Amsterdam: Faculty of Economic Science, University of Amsterdam, 1984).

14. Capecchi, Vittorio, "The Informal Economy and the Development of Flexible Specialization in Emilia-Romagna," in Portes, Castells, and Benton, *The Informal Economy*.

15. Scott and Storper, *Production, Work, Territory*; Blumberg, Paul, *Inequality in an Age of Decline* (New York: Oxford University Press, 1980).

16. Today many industries must accommodate rapid changes in output levels and product characteristics. Production of basic goods and consumer durables, the leading growth industries in manufacturing in the postwar period, has declined. The most rapidly growing manufacturing sectors within manufacturing are the high-technology complex and craft-based production in traditional branches such as furniture, footwear, and apparel.

17. It is the result of several concrete developments besides the more general processes cited above. In the case of the garment industry, the city's largest manufacturing sector, the biggest shops with mechanized production were the ones to move. Less mechanized, specialized shops and the industry's marketing and design operations have remained in the city. The greater demand for specialty items and limited edition garments has promoted the expansion of small shops and industrial homework for highly priced garments and accessories in the city because small runs and proximity to design centers are important locational constraints (Sassen, Saskia, "Immigrant Women in the Garment and Electronics Industries in New York." Third Research Report presented to the Revson Foundation, New York City (May 1989)). A parallel argument can be made for furniture, furs, and footwear. Small-scale, immigrant-owned plants have also multiplied because of their easy access to cheap labor and, more importantly, because of a growing demand for their products in the immigrant communities and in the city at large.

18. In the case of New York City, three kinds of activity seem to be taking place. First, manufacturing firms producing things ranging from hand tools through furniture to boxing gloves appear to be healthy. Second, small-scale production for retailers with high-income markets has increased in businesses ranging from gourmet carry-out to boutique clothing and accessories. Cheap labor and large markups make this production profitable. The availability of plants

willing to undertake short production runs on a subcontract basis also contributes. Third, production takes place for the newly expanded low-income mass market, much of it sold on the street. In large cities like New York and Los Angeles, this market is largely supplied by local or overseas sweatshops facilitated in turn by a large immigrant work force. (Fernández-Kelly, M. P., and Saskia Sassen, "Collaborative Study on Hispanic Women in the Garment and Electronic Industries in New York and California." Final Report. It is not easy to measure these three kinds of activities; this is merely a tentative organization of fragmentary evidence.

19. Using BLS data and census data, Blumberg, *Inequality in an Age of Decline,* estimated net spendable average weekly earnings of production or nonsupervisory workers with three dependents for several industries. Of the six major industry groups, all recorded increases from 1948 to 1968. From 1968 to 1978, all except FIRE and trade recorded gains though at much lower levels than in previous decades. FIRE recorded a decline of 5 percent and trade of 3.6 percent. Manufacturing, which had experienced increases of 20 percent from 1948 to 1958 and of 18 percent in the subsequent decade, had an increase of only 7.4 percent from 1968 to 1978. FIRE and trade had increases of about 20 percent in the first postwar decade and about 13 percent in the subsequent decade to arrive at negative rates in the 1970s.

20. Sheets, Robert, G., Stephen Nord, and John J. Phelps, *The Impact of Service Industries on Underemployment in Metropolitan Economies* (Lexington, MA: D.C. Heath, 1987).

21. Harrison and Bluestone, *The Great U-Turn*, Organization for Economic Cooperation and Development, *OECD Employment Outlook* (Paris: OECD, September 1985), pp. 90–91; Bell, Linda, and Richard Freeman, "The Facts About Rising Industrial Wage Dispersion in the U.S.," Industrial Relations Research Association, *Proceedings* (May 1986). Using census data and the 1976 survey on income and education, Stanback and Noyelle, *Cities in Transition,* showed that there is a high incidence of the next to lowest earning class in all services except distributive services and public administration. Almost half of all workers in the producer services are in the two highest earnings classes; but only 2.8 percent are in the middle earnings class compared with half of all construction and manufacturing workers.

22. Borjas, George, and Marta Tienda, "The Economic Consequences of Immigration," *Science* 235 (February 6, 1987); Wilson, William J., "The Urban Underclass in Advanced Industrial Societies," and Kasarda, John D., "Urban Change and Minority Opportunities," in Paul E. Peterson, ed., *The New Urban Reality* (Washington, DC: The Brookings Institution, 1985); Wilson, William J., *The Truly Disadvantaged: The Inner City, the Underclass, and Public Policy* (Chicago: University of Chicago Press, 1987); Freedman, Richard B., and Harry Holzer, eds., *The Black Youth Employment Crisis* (Chicago: University of Chicago Press, 1986); Tienda, Marta, "Puerto Ricans and the Underclass Debate," *Annals of the American Academy of Political and Social Science* 501 (January 1989).

23. During the post–World War II period the real inflation-adjusted average weekly wages of workers increased from $67 to almost $92 in 1965 and declined slightly to $89 in 1979. BLS data shows that from 1947 to 1957 real spendable earnings grew over 20 percent; from 1957 to 1967 by 13 percent, and from 1967 to 1977 by 3 percent. Blumberg, *Inequality in an Age of Decline,* p. 71.

24. Harrison and Bluestone, *The Great U-Turn,* Bell and Freeman, *Black Youth Unemployment,* OECD, *OECD Employment Outlook,* pp. 90–91. Some analysts argue that the increase in inequality in the earnings distribution has been driven by demographic shifts, notably the growing participation of women in the labor force and the large number of young workers due to the baby boom generation, two types of workers traditionally earning less than white adult males. Lawrence, Robert Z., "Sectoral Shifts and the Size of the Middle Class," *Brookings Review* (Fall 1984). Harrison and Bluestone counter this argument by showing (Chapter 5) that the increased inequality remained after controlling for various demographic factors as well as the shift to services. Inequality increased within such groups as white women, young workers, white adult men, and so on. While the sectoral shift accounted for one-fifth of the increase in inequality, most of the rest occurred *within* industries. (See their appendix Table A.2 for 18 demographic, sectoral, and regional factors.) The authors explain the increased inequality in the earnings distribution in terms of the restructuring of wages and work hours (Chapters 2 and 3).

25. Notwithstanding the increase in multiple-earner families and transfer payments, family income distribution has also become more unequal. Using CPS data on family income, Blumberg, *Inequality in an Age of Decline,* found that real family income increased by 33 percent from 1948 to 1958; by 42 percent from 1958–1968; but by only 9 percent from 1968–1978. By 1984, the Gini coefficient of income inequality stood at its highest since the end of World War II, having sharply increased in the 1980s after only slight increases in the 1970s. A June 1989 House Ways and Means Committee staff report found that from 1979 to 1987 the average income of the bottom fifth of families declined 8 percent while that of the top fifth increased 16 percent. Adjusting for inflation and family size, the bottom fifth suffered a 1 percent decline from 1973 to 1979 and a 10 percent decline from 1979 to 1987; the top fifth increased 7 percent from 1973 to 1979 and 16 percent 1979 to 1987. It should be noted that 1979 and 1987 were both years of prosperity and low unemployment.

26. Part-time work increased from 15 percent in 1955 to 22 percent in 1977. See Blumberg, *Inequality in an Age of Decline,* pp. 67 and 79, references, p. 267; Harrison and Bluestone, *Great U-Turn,* p. 102.

27. Deutermann, W. V., Jr., and S. C. Brown, "Voluntary Part-Time Workers: A Growing Part of the Labor Force," *Monthly Labor Review* 101 (June 1978).

28. U.S. Department of Commerce, Bureau of the Census, *County Business Patterns,* various years.

29. Sheets, Nord, and Phelps, *The Impact of Service Industries.*
30. Note that in individual industries, security brokers ranked among the highest with $69,670, and domestic household workers ranked lowest with $10,110.
31. These data cover all 791,000 workers in the financial service industry in New York State in 1987. Since 576,000 of these are in New York City, we can assume the occupational distribution is similar in the city.
32. For example, in 1980 the highest-paid category of secretaries earned $335.50 in manufacturing and $326 in nonmanufacturing (although they did earn $353 in public utilities). The same pattern held for 3 of the remaining 4 categories of secretaries, as did most of the other 35 office clerical categories and 21 technical categories. The pattern changed somewhat in 1988; while manufacturing still paid higher average wages, this was more true for the highest-paid categories and much less so in the lower-paid categories. For example, the highest-paid category of secretaries, accounting for 10 percent of all secretaries, earned an average of $621 in manufacturing and $571 in nonmanufacturing; the highest-paid category of word processor earned $442 in manufacturing and $375 in nonmanufacturing. But in the lowest-paid occupational categories, nonmanufacturing paid slightly higher average weekly earnings.
33. Sassen, Saskia, *The Mobility of Labor and Capital* (Cambridge: Cambridge University Press, 1988).
34. Complaints of businesses in violation of legally defined uses of building or zoning ordinances are normally registered with local development corporations and community boards before being referred to the Department of Buildings.
35. Columbia University, "The Informal Economy in Low-Income Communities in New York City" (New York: Columbia University, Program in Urban Planning, 1987).
36. For a detailed account see Sassen, S., and W. Grover, "Unregistered Work in the New York Metropolitan Area" (New York: Columbia University, Program in Urban Planning, Papers in Planning, 1986; Columbia University, "The Informal Economy in Low-Income Communities in New York City" (New York: Columbia University, Program in Urban Planning, 1987); Columbia University, "Immigration Research Project" (New York: Columbia University, Program in Urban Planning, 1989).
37. For each of the industry examples, the number of firms, firm size, and number of employees is derived from the New York State Department of Labor, ES202 ensured employment file.
38. The amount of additions and alterations to residential dwellings in New York City is very high. The State Division of Housing and Community Renewal estimated that there were more than 1,500 documented instances of major capital improvements (window replacements, roof and boiler replacements, etc.) made to apartment buildings, affecting some 60,000 rental units in the first half of 1986 alone, according to Marcuse, Peter, "Abandonment, Gentrification, and Displacement: Linkage in New York City," in Smith, N., and P.

Williams, *Gentrification of the City* (Boston: Allen & Unwin, 1986). Fieldwork by our team in Washington Heights in 1987 found a significant volume of alterations.

39. Balmori, D., "Hispanic Immigrants in the Construction Industry" (New York University Center for Caribbean and Latin American Studies. Occasional Paper No. 38, 1983).

40. The Building Trades Employers Association is the representative body for unionized contractors. Its major function is collective bargaining with the unions that are represented in the Building and Construction Trade Council. William Canavan, the Association's president, estimated that alterations account for about half of the building construction activity in the city and that the alterations sector contains significant elements of informal activity. Mr. Canavan speculated that the declining labor pool of construction workers in the metropolitan area would eventually permit the absorption of parts of the informal sector.

41. The widespread conversion of rental units to cooperatives and gentrification of neighborhoods in the late 1970s and early 1980s engendered a rapid increase in the demand for rehabilitation and renovation work. If the office building construction boom ends, many unionized workers may become interested in smaller projects again. Gallo, Carmenta, "The Construction Industry in New York City: Immigrant and Black Entrepreneurs" (Conservation of Human Resources Project, Research Program on Newcomers to New York City, January 1981).

42. A recent accident in a major construction site in midtown Manhattan illustrates some of these trends. A crane operator was found to be unlicensed. The accident led to a citywide inspection of high-rise construction sites, which revealed widespread use of nonunion subcontractors and an unexpectedly high incidence of subcontractors without the requisite permits or in violation of one or more codes. See also Balmori, "Hispanic Immigrants in the Construction Industry," and Gallo, "The Construction Industry in New York City."

43. Sassen, Saskia, "Immigrant Women in the Garment and Electronics Industries in New York." Third Research Report presented to the Revson Foundation, New York City (May 1989).

44. Sassen, 1989b. There is a vast literature on the garment industry in New York City. The sources documenting these trends include studies by the New Jersey Department of Labor, "Study of Industrial Homework" (Trenton, NJ: Office of Wage and Hour Compliance, Division of Workplace Standards, 1982), the New York State Department of Labor, "Study of State-Federal Employment Standards for Industrial Homeworkers in New York City" (Albany, NY: Division of Labor Standards, 1982), New York State Department of Labor, "Report to the Governor and the Legislature on the Garment Manufacturing Industry and Industrial Homework" (Albany, NY: Division of Labor Standards, 1982); Abeles, Schwartz, Hackel, and Silverblatt, Inc., *The Chinatown*

*Garment Industry Study* (Report to ILGWU Locals 23–25 and the New York Sportswear Association, 1983); Leichter, Franz, "Return of the Sweatshop: A Call for State Action" (New York, 1979) and Leichter, Franz, "Return of the Sweatshop: Part II of an Investigation" (New York, 1981); City of New York, Office of Economic Development, "Garment Center Study" (New York, 1987).

45. It is impossible to evaluate the adequacy of these figures, but union organizers and members of various immigrant communities confirm a sharp increase in the number of such jobs. The figures for special permits and certificates for homework issued by the Division of Labor Standards for New York City provide an equally inadequate picture because such permits and certificates are no longer issued in women's wear, where the largest number of homeworkers are employed, and because authorized homeworkers represent only the tip of the iceberg.

46. Leichter, "Return of the Sweatshop I and II"; Abeles, Schwartz, *Chinatown Garment Industry*; Sassen, "Immigrant Women in the Garment and Electronics Industries"; Columbia University, "Informal Economy."

47. New Jersey Department of Labor, "Study of Industrial Homework."

48. Sassen, "Immigrant Women in the Garment and Electronics Industies."

49. The main source for this industry is research in progress by the author. This project seeks to identify general patterns, subcontracting arrangements and use of homeworkers in the electronics industry in 8 four-digit level branches in the SIC 35, 36, and 38 groups. It is based on a survey of a random sample of 100 electronics manufacturing firms in the New York metropolitan area and a study of homework.

50. Sassen, "Immigrant Women in the Garment and Electronics Industries."

51. A similar study carried out in California (Fernández-Kelly, M. P., and Saskia Sassen, "Collaborative Study on Hispanic Women in the Garment and Electronic Industries in New York and California," found a different pattern: extensive use of homeworkers to assemble and clean electronics components. This would suggest that a large supply of low-wage immigrant women does not inevitably lead to their use in a given industry.

52. The most thorough study of private regulated and unregulated transportation in New York City was carried out by Grava, Sclar, and Downs, from Columbia University, for the Metropolitan Transportation Authority. They found that virtually every black or ethnic neighborhood had some form of "gypsy" and "livery" car service, and that these were typically run by members of the community: thus there are black, Puerto Rican, Haitian, Korean, and Hassidic Jewish "livery" car services. They estimated the current livery car service fleet at 22,000 vehicles. While many of these are in compliance, many are not. None of the estimated 8,000 gypsy cabs, on the other hand, are in compliance.

53. Columbia University, "The Informal Economy."

54. Sassen, Saskia, *The Global City.*

# 4

# The Public Sector

## Charles Brecher / Raymond D. Horton

## Introduction

The terms *dual city* and *postindustrial city* are intended to capture those economic and demographic characteristics that distinguish modern urban centers, such as New York, from cities that retain large manufacturing activities and from earlier versions of themselves. The people and businesses in New York City today are markedly different not only from those in Peoria, but from those in New York City one-quarter century ago. This chapter describes how the local public sector has responded to these socioeconomic changes.

A complete answer to the question requires some explicit assumptions about what local government is able to do. What are the important ways in which the city's activities could have changed? Social scientists concerned with cities generally point to three forms of local public activity over which government officials exercise discretion and, hence, for which it is possible to expect and observe change. These "stakes and prizes" of local politics involve the expenditure of public funds, the raising of revenues through taxation, and regulation.[1] For each of the three types of government action it is possible to identify segments of the community who benefit or are "winners" and those who pay added costs or are "losers" as a result of specific policy changes.

Public expenditure policies have two fundamental dimensions—how much to spend and what to spend it on. The scale of spending is a basic indicator of the size of local government, and over time city spending may shrink or expand. Who benefits from the expansion or contraction of the budget is largely a function of how the money is used. The distribution of expenditures among types of services and classes of beneficiaries also may change. Such trends can be interpreted as indicators of changing municipal priorities and of shifts in the relative capacity of different beneficiaries to influence city officials.[2]

Government officials also decide who pays for the city government's activities. These decisions generally involve choices between "exporting" taxes and placing a burden primarily on local residents. For example, hotel taxes, commuter income taxes, and federal grants are revenue sources that "export" the fiscal burden; in contrast, most sales taxes and most residential property taxes are paid by local residents. Since there often are effective economic limits on how much of the tax burden can be exported, a second set of critical tax policy decisions involves how the local tax burden is distributed among groups of residents. Over time, changes in the share of the local tax burden that is "exported" and in distribution of the remaining tax burden measure priorities and power relationships among different groups of taxpayers.

Cities also regulate a wide range of individual and business behavior. These regulatory activities include the establishment and enforcement of building and health codes, the licensing of contractors and of workers in a range of occupations, and the enforcement of statewide criminal laws. The range of local regulatory authority and the manner in which it is enforced can be expected to change over time, but, in many if not most cases, such shifts in regulatory policy are minor and derive from state and federal action rather than local initiative.

In the regulatory arenas most subject to local authority, it is possible to discern changed practices by city officials. Police chiefs exercise great discretion in selecting the types of crimes and neighborhoods on which to focus enforcement; and local legislative bodies may use licensing and other rules to encourage or discourage new entrants to a variety of business activities, including electrical contracting, street vending, and taxis.

Although the numerous arenas of city regulation are significant, few would disagree that one local regulatory power has a great potential for shaping the development of an urban area—zoning. Land use regulation has been recognized as a legitimate local government activity since early in this century, and significant changes have taken place since then.

A second important arena of regulation in New York is so-called rent control. Since the elimination of federal price controls at the end of World War II, New York City is one of a few places that has continuously exercised the local option to regulate residential rents. But the character and locus of administrative responsibility for rent regulation have changed significantly during the period, with serious implications for past and potential investors in residential property and their tenants.

In sum, to learn if and how local government has changed, it is necessary to examine important city policy decisions or "outputs." The major areas of potential change for New York or any other major American city are the size and distribution of local expenditures, the structure of the local revenue system and the burden it places on residents in different groups, and the patterns of land use and rent regulations and their impacts on competing interest groups. These do not include all or even most of the policy arenas of local government, but they are the most important.

## Expenditure Policies

The size and character of the city's spending have changed significantly—and sometimes abruptly—during the three decades since 1960. Alterations in local expenditure policy are evident in both the scale of such activity and its distribution among alternative functions and beneficiaries.

### The Size of Local Government

The size of local government is not measured well by the amount of money it spends. Inflation and economic growth make simple dollar amounts misleading. Constant (i.e., inflation-adjusted) dollar expenditures and expenditures as a share of the local economy are more appropriate yardsticks. The City of New York's constant dollar expenditures grew substantially each year between 1961 and 1975, as Table 4.1 shows. In this period, local government more than doubled. In constant (1982) dollars the city spent over $21.1 billion in 1975 compared to $8.6 billion in 1961. Since the city's population fell by roughly one million people over the same period, real per capita spending nearly tripled.

The growth was concentrated in the decade from 1961 to 1971. In these 10 years real spending more than doubled, with annual increases averaging 7.6 percent. In subsequent years, spending increases slowed but remained substantial.

The continued growth of city expenditures after 1971 is particularly important because the local economy was shrinking in that period. From 1969 to 1975, the real value of goods and services produced in the city fell about 11 percent; in the same period real spending by local government expanded 30 percent. As a result, the local government share of the local economy rose rapidly, jumping from 16 to 22 percent between 1970 and 1975. From 1961 to 1975, city government's relative size had grown from

**Table 4.1**  **Total Spending by the City of New York: Fiscal Years 1961–1989 (dollars in millions)**

| Fiscal Year | Current Dollars | Constant (1982) Dollars | As a Percentage of Local Value Added |
|---|---|---|---|
| 1961 | 2,734.4 | 8,572.0 | 9.7 |
| 1962 | 2,958.9 | 9,185.1 | 10.2 |
| 1963 | 3,237.3 | 9,856.7 | 10.7 |
| 1964 | 3,540.9 | 10,545.2 | 11.2 |
| 1965 | 3,844.2 | 11,342.2 | 11.8 |
| 1966 | 4,240.5 | 12,209.1 | 12.5 |
| 1967 | 4,977.6 | 13,870.3 | 14.0 |
| 1968 | 5,517.5 | 14,938.0 | 14.8 |
| 1969 | 6,329.9 | 16,216.1 | 15.7 |
| 1970 | 6,893.0 | 16,546.7 | 15.9 |
| 1971 | 7,938.6 | 17,843.1 | 17.5 |
| 1972 | 8,820.0 | 18,846.3 | 18.5 |
| 1973 | 9,525.6 | 19,480.5 | 19.1 |
| 1974 | 10,721.9 | 20,114.1 | 20.2 |
| 1975 | 12,377.3 | 21.139.0 | 22.2 |
| 1976 | 12,261.3 | 19,638.7 | 21.0 |
| 1977 | 12,989.7 | 19,775.1 | 21.2 |
| 1978 | 13,090.1 | 18,958.8 | 20.1 |
| 1979 | 13,216.4 | 17,891.0 | 18.8 |
| 1980 | 14,290.2 | 17,482.1 | 18.4 |
| 1981 | 15,108.5 | 16,742.3 | 17.4 |
| 1982 | 16,370.8 | 16,793.7 | 17.4 |
| 1983 | 16,992.3 | 16,524.0 | 17.0 |
| 1984 | 18,537.0 | 17,251.8 | 17.2 |
| 1985 | 20,484.2 | 18,278.5 | 17.8 |
| 1986 | 21,745.2 | 18,737.0 | 17.9 |
| 1987 | 23,289.2 | 19,350.1 | 18.0 |
| 1988 | 24,647.0 | 19,428.1 | 17.8 |
| 1989 | 27,624.9 | 20,713.2 | 19.1 |

*Sources:* Expenditure data are from annual reports of the Comptroller of the City of New York. The expenditure totals include operating and capital expenses. The totals for fiscal years 1968–1980 have been adjusted by the authors to take into account changed practices in the reporting of the state and federal portions of expenditures under the Medicaid program. Constant dollar conversions are based on the Consumer Price Index for the New York–Northeastern New Jersey region. Constant dollar value added calculations are based on estimates provided by Matthew Drennan, based on the econometric model described in his *Modeling Metropolitan Economics for Forecasting and Policy Analysis* (New York: New York University Press, 1985).

the equivalent of about one-tenth to nearly one-quarter of the city's economic output.

After 1975, local government began to shrink. Sharp cutbacks in 1976 were followed by more modest real reductions in almost every year between 1976 and 1983. The constant dollar value of city expenditures fell more than one-fifth during this period of contraction. Since the local economy began a significant recovery after 1977, the real reductions in city expenditures represented an even greater reduction in local government as a share of the local economy. From 1975 to 1983 the relative size of city government shrank from over 22 percent to 17 percent of the city's total economic output. By 1983 local government had returned to about the same absolute and relative size as it was at the start of the 1970s.

It appears that 1983 was another turning point in New York City's expenditure policy. In the 1983–1989 period, the real value of city spending rose 25 percent. However, the local economy also grew during these years, so government's share grew more slowly.

## Expenditure Priorities

The distinct periods of expansion and contraction in the size of local government were accompanied by differing priorities in the mix of spending among service activities. The functions of local government often are described in terms of three broad categories—developmental, redistributive, and allocative.[3]

Developmental spending is intended primarily to enhance the attractiveness of an urban area for business activity. Developmental expenditures include infrastructure investments, subsidies for industrial parks, and, particularly significant in New York City, the maintenance and improvement of transportation facilities, including mass transit. While all residents of a community, including future residents, potentially benefit from the economic growth stimulated by successful developmental projects, owners of land and commercial facilities typically reap the greatest and most direct benefits.

Redistributive expenditures are aimed at improving the living conditions of residents at the low end of the income distribution. The major redistributive items in the New York City budget are cash transfers or "welfare" payments, medical care, housing subsidies, and social services for the poor.

The remaining city services are considered allocative. These expenditures are not viewed as having differential impacts among income groups or classes; rather they are viewed as collective "housekeeping" functions required by residents generally. Examples include refuse collection and fire protection. Political disputes over this type of spending are, in this view, confined to competition among different geographic areas or neighborhoods within the city rather than among other types of interest groups.

However, in New York City the remaining allocative functions include a wide range of activities, some of which have significant developmental or redistributive impacts. Specifically, it is important to separate educational and criminal justice expenditures from the other "housekeeping" functions of local government.

Education in all cities has an important developmental benefit in the sense that it is an investment in the future labor supply. In addition, education expenditures have an important redistributive quality because the student population is disproportionately poor. Moreover, in New York City upper-income families rely heavily on private schools, making the public schools an even more redistributive enterprise.[4]

Criminal justice also has strong developmental and redistributive implications. To the extent that these services promote public safety, they contribute to the city's economic competitiveness. They are also redistributive. The poor are disproportionately represented among the victims of crime and those who are arrested, tried, and incarcerated by criminal justice agencies. Thus it is appropriate to examine the mix of city spending in terms of five categories—predominantly developmental, predominantly redistributive, educational, criminal justice, and other allocative services.

Analysis of the relevant data reveals that New York City's spending priorities changed during the nearly three decades since 1960 (see Table 4.2). Nearly all services received higher allocations as a result of the growth in the local public sector, but the added resources were not divided equally.[5]

Redistributive services benefited most. In 1961, these activities accounted for just over one-quarter (25.8 percent) of city spending; by 1969, the share exceeded one-third (35.8 percent); and in 1975, it was still 33 percent. The growth in redistributive spending was concentrated in the 1961–1969 period, when welfare payments—already a large item—virtually exploded and more than quadrupled in the 8-year period. Public assistance spending growth subsequently slowed in the early 1970s, in part because the federal government assumed responsibility for aged and disabled individuals under the Supplementary Security Income program enacted in 1972. However, spending under the Aid to Families with Dependent Children program continued to rise during these years, as did spending for medical care for the poor.

In contrast, there was little change in the share of spending devoted to education and criminal justice during the period of growth, and the other

**Table 4.2    City of New York Expenditures by Function:
Selected Fiscal Years (percentage distribution)**

|  | 1961 | 1969 | 1975 | 1983 | 1989 |
|---|---|---|---|---|---|
| Primarily Redistributive Functions | 25.8 | 35.8 | 32.6 | 33.2 | 30.8 |
| Public Assistance | 8.7 | 15.9 | 11.5 | 9.2 | 6.5 |
| Health | 11.0 | 11.7 | 9.6 | 9.9 | 9.9 |
| Social Services | 5.3 | 7.5 | 9.8 | 11.8 | 11.0 |
| Housing | 0.8 | 0.7 | 1.6 | 2.3 | 3.4 |
| Primarily Developmental Functions | 11.0 | 5.6 | 11.2 | 8.4 | 9.5 |
| Infrastructure | 5.2 | 4.9 | 8.6 | 4.4 | 4.8 |
| Transportation | 5.8 | 0.7 | 2.6 | 4.0 | 4.7 |
| Education | 27.4 | 29.0 | 28.6 | 26.9 | 25.6 |
| Elementary and Secondary | 24.9 | 25.6 | 24.0 | 25.7 | 24.3 |
| Higher | 2.5 | 3.3 | 4.5 | 1.2 | 1.3 |
| Criminal Justice | 13.7 | 11.3 | 12.7 | 12.3 | 14.7 |
| Police | 10.6 | 9.1 | 9.9 | 9.7 | 10.3 |
| Other | 3.1 | 2.2 | 2.8 | 2.7 | 4.5 |
| Other Allocative Functions | 22.2 | 18.4 | 15.0 | 19.1 | 19.4 |
| Total | 100.0% | 100.0% | 100.0% | 100.0% | 100.0% |
| Total Expenditure ($ millions) | $2,290.6 | $5,800.7 | $10,444.8 | $15,353.3 | $25,656.1 |

*Sources:* See Table 4.1. Details on the allocation of items to each function are available from the authors; the method follows closely that presented in Charles Brecher and Raymond D. Horton, "Expenditures," in Charles Brecher and Raymond D. Horton, editors, *Setting Municipal Priorities: American Cities and the New York Experience* (New York: New York University Press, 1985).

*Notes:* Total includes capital and operating expenses. Total adjusted by authors to account for change in Medicaid reporting. Total excludes debt service; see Note 5.

allocative functions also received a reduced priority during these years. In 1961 and in 1975, education accounted for about 27 and 29 percent, respectively, of city spending. Similarly, criminal justice activities consumed under 14 percent of city spending in 1961 and a nearly identical share in 1975. The big losers, at least in a relative sense, during the period of growth were the other "housekeeping" services, such as sanitation and fire protection; these activities fell from 22 to 15 percent of local expenditures.

Developmental activities were never a very large share of the city's budget, accounting for about 11 percent of the total in both 1961 and 1975. However, their relative priority fell in the intervening years, largely because of reduced city investments in transportation services.

In sum, in the period of expanding city government, aid to the poor received disproportionately large increments while the traditional housekeeping functions of local government were assigned a low priority. These priorities shifted when city government entered a period of contraction.

The most dramatic initial contraction took the form of a two-thirds reduction in capital project spending between 1975 and 1978. Virtually all city-funded construction was halted, because the local government could not borrow in public markets to finance its capital projects and chose not to substitute "operating" funds for "capital" funds. As a consequence, a major change in priorities during the 1975–1983 period was the reduction of developmental activities from 11 to 8 percent of the budget. Also during the 1975–1983 period, welfare spending was curbed, and other allocative functions grew from 15 percent of the budget in 1975 to over 19 percent in 1983.

Further shifts occurred in the growth period of 1983–1989. The share of spending devoted to redistributive functions again fell, reaching 30.8 percent in fiscal year 1989. The highest priority was assigned to criminal justice; the share of total spending allocated to this function rose from 12.3 to 14.7 percent in the 1983–1989 period. The other categories retained relatively stable shares.

It is also useful to look at changing budget priorities across these periods according to the objects of expenditure, although consistent data are available only from 1970 to 1985. Government spends money not only for direct services (through the number of its employees and their compensation rates) and capital (through debt payments on bonds that finance infrastructure construction and the purchase of equipment), but also for transfer payments to individuals and for "other than personal service" (OTPS) contracts. This latter category has become quite large in city budgets, amounting to perhaps one-quarter of the total. OTPS ranges from small contracts for accounting or consulting services to large purchases of public services from third party providers, typically private, nonprofit agencies. For example, New York City pays hundreds of millions of dollars annually to foster care agencies to care for children and to home care agencies to assist the frail elderly.

In addition to considering shifting priorities according to functional area, it also is instructive to consider two issues related to these objects of expenditures: how priorities have changed over time first with respect to the trade-off between number of employees and per-employee compensation rates and second with respect to the trade-off between direct labor spending and the indirect provision of services through "third party government" as sustained by the OTPS budget.[6] It was already noted that government spending grew rapidly in the pre-fiscal crisis period, declined during the fiscal crisis, and accelerated once more between 1983 and 1989. Since city government is labor-intensive, the number of employees on the city's payroll reflected these trends, rising from 275,211 in 1970 to a peak of 285,856 in 1975, then falling back to 236,057 in 1983 as a result of retrenchment, then rising once more to 251,720 in 1985.[7] By 1988, employment peaked once more at about 280,000.

As Bailey and Waldinger show in their chapter, blacks, and to a lesser extent Latinos (and black and Latino women more than men), benefited from the pre- and post-fiscal crisis growth of the public sector labor force in New York City. But these gains have been mediated by the trade-off between jobs and wages, the traditional pattern of paying uniformed employees more than others, and the continued concentration of blacks, Latinos, and women in lower-paying job categories and agencies.[8]

In the first part of the 1970s, rising compensation per employee accounted for 54 percent of the increase in personnel costs while growth in the number of employees accounted for 45 percent. Uniformed employees also gained pay relative to civilians in this period. During the 1975–1983 fiscal crisis period, however, staffing reductions accounted for 82 percent of the decline in labor costs, and coalition bargaining led to a compression both of the differential between uniformed employees and others and of the range of pay among civilians. But after the fiscal crisis, from 1983 to 1985, compensation once more accounted for 58 percent of the rise in payroll costs, coalition bargaining broke down, and the uniform differential again increased.[9] These trends obviously benefited the blacks and Latinos who made up a large fraction of the new hires. But this conclusion must be tempered by the observation that though white males were a declining fraction of the work force, they retained the overwhelming share of better paid jobs. Moreover, during the fiscal crisis, the trade-off between jobs and wages was made to protect the organized workers' compensation at the cost of reducing the number of employees (and, in many cases, the volume of services they could provide).

The rise of OTPS spending is equally significant. Direct labor costs actually fell from 59.5 percent of total expenditures in 1970 to 49.3 percent in 1983, though in recent years it regained a fraction of this loss. As Table 4.2 showed, public assistance transfer payments also fell from 15.8

percent of expenditures in 1971 to only 7.2 percent in 1988. In other words, the gain in redistributive spending does not stem from transfer payments, nor even primarily from the growth of the city payroll, but from the sharp rise in OTPS for social services. Between 1966 and 1975, public assistance payments rose from 10.1 to 12.9 percent of the total city budget exclusive of debt payments, while OTPS spending excluding public assistance declined slightly from 23.6 to 22.1 percent, for an overall growth in the OTPS share of the budget. After the fiscal crisis, between 1975 and 1983, public assistance dropped to 10.2 percent of spending exclusive of debt payments, but OTPS spending excluding public assistance rose from 22.1 to 29.7 percent of the total.[10] Since 1983, such spending has continued to rise.[11] Thus, like their counterparts on the city payroll, third party service providers benefited from the post-fiscal crisis expansion of public spending.

## Who Pays?

These expenditures must be financed, and selecting revenue sources is an equally important city policy. "Who pays?" is the critical question in considering the political implications of alternative sources. Three conventional revenue options are available—borrowing, intergovernmental aid, and locally derived sources.

Borrowing typically takes the form of issuing long-term bonds. This transfers the burden from current city residents to future city residents. It is regarded as an appropriate financing mechanism when the benefits of the expenditures also are received primarily by future residents, as is the case for capital improvements. However, capital improvements also may be financed from current revenue sources, and borrowing is sometimes used to finance current operations that provide no benefits to future residents.

Intergovernmental aid shifts the financial burden from city residents to taxpayers in the "outside world." Although city residents obviously pay taxes to the state and federal governments, these payments need not be returned in the form of aid. Thus most federal aid, and even most state aid, is viewed as "free" money.

Locally derived revenues consist primarily of taxes, but also include user charges, such as license fees, water bills, and a variety of other items. The burden of taxes varies with the type of tax. Some taxes, such as the local personal income tax, residential property taxes, and sales taxes on items consumed by residents, are clearly paid by residents. Others, such as the hotel occupancy tax, the commuter income tax, and taxes on some business income earned by selling goods or services to nonresidents, are clearly "exported." For other taxes, such as the commercial occupancy tax, the ultimate burden is a source of controversy among economists. The mix of taxes selected by a local government strongly influences the extent to which its residents will pay for city expenditures.

Local taxes also have distributive consequences. A progressive local income tax requires higher-income residents to finance a greater share of local expenditures than does a sales tax. And the residential property tax, which has been characterized as a "rent tax," places a highly dispropor-tionate burden on low-income households because so much of their in-come is devoted to housing costs. The choice of different taxes thus creates different sets of winners and losers.

### Getting Others to Pay

Although precise estimates of how the burden of local taxes is distributed are beyond the scope of this chapter, Table 4.3 indicates changing pat-terns of borrowing and intergovernmental aid. Use of these two "exter-nal" funding sources rose substantially and almost steadily from the start of the 1960s to 1975. Reliance on intergovernmental aid practically dou-bled, growing from about 18 to 30 percent of the city's revenues. Reliance on borrowing was more variable but generally increased from the late 1960s until 1975, when the city lost access to public credit markets. Con-versely, locally imposed taxes fell from 71 percent of the city's revenues in 1961 to just 50 percent in 1976.

After 1976 this trend was reversed. Local revenues have risen nearly steadily to reach about 61 percent of the total by the late 1980s. Intergov-ernmental aid declined, particularly in the 1980s. Borrowing was curtailed in the years after the 1975 fiscal crisis; in 1981 it accounted for less than 4 percent of city resources compared with between 12 and 19 percent in the first half of the 1970s; by 1989 borrowing was about 9 percent of total revenues.

### Which New Yorkers Pay?

The decline and subsequent resurgence of locally imposed taxes was ac-companied by important changes in the nature of the city's tax system (see Table 4.4). In 1961, New York, like most other cities, relied on a local property tax for nearly two-thirds of all local revenue. In the depression of the 1930s, the state legislature had expanded local taxing authority to include a sales tax of 3 percent and a relatively low gross receipts tax. In

Table 4.3    City of New York Revenue Sources: Fiscal Years 1961–1989
(percentage distribution)

| Year | Total % | Local % | Borrowing % | Intergovernment % |
|------|---------|---------|-------------|-------------------|
| 1961 | 100.0 | 71.2 | 10.6 | 18.2 |
| 1962 | 100.0 | 70.2 | 10.9 | 18.9 |
| 1963 | 100.0 | 65.5 | 13.8 | 20.7 |
| 1964 | 100.0 | 65.0 | 14.9 | 20.1 |
| 1965 | 100.0 | 65.8 | 14.0 | 20.2 |
| 1966 | 100.0 | 64.3 | 12.0 | 23.7 |
| 1967 | 100.0 | 61.7 | 10.2 | 28.1 |
| 1968 | 100.0 | 59.4 | 11.3 | 29.4 |
| 1969 | 100.0 | 58.5 | 9.0 | 32.6 |
| 1970 | 100.0 | 58.1 | 12.2 | 29.7 |
| 1971 | 100.0 | 54.9 | 13.8 | 31.3 |
| 1972 | 100.0 | 54.6 | 15.8 | 29.6 |
| 1973 | 100.0 | 55.6 | 14.6 | 29.7 |
| 1974 | 100.0 | 51.2 | 19.3 | 29.5 |
| 1975 | 100.0 | 54.1 | 16.0 | 29.8 |
| 1976 | 100.0 | 50.4 | 15.3 | 34.2 |
| 1977 | 100.0 | 52.0 | 15.8 | 32.2 |
| 1978 | 100.0 | 54.5 | 7.6 | 37.9 |
| 1979 | 100.0 | 53.8 | 6.8 | 39.4 |
| 1980 | 100.0 | 56.1 | 5.0 | 38.9 |
| 1981 | 100.0 | 58.0 | 3.9 | 38.1 |
| 1982 | 100.0 | 56.1 | 6.5 | 37.4 |
| 1983 | 100.0 | 58.5 | 5.3 | 36.2 |
| 1984 | 100.0 | 58.6 | 5.7 | 35.8 |
| 1985 | 100.0 | 59.1 | 5.1 | 35.8 |
| 1986 | 100.0 | 58.2 | 7.9 | 33.8 |
| 1987 | 100.0 | 62.1 | 6.4 | 31.6 |
| 1988 | 100.0 | 61.0 | 8.3 | 30.7 |
| 1989 | 100.0 | 60.7 | 8.9 | 30.4 |

*Sources:* See Table 4.1.

1961, these sources accounted for 19 and 13 percent, respectively, of local revenues.

In the next few years the city continued to rely principally on these same sources, but it imposed a new commercial rent tax in 1962. By 1966 this yielded nearly $72 million, or over 3 percent of local revenues. Also, the sales tax was increased from 3 to 4 percent in 1963.

Major tax policy changes occurred in the 1966–1971 period. A new personal income tax (and commuter earnings tax) was enacted in 1966. At the same time the sales tax was lowered to 3 percent (to be collected by the state for the city), and the gross receipts tax was transformed into a series of corporate taxes with income rather than receipts as the base. As a result of these changes, by 1971 the property tax accounted for less than 58 percent of local revenues and the sales tax share fell to 14 percent. The new personal income tax accounted for nearly 6 percent and business income taxes about 9 percent.

The general trend since 1971 has been for the property tax to continue to fall as a share of revenues and for all other sources to increase. By 1989, the property tax was about 41 percent of local revenues compared to the 1961 level of 64 percent. This relative decline was *not* the result of reduced statutory or nominal property tax rates. In fact, the City Council increased the nominal tax rate in each year but four (1978–1980 and 1986) of the 1960–1989 period. However, growth in the property tax yield was constrained by local assessment practices that did not update the assessed value of property to fully reflect market values. This lag in assessment practices meant that owners' tax bills tended to grow more slowly than their property values despite the increase in the nominal rate. The effective tax rate, defined as the rate per dollar of market value, rose only gradually and irregularly between 1961 and 1977; since then it has fallen in most years, and in 1988 was $2.24 or just 53 percent of the 1977 high.

Due to its elasticity, progressive nature, and responsiveness to inflation, the personal income tax grew in relative importance to account for over 17 percent of all local tax revenues in 1989. The sales tax share has risen due to an increase in the rate to 4 percent in 1975 and its responsiveness to inflation and economic growth. In the early 1970s some business income tax rates were increased, and these measures helped increase those taxes' share from 9 to 14 percent of the total between 1971 and 1976. Despite some modest rate reductions late in the 1970s, business income taxes continued to rise due to economic growth and comprised over 14 percent of local revenues in the late 1980s.

The introduction of and increased dependence on the personal income tax has probably had the biggest distributional impact. This tax generally cannot be exported and is paid by local residents.[12] Thus, it has probably lowered the share of the tax burden that is exported. Nonetheless, nonresidents probably pay a significant share of the "local" taxes when they purchase items in the city, pay a portion of business income taxes, and pay a portion of the property tax on commercial enterprises. Even if business owners are not able to shift their tax costs to consumers, nonresidents still pay if stockholders, partners, or proprietors live elsewhere.

**Table 4.4  City of New York Sources of Local Tax Revenues (percentage distribution)***

| Fiscal Year | Total % | Real Estate % | Sales % | Personal Income % | Business Income % | Commercial Rent % | Other % |
|---|---|---|---|---|---|---|---|
| 1961 | 100.0 | 63.9 | 19.4 | — | 13.1 | 0.0 | 3.6 |
| 1962 | 100.0 | 63.3 | 19.3 | — | 11.6 | 0.1 | 5.7 |
| 1963 | 100.0 | 62.7 | 18.5 | — | 13.3 | 0.1 | 5.4 |
| 1964 | 100.0 | 59.9 | 21.1 | — | 9.9 | 3.3 | 5.8 |
| 1965 | 100.0 | 59.0 | 20.4 | — | 11.4 | 3.2 | 6.0 |
| 1966 | 100.0 | 61.5 | 17.1 | — | 10.9 | 3.2 | 7.3 |
| 1967 | 100.0 | 57.9 | 14.6 | 5.0 | 9.7 | 2.8 | 10.0 |
| 1968 | 100.0 | 54.8 | 14.1 | 5.8 | 10.8 | 2.7 | 11.8 |
| 1969 | 100.0 | 54.1 | 14.3 | 6.5 | 11.2 | 2.6 | 11.3 |
| 1970 | 100.0 | 56.8 | 14.5 | 6.4 | 11.5 | 2.9 | 7.9 |
| 1971 | 100.0 | 57.6 | 14.3 | 5.8 | 8.7 | 4.0 | 9.6 |
| 1972 | 100.0 | 51.6 | 12.8 | 10.9 | 10.6 | 3.8 | 10.3 |
| 1973 | 100.0 | 54.4 | 12.8 | 10.2 | 10.0 | 3.9 | 8.7 |
| 1974 | 100.0 | 55.4 | 12.8 | 10.1 | 9.7 | 3.9 | 8.1 |
| 1975 | 100.0 | 53.6 | 16.0 | 9.4 | 10.8 | 3.9 | 6.3 |

| Year | | | | | | |
|------|-------|------|------|------|-----|-----|
| 1976 | 100.0 | 51.5 | 14.3 | 9.2  | 13.6 | 3.4 | 8.0 |
| 1977 | 100.0 | 51.4 | 13.8 | 9.9  | 13.1 | 3.2 | 8.6 |
| 1978 | 100.0 | 50.3 | 14.5 | 10.9 | 12.5 | 3.0 | 8.8 |
| 1979 | 100.0 | 48.8 | 15.7 | 11.2 | 12.4 | 3.2 | 8.7 |
| 1980 | 100.0 | 45.9 | 16.4 | 12.6 | 13.6 | 3.1 | 8.4 |
| 1981 | 100.0 | 42.8 | 17.0 | 13.2 | 15.0 | 3.1 | 8.9 |
| 1982 | 100.0 | 43.6 | 17.1 | 14.1 | 14.5 | 3.4 | 7.3 |
| 1983 | 100.0 | 43.3 | 17.3 | 15.2 | 14.0 | 3.8 | 6.4 |
| 1984 | 100.0 | 41.3 | 17.6 | 16.2 | 14.5 | 4.1 | 6.3 |
| 1985 | 100.0 | 39.9 | 17.3 | 16.5 | 15.3 | 4.1 | 6.9 |
| 1986 | 100.0 | 40.9 | 17.0 | 16.2 | 14.5 | 4.2 | 7.2 |
| 1987 | 100.0 | 39.1 | 16.1 | 17.1 | 15.3 | 4.1 | 8.3 |
| 1988 | 100.0 | 40.4 | 16.7 | 15.8 | 15.4 | 4.4 | 7.3 |
| 1989 | 100.0 | 41.3 | 16.2 | 17.1 | 14.4 | 4.5 | 6.5 |

*Sources:* City of New York, Annual Report of the Comptroller, fiscal years 1961 through 1989 editions.

* Individual items shown as a percentage of total taxes, rather than total local revenue. Total local revenue, as shown in Table 4.3, includes non-tax revenues.

Precise estimates of tax exports are not possible with available data, but some observations on their potential magnitude can be offered. Although the city has a thriving tourist industry, the nonresident share of the sales tax is probably small—perhaps no more than 10 percent of the tax's yield, or under 2 percent of all local revenues. It is estimated that approximately one-quarter of the city's economic output is exported; perhaps the same share of the business incomes taxes also is exported. This would equal about 4 percent of total tax revenues.

A significant share of the real property tax may be exported. Only about 37 percent of the tax's yield is from residential property; the remainder is from utility property (about 17 percent) and other commercial property (about 46 percent).[13] If roughly one-quarter of the nonresidential property tax (and commercial rent tax) burden is shifted to nonresident consumers or owners, this would represent about 6 percent of total local revenues.

In sum, the export of "local" taxes may represent about 11 percent of all local tax revenues. If these revenues are combined with borrowing and intergovernmental aid, the remaining sources of "truly local" revenues comprise only about 50 percent of all funds which the city raises. That is, New Yorkers finance only about half the cost of their local government.

Finally, the changes in the tax structure since 1960 have altered how the tax burden is distributed across income classes. The general trend is towards a more progressive tax system. The two most regressive revenue sources—the residential property tax and the sales tax—have declined significantly as a share of local revenues. At the same time, the more progressive personal income tax has increased its role. Business income and rent taxes, which are either quite progressive or largely exported, have also played an increased role. However, the general trend has been marked by abrupt shifts, such as the 1966 reforms, and occasional reversals, such as the reductions and increases in sales tax rates and the increases and later reductions in business income tax rates.

## Regulatory Policies

Like spending and taxing policies, regulatory activities have changed over the past three decades. The extent and character of the regulatory policy changes are evident in histories of the two most significant arenas—zoning and rent control.

*Land Use Regulation*

Government "outputs" are harder to quantify in the regulatory arena than in fiscal policy. In one sense, the decisions may be viewed as the laws themselves. In this interpretation changes in zoning regulations may be viewed as changes in government policy. But the laws alone may be misleading, because they may have little impact on shaping actual land use. This could occur if zoning rules permit more dense development than builders actually seek or if variances to the rules are granted frequently. Thus it is important to examine changes in the actual pattern of development as well as in the provisions of the laws intended to regulate land use.

The period since 1960 has seen frequent changes in New York City's zoning laws.[14] In 1961, a new comprehensive zoning ordinance was passed replacing the rules established in 1916. The revisions generally lowered the density permitted under the earlier rules, but at the same time the new law was intended to accommodate significant expansion in housing and office jobs from then-current levels. The revised rules in Manhattan permitted construction of office towers in the "international style"— rising straight up from the street and permitting relatively inexpensive and flexible large open spaces needed for modern corporate uses.

The comprehensive revisions of 1961 were followed by four important changes or additions: the creation of special districts, the legalization of residential lofts in manufacturing districts, landmarks preservation requirements, and a new midtown zoning ordinance in 1982. Special districts were used frequently in the late 1960s and 1970s for a variety of purposes. A special Theater District was established to preserve this area's stages. The new provision permitted increased office space for developers keeping a theater in their building. A special Fifth Avenue District required certain design features and encouraged covered retail galleries; in exchange, developers could increase their bulk provided the additional space was allocated to residential use. A special United Nations District encouraged certain public amenities by allowing increases in floor areas for such development.

Three other special districts were created in anticipation of public development projects that never materialized. A special Transit Land Use District was created along the route of the planned Second Avenue subway to encourage development that fit with the planned subway entrances. A special Convention Center District was created to accommodate a new convention center at the Hudson River in the West 40s, but the center was eventually built elsewhere. The plans for the never-constructed convention center also generated a special Clinton District intended to protect the residential character of the Clinton neighborhood following completion of the convention center (ultimately built elsewhere).

Four additional special districts were created in conjunction with largely public sector development projects. The Battery Park City District creates rules for development of this landfill area, which is carried out by a state development authority. The Greenwich Street Development District provides floor space bonuses to encourage pedestrian circulation improvements in the area adjacent to the Battery Park City District. The South Street Seaport District establishes special rules for redevelopment of this historic district. It permits transfer of development rights from historic buildings to designated commercial lots in the area. The Manhattan Landing District sets forth development rules for "offshore" development along the East River south of the Manhattan Bridge.

Although the special districts are clearly a form of land use control, they have generally relied more heavily on incentives than on prohibition of private behavior. They promoted specific goals for an area by allowing more dense development than the general zoning laws would allow, in exchange for the desired type of development.

The zoning changes related to lofts were an effort to accommodate mixed residential and manufacturing uses. The 1961 rules established a strict division between manufacturing and residential areas. However, exceptions were made in 1971 for artists living and working in parts of previously manufacturing lofts in sections of lower Manhattan. The exceptions were extended to additional areas in 1976. In 1981, broader revisions extended the areas where mixed industrial and residential use was permitted, but conditioned conversion of manufacturing to residential use on the developer's payment to a relocation fund that would benefit manufacturing firms leaving the converted space for other parts of New York City.

New York City landmark preservation legislation was passed in 1968. The local law established a Landmarks Preservation Commission, consisting of eleven mayoral appointees, which can designate buildings as landmarks based on their special historic or aesthetic character. Designated landmarks must be kept in good repair by their owners and cannot be demolished or altered by their owners without Commission approval. While not technically a zoning rule, the effect of the legislation is to shape development by restricting use of certain properties. Designation of numerous landmarks in an area could limit the density of its development. However, the potential for landmarks preservation decisions to affect broad development patterns is limited by the accompanying changes in the zoning laws; new rules permitted a landmark property owner to transfer unused development rights from a landmark to nearby properties. This means that landmark designation within a neighborhood does not necessarily reduce the aggregate density of development in that neighborhood.

The combination of potential bonuses under the special district provisions and the granting of variances under negotiated arrangements led to a perception that more comprehensive changes in midtown Manhattan zoning were needed, and such reforms were enacted in 1982. The new zoning rules modified the bonuses available under the special district rules, lowered the general levels of density permitted in much of midtown, and increased permissible density on parts of the West Side in order to encourage development in that area. The intention was to "spread" office tower development westward.

It is hard to say how these changes have affected actual patterns of land use. Data on the construction of new office space in Manhattan suggest that zoning did not impede development or alter the developmental path established by market forces. While new construction of office space followed a cyclical pattern, substantial increases in the Manhattan office stock took place. In the 1960–1987 period, over 150 million square feet of space was constructed, more than doubling available space.[15] Although only 241 buildings went up, they are giant structures with an average of over 620,000 square feet of rentable space each. Thus, zoning has generally been consistent with extremely dense development of office space in a relatively small portion of Manhattan, a pattern driven by market forces.

Conflicts between zoning rules and market forces appear more significant in the allocation of land to manufacturing functions in Manhattan. A major portion of Manhattan is zoned for manufacturing purposes. Pressures for close-to-work housing among the white collar work force have made parts of these areas desirable for upper-income housing development. The loft conversion provision partially reconciles the previous zoning rules to new market pressures, but serious tensions remain between residential developers and the remaining manufacturing users.

Although the zoning rules deter residential development in a portion of Manhattan, they probably had little influence on the overall supply and distribution of housing units in the city. Despite local population decline, the total number of housing units in the city increased almost 180,000, or over 6 percent, in the 1960–1980 period, with most of the expansion during the first decade. However, Manhattan lost units in the 1960s and expanded more rapidly than the citywide average in the 1970s. The most rapid development took place in Queens and Staten Island with the latter borough nearly doubling its housing supply in the two decades. The

Bronx is the only borough that experienced a net loss of housing units over the period, and all of this decline was concentrated in the 1970s. Brooklyn retained a relatively stable aggregate housing supply, accounting for about three of every ten housing units in both 1960 and 1980.

In general, it is difficult to make causal links between the zoning regulations and the pattern of residential development in the city. Rather, both private market forces and another form of regulation, rent control, are more widely perceived as playing stronger roles in shaping the local housing supply.

## Rent Regulations

Rent regulations create winners and losers in the classic battles between landlords and tenants. Rent control is often viewed as a distinctly New York phenomenon related to the city's uniquely high proportion of renters in a nation that values home ownership. But, in fact, the contemporary system of rent control has its origin in federal legislation and has been altered significantly by state as well as local action.

Current rent regulations began in the national system of price controls established during World War II. These rules were applied to housing in New York City (and elsewhere) in 1943, and federal controls remained in effect until 1950 in order to prevent excessive rent increases during the postwar period of economic adjustment. However, new construction was encouraged by the exemption of units built after 1947 from any rent controls.

The federal legislation terminating national rent regulation after World War II permitted states to establish programs of rent control. New York State pursued this option. State legislation passed in 1950 created a state agency to administer a statewide system that tightly regulated rent increases in units which remained occupied by the same tenant, but permitted higher rent increases for units which became vacant. As under the federal rules, units built after 1947 remained uncontrolled.

During the 1950s most areas of the state experienced significant expansion of the housing supply. The improved market conditions as well as the relatively small share of residents who were renters led to the elimination of state rent controls for virtually all localities except New York City. Consequently, in 1962 state legislation transferred administrative responsibility for the rent control program from the state to a city agency.

The city-run program continued to be restricted to buildings built before 1947 and to follow the principle of lower rent increases for units occupied by the same tenant than for those which became vacant. City administration also was characterized by permissible rent increases which substantially lagged increases in operating costs. The result was often criticized because rents were determined primarily by turnover in an apartment, and landlords faced difficulty achieving desired rates of return without neglecting maintenance needs.

Rent control was attractive because it protected tenants satisfied with their current housing. When the New York City housing market became very tight in the later part of the 1960s, tenants sought such protection in newly constructed buildings. In response, in 1968 city officials used the authority granted in the state law to expand the local program to include "rent stabilization." These new regulations applied limits to rent increases in approximately 350,000 units built after 1947. Following the principles of the initial rent control program, permissible rent increases were set at lower rates for tenants remaining in their apartments than for those newly entering an apartment. However, even for tenants remaining in their units, rent increases were typically higher for the newer rent stabilized units than for the original rent controlled units.

In order to rationalize the regulation of rents in the pre-1947 buildings, city officials modified the rent control program in 1969. For each rent controlled unit a Maximum Base Rent (MBR) was established based on estimated operating costs and a competitive return on the owner's investment. Rents for apartments that became vacant could be set at the MBR, but tenants continuing to occupy their apartments were protected against large rent increases by an annual limit of 7.5 percent on their rent increase.

State legislation modified both the MBR and the rent stabilization programs in 1971. The state effectively ordered the city to gradually end rent regulation through the Vacancy Decontrol Law. This mandated that any unit that became vacant would no longer be subject to any rent regulation. Only tenants continuing to occupy their apartments would be protected by either the rent stabilization or MBR programs. Since eventually all units would become vacant, the intent over the long run was to eventually eliminate rent control in New York City.

The state reversed its policy in 1974. New legislation reestablished rent stabilization for all units decontrolled during the 1971–1974 period and applied the rent stabilization rules to units that became vacant in the future. Thus, tenants in pre-1947 units that had not become vacant remained under the MBR program and all other apartment units were made subject to the rent stabilization program.

From 1974 to 1983 the city's Rent Guidelines Board continued to set permissible limits on rent increases for most apartments in the city. The rates of increase were linked to rates of increase in operating costs, but annual battles between landlords and tenants over the magnitude of these changes were often bitter. In 1983, the State Division of Housing and Community Renewal assumed the responsibility for establishing permissible rent increases for rent control and for handling the administrative details in connection with both controlled and stabilized apartments. However, the city's Rent Guidelines Board continued to determine permissible rent increases for the rent stabilized component.

In sum, rent regulation policy in New York City has been altered often and in different directions. In the early 1960s the previously state-run program was taken over by the city, and in the later part of that decade the program was both given new principles for regulation and expanded in scope to cover newer units. This local policy was superseded by state policy in 1971 that sought to end rent control, but the state reversed itself in 1974. For the next decade more consistent policies were followed by local authorities, but in 1983 the state once again assumed a larger role in the program.

## Summary

This chapter has sought to define the most important arenas of local government activity and to describe the changes that have taken place in them since 1960. Expenditure policies have changed in four distinct periods. From 1960 to 1969, spending increased rapidly and was allocated in favor of redistributive activities. Public assistance alone rose from 8.7 percent of the budget in 1961 to 15.9 percent in 1969. The number of employees, their compensation, and payments to third party providers also increased. From 1969 to 1975 spending continued to increase, but less priority was assigned to redistribution and greater reliance was placed on borrowing as a source of revenue. From 1975 to 1983, spending was reduced and developmental activities were curbed, while the allocative functions were favored. Employment declined much more than compensation, while OTPS held steady. Since 1983, expenditures have been growing in constant dollars and remaining a gradually rising share of the local economy.

Revenue policies have changed in two distinct ways. Initially, the capacity to transfer the burden of financing local government to nonresidents was expanded through greater reliance on intergovernmental aid and borrowing, but this trend has not been consistent. Reliance on borrowing has slowed since the mid 1970s, and intergovernmental aid has become less significant in the 1980s. The city is thus raising more from its own resources. Second, the tax burden among local residents has been altered. The incidence of city taxes has become more progressive largely due to the enactment of a local personal income tax.

Land use regulations appear to have had a limited impact on changing land use patterns from what the market would have produced. The overall pattern of dense office development in a relatively small area of Manhattan has not been significantly altered by these regulations. Zoning restrictions seem not to have played much role in shaping the pace or distribution of residential development.

Rent controls have had a more significant impact on housing economics, though the responsibility for administration has shifted back and forth between the state and city. There was a brief period during which complete decontrol was sought, but this proved a fleeting policy.

It is not easy to say how these trends helped or hurt the various interests that make up the city, in part because it is hard to measure all the benefits and burdens in the different arenas and reduce them to comparable figures and, in part, because "interests" can be defined in many different ways. We can, nevertheless, reach some tentative conclusions. Following Sayre and Kaufman, we can distinguish between "revenue providers," namely property owners and recipients of taxable income, and "service demanders," namely organized producer interests like city employees and third party providers and the less organized citizenry who consume public services. The latter may be politically articulated in spatial "neighborhoods," or in groups defined primarily by income levels, with poorer consumers oriented to redistributive services and higher income consumers oriented primarily to allocative services. Two basic cleavages thus operate: between those who pay taxes but do not rely heavily on public service production or consumption and those who do; and, within this latter group, between producer and consumer interests.

Along the dimension of spending, the fiscal crisis dramatically reversed, at least for a time, a trend that had favored both public service producers and consumers over owners of property and possessors of income. It certainly focused attention on the need for local government to provide a favorable climate for private investment. But while the fiscal crisis slowed the trend toward social spending, it did not reverse it. The post-fiscal crisis spending pattern still favors social services, but it gives greater emphasis to producer interests than to consumer interests. That is to say, transfer payments to individuals have declined relative to the social services payroll and the compensation of public employees has risen faster than their numbers. Although much more needs to be known about the distributional consequences of the OTPS budget, private providers under contract to city government also seem to have gained.

On the dimension of taxation, city government has reduced its total claim on local value added, become more reliant on its own resources, and shifted away from property taxes to income taxes. Most important, in contrast to the 15 years leading up to the fiscal crisis, the New York City economy grew faster than its government's revenue exactions between 1975 and 1983 and at almost the same rate since. Moreover, property owners gained (i.e., paid less) relative to other taxpayers, and greater reliance on the income tax has distributed the tax burden more progressively.

Turning to regulation, land use policy has not substantially altered the market-driven pattern of dense development of the central business district for office use. In contrast, residential rent regulation, which has shifted back and forth between state and city government, has probably restricted investment in rental housing.

If an overall conclusion can be drawn, it is that private property interests and organized public producer interests have both gained from the post-fiscal crisis patterns of government action in New York City. Among both revenue providers and service consumers, less organized, more diffuse interests have done relatively less well, and, as in the case of the dependent poor, sometimes absolutely less well.

## Notes

1. The "stakes and prizes" approach is used in Sayre, Wallace, and Herbert Kaufman, *Governing New York City: Politics in the Metropolis* (New York: Russell Sage Foundation, 1960), Chapter 2.

2. This mode of analysis is developed further in Brecher, Charles, and Raymond D. Horton, "Community Power and Municipal Budgets," in Lurie, Irene, ed., *New Directions in Budget Theory* (Albany: State University of New York Press, 1988), pp. 148–164.

3. For a more complete discussion of these categories, see Peterson, Paul, *City Limits* (Chicago: University of Chicago Press, 1981), especially Chapter 3.

4. For an elaboration of these points, see Berne, Robert, and Emanuel Tobier, "The Setting for School Policy," in Brecher, Charles, and Raymond D. Horton, eds., *Setting Municipal Priorities, 1988* (New York: New York University Press, 1987).

5. The data in Table 4.2 reflect total spending net of debt service. This is most appropriate because it is not possible to allocate debt service among the functions and because the figures include capital spending financed through borrowing. Counting both debt service and capital spending could be interpreted as "double counting" for this analysis.

6. The concept of "third party government" has been elaborated and analyzed by Salamon, Lester, "Rethinking Public Management: Third-Party Govern-

ment and the Changing Forms of Government Action," *Public Policy* 29 (Summer 1981): 255–276.

7. For further discussion, see Horton, Raymond D., "Fiscal Stress and Labor Power." Paper presented to the Industrial Relations Research Association Annual Meeting, New York (December 28–30, 1985).

8. Stafford, Walter W., with Edwin Dei, *Employment Segmentation in New York City Municipal Agencies* (New York: Community Service Society, 1989); Urban Research Center, New York University, "Wage Discrimination and Occupational Discrimination in New York City's Municipal Workforce: Time for a Change" (1987).

9. Horton, "Fiscal Stress and Labor Power," Table 1.

10. Brecher and Horton, "Community Power and Municipal Budgets," Table 7-2, p. 159. Major categories of OTPS aside from public assistance include Medicare and Medicaid, daycare, foster care, and Health and Hospital Corporation affiliations contracts with private, nonprofit hospitals.

11. Grossman, David A., Lester M. Salamon, and David M. Altschuler, *The New York Nonprofit Sector in a Time of Government Retrenchment* (Washington, DC: The Urban Institute Press, 1986), reports that government funding for nonprofits in the early 1980s rose only in New York out of the sixteen jurisdictions studied.

12. The principle exception is the part of the tax paid by commuters on income earned in the city, but this is estimated at less than 10 percent of the tax's yield or under 2 percent of total local revenues.

13. These data are 1987 figures from City of New York, Executive Budget, Fiscal Year 1989, *Message of the Mayor* (May 9, 1988), p. 25.

14. The material in this section draws from an unpublished and untitled manuscript on the history of zoning in New York City by Gerard George.

15. See the Real Estate Board of New York, "Rebuilding Manhattan: A Study of New Office Construction" (October 1985), and *Fact Book 1985* (March 1985).

# 5

# The Geography
# of Employment and Residence
# in New York Since 1950

## Richard Harris

Almost thirty years ago, Edgar Hoover and Raymond Vernon wrote a definitive study of the geography of homes and workplaces in the modern metropolis.[1] Their analysis of the New York metropolitan region has come to be viewed as a classic of its kind. Since they wrote, however, much has changed. The forces of economic restructuring have led to a decline of manufacturing, a growth of offices, and in some urban areas, the gentrification of the inner city. No place exemplifies these trends better than New York. In the 1970s, New York lost more manufacturing jobs than most United States metropolitan centers possessed. Partly for this reason it almost went bankrupt. In the next decade, however, job losses were counterbalanced by the growth of finance and business service employment, notably in Manhattan where an extraordinary office boom helped to make the fortunes of men like Donald Trump. This boom has produced a trend towards gentrification that is so marked that some observers now describe the social transformation of the modern inner city as "Manhattanization."[2] In so doing, they continue a long tradition of viewing New York as the exceptional epitome of the modern metropolis.

In fact, little is known about the current, and changing, geography of employment and residence in New York. In both the popular and the academic press a great deal has been written about certain types of change. Inner-city gentrification, especially as it has affected specific neighborhoods, has been quite well studied. But no attempt has been made to examine the larger geographical and historical context within which such trends have occurred. This chapter attempts to fill part of this gap in our knowledge by presenting an outline of the changing geography of employment and residence in the New York metropolitan region over the postwar period. The scope of the subject, coupled with the limitations of data, resources, and space, limit this outline to a rough sketch. As such, however, it serves to highlight the magnitude of the geographical shifts that have occurred.

## The Geography of Job Restructuring

To most outsiders, "New York" conjures up images of the skyscrapers of Manhattan, but New York extends beyond New York County, beyond New York City, and indeed beyond the boundaries of the Standard Metropolitan Statistical Area (SMSA). Although any boundary is arbitrary, in some ways the most meaningful unit is the Regional Metropolitan Area (RMA) (Figure 5.1). Consisting of twenty-two counties, twelve in New York State, nine in New Jersey, and one in Connecticut, it is an almost continuously built-up area. Except where specified, this chapter is concerned with the RMA. The RMA may be divided into three successive rings, on the basis of the age of the physical infrastructure and also of building and population density, each surrounding the central core of Manhattan (New York County). The "outer core," consisting of the boroughs of Brooklyn (Kings County), the Bronx, and Queens, as well as Hudson County in New Jersey, was developed mainly between the late nineteenth century and the 1920s. The "inner (suburban) ring" was settled largely in the interwar and immediate postwar years, while the "outer ring" has been developed for the most part since the Second World War. Since Hoover and Vernon's study, the outer ring is the only one to have experienced significant growth. Between 1956 and 1975 the population of the RMA increased from 14.7 to 16.8 million, since when it has stabilized. The relative population share of Manhattan, the outer core, and even the inner ring have all fallen since 1956, while that of the outer ring has almost doubled to 31 percent (Table 5.1). The suburbanization of employment has been even more striking than that of population, as the outer ring increased its employment share from 12.3 percent to 28.7 percent over the same period. Even so, in 1985 Manhattan still accounted for almost one-tenth of all residents and over one-quarter of all jobs in the tri-state area.

### Industries

The postwar period has seen the stagnation and decline of manufacturing in America, especially in the Northeast and very dramatically in the New

**Figure 5.1   The New York Metropolitan Region**

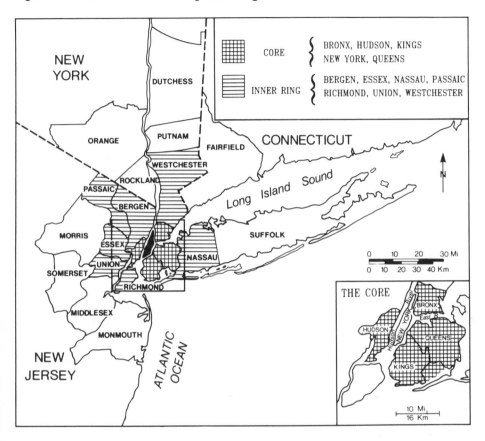

*Source: 1980 Census of Population,* Harris, after Hoover and Vernon.

York RMA.[3] Until the mid-1970s the decline of manufacturing almost equaled, and in the early seventies actually exceeded, job growth in other sectors. With the local recovery that began in 1977, however, the loss of blue collar jobs has been heavily outweighed by the expansion, in particular, of employment in finance and related industries.

The shift away from manufacturing towards office work has had a profound effect upon the geography of employment. All through the postwar period, manufacturing has been concentrated in the suburbs. For 1956, Hoover and Vernon measured the varying concentration of jobs with an index of specialization, or location quotient, which measures the extent to which a particular type of employment is over- or underrepre-

Table 5.1 Population and Employment in the New York Metropolitan Region: 1956–1985

| | Percentage Distribution | | | | | |
|---|---|---|---|---|---|---|
| | Population | | | Employment | | |
| | 1956 | 1975 | 1985 | 1956 | 1975 | 1985 |
| Manhattan | 11.8 | 8.0 | 8.1 | 40.6 | 29.1 | 27.2 |
| Rest of Core | 41.8 | 32.1 | 32.4 | 23.6 | 19.0 | 16.2 |
| Inner Ring | 29.7 | 28.8 | 28.5 | 23.5 | 27.9 | 27.9 |
| Outer Ring | 16.7 | 31.1 | 31.0 | 12.3 | 24.0 | 28.7 |
| NYMR (in thousands) | 15,375 | 18,394 | 18,304 | 6,700 | 7,218 | 8,392 |
| NYMR (in thousands) (excluding Connecticut) | 14,671 | 16,774 | 16,635 | 6,450 | 6,602 | 7,604 |

Sources: Hoover and Vernon, Anatomy of a Metropolis, 1959, p. 6; calculated from New York Metropolitan Transportation Council, Metromonitor, 1986.

Note: The 1975 and 1986 data are for a tri-county region which includes parts of Connecticut in addition to Fairfield County.

sented in specific areas of the city. The quotient (LQ) ranges from zero to infinity, with 100 representing the metropolitan average. Figures greater than 100 indicate an overrepresentation of the job type in question. In 1956 manufacturing jobs were underrepresented in Manhattan (LQ=69) and overrepresented elsewhere (Table 5.2). By 1980 the suburban concentration of manufacturing had become even more apparent. Most striking was the relative decline of employment within the core outside Manhattan. In 1956 manufacturing was heavily overrepresented in the outer boroughs and Hudson County (LQ=121), but by 1980 it was noticeably underrepresented (LQ=86). The absolute decline of manufacturing within the RMA as a whole, then, has had by far its greatest impact within the oldest industrial suburbs, notably Brooklyn and the Bronx.[4]

The only area to have seen a growth in manufacturing is the outer ring. Its share of manufacturing jobs rose from 13 percent to 30 percent between 1956 and 1980, and has probably grown since. The links between manufacturing and wholesaling are close, and as the one has moved to the suburbs so has the other. In the case of wholesaling the shift is very striking indeed. In 1956 Manhattan retained 62 percent of all wholesaling jobs in the RMA, down from about 77 percent in 1929.[5] In the next 25 years, as the port declined, Manhattan's share was halved to barely 29 percent, while the shares of both of the suburban rings increased greatly. Manufacturing and wholesaling have relied increasingly on the truck and

**Table 5.2    Industrial Specialization Within the New York Metropolitan Region: 1956 and 1980**

| | Percentage Distribution | Location Quotient (NYMR=100) | | | |
|---|---|---|---|---|---|
| | | Manhattan | Rest of Core | Inner Ring | Outer Ring |
| **1956** | | | | | |
| Manufacturing | 28.2 | 69 | 121 | 117 | 128 |
| Wholesaling | 6.8 | 145 | 83 | 66 | 45 |
| Finance | 4.8 | 169 | 46 | 68 | 35 |
| **1980** | | | | | |
| Manufacturing | 21.5 | 78 | 86 | 111 | 122 |
| Transport | 9.1 | 102 | 158 | 81 | 71 |
| Wholesaling | 5.1 | 110 | 94 | 112 | 78 |
| Retailing | 14.1 | 70 | 101 | 114 | 113 |
| Finance | 9.5 | 195 | 57 | 75 | 62 |
| Business services | 5.9 | 144 | 66 | 95 | 88 |
| Personal services | 2.6 | 108 | 104 | 100 | 85 |
| Prof. Services | 22.1 | 87 | 118 | 97 | 102 |
| Public administration | 4.8 | 104 | 117 | 88 | 94 |
| **NYMR** | 100.0 | 100 | 100 | 100 | 100 |

*Sources:* Calculated from Hoover and Vernon, *Anatomy of a Metropolis*, 1959, p. 248; U.S. Bureau of the Census, *Place of Work*, New York, 1984, Table 1.

less upon rail and ship, so that suburban locations close to interstate highways have proven to be all but indispensable.

In contrast to the suburban trend in manufacturing, the finance and business service sectors have become even more concentrated in Manhattan. In 1956, employment in the financial sector was heavily concentrated in Manhattan (LQ=169) and underrepresented elsewhere (Table 5.2). By 1980 its overrepresentation in Manhattan had risen (LQ=195), while related business services also had an especially strong presence within the central core. It is not clear whether these sectors can remain so highly concentrated. For many years the head offices of *Fortune* 500 corporations have been moving out of Manhattan.[6] Companies cite the high costs of land, taxes, and housing as the reasons for moving. As they move, business services may follow, and even the financial sector is not immune to the costs of a core location.

Suburban office growth has been encouraged by a new communications technology that makes it possible to separate routine from head office functions. A suburban location is often advantageous since office space is more expensive in Manhattan than elsewhere, while the clerical force is concentrated in the outer core. Cheap electricity has made the New Jersey suburbs more attractive than the boroughs, and is contributing to the success of places such as the Secaucus Meadowlands.[7] As a result, the city has offered incentives to draw employers to office centers such as Fordham Plaza in the Bronx and College Point in Queens.[8] It has met with some success, for example, in persuading Chase Manhattan Bank to move to Brooklyn. The costs in terms of taxes forgone are high, however, and the city may be better advised trying to keep jobs in Manhattan, which is still at the center of the admittedly congested metropolitan transportation network.[9] Although many back- and head offices continue to move out to the suburbs, the Manhattan office boom that began in the late 1970s did not slow down until 1990. As a result, the complementary concentration of offices in Manhattan and of manufacturing and wholesaling in the suburbs is, if anything, even more marked than ever.

*Occupations*

The restructuring of industry has affected the occupational composition of the labor force. The decline of manufacturing has led to an erosion of jobs for blue collar workers. At the same time, the growth of finance and service sectors has created opportunities for clerical workers, professionals, and managers. These shifts have been uneven in their impact, being greatest in Manhattan and the rest of the core. The inner and outer suburban rings contained a fairly balanced cross-section of jobs in 1980, as they had done in 1950 (Table 5.3). Only clerical positions have been underrepresented there while, as industry suburbanized, skilled manual jobs are still overrepresented. Yet marked contrasts have emerged within the city's core. Since the Second World War, Manhattan has strengthened its role as a place of employment for all types of office workers. Between 1950 and 1980 the location quotient for managerial and professional jobs in Manhattan rose from 102 to 120, while that for clerical workers increased from 114 to 128 (Table 5.3). Conversely, the borough's share of blue collar jobs reached an all-time low. By 1980, the proportion of Manhattan's labor force that was blue collar workers was barely three-fifths of the share that these occupations constituted in the metropolitan region as a whole.

The opposite has been happening in the boroughs. The boroughs (with Hudson County) have always been a place for blue collar, as opposed to white collar, jobs. In 1950 they contained slightly less than their share of clerical jobs (LQ=90), and more than their share of manual jobs (LQ=107)

Table 5.3    The Occupational Specialization of Jobs
Within the New York Metropolitan Region: 1950, 1970, and 1980

| | Location Quotient (NYMR=100) | | | | | |
| --- | --- | --- | --- | --- | --- | --- |
| | Manhattan | | | Rest of Core | | |
| | 1950 | 1970 | 1980 | 1950 | 1970 | 1980 |
| Managers/Professionals | 102 | 122 | 120 | 98 | 82 | 84 |
| Clerical | 114 | 141 | 128 | 90 | 77 | 83 |
| Sales | 106 | 108 | 98 | 96 | 89 | 93 |
| Crafts | 86 | 73 | 59 | 108 | 115 | 119 |
| Operatives and Laborers | 87 | 61 | 60 | 107 | 134 | 132 |
| Service | 116 | 100 | 86 | 91 | 107 | 121 |
| | Inner Ring | | | Outer Ring | | |
| | 1950 | 1970 | 1980 | 1950 | 1970 | 1980 |
| Managers/Professionals | 99 | 93 | 95 | 97 | 98 | 97 |
| Clerical | 88 | 117 | 96 | 85 | 77 | 89 |
| Sales | 95 | 102 | 103 | 93 | 99 | 105 |
| Crafts | 114 | 110 | 109 | 115 | 110 | 116 |
| Operatives and Laborers | 114 | 107 | 108 | 112 | 100 | 109 |
| Service | 82 | 92 | 99 | 85 | 111 | 98 |

Sources: Hoover and Vernon, Anatomy of a Metropolis, 1959, p. 148; Kamer, "The Changing Spatial Relationship Between Residences and Worksites in the New York Metropolitan Region," 1977, pp. 448–449; calculated from U.S. Bureau of the Census, Place of Work, New York, Table 1.

Note: Data for 1970 pertain to a 17-county region that excludes Dutchess, Fairfield, Monmouth, Orange, and Putnam counties.

(Table 5.3). Since then, the boroughs have come to rely even more heavily on blue collar jobs. By 1980 they contained less than 85 percent of their share of managerial, professional, and clerical employment, but 119 percent of their share of skilled manual jobs, and fully 132 percent of their regional share of jobs for operatives and laborers. Over the postwar period as a whole, then, the historic contrast in the types of jobs available in Manhattan as opposed to the rest of the core has become greater.

The movement of back offices out of Manhattan is modifying this picture. The concentration of managerial and professional jobs in Manhattan stabilized in the 1970s, indicating that the center remains attractive for head office work (Table 5.4). But the concentration of clerical jobs declined in the 1970s, and this decline has probably continued.[10] At the same time, the share of clerical jobs in the rest of the core has risen slight-

Table 5.4   Changes in the Occupational Specialization of Jobs
in the New York Metropolitan Region: 1950–1980

| | Changes in Location Quotient | | | |
| --- | --- | --- | --- | --- |
| | Manhattan | | Rest of Core | |
| | 1950–1970 | 1970–1980 | 1950–1970 | 1970–1980 |
| Managers/Professionals | 20 | −2 | −16 | 2 |
| Clerical | 27 | −13 | −13 | 6 |
| Sales | 2 | −10 | −7 | 4 |
| Crafts | −13 | −14 | 7 | 4 |
| Operatives and Laborers | −26 | −1 | 27 | −2 |
| Service | −16 | −14 | 16 | 14 |
| | Inner Ring | | Outer Ring | |
| | 1950–1970 | 1970–1980 | 1950–1970 | 1970–1980 |
| Managers/Professionals | −6 | 2 | 1 | −1 |
| Clerical | 29 | −21 | −8 | 12 |
| Sales | 7 | 1 | 6 | 6 |
| Crafts | −4 | −1 | −5 | 6 |
| Operatives and Laborers | −7 | 1 | −12 | 9 |
| Service | 10 | 7 | 26 | −13 |

Sources: See Table 5.2.

ly. The partial decentralization of clerical jobs within the city has helped mitigate the effects of job loss in manufacturing and holds out some hope for a partial rejuvenation of the boroughs.

## The Social Geography of New York

Recent changes in the nature and location of jobs have reshaped the social geography of New York at all scales, ranging from that of the metropolitan area down, in many cases, to the block. Thirty years ago, Hoover and Vernon noted the existence of broad differences in the social composition of Manhattan, the outer core, and the suburban rings.[11] Manhattan's residents included more than its share of professionals (LQ=128) and service workers (LQ=190), but barely half its share of skilled blue collar workers (LQ=57) (see Table 5.5). As a result, the income distribution among the borough's residents was polarized, with the middle cate-

**Table 5.5    The Occupational Specialization of the Resident Labor Force in the New York Metropolitan Region: 1950, 1970, and 1980**

| | Location Quotient (NYMR=100) | | | | | |
| | Manhattan | | | Rest of Core | | |
| | 1950 | 1970 | 1980 | 1950 | 1970 | 1980 |
|---|---|---|---|---|---|---|
| Managers | 93 | 112 | 127 | 93 | 77 | 76 |
| Professionals | 128 | 148 | 163 | 82 | 79 | 74 |
| Clerical | 95 | 94 | 82 | 115 | 117 | 122 |
| Sales | 93 | 90 | 94 | 104 | 91 | 87 |
| Crafts | 57 | 50 | 43 | 102 | 101 | 96 |
| Operatives | 94 | 77 | 74 | 104 | 114 | 116 |
| Laborers | 92 | 67 | 57 | 94 | 109 | 117 |
| Service | 190 | 130 | 105 | 84 | 102 | 116 |

| | Inner Ring | | | Outer Ring | | |
| | 1950 | 1970 | 1980 | 1950 | 1970 | 1980 |
|---|---|---|---|---|---|---|
| Managers | 122 | 120 | 109 | 84 | 114 | 106 |
| Professionals | 113 | 106 | 99 | 106 | 120 | 107 |
| Clerical | 90 | 90 | 96 | 72 | 74 | 85 |
| Sales | 102 | 113 | 109 | 88 | 107 | 106 |
| Crafts | 107 | 107 | 103 | 127 | 128 | 119 |
| Operatives | 92 | 96 | 94 | 109 | 83 | 98 |
| Laborers | 99 | 100 | 100 | 133 | 102 | 94 |
| Service | 81 | 88 | 90 | 93 | 100 | 94 |

*Sources:* Hoover and Vernon, *Anatomy of a Metropolis*, 1959, p. 148; Kamer, "The Changing Spatial Relationship Between Residences and Workplaces in the New York Metropolitan Region," 1977, pp. 448–449; Calculated from U.S. Bureau of the Census, *General Social and Economic Characteristics*, Connecticut, New Jersey, and New York, Table 177.

gories being underrepresented (Figures 5.2 and 5.3a). The core counties outside Manhattan had more than their share of working class residents, notably clerical workers (LQ=115), and to a lesser extent sales workers and operatives (LQ=104). Their income distribution mirrored that of Manhattan, with a solid bulge of middle income earners. The inner ring suburbs were different again. Containing a high proportion of managers and professionals (LQs=122, 113), as well as the skilled blue collar workers (LQ=107), their income distribution was skewed towards the affluent end of the spectrum. The outer ring came closest to being typical of the metropolitan area as a whole. With a high proportion of all types of blue collar workers, it contained roughly its share of people in all income categories (Figure 5.3a).

Figure 5.2   Median Household Income, by Sub-Borough District

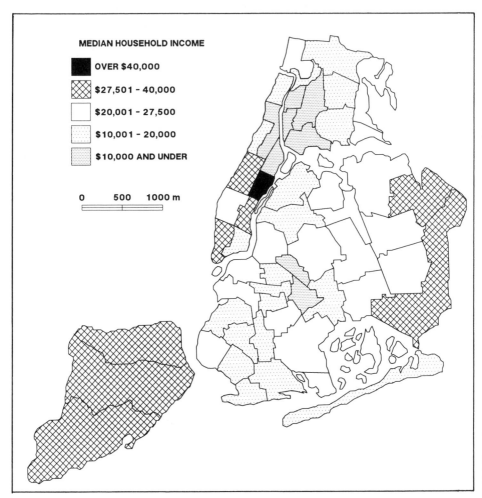

MEDIAN HOUSEHOLD INCOME

■ OVER $40,000

▨ $27,501 – 40,000

☐ $20,001 – 27,500

▨ $10,001 – 20,000

▨ $10,000 AND UNDER

0      500    1000 m

*Source:* Stegman, 1988.

In the past thirty years Manhattan, and each of the three surrounding rings of counties, have changed. In the suburban rings these changes have been quite subtle. The inner ring has lost some appeal for the afflu-ent. Its share of managers and professionals has dropped, in the case of the latter to a point of parity (LQ=99) with the metropolitan area (Table 5.5). Even so, its income distribution is still skewed upwards (Figure 5.3*b*). In contrast, the outer ring has gained a disproportionate number of man-

**Figure 5.3   Geographic Distribution of Households, by Income, New
York Metropolitan Region**

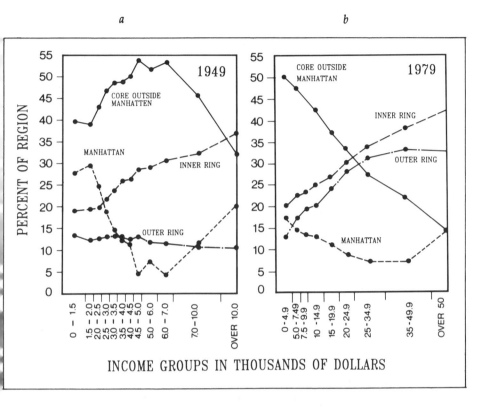

INCOME GROUPS IN THOUSANDS OF DOLLARS

*Sources: U.S. 1950, 1980 Census of Population,* from Hoover and Vernon, 1959, p. 158.

agers, professionals, and skilled blue collar workers. As a result, its income distribution is now skewed upward. In terms of income, although
rather less in terms of the specific mix of occupations, the two suburban
rings are now more similar than they were in 1950.

In becoming more similar, the rings have differentiated themselves
even more from Manhattan and from the remainder of the core. By 1980
Manhattan had become, preeminently, the place of residence of both professionals (LQ=163) and of managers (LQ=127) (Table 5.5). Its share of
service workers had fallen precipitously while all types of blue collar
workers, now including operatives and laborers, were markedly underrepresented. Owing to inflation, and changes in the income categories
used by the census, it is difficult to say whether Manhattan's income dis-

tribution has become more polarized since 1950. But the data do reveal a continuing underrepresentation of middle income households. The rest of the core, by contrast, shifted from being dominated by the middle to being dominated by the poor (Figure 5.3*b*).

The growth of affluent households downtown is usually referred to as gentrification. This process has entailed changes in the social composition of inner residential areas, the redevelopment or renovation of the housing stock, and a transition from rental to owner-occupancy. The presence of affluent households within the inner city is not a novelty in New York. The Upper East Side, in particular, has long been a bastion of wealth. But, in New York as in other cities, gentrification gained momentum in the 1970s. In the 1950s and 1960s many executives, and especially those with children, chose to live in the suburbs. In that 20-year period the relative concentration of managers and professionals in the outer ring increased by 30 and 14 percentage points, respectively (Table 5.6). But this pattern of suburbanization was reversed in the 1970s, when the relative concentration of both groups went into a decline at the metropolitan fringe. This does not mean that the numbers of executives living in the outer ring actually declined, or that significant numbers decided to move to Manhattan. Most likely, the falling concentration in the suburbs was due to an absolute growth in Manhattan as baby boomers established careers.

By 1980, gentrification had left its marks on the landscape of Manhattan, as neighborhoods of new prosperity were added to the established wealth and status of the Upper East Side. Starting in the late sixties, renovation and redevelopment activity was brought to Greenwich Village, SoHo, the Lower East Side, the "Yupper" West Side, Battery Park City, and to accessible districts in the outer boroughs such as Park Slope, Cobble Hill, and on a more modest scale, Clinton and Fort Greene in Brooklyn.[12] In many cases it was initiated by impecunious pioneers, including artists and young professionals willing to invest labor on their own homes. The pioneers were followed by more affluent and apparently more permanent settlers, including executives and better-paid professionals. Between 1950 and 1980 the overrepresentation of these two groups in Manhattan increased by 34 and 35 percentage points, respectively. In each case almost half of the increase occurred between 1970 and 1980 alone (Table 5.6).

As far as it is possible to judge, the trend towards inner city gentrification has increased since the late 1970s. The fiscal crisis of the early- and mid-seventies brought cuts in city services, which surely might have made a suburban home seem doubly attractive to those able to commute. A local economic recovery began in 1977, and the pace of gentrification has been rapid ever since. Apartments and manufacturing loft space has

**Table 5.6    Changes in the Occupational Specialization
of the Resident Labor Force
in the New York Metropolitan Region: 1950–1980**

| | Change in Location Quotient | | | |
|---|---|---|---|---|
| | Manhattan | | Rest of Core | |
| | 1950–1970 | 1970–1980 | 1950–1970 | 1970–1980 |
| Managers | 19 | 15 | −16 | −1 |
| Professionals | 20 | 15 | −3 | −5 |
| Clerical | −1 | −12 | 2 | 5 |
| Sales | −3 | 4 | −13 | −4 |
| Crafts | −7 | −7 | −1 | −5 |
| Operatives | −17 | −3 | 10 | 2 |
| Laborers | −25 | −10 | 15 | 8 |
| Service | −60 | −25 | 18 | 14 |
| | Inner Ring | | Outer Ring | |
| | 1950–1970 | 1970–1980 | 1950–1970 | 1970–1980 |
| Managers | −2 | −11 | 30 | −8 |
| Professionals | −7 | −7 | 14 | −14 |
| Clerical | 0 | 6 | 2 | 11 |
| Sales | 11 | −4 | 19 | −1 |
| Crafts | 0 | −4 | 1 | −9 |
| Operatives | 4 | −2 | −26 | 15 |
| Laborers | 1 | 0 | −31 | −8 |
| Service | 7 | 2 | 7 | −6 |

*Sources:* See Table 5.4.

steadily been converted to condominium ownership. Between 1981 and 1987 the proportion of households that own their homes increased by 2.5 percentage points in all of New York City, but by 5.9 points in Manhattan.[13] Most of this increase was due to the conversion of existing rental units to co-op or condominium ownership and, on the whole, the occupants of these newly converted units have been relatively affluent. In the city as a whole in 1986, the median household incomes of tenants and owners were $16,000 and $30,000, respectively.[14] Those who bought converted units between 1983 and 1986, however, had a median income of $36,000.[15] The latter households were mainly (77 percent) white, and most (78 percent) had no children.[16] Lately, the search for improvable properties has extended to the fringes of Harlem. The pool of black and Puerto Rican gentrifiers is quite small, however, and any large-scale change in the social class composition of this area will depend upon the willingness of whites to move into one of North America's largest ghettoes. It is not clear whether enough whites are willing to do this.[17]

Directly or indirectly, gentrifiers displace lower-income households. Apartments are renovated and then rented or sold at prices well beyond the means of the previous occupants.[18] In the short run, this process leads to greater mixing of people at the scale of the neighborhood, and within specific buildings. Indeed, upgraded and abandoned housing units coexist on the same blocks.[19] But this situation is not stable even in New York, where the close juxtaposition of poverty and wealth has a long history and where the wealthy have developed the requisite strategies for social avoidance. At the time of writing, renovation and displacement are beginning to transform the Lower East Side, historically the reception area for immigrants and today the last major area of low-income settlement in lower Manhattan.[20] In Manhattan as a whole, median household incomes are rising more rapidly than in any other borough. In constant dollars, the increase between 1983 and 1986 alone was 18.3 percent.[21] It is not difficult to foresee a time when Manhattan below 96th street will be homogeneously affluent.

Up to now, economic restructuring has generally had the effect of exaggerating the polarized social composition of Manhattan. Its effect on the outer core has been to bring about a qualitative change. In 1949 the boroughs and Hudson County contained a solid bulge of middle-income households. They now contain only three-quarters of their share of managers and professionals, but more than their share of clerical and service workers, together with operatives and laborers. Employees in all of the latter occupational categories are, in general, poorly paid. As a result, the income distribution within the outer core is consistently weighted towards the bottom end of the spectrum. In 1979, the outer core contained 14 percent of all households within the metropolitan area that received incomes in excess of $50,000. In contrast, they were home to exactly half of those households that received less than $5,000.

Data at the borough scale understate the true contrasts between the gentrifying center, much of the outer core, and the suburbs. In social terms, the emerging contrast is that between the affluence of lower Manhattan and adjacent parts of Brooklyn, and the poverty of northern Manhattan, the south Bronx, and most of northern Brooklyn.[22] The ring of poverty around the growing, affluent center is not complete. Much of Queens, even those parts that are closest to lower Manhattan, is quite prosperous. With this exception, however, the pattern is quite striking.

The occupational pattern of settlement has strong racial and ethnic associations. Within the city, affluent Manhattan is mostly white and concentrated south, east, and west of Central Park.[23] As Manhattan is gentrified it is likely to become more white. The poor are mostly black or Hispanic and live north of 96th street in Harlem and Washington Heights-Inwood. The decline of the outer core has gone hand in hand with the influx of blacks, notably to Bedford-Stuyvesant in northern Brooklyn, now New York's largest black ghetto, and of Hispanics into numerous smaller pockets of settlement.[24] These trends have created neighborhood conflicts and white resistance in places such as Forest Hills, Canarsie, and Howard Beach.[25] They have also led to white flight, with the result that the boroughs have become the home for a growing proportion of ethnic and racial minorities, including a new generation of immigrants from Latin America and East Asia.

In part new immigrants have followed their predecessors, settling first in the city, and specifically in inner areas such as the Lower East Side.[26] In 1980 the proportion of foreign-born residents in suburban counties nowhere exceeded 15 percent, while the figure for New York City was 23.6 (Figure 5.4). Increasingly, however, new immigrants are settling outside of the traditional reception areas. Koreans are a case in point.[27] Thus in 1980, Queens contained a higher proportion of first generation immigrants than did Manhattan or Brooklyn. Indeed, a growing number of immigrants are finding their way into the suburbs. In 1980, foreign-born residents made up at least 5 percent of the population in every metropolitan county. Many of the new immigrants are upwardly mobile.[28] As a result, the association of class with race or ethnicity remains strongest for blacks and Hispanics, and the largest slums are black or Hispanic ghettos.

## The Influence of Employment Location on Residence

The social contrasts between Manhattan, the outer core, and the suburban rings are the result of millions of decisions to move, settle, or stay put. These decisions have been shaped by many considerations. One of the most important has been the changing distribution of different types of paid employment.

In a general way, the influence of work on the location of the home may be seen by comparing, for specific occupations, the areas of concentration of people and jobs. If people follow jobs, the same counties that contain more than their share of certain types of work will also contain more than their share of the people who do that work. In general, such an association is apparent. In the case of semiskilled and unskilled manual

Figure 5.4   **Proportion of Population Foreign-Born: 1980**

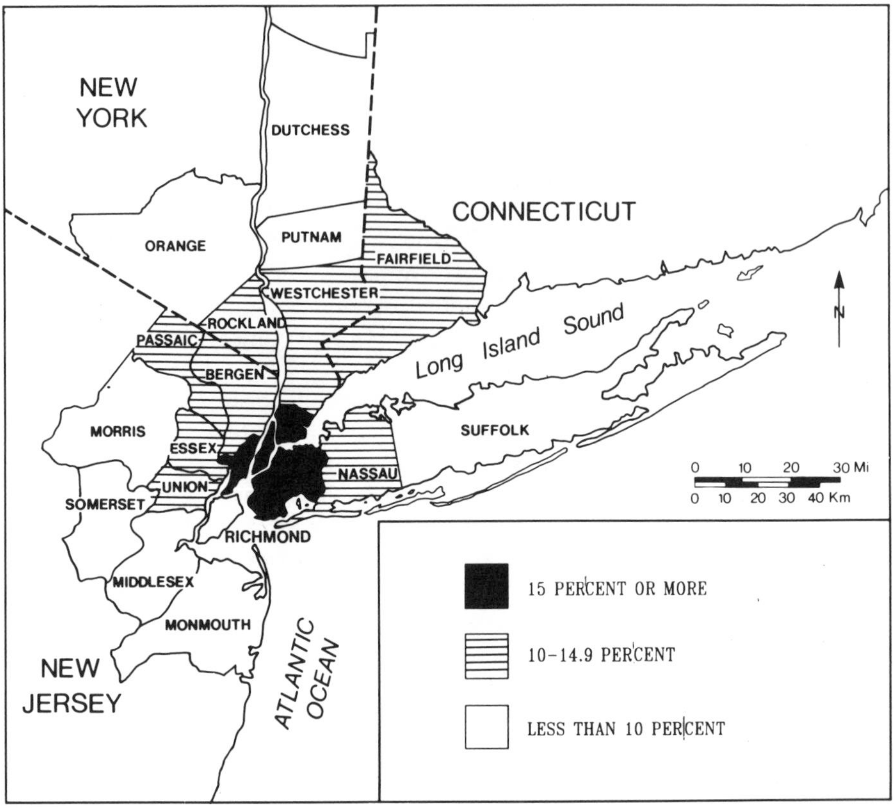

*Source: 1980 Census of Population,* Harris, after Hoover and Vernon.

work, for example, the same three counties that contain a marked over-representation of jobs also contain a lot more than their share of employees (Figure 5.5). Another six counties contain slightly more than their share of both people and jobs. Only one county, Bergen, has a slight excess of jobs, but not of people, and none has an excess of people but not of jobs. It is possible, of course, that the jobs followed the people, but the reverse is far more probable.

The association between work and home is apparent, though weaker, for most other occupational groups. Among skilled workers, three counties contain an excess of both people and jobs, but nine have a slight excess of people but not of jobs (Figure 5.6). It is likely that skilled work-

**Figure 5.5    Semiskilled and Unskilled Occupations: 1980**

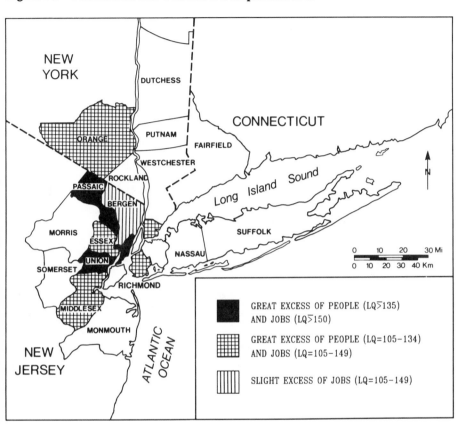

*Source: 1980 Census of Population,* Harris, after Hoover and Vernon.

ers are able and willing to travel farther to work. The same is also true of those in managerial and professional occupations. Manhattan aside, three counties, Putnam, Westchester, and Morris, contained an excess of both people and jobs in these lines of work (Figure 5.7). A further six contained residential clusters, but none had concentrations of work. Many of the professionals and managers in these six counties probably worked in Manhattan. Thirty years ago, where workplaces and residences did not coincide, the residences were generally suburban.[29] The same is true to-day. In the case of managers and professionals this is inevitable, since the jobs are concentrated in lower Manhattan. In the case of the skilled blue collar workers, however, it is not. Presumably, many of the workers who

**Figure 5.6  Skilled Occupations: 1980**

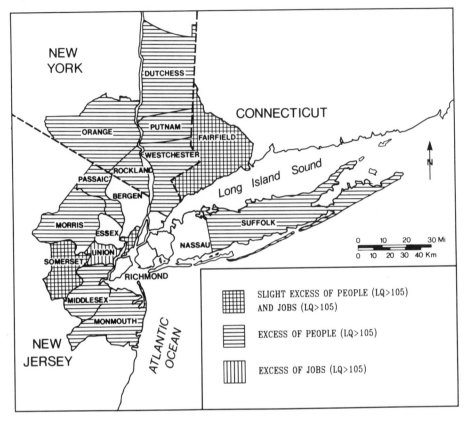

*Source: 1980 Census of Population,* Harris, after Hoover and Vernon.

live farther away from Manhattan than their jobs do so in order to take advantage of cheaper land and more modern housing.

In terms of the broad occupational classification for which data are available, one group stands out. There are no counties that contain more than their share of both clerical jobs and employees. Manhattan has the jobs; the outer boroughs house the workers (Figure 5.8). In part, this is because most clerical workers are poorly paid and are unable to afford Manhattan rents. But gender also plays a vital role. Within the entire metropolitan area in 1980, women were 44 percent of the labor force. In most occupational groups this proportion was less than 50 percent, but among clerical workers women were in a majority (Table 5.7). Many female clerical workers would have been single and, subject to limitations imposed by

**Figure 5.7   Managerial and Professional Occupations: 1980**

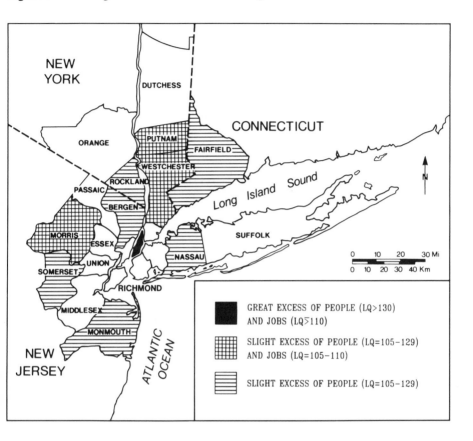

*Source: 1980 Census of Population, Harris, after Hoover and Vernon.*

their income, able to make their own choice of residence. But many would have been married. Typically, the latter would have lived in households in which proximity to the man's place of work would have been given top priority.

The combined effect of gender and income can explain the difference in the commuting patterns of clerical workers, as opposed to those of managers and professionals. Although the place of work for a high proportion of both groups of workers was located in Manhattan, each lived in different parts of the metropolitan area. Varying patterns of settlement imply differences in commuting. Published data do not make it possible to trace actual commuting patterns within the entire 22-county region.

**Figure 5.8    Clerical Occupations: 1980**

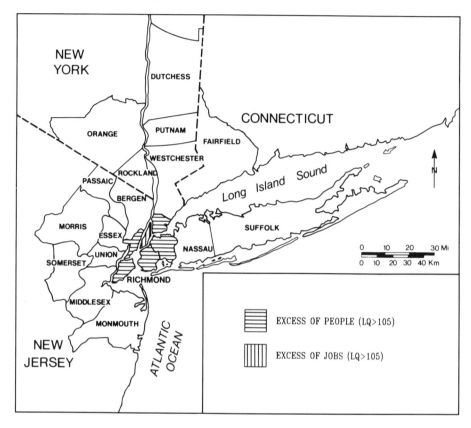

*Source: 1980 Census of Population, Harris, after Hoover and Vernon.*

However, they do provide information about commuting, broken down by county within an SMSA that included Putnam, Rockland, and Westchester counties as well as the city itself. Census data show that, by New York standards, clerical workers travel moderate distances to work and that managers and professionals may travel quite far. The majority of clerical workers in each of the outer boroughs works in Manhattan, and almost all of the remainder work within their borough of residence. Very few of those that lived in the suburban ring counties commute downtown. Even in Westchester County the proportion was only 16 percent. By contrast, a significant minority of managers and professionals who lived in the suburban ring worked in Manhattan, the proportion in Westchester being 27 percent.

**Table 5.7    The Gender Composition of the Resident Labor Force, by Occupation: New York Metropolitan Region, 1980**

| | Location Quotient (NYMR=100) | | | Proportion of the Labor Force That Are Women | | | |
|---|---|---|---|---|---|---|---|
| | Manhattan | | | Rest of | Inner | Outer | |
| | Men | Women | Manhattan | Core | Ring | Ring | NYMR |
| Managers | 115 | 168 | 39.4 | 31.6 | 25.1 | 23.4 | 27.8 |
| Professionals | 170 | 153 | 48.3 | 50.7 | 46.6 | 45.1 | 47.4 |
| Clerical | 107 | 70 | 67.6 | 69.5 | 77.2 | 76.8 | 73.4 |
| Sales | 101 | 86 | 42.8 | 42.1 | 43.0 | 45.2 | 43.5 |
| Crafts | 39 | 105 | 21.3 | 9.3 | 7.2 | 6.4 | 8.2 |
| Operatives | 62 | 99 | 48.3 | 35.5 | 30.4 | 32.2 | 34.0 |
| Laborers | 59 | 59 | 22.9 | 19.1 | 21.2 | 21.8 | 20.8 |
| Service | 124 | 86 | 42.4 | 45.3 | 49.1 | 51.5 | 47.8 |
| | | | 47.3 | 45.1 | 43.4 | 42.0 | 43.9 |

*Source:* U.S. Bureau of the Census, *General Social and Economic Characteristics*, 1983, Connecticut, New Jersey, New York, Table 177.

Distance is not necessarily equivalent to time. A recent survey conducted by the Regional Plan Association showed that although many executives travel far to work, they do not spend much more time commuting than clerical workers.[30] Clerical workers commute by bus or subway, while executives depend more heavily on the suburban rail service, which is faster, if more expensive. If low income prevents many clerical workers from living in Manhattan, it also prevents them from following the example of the suburban executive.

As the determinant of commuting patterns, gender helps to explain differences between occupational groups as well as within groups. Executives are a case in point. A majority of managers are men (Table 5.7). This is most apparent in the outer ring suburbs, however, and least in Manhattan. Indeed, in relative terms Manhattan contains a much greater concentration of female managers (LQ=168) than of male (LQ=115). The evidence is suggestive, indicating that male executives are part of a traditional or compromise work strategy. Their homes are in the suburbs; their wives work at home or take an available job in the vicinity. In contrast, female executives are likely to be single or, if married, part of a dual wage-earning household. To work and build a career they, more than their male counterparts, must live in an environment that minimizes commuting and unpaid domestic work. Some, of course, are able to sustain a suburban life by employing servants. But many find that to pursue their careers they have to live close to work. This is likely to be especially true for the growing number of self-employed women in consulting and related occupations, for whom easy access to sources of information, services, and employment contacts is critical. In this manner women, including those with careers, are playing an important part in the process of gentrification.[31]

## Conclusion

The restructuring of New York's economy in the past 30 years has significantly changed the industrial and social geography of the metropolitan area. The steady loss of manufacturing jobs has been geographically selective, having its greatest impact upon the boroughs. More recently, office growth has occurred virtually everywhere, but most strikingly in Manhattan. These shifts in the geography of employment have reshaped the social geography of the metropolitan area. Large-scale contrasts between Manhattan, the remainder of the core, and the suburbs, have increased. With office growth, much of Manhattan below 96th Street has been, or is in the process of being, gentrified, as are adjacent areas of Brooklyn. In contrast, the effects of the loss of manufacturing is still very apparent in parts of Brooklyn and Queens, together with a large swath of the Bronx.

The United States city in the postwar period has been likened to a ring donut, with a hole of poverty in the middle. In New York the poverty is being displaced outwards as a core of affluence grows. In the process, many neighborhoods are undergoing a process of upward transition, with associated conflicts and problems of displacement. There are limits to this trend. The most critical limit is likely to be the capacity—in terms of time and money—of low-wage workers to get to work. Both at work and at home, the affluent need the services that are provided by cleaners, nannies, secretaries, clerks, and waitresses. Many of these workers work long hours for low pay and, as they are displaced from the gentrifying center, they are likely to find their journeys to work increasingly onerous. At the limit they may be unable or unwilling to make the necessary commute. For many, of course, commuting in New York is already a nightmare: costly, time-consuming, stressful, and sometimes dangerous. But it is not clear that the limits have yet been reached. For the present, at least until the next major recession, the geographical transformation of New York continues apace.

# Notes

I would like to thank members of the Dual City working group, especially Manuel Castells and Frank DeGiovanni, for their comments on an earlier draft, and Rick Hamilton for drawing the maps.

1. Hoover, Edgar, and Raymond Vernon, *Anatomy of a Metropolis* (Cambridge: Harvard University Press, 1959).

2. Smith, Neil, and Peter Williams, eds., *Gentrification of the City* (Boston: Allen & Unwin, 1986), pp. 217–219.

3. Ross, Robert, and Kent Trachte, "Global Cities and Global Classes: the Peripheralization of Labor in New York City," *Review* 6,3 (1983): 393–431; Rubin, Marilyn, Ilene Weber, and Pearl Kamer, "Industrial Migration: A Case Study of Destination by City-Suburban Origin within the New York Metropolitan Area," *Journal of the American Real Estate and Urban Economics Association* 6 (1978): 417–437.

4. Rubin, Weber, and Kamer, "Industrial Migration."

5. Chinitz, Benjamin, *Freight and the Metropolis* (Cambridge: Harvard University Press, 1960).

6. Quante, Wolfgang, *The Exodus of Corporate Headquarters from New York City* (New York: Praeger, 1976); Conservation of Human Resources, *The Corporate Headquarters Complex in New York City* (Montclair, NJ: Allanheld Osmun, 1977); Scardino, Albert, "Changing Era for New York's Economy," *New York Times* (18 May 1987): B1–2.

7. Armstrong and Milder, "Employment in the Manhattan CBD"; Peterson, Iver, "The Meadowlands, Symbol of Region's 'Border Wars,'" *New York Times* (29 June 1987): B1,4; Roberts, Sam, "If Companies Move to Suburbs It Still Hurts," *New York Times* (28 May 1987): B1.

8. Spinola, Steven, "Promoting Back Office Development in New York City," *City Almanac* 18,1–2 (1984): 23–28.

9. Smith, Neil, "Of Yuppies and Housing: Gentrification, Social Restructuring, and the Urban Dream," *Environment and Planning D: Society and Space* 5 (1987): 151–172.

10. Moss, Mitchell L., and Andrew Dunau, "Will the Cities Lose Their Back Offices?" *Real Estate Review* 17,1 (1987): 62–68.

11. Hoover and Vernon, *Anatomy of a Metropolis*, pp. 162ff.

12. Blauner, Robert, "Oh Pioneers. Life in the Newest Neighborhood," *New York* (June 16, 1987), p. 39; Chall, Daniel, "Neighborhood Changes in New York City during the 1970s. Are the Gentry Returning?" *Federal Reserve Bank of New York Quarterly Bulletin* (Winter 1983–1984): 38–48; Community Service Society of New York, "Displacement Pressures in the Lower East Side." Working Paper (1987); Trillin, Calvin, "US Journal: Greenwich Village. Thoughts on the Shape of Neighborhood History" *New York* 58 (June 7,

1982), p. 104; Unger, Craig, "The Lower East Side. There Goes the Neighborhood," *New York* (May 28, 1984), pp. 32–41; Zukin, Sharon, *Loft Living: Culture and Capital in Urban Change* (Baltimore: Johns Hopkins University Press,
1982).

13. Stegman, Michael A., *Housing in New York: Study of a City, 1984* (New York:
Department of Housing Preservation and Development, City of New York,
1984), p. 45; Stegman, *Housing and Vacancy Report*, p. 26.

14. Stegman, *Housing and Vacancy Report*, p. 100.

15. Ibid., p. 185.

16. Ibid., pp. 182, 185.

17. Schaffer, Robert, and Neil Smith, "The Gentrification of Harlem?" *Annals of
the Association of American Geographers* 76,3 (1987): 347–365.

18. Marcuse, Peter, "Abandonment, Gentrification, and Displacement: Linkage
in New York City," in Smith, N., and P. Williams, eds., *Gentrification of the
City* (Boston: Allen & Unwin, 1986); "Homelessness, Poverty, Race and Displacement," (New York: New York Civil Liberties Union Foundation, March
1986). See also Chapter 11.

19. Marcuse, "Abandonment, Gentrification."

20. Community Service Society of New York, "Displacement Pressures."

21. Stegman, *Housing and Vacancy Report*, p. 100.

22. Tobier, Emanuel, *The Changing Face of Poverty: Trends in New York City's Population in Poverty 1960–1990* (New York: Community Service Society of New
York, 1984).

23. City of New York, Department of City Planning, *Atlas of the Census* (1985).

24. Ibid., pp. 11–12.

25. Cuomo, Mario, *Forest Hills Diary* (New York: Random House, 1974); Rieder,
Jonathan, *Canarsie: The Jews and Italians of Brooklyn Against Liberalism* (Cambridge: Harvard University Press, 1985).

26. City of New York, *Atlas*, p. 18.

27. Kim, Ilsoo, "The Koreans: Small Business in an Urban Frontier," in N. Foner,
ed., *New Immigrants in New York* (New York: Columbia University Press,
1987).

28. Waldinger, Roger, "Changing Ladders and Musical Chairs: Ethnicity and Opportunity in Post-Industrial New York," *Politics & Society* 15,4 (1986–1987):
369–402.

29. Hoover and Vernon, *Anatomy of a Metropolis*, p. 149.

30. Regional Plan Association of New York, "The Effects of Headquarters Office
Locations on Travel," *Technical Report No. 2* (New York: Regional Plan Association, 1983).

31. Rose, Damaris, "Rethinking Gentrification: Beyond the Uneven Development
of Marxist Theory," *Environment and Planning D. Society and Space* 2,1 (1984):
62; Smith, "Of Yuppies and Housing," p. 158.

# PART III

# The New Dominant
# Occupational Strata

# 6

# Upper Professionals: A High Command of Commerce, Culture, and Civic Regulation

## Steven Brint

## Introduction

Even in the antebellum period, the distinctive industries of New York City—shipping, wholesale trade, and finance—required a relatively sizeable body of professional experts and salaried managers. Yet these upper white collar workers left but a weak social imprint in the days of New York's rise to prominence as the nation's premier commercial city. They were overshadowed by the triumphant entrepreneurs and financiers who employed them, by the colorful and often corrupt politicians who represented the people of the port city as it grew into a great economic center, and by the laboring masses who dwarfed them in numbers and collective influence. Some roles were left to professional men, especially lawyers, in campaigns for civic betterment and as patrons (and indeed as contributors) to arts and letters, but, for the most part, the early history of New York is dominated by other more numerous and powerful classes.

The contemporary period presents a very different and more controversial picture. Where salaried professionals and managers, as classified by the Census Bureau, accounted for something under 5 percent of the working population throughout the nineteenth century and early twentieth century,[1] they now represent nearly 30 percent of the labor force.[2] At the higher end of the professional and managerial spectrum, affluent professional people are now so numerous, visible, and influential that some observers have characterized them as the "new dominant class" of the postindustrial city.[3] On the surface, these images are compelling. New Yorkers have become accustomed to associating the brisk, confident

155

strides of the upper classes with highly educated brokers, lawyers, architects, even the once-tawdry metropolitan journalists—and not necessarily with the business tycoons, financiers, and politicians of years gone by. Apart from their evident sense of purpose and confidence, there are other "class-like" characteristics that upper-level professionals seem also to share. To some observers, they look strikingly similar in their support for civil liberties, moderate social reform, and vigorous business development policies. And, as is so often the case with the leading classes, the younger cohorts of the professional group, the so-called Yuppies (young urban professionals), have been hailed in recent years as fashion-makers and trendsetters in the city and indeed in the nation at large.[4] This chapter will provide a sociological evaluation of these popular images, concentrating on where New York's salaried professional people fit into the class structure and political divisions of the modern metropolis.

*Professional Strata*

To do so, the professional and managerial categories, as defined by the Census Bureau, have been divided into four broad strata. The first is an *Upper Professionals* group, composed of people with highly valued intellectual resources, who typically work for powerful organizations and are involved with the cosmopolitan side of the economic and cultural life of the city. These people include, for example, many corporate lawyers, accountants in the leading accounting firms, numbers of the major architectural firms, television executives, leading artists and designers, doctors in leading medical research hospitals, and researchers involved with important civic planning activities. The second group is a *Rank-and-File Professionals* stratum, composed of salaried people with less highly valued intellectual resources, who typically work for less powerful individuals or organizations and whose orientations are more local than cosmopolitan. These people include, for example, many teachers, social workers, engineers, government lawyers, internists in local practice, suburban journalists, and accountants for small and medium-size businesses. The third group is a *Small Employers* group, which includes self-employed business and professional people of solidly middle- and upper-middle incomes. The fourth is a *Lower-level Professionals* group—people with professional or managerial occupational titles, but without the incomes to sustain a securely middle class standard of living.

The structure of stratification among New York's professionals and managers is steeply pyramidal. In my calculations, just over 1 percent of New York City's labor force in 1980 qualified as Upper Professionals, using an annual income cutoff of $40,000 for purposes of categorization.

Another 1 percent qualified as Small Employers, again using a $40,000 per year cutoff. Approximately 10 percent of the city's labor force qualified as Rank-and-File Professionals, using an annual income of $20,000 as a cutoff. A surprisingly large proportion—almost 20 percent of the labor force (and almost two-thirds of the census professionals and managers)—fell into the Lower-level Professionals category.

This chapter will focus on the top group—the Upper Professionals—because this group is central to our popular images of a "new class" of highly educated professionals who provide social and economic direction from the command posts of a knowledge-based society.

*Institutional Bases*

Using a framework suggested by Matthew P. Drennan's chapter in this volume,[5] my analysis focuses on four major institutional complexes that employ upper-level professional workers: (1) the corportate and business services (or C&BS) complex; (2) the culture and communications (C&C) complex; (3) the civic (CIV) complex; and (4) the human capital services (HCS) complex. These four institutional complexes are the central and most powerful sectors in the city's economic and political life, and they are, at least in some important respects, self-consciously knowledge- and information-based.

The principal reason for the fourfold division is that separate social and economic forces are at work in the rise of these four institutional complexes, and these forces have important implications for the socioeconomic situation, identifications, and politics of Upper Professionals. A functional terminology provides the best shorthand way to indicate the nature of these forces in a sufficiently brief space. The corporate and business services complex is driven by the developing production needs and capacities of the advanced sectors of the economy. The culture and communications complex is driven by consumer information and recreational interests. The civic complex is driven by the need to maintain and regulate the urban environment through administrative and political decision-making. The human capital services industries—health, education, and social services—are united by a common focus on maintaining (and, where possible, improving) the social and economic situation of individuals so that they can meet accepted standards as productive members of the society.

In 1980, the corporate and business complex employed almost two-thirds of Upper Professionals in New York City (see Table 6.1). The group was divided almost equally between those working in corporate headquarters per se (31.5 percent) and those working in financial and business services (34.5 percent). The corporate segment was dominated, not surprisingly, by executive officers, who comprised half of the total. The business services segment was more heterogeneous occupationally. Again, executive officers were a large group (29 percent), but so were lawyers (16 percent) and securities brokers (also 16 percent).

The other complexes were much smaller. The culture and communications complex employed approximately one out of ten Upper Professionals in 1980. Of this group, two-thirds (69 percent) were artists or writers. Approximately 5.5 percent of all Upper Professionals were members of the civic complex by direct organizational affiliation.[6] Of these, the great majority were part of the administrative apparatus of government. One-quarter were administrators, and 22 percent were lawyers or judges. Approximately 13 percent of Upper Professionals were employed in the HCS complex in 1980. About two-fifths of these were physicians, and 10 percent were educators.

## Socioeconomic Situations

There are three important questions about the social class sitation of the professional groups in New York:

1. Are the Upper Professionals a "new dominant class," as the heralds of the postindustrial society would have it?
2. Are the Upper Professionals, divided as they are by institutional sector and average life chances, really a class at all?
3. Where do the other professional and managerial strata—the Small Employers, Rank-and-File Professionals, and Marginal Professionals—fit into the class structure of the postindustrial city?

### A "New Dominant Class"?

The first question is the easiest to answer. In spite of their impressive credentials and relatively privileged economic situations, Upper Professionals cannot be seriously considered a "new dominant class" in New York City (or indeed anywhere else). The top class in New York is, as it has long been, the thin ribbon of wealthy entrepreneurs, corporate officers, financiers, and investors who own the largest proportion of economic resources in the city. The Upper Professionals are a "high command" of commerce, culture, and civic regulation, but not the highest command.

It seems likely that the role of highly educated professionals in New York is magnified because of the influence of suburbanization. Many of

**Table 6.1  Major Occupations of Upper Professionals, by Institutional Complex, New York City: 1980**

| Institutional Complex | Percentage of Category | (N) |
|---|---|---|
| Corporate (31.5% of total for 5 institutional complexes) | | |
| Managers, n.e.c. | 37.1 | (227) |
| Publicity and marketing | 20.4 | (125) |
| Sales Reps and supervisors | 16.2 | (99) |
| Lawyers | 5.2 | (32) |
| Financial and Business Services (34.4% of total) | | |
| Managers, n.e.c. | 19.1 | (128) |
| Lawyers | 16.3 | (109) |
| Securities brokers | 16.0 | (107) |
| Financial officers | 11.1 | (74) |
| Advertisers | 5.6 | (37) |
| Sales mgrs and sales reps. | 5.1 | (34) |
| Accountants | 3.1 | (21) |
| Management analysts | 3.0 | (20) |
| Communications and Culture (15.6% of total) | | |
| Actors | 21.8 | (66) |
| Designers | 12.5 | (38) |
| Managers, n.e.c. | 12.2 | (37) |
| Authors | 10.0 | (31) |
| Painters and sculptors | 7.9 | (24) |
| Musicians | 7.9 | (24) |
| Editors and reporters | 6.9 | (21) |
| Civic (5.4% of total) | | |
| Public administrators | 25.0 | (26) |
| Managers, n.e.c | 16.3 | (17) |
| Lawyers | 11.5 | (12) |
| Judges | 9.6 | (10) |
| Human Capital Services (12.8% of total) | | |
| Physicians | 40.4 | (98) |
| Professors | 9.9 | (23) |
| Psychotherapists | 9.1 | (22) |
| Educational administrators | 7.0 | (17) |
| Managers, n.e.c. | 7.0 | (17) |
| Health administrators | 4.0 | (10) |

*Source:* 1980 Public Use Microdata Sample (PUMS), U.S. Census.

the most powerful people in the city do not live regularly in New York. By concentrating exclusively on people who do live in New York, social scientists can convey the (wrong) impression that upper-level professionals dominate. As Andrew Hacker has observed, top corporate executives are not usually urbanites.[7] They typically come from small town and midwestern backgrounds, and they are more often interested in good golf courses than good museums. In 1975, three-quarters of the presiding officers of corporations with offices in New York lived outside the city.

Even among city residents, however, it should be evident that the distributional structure is not dominated by the Upper Professionals. There is a thin but powerful stratum of millionaires (and, indeed, billionaires)[8] who remain resident in New York. At the apex of this group are a few extremely wealthy people, like Estee Lauder, Harry Helmsley, and David Rockefeller, who started large businesses or descended from those who did, and the great real estate magnates, like Donald Trump and Sol Lefrak, who are the functional heirs of the Astor approach to acquisition.

## Stratum or Class?

We are left, then, with the Upper Professionals as a next-to-the-top layer. Is this next-to-the-top layer also a "class"? There are clearly some reasons for believing that Upper Professionals share enough commonalities in social situation, interests, and culture to constitute a definable class.

The Upper Professionals are distinguished by their backgrounds, levels of education, relative youth, and chances for capital accumulation. According to 1980 census data, almost 90 percent of the Upper Professionals were non-Hispanic whites (compared to 80 percent of the Rank-and-File Professionals and 57 percent of the Lower-level Professionals). Eighty percent of the Upper Professionals were college graduates, compared to two-thirds of the Rank-and-File Professionals and less than half of the Lower-level Professionals. Some 55 percent of the Upper Professionals were 45 or younger, compared with 40 percent of professionals at the same income level living outside Manhattan. Over 7 percent of the Upper Professionals reported earnings from dividends and interest of over $25,000 in 1980, compared to 1 percent of the Rank-and-File Professionals and none of the Lower-level Professionals.

It is possible to argue that Upper Professionals are united, to a considerable degree, by training, work experiences, and taste. Their educational credentials provide a common basis for access to higher-level positions. The experience of higher education encourages a willingness to research facts and to draw on expert sources of information. Professional work in each of the four complexes typically involves many snap decisions, deadline pressures, and the ability to control quantities of information and think through the effects of many variable forces. This is not exactly the "culture of critical discourse," which sociologist Alvin Gouldner has described; it is more a "culture of quick-witted discourse."

Survey evidence indicates that the taste of Upper Professionals runs toward expensive designer goods and avid consumption of the arts. On the latter point, national surveys indicate that participation and consumption of the arts is an additive function of urban residence, high levels of education, high incomes, and professional occupations. In other words, arts consumption is correlated with each of the characteristics used to define the Upper Professional group.[9]

An important point about the taste of the Upper Professionals is not that it is distinctively channeled in any particular way, but that there is simply more of it and more diversity in it. Data from the Consumer Expenditures Survey found that spending on lifestyle purchases of all types increased from 9 to 20 percent from the lowest to the highest quintiles.[10] The consumption data indicate that better-educated and higher-income people do not enjoy any particular style of music or art over that enjoyed by other groups, they enjoy all styles more than other groups.[11]

In spite of these commonalities, it seems unlikely that these professionals truly constitute a class in any meaningful sense of the term. Perhaps the most important argument against thinking of the Upper Professionals as a class is the considerable variation in ties to other classes that exists among the Upper Professionals in the different complexes. Professionals in the corporate and business services complex are closely tied in terms of function and also background to the upper class of wealthy entrepreneurs and investors. These are the people they directly or indirectly represent and for whom the success of their activities counts most directly. Corporate lawyers work on behalf of the top executives of the corporations, as do advertising executives, accountants, investment bankers, and management consultants. Professionals in the civic and human capital services complexes, by contrast, are tied functionally to political organizations, government administration, and community activists. These are very different institutional milieus from those served by corporate headquarters professionals. The culture and communications complex is tied not only to corporate business but also to the popular arts and popular arts audiences.

Professionals in the different institutional complexes also have decidedly different earnings curves. As Stanback and his colleagues have noted about producer services nationally, the size of the GNP originating in this sector tends to be much higher than the sectors' corresponding share of employment.[12] As this observation would lead us to predict, the professionals and managers of New York's corporate and business services complex were not only the largest of the Upper Professional sectors, they were also, to an even greater degree, the most advantaged. Of the Upper Professionals who reported earnings of $75,000 or more in 1980, three-quarters were tied to the C&BS complex.[13] Of those who reported capital gains of $25,000 or more, 70 percent were from this sector. If we can take them at their word (clearly a dubious assumption in some cases), the civic professionals were the least advantaged of the Upper Professional groups. One-quarter reported earning over $60,000 or more in 1980, compared to 40 percent of Upper Professionals at large. Upper Professionals in the HCS complex—the other predominantly nonprofit sector—were also somewhat less advantaged. Thirty percent of them reported incomes above $60,000 in 1980. Since physicians in the complex earned at a rate comparable to Upper Professionals in other sectors, these figures represent significantly lower average earnings for the other occupational groups included there.

Significant differences also exist in the ethnic composition of the main institutional complexes. The corporate and business service complex is disproportionately composed of whites, and especially those from British, Italian, Irish, and Russian ancestry. Blacks, Puerto Ricans, and Asians are extremely underrepresented in this complex. The culture and communications complex is not quite as skewed toward white groups, but it is very nearly so. Here people from British and Russian backgrounds (many of the latter of whom are Jewish) are especially prevalent. Only the civic and human capital service complexes were at all likely to employ black and Asian professionals.

Taken together, these divisions in ties to other classes, life chances, and background characteristics seem to override the commonalities shared by the Upper Professionals. These people are a distinct stratum of business and professional New York, but they are too institutionally divided to be usefully considered a class.

### The Other Strata of Business and Professional New York

A few words should be said about the third, fourth, and fifth layers of business and professional New York—the Small Employers, Rank-and-File Professionals, and Lower-level Professionals—and where they fit into the class structure of the dual city.

The Small Employers class includes business owners in goods production, wholesale and retail trade, and it also includes self-employed professional people (mainly doctors and lawyers). As constructed, the Small Employers have incomes which approximate those of the Upper Professionals, but different organizational and market attachments.

The Small Employers are their own bosses, and they are typically involved in goods and services production to local or regional consumers. The Upper Professionals, by contrast, are attached to organizations and are typically involved in goods and services production for national or even international consumers. The differing average educational levels of the Upper Professionals indicate something about the information-processing requirements of working in high-level positions in complex organizations with this broad market scope. Some 80 percent of Upper Professionals were college graduates. If we look at only the business people among the small employers (leaving out the self-employed professionals), only about 40 percent were college graduates.

Goods production and distribution establishments are still one of the backbones of the New York economy, but they are less important than they had been. The New York State Department of Labor showed a modest (.86 percent) annual decline in goods production and distribution as a locus of employment in the 1977–86 period, continuing a trend from the 1950s and 1960s. Manufacturing is responsible for the majority of the job loss. Although New York remains relatively strong in some light manufacturing industries, and in production of some relatively unstandardized goods (clothes, jewelry, leathers, furs, and toys, in particular), especially for luxury markets, it has not grown in manufacturing employment since the 1940s. The retail trade sector has been generally stable for the last decade as a contributor to New York's economic activity, but it also lacks the market scope of the industries and organizations employing the Upper Professionals.

Rank-and-File Professionals include the army of managers and professionals who keep public sector activities and private businesses organized and operating, but who are not handsomely rewarded for their efforts. The largest single group in the Rank-and-File are managers (one-third of the total). A large proportion of these managers come from manufacturing and wholesale trade or from financial and business services (each nearly 10 percent of the total). Also well represented are business professionals, such as accountants, public relations experts, and sales representatives, who account for 18 percent of the Rank-and-File total, and human services professionals, such as teachers, nurses, and social workers, who account for 15 percent of the total.

The Rank-and-File Professionals were much more likely to be employed by government and nonprofit organizations than were the Upper Professionals. In particular, the Rank-and-File Professionals were much more likely to be working for consumer service organizations (26 to 13 percent of the Upper Professionals). They were also much less likely to be in the financial and business service sector (25 to 38 percent of the Upper

Professionals), or in culture and communications (6 to 10 percent) (see Table 6.2).

Rank-and-File Professionals were somewhat younger than the Upper Professionals (33 percent were under the age of 35, compared to 25 percent of the Upper Professionals), more likely to be from minority groups (23 percent compared to 13 percent), and more likely to be female (30 percent compared to 20 percent).

Most of these Rank-and-File Professionals should probably be classified as part of New York's dwindling middle class; some of them no doubt have family incomes that would place them in the top categories. A fair estimate would be to place two-thirds to three-quarters of the group into the middle class, and the rest above.

In terms of style and identity, many of these Rank-and-File Professionals emulate the designer tastes of the Upper Professional class, while others choose either more of a "intellectual" or more of a standard "middle American" style. Some of these Rank-and-File Professionals will become Upper Professionals, and consumption styles that emulate the Upper Professionals make a good deal of sense for them. For others, choices will be associated with generation, family ties, religiosity, ethnicity, and educational level. Older, more family-oriented, and more religious professional people are likely to share the values and consumption styles of "middle Americans" (the favored style of Small Employers as well). Younger, less religious, and better-educated professional people will sometimes take on the cosmopolitan and critical style of the intellectual stratum (which is presumably found more frequently among the Lower-level Professionals, who have, in fact, a good deal to complain about in terms of their status and economic situation).

The Lower-level Professionals are a particularly interesting group, because they so confound our conventional expectations about the status-meaning of professional and managerial work. The cutoff point for the Rank-and-File Professionals was set as $20,000 because $20,000 was the median family census income for 1980 in New York City. This amount may be considered to represent the norm for a comfortably middle class standard of living for an average family. The people falling below this cutoff, the Lower-level Professionals, are the fourth, and by far the largest, layer of business and professional New York.

The Lower-level Professionals included private sector managers (28 percent of the total), artists and writers (10 percent), elementary and secondary school teachers (8 percent), nurses (8 percent), accountants (4.5 percent), and social workers (almost 4 percent). The Lower-level Professionals were disproportionately linked to the non-profit sector. They

**Table 6.2** Social and Economic Characteristics, by Strata, Professionals and Managers, New York City: 1980

| | Upper Professionals (N=1943) % | Small Employers (N=1305) % | Rank-and-File Professionals (N=15248) % | Lower-level Professionals (N=30582) % |
|---|---|---|---|---|
| Occupation[a] | | | | |
| Manager | 38.5 | 32.1 | 34.6 | 27.9 |
| BusProf | 18.3 | 22.8 | 18.3 | 19.1 |
| TechProf | 3.1 | 1.9 | 11.0 | 10.0 |
| SocCult | 23.3 | 0.0 | 12.2 | 15.1 |
| Classical | 15.0 | 42.5 | 8.4 | 3.1 |
| HumServ | 1.9 | .8 | 15.6 | 24.8 |
| | | | | |
| Industry[b] | | | | |
| MfgFirm | 24.5 | 20.5 | 22.0 | 16.4 |
| Retail | 8.6 | 10.0 | 8.6 | 14.2 |
| BusServ | 35.4 | 42.2 | 25.3 | 20.1 |
| OthBus | 1.8 | 1.4 | 4.3 | 2.5 |
| C & C | 9.7 | 1.6 | 5.5 | 5.9 |
| Civic | 8.3 | .3 | 2.3 | 3.7 |
| HumCapServ | 12.8 | 24.0 | 26.6 | 32.6 |
| | | | | |
| Age | | | | |
| Under 35 | 24.8 | 10.8 | 33.6 | 42.5 |
| 36–45 | 30.8 | 27.0 | 24.5 | 33.3 |
| 46–55 | 23.1 | 26.4 | 22.1 | 12.6 |
| 56–65 | 14.6 | 21.1 | 14.9 | 8.5 |
| Over 65 | 6.7 | 15.5 | 4.8 | 3.0 |
| | | | | |
| Sex | | | | |
| Male | 80.5 | 93.6 | 70.1 | 50.1 |
| Female | 19.5 | 6.4 | 29.9 | 49.9 |
| | | | | |
| Education | | | | |
| Non-College | 19.3 | 28.0 | 36.4 | 53.5 |
| College Graduate | 80.7 | 72.0 | 63.6 | 46.5 |
| | | | | |
| Capital Gains[c] | | | | |
| $5000+ | 28.0 | 37.8 | 9.1 | 1.4 |
| $10000+ | 19.1 | 24.6 | 3.5 | .3 |
| $25000+ | 7.6 | 8.1 | .4 | 0.0 |

**Table 6.2** (*continued*)

|  | Upper Professionals (N=1943) % | Small Employers (N=1305) % | Rank-and File Professionals (N=15248) % | Lower-level Professionals (N=30582) % |
|---|---|---|---|---|
| Ethnicity |  |  |  |  |
| West Indian | 0.0 | 1.6 | 2.1 | 5.6 |
| Puerto Rican | 1.0 | 2.2 | 3.3 | 7.1 |
| Native Black | 6.4 | 1.8 | 9.7 | 18.6 |
| Other Hispanics | 2.5 | 2.7 | 3.0 | 5.4 |
| Asian | 4.1 | 3.4 | 5.5 | 6.2 |
| Greek | 1.0 | 1.1 | 1.2 | 1.2 |
| Irish | 12.2 | 8.7 | 17.1 | 14.6 |
| Italian | 12.8 | 20.9 | 28.1 | 22.2 |
| Russian | 41.2 | 47.5 | 23.7 | 14.7 |
| British | 18.8 | 10.1 | 6.3 | 4.3 |

*Source:* 1980 PUMS Census data.

*Notes:*

[a]Occupational categories are Mgr (manager); BusProf (business professionals, such as accountants, advertising people, and public relations specialists); TechProf (technical professionals, such as scientists and engineers, and also high-earning technicians); SocCult (social and cultural professionals (such as artists, writers, social scientists, and university teachers and researchers); Classical (classical professionals such as doctors, dentists, lawyers, and judges); and HumServ (human services professionals, such as elementary and secondary school teachers, nurses, social workers, and clergy).

[b]Industrial categories are: MfgFirm (manufacturing and wholesale trade); Retail (retail trade); OthBus (agriculture, mining, transportation, and utilities); BusServ (Business Service Firms, including law firms, engineering firms, management consulting firms, accounting firms, etc.); C & C (culture and communications firms and organizations, such as publishers, radio and television, and museums); Civic (nonprofit and government); and HumCapServ (human capital services, including health, education, and social welfare firms and agencies).

[c]CapGains (Capital Gains) includes earnings from dividends, interest, and net gains on rental property.

were also considerably younger, less educated, more often female, and more often nonwhite than the other professional strata (see Table 6.2).

Unlike the higher professional strata, these people clearly do not, in the great majority of cases, represent a segment of the "city of the rich." Considering the significant incidence of working spouses in this group, the majority probably ought to be classified as part of New York's middle class. However, many of them fall below even this level, and are best counted as part of the "city of the poor." In 1980, 40 percent of the Lower-level Professionals reported incomes of $10,000 or less to the census. Some of these people also had working spouses who lifted them into the middle class. But if even one-third of the Lower-level Professionals were, in fact, part of the "city of the poor" (a not unlikely figure), this means that fully one in seven census-designated professionals and managers had economic situations similar to those of the city's large and predominantly minority lower working and poverty classes. This is one of the tricks that an increasingly misleading occupational terminology now plays on us.

## Politics

The most important questions about the politics of New York's professional strata are whether they represent: (1) a predominantly liberal group, as some Republican and neoconservative writers have argued; (2) a predominantly conservative group, as some liberal writers have avowed; or (3) whether they are divided by sector of employment and other factors, as some social scientists have alleged. This section will attempt to answer these questions and to show where the lines of commonality and difference actually exist.

### The Importance of Fiscal Conditions

One point is clear: the politics of New York's professional people have been highly changeable. Indeed, one of the more interesting turnabouts in American politics in the last 15 years is the apparent reversal of the political position of the professional classes in New York. In the 1970s, the "cosmopolitan constituency," as Andrew Hacker called it, appeared markedly liberal and it disproportionately supported liberal politicians like John Lindsay, Robert Kennedy, and George McGovern. In the late 1970s and early 1980s, the same group appears markedly conservative and tended to support politicians like Ed Koch and Ronald Reagan.

A similar kind of shift occurred across the country, of course, but in New York, it appears that higher-level professionals and managers shifted somewhat more dramatically than other segments of the population. This is because they started in the 1960s and early 1970s more liberal, and sometimes far more liberal, than the norm and then moved to a position that was very nearly as conservative as the norm. In the country at large, all segments shifted to the right, but at roughly similar rates. The analysis of three General Social Survey (GSS) national spending items reported in Table 6.3 provides a suggestive sense of how upper and middle city professionals in the New York region diverge from those of GSS respondents at large.[14]

One interesting analysis of the electorate during the earlier, pre-fiscal

Table 6.3 Attitudes on Three Social Issues: 1972–1986,
National Norms and New York Region City Professionals

| | Government Spends Too Little % | Government Spends About Right % | Government Spends Too Much % |
|---|---|---|---|
| **I. How much should the federal government be spending on improving the condition of blacks?** | | | |
| 1972–1974 | | | |
| Everyone (N=2781) | 34.0 | 43.4 | 22.7 |
| NY Region Profs* (N=25) | 80.0 | 20.0 | 0.0 |
| 1977–1980† | | | |
| Everyone (N=4166) | 26.6 | 46.8 | 26.6 |
| NY Region Profs (N=17) | 23.5 | 58.8 | 17.6 |
| 1984–1986 | | | |
| Everyone (N=1820) | 35.3 | 45.9 | 18.8 |
| NY Region Profs (N=16) | 70.0 | 30.0 | 0.0 |
| **II. How much should the federal government be spending on welfare programs?** | | | |
| 1972–1974 | | | |
| Everyone (N=2854) | 21.9 | 29.3 | 48.8 |
| NY Region Profs (N=25) | 33.3 | 13.3 | 53.3 |
| 1977–1980 | | | |
| Everyone (N=4323) | 13.3 | 25.7 | 60.8 |
| NY Region Profs (N=17) | 0.0 | 29.4 | 70.6 |
| 1984–1986 | | | |
| Everyone (N=1890) | 22.1 | 34.5 | 43.4 |
| NY Region Profs (N=16) | 20.0 | 60.0 | 20.0 |
| **III. How much should the federal government be spending on military arms and defense?** | | | |
| 1972–1974 | | | |
| Everyone (N=2787) | 15.0 | 48.2 | 36.8 |
| NY Region Profs (N=25) | 6.7 | 6.7 | 86.7 |
| 1977–1980 | | | |
| Everyone (N=4187) | 38.2 | 41.5 | 20.3 |
| NY Region Profs (N=17) | 31.3 | 31.3 | 37.3 |
| 1984–1986 | | | |
| Everyone (N=1882) | 16.4 | 42.2 | 41.4 |
| NY Region Profs (N=16) | 10.0 | 30.0 | 60.0 |

*Source:* Cumulative General Social Survey, 1972–1986.
*NY Region Profs includes all middle- to high-income (above $15,000 in 1972–1974; above $20,000 in 1977–1980; and above $25,000 in 1984–1985) census-designated professionals and managers living in cities (250,000 population or more) in the Middle Atlantic region (which includes New York and other large cities in the region).
†Four survey years are grouped, because no survey was conducted in 1979.

crisis period is provided by Andrew Hacker. Hacker concluded that Lindsay's reelection in 1969 rested on extraordinary increases in the pro-Lindsay vote from white neighborhoods surrounding Central Park. The net gain he made in Manhattan's East and West sides "outdistanced the advances he made in all of Brooklyn and Queens put together."[15] In addition, Lindsay made gains among "younger and better-educated Catholics, particularly in Queens, [who] had developed values compatible with the Lindsay candidacy."[16]

The unity of the "cosmopolitan constituency" was broken in the mid and late 1970s, in the wake of the city's fiscal and economic development crises. This was especially true in 1977, when many liberal professionals voted for Mario Cuomo over Edward Koch, who had become identified with the city's business establishment. This trend continued in the 1980s, with professionals and managers increasingly preferring conservative candidates like Ed Koch and Ronald Reagan.

Analysis of voting patterns in New York's sixty assembly districts provides useful data on the recent period. These data show that, among whites, Ed Koch and Ronald Reagan were quite popular in districts with high proportions of professionals and managers; Koch, in particular, was nearly as popular there in 1985 as he was in lower white collar and working class districts.

In recent years, fiscal conditions and the reigning political climate have made professionals look liberal in one era and conservative in another. Professionals and managers tended to be moderate "cosmopolitan" reformers during the 1950s and 1960s, periods of sustained economic growth, but they tended to be more conservative after the fiscal crisis period of economic uncertainty. Yet it is worth noting that (measured by their voting behavior) white professionals and managers have been slightly less conservative than most other whites, even in recent years, presumably because their relative security encourages them to express a degree of reformist sentiment.

## The Influence of Occupation, Sector, and Race

These temporal shifts are not the only feature of the politics of professionals that bears emphasizing. Within the professional strata, there are also important occupational, sectoral, and, especially, racial bases of division.

Applying the national survey findings to New York would suggest that Upper Professionals in the corporate headquarters complex should tend to be comparatively conservative, while Upper Professionals in the cultural, civic, and social services complexes should tend to be relatively liberal.

Unfortunately, data to test these propositions directly do not exist. As a proxy, data from the assembly district level can be used to identify five professional and managerial groups on the basis of occupation and a simpler version of industrial sector. The five groups are: (1) private sector managers; (2) technical and business service professionals (including such occupations as engineers, consultants, advertisers and accountants); (3) "classical" professionals (doctors, lawyers, and judges); (4) public sector managers; and (5) social and cultural professionals (including arts professionals, writers, journalists and editors, professors, teachers, and social workers).

Although the expected divisions among professionals and managers may have become attenuated by 1985, they were still at least weakly evident. Among white professionals and managers in 1985, Koch was most popular in assembly districts with high proportions of business and technical professionals and in those with high proportions of private sector managers. He was somewhat less popular in assembly districts with high proportions of human service and arts professionals, public managers, and professionals in the "classical" high status professions of medicine and law (see Table 6.4).

The assembly district data suggest that occupational and sectoral divisions were more important in recent national electoral contests. Among whites, the data in Table 6.4 suggest that human service, arts, and "classical" professionals were considerably less favorable to President Reagan than were other professionals and managers, although all groups were at least moderately supportive.

These socioeconomic divisions, however, pale in comparison to the racial divisions found in the same data. In the case of Mayor Koch, these no doubt reflected the matter of Koch's ethnic loyalties, with a great majority of black professionals and managers and many Hispanic professionals opposing the mayor, whom they perceived as relatively unsympathetic to their concerns. Where all predominantly white assembly districts were at least moderately favorable to the mayor in 1985, all assembly districts with high proportions of black professionals and managers were strongly antagonistic, indeed nearly as antagonistic as black working class districts. Class made an important difference only among Hispanics. Assembly districts with high proportions of Hispanic professionals and managers were weakly favorable toward the mayor, while those with high proportions of Hispanic white and blue collar workers were mildly unfavorable.

Similarly, in the presidential election of 1984 and the Democratic primary of the same year, occupational and organizational sectoral divisions were much less important than racial divisions. Whites, regardless of class and occupation, tended to support Reagan, while blacks, regardless of class and occupation, tended to oppose him. Similar patterns were found

**Table 6.4**  Votes, by Occupational Composition of Assembly Districts: 1984 and 1985 (simple $R$)

| | Reagan Presid. Vote 84 | Jackson Democ. Primary Vote 84 | Mondale Democ. Primary Vote 84 | Hart Democ. Primary Vote 84 | Koch Democ. Primary 85 |
|---|---|---|---|---|---|
| **1. Whites** | | | | | |
| Soc/Cult Profs. | .350 | -.335 | .589 | .916 | .463 |
| "Classical" Profs. | .355 | -.300 | .498 | .826 | .424 |
| Public Managers | .519 | -.441 | .480 | .761 | .449 |
| Private Managers | .624 | -.527 | .605 | .874 | .553 |
| Tech/Bus Profs. | .784 | -.649 | .650 | .838 | .584 |
| Sales Workers | .791 | -.681 | .685 | .832 | .659 |
| Clerical Workers | .911 | -.831 | .627 | .645 | .609 |
| Service Workers | .785 | -.782 | .433 | .624 | .405 |
| Craft Workers | .838 | -.749 | .358 | .297 | .373 |
| Operatives | .580 | -.681 | .130* | .104* | .153* |
| **2. Blacks** | | | | | |
| Soc/Cult Profs. | -.724 | .898 | -.477 | -.491 | -.566 |
| "Classical" Profs. | -.468 | .653 | -.156 | -.083* | -.315 |
| Public Managers | -.602 | .780 | -.403 | -.380 | -.479 |
| Private Managers | -.729 | .875 | -.471 | -.485 | -.560 |
| Tech/Bus Profs. | -.605 | .754 | -.461 | -.457 | -.544 |
| Sales Workers | -.791 | .894 | -.574 | -.602 | -.629 |
| Clerical Workers | -.782 | .902 | -.588 | -.641 | -.630 |
| Service Workers | -.782 | .906 | -.594 | -.640 | -.636 |
| Craft Workers | -.764 | .892 | -.604 | -.648 | -.640 |
| Operatives | -.788 | .909 | -.617 | -.661 | -.646 |
| **3. Hispanics** | | | | | |
| Soc/Cult Profs. | -.244 | .014* | .138* | .335 | .063* |
| "Classical" Profs. | .214* | -.242 | .315 | .624 | .241 |
| Public Managers | -.035* | -.146* | .175* | .338 | .200* |
| Private Managers | -.070* | -.208* | .094* | .247 | .065* |
| Tech/Bus Profs. | .267 | -.355 | .188 | .288 | .170 |
| Sales Workers | -.392 | .040* | -.178* | -.152 | -.124 |
| Clerical Workers | -.416 | .041* | -.260 | -.281 | -.200 |
| Service Workers | -.526 | .179* | -.255 | -.229* | -.235 |
| Craft Workers | -.432 | .079* | -.339 | -.332 | -.282 |
| Operatives | -.503 | .142* | -.357 | -.339 | -.308 |

*Source:* Mollenkopf-CUNY New York Assembly District Data Base.

*Note:* All correlations are between proportion of the occupational category in an assembly district and percentage vote for the designated candidates. The Reagan vote includes all voters. The last four columns include only Democratic voters. Whites include some Hispanics.

* = Correlation is *not* significant at p < .05.

on the Jackson vote in the Democratic primary of 1984. Yet different professional groups varied substantially within this basic tendency. The analyses reported in this section indicate that the view of the politics of professionals as essentially conservative and business-oriented during times of fiscal stress is realistic for the recent years. The divided upper-middle view also has some merit, although divisions, in recent years at least, appear to be relatively minor. Neither view, however, is fully adequate, because both fail to take into account the two major factors that have conditioned the politics of professionals and managers: the fiscal condition of the city and race.

### Four Political Cultures?

In the end, a satisfying treatment of the politics of professional people will likely need to pay attention to four important political cultures which have roots in the professional and managerial strata, broadly considered. Sophisticated New Yorkers may be able to speak in the idiom of all four cultures depending on the situation, but it is unlikely that the assumptions of the cultures have equal weight even for the most situationally oriented people. Instead, the likelihood is that their centrality to self-definition and political behavior varies considerably among professionals.

Concentrated to a greater degree among higher-income professionals and managers, there is a *business culture*, oriented primarily to policies promoting a favorable business climate in the city; and there is also a *liberal professional culture*, oriented to "humanistic values," liberal social reform, cultural activities, and the preservation of the physical and social fabric of the city. These cultures have clearly differing social bases. The business culture, not surprisingly, is located principally in the corporate headquarters complex, and among higher-income professionals and managers in other for-profit firms and enterprises. It is associated with the ambiance of the Upper East Side and the more conservative suburban communities. The liberal professional culture is located principally in the nonprofits, the universities, cultural organizations, and government. It is associated with the ambiance of Greenwich Village, Morningside Heights, and the Upper West Side.

It seems likely that in recent years, many liberal professionals have accommodated to the prerogatives of the dominant business sector, just as in the 1960s and 1970s many business people accommodated to the then-ascendant rhetoric of the "service society," the "knowledge class," social reform, and community control. Together with these accommodations, however, are also persistent tensions arising from conflict between two status cultures: the utilitarian and profit-oriented concerns of people close to the financial and business worlds, and the intellectual, expressive, and culturally cosmopolitan concerns of people close to the liberal professional world of the universities, the arts, the nonprofits, and government social services.

Concentrated to a greater degree among lower-income professionals and managers is an *egalitarian culture*, which more completely identifies with the problems of the poor and minority racial and ethnic groups; and there is also the *white ethnic culture*, which is largely Democratic, but worried about crime and resistant to perceived preferential treatment of the poor and minorities. The latter two cultures extend far beyond the professional and managerial categories, of course, but they clearly encompass many middle and lower middle income professionals and managers as well.

In recent New York elections, the status tensions between conservative executives and reformist professionals have been overshadowed by the anger of people in the third and fourth cultures, the people who represent those essentially left out of both the economic and cultural riches of New York. Blacks and whites are more internally united by race than they are internally divided by class and institutional location. Because of this, political conflict in the professional and managerial strata in recent years, at bottom, looks much like political conflict in the city at large; whites are, by and large, conservative and business-oriented, while blacks (and to a much lesser degree Hispanics) are liberal and "social justice"-oriented.

Against the sharp and quite generally shared antagonism of most black and some Hispanic professionals, the difference in emphasis between the white captains of commerce and the white captains of reform seemed somewhat pallid during most of the 1980s. The anger of the minority culture was blocked by the equally intense feelings, and more effective political voice of lower and middle income whites, professional or otherwise, who formed the solid core of the Koch constituency. In 1989, however, the minority of reform-oriented white Upper Professionals may well have provided Mayor Dinkins with a small but potent constituency.

## Conclusion

The theorists of "postindustrial society" often describe the Upper Professional group—people with high-level intellectual credentials and powerful organizational positions—as the most important class in an increasingly "knowledge-based" economy and society. This chapter has argued that Upper Professionals in New York are neither dominant in this way, nor even socially cohesive in any clear and obvious sense.

It is a mark of our increasingly organizations-dominated society that occupational activities are yoked to distinctive organizational powers and purposes. Both organizational powers (as measured by level of resources and market scope) and organizational purposes (as measured by goals and functions) are important in defining important cleavages in the modern metropolis, but for different reasons.

Organizational powers are most important for understanding the stratification of professional workers. The scope of organizations—in the case of New York City, whether they are national (or even international) in scope or essentially local in orientation—provides one fundamental criterion that helps us place professionals on one side or the other of the Upper and Rank-and-File divide. The Upper Professionals are precisely those people who have not only highly valued intellectual resources, but who also work for resource-rich organizations. It is the combination, not one or the other, that is important.

Differences in organizational purposes, by contrast, are important for understanding political and cultural divisions among professional people. Although there are some broad commonalities in the experiences and expectations of economists and lawyers working for international business firms and those working for civic organizations, their outlooks are influenced also by the distinctive purposes and means of the organizations for which they work. Daniel Bell has written about the (upper) professional class, "(T)he actual play and conflict of interests exist between the organizations to which men belong, rather than between the more diffuse class or status identities."[17] This chapter has not downplayed shared aspects of the Upper Professionals' social situation as much as Bell does in this passage, but it nevertheless recognizes an important element of truth in his emphasis on the shaping influence of organizational attachments.

Numerically, the main component of the city's Upper Professionals are the members of the corporate and business service complex, who serve as the main support staff for American financial and business organizations and the nation's wealthiest investors. This is an important group, to be sure, but its members, although privileged, cannot be realistically described as residing at the apex of the city's social structure. This apex is dominated, as it has long been, by wealthy investors and entrepreneurs (joined by a few political and entertainment celebrities). The other institutional arms of the Upper Professsional stratum provide service for consumer interests in information and entertainment, political interests in civic regulation, development and conflict resolution, and citizen expectations concerning health, education, and welfare. They are, for the most part, still less dominant than the members of the corporate and business services group.

The culture and politics of the Upper Professionals partly reflect their primary institutional locations. The fashionable trends in consumption are set mainly by the members of the corporate and business service complex, but extend now also to the other sectors as well. Similarly, in politics, the centers of business-oriented conservatism are, not surprisingly, in the corporate and business services complex. Remaining centers of liberal reform exist principally in the other three complexes.

The politics of the group have been greatly determined by the city's fiscal condition and the reigning political climate. In the years before the fiscal crisis of the mid 1970s, business professionals tended to accommodate to the views of liberal reformers. In the years following the fiscal crisis, the opposite has tended to occur. Racial divisions have also been extremely important in shaping the politics of Upper Professionals. Whites gradually became an overwhelmingly security-conscious and business-oriented group, while high-achieving nonwhites have taken on the lion's share of such "social justice"-oriented opposition as continues to be found among the city's Upper Professionals.

# Notes

1. See Rosenkwaite, Ira, *A Population History of New York* (Syracuse: Syracuse University Press, 1972).

2. Calculated from the 1980 PUMS data from the U.S. Bureau of the Census. Obviously, not all professionals and managers are salaried. Self-employed professionals, a generally elite group, now account for 1 percent of the New York City labor force, while self-employed managers, many of whom are economically marginal small proprietors, represent about 3 percent. The total professional-managerial proportion is, thus, 28.5 percent of the total labor force, according to the 1980 PUMS data (and a little higher, if high-income technicians are included, as they probably should be). See also U.S. Department of Commerce, Bureau of the Census, 1984.

3. Bell, Daniel, *The Coming of Post-Industrial Society* (New York: Basic Books, 1973).

4. See, for example, Hammond, John L., "Yuppies," *Public Opinion Quarterly* 50 (1986): 457–501.

5. See also Drennan, Matthew, "Local Economy and Local Revenues," in Brecher, Charles, and Raymond D. Horton, eds., *Setting Municipal Priorities, 1988* (New York: New York University Press, 1987).

6. My calculations are based on defining as Civic Complex Upper Professionals all salaried professionals and managers earning over $40,000 annually and working in nonprofit organizations, voluntary membership organizations,

and government executive, legislative, and judicial departments. The operational definition is far from perfect, for it leaves out many university professors and religious leaders who are members of the civic complex. It also leaves out the many business and professional people who are employed elsewhere, but are influential in the deliberations of civic leaders.

7. Hacker, Andrew, *The New Yorkers: Profile of An American Metropolis* (New York: Mason-Charter, 1975).

8. Of the 100 billionaires listed by *Fortune* magazine in 1987, 15 percent were listed as residents of New York City.

9. On the taste of Upper Professionals, see DiMaggio, Paul, and Michael Useem, "Social Class and Arts Consumption," *Theory and Society* 5 (1978): 141–162; Hughes, Michael, and Richard A. Peterson, "Isolating Patterns of Cultural Choice," *American Behavioral Science* 26 (1983): 459–479; and Bourdieu, Pierre, *Distinction* (Cambridge: Harvard University Press, 1984).

10. Stanback, Thomas M., Jr., Peter J. Bearse, Thierry J. Noyelle, and Robert A. Karasek, *Services: The New Economy* (Totowa, NJ: Allanheld, Osmun, 1984), p. 35.

11. DiMaggio, Paul, "Classification in Art," *American Sociological Review* 52 (1987): 440–455.

12. Stanback et al, *Services*. By contrast, the share of GNP for government, nonprofits, and human capital services tend to be lower than their respective employment share. This reflects some combination of differences in levels of wage rate, capital intensiveness, and productivity in the various industries.

13. Unfortunately, these are almost certainly quite inexact estimates of the proportion of affluent professionals and managers. Apparently there is a strong tendency among wealthier New Yorkers to underestimate their income and property holdings. It seems impossible, for example, that only 1300 New Yorkers earned at least $75,000 per year in 1980 and had incomes that were at least half based on investment earnings. Yet this is the estimate that we obtained from the 1980 census data for New York.

14. Unfortunately, the number of upper-income professionals in New York City itself could not be obtained from the General Social Survey. We have had to combine professionals living in large cities from throughout the Middle Atlantic region.

15. Hacker compares the vote received by Lindsay in 1969 with the "No" vote on the 1966 referendum to abolish the civilian review board, a Lindsay-backed program.

16. Hacker, *The New Yorkers*, pp. 61–62.

17. Bell, *Coming of Post-Industrial Society*, p. 376.

# 7

# Women Clerical Workers

Cynthia Fuchs Epstein / Stephen R. Duncombe

## Introduction

A vision of the American workplace once brought to mind men handling machinery in factories. Actually, white collar work now comprises over half of the American economy; the largest occupational group, clerical workers, now totals 20 million workers.

Four out of five people who work in offices processing the records of business and government are women. The sex segregation that characterizes clerical work has become stronger, rising from just over 60 percent of clerical jobs in 1950 to nearly 80 percent in 1980.[1]

The economy's long-term growth in clerical jobs has provided employment for the many millions of women who have flocked to the workplace at an unprecedented rate since the 1950s. It also has enabled black and Latina women workers, formerly concentrated in domestic and agricultural work, to take a step up in occupational status. Minority women have expanded their representation among clerical workers noticeably in the last 15 to 20 years.[2]

These trends have been dramatically evident in New York City. As Drennan's chapter has shown, New York's economic rebound since 1977 has centered on information processing, the coordination of large organizations and the management of financial markets. These developments have created a large number of professional and clerical jobs in the city. In an environment in which affirmative action opened recruitment to women and members of minority groups, some women—usually white middle class women—made their way out of the clerical ghettos to enter

177

mobility tracks into management and professional work. Other women—many of them black—found their way into the clerical positions white women left behind and into the new positions created by the thriving economy, as Bailey and Waldinger's chapter has shown.

However, the development of white collar clerical work has proved a mixed blessing, affecting women workers in disparate ways, depending on their education, race, ethnicity, and work history. Waldinger and others have argued that as the proportion of white workers declines, the resulting vacancy chain allows nonwhites to move up the job hierarchy.[3] But while minorities are indeed moving into white collar jobs, managers seem reluctant to bring them very far up the ladder.

The clerical workplace is also being rapidly transformed. Computerization has decreased the need for workers in some jobs; a recent decrease in the national percentage of clerical workers is one example of that change.[4] The advances in microelectronic and telecommunications technology over the past few decades also "have revolutionized information storage, processing, and retrieval, with immediate and long-range consequences for clerical work."[5] The U.S. Department of Labor estimates that more than 7 million workers in the United States use computer-based video display terminals (VDTs) to do word and data processing, and that nearly all the jobs classified as "administrative support, including clerical" deal with information processing to some extent and involve tasks that lend themselves to various levels of computerization.[6] Women clerical workers, and especially minority women clerical workers, the most recent entrants into the labor force, are disproportionately represented among those likely to be directly affected by office automation.[7]

Technological change also affects the pace and quality of work life. Computers not only permit the breaking down of jobs into small components, reducing worker discretion, but they also permit electronic surveillance of workers' productivity. Supervision may also be faceless, through the medium of a computer printout. Thus, many jobs have become deskilled, and many have become highly controlled. This is true not only for lower level employees, but, as Barbara Garson has observed, "office automation [is] rising almost floor by floor to engulf higher and higher strata of white collar workers."[8] Of course, the computer has also enhanced some jobs, offering employees the opportunity to increase their skills and understanding. Shoshana Zuboff has pointed out that whether computerization of the workplace will create a more challenging work environment or a more degrading one rests on employer policy.[9]

New York City is an excellent site to study the problems of clerical workers generally. Many of the problems clerical workers face there may be found in any office situation. Some conditions are typical of other large urban centers, especially those composed of a heterogeneous work force. Some, of course, are unique to New York, and represent both opportunities and liabilities. On the one hand, New York has a large minority population which is finding employment in the clerical labor force. On the other, the high cost of office space and housing and the problems of education (e.g., an exceptionally high dropout rate among minority youth) constrain both supply and demand for labor for many jobs. Minority workers often enter the economy with different linguistic traditions or different educational preparations than those of the traditional non-Hispanic white woman worker. Yet, many reports suggest that the new technology utilized in clerical work demands higher educational achievement among clerical workers.[10]

The local economy of New York City reflects the national economy. The largest job growth in the post-1977 recovery period in New York has been in services and in the finance, insurance, and real-estate sectors (commonly referred to as FIRE), which together added some 340,000 jobs by 1986.[11] These fields rely heavily on clerical labor. While the decline of manufacturing reduced the need for some attendant clerical support, the growing sectors far outweighed this loss, and some 42,000 clerical jobs were created in the past 10 years. The New York State Department of Labor's "Occupational Needs for the 1980's" report predicted that employment in New York City was expected to increase 4.6 percent between 1980 and 1990. Clerical jobs, however, were expected to increase at an average rate of 7.7 percent over the 10-year period, yielding a total of 1,055,000 clerical jobs in the city by 1990.[12]

This growth of clerical work has created some excellent jobs for women and some others that are dead-end. White, black, and Latina women typically face different prospects in clerical employment. The story is one of both advantage and disadvantage, and it is not clear-cut. Disadvantages to one group of workers are often advantages to another in the changing dynamic of gender, ethnic and racial succession patterns, and changing skill requirements in various realms of the workplace.

### Work Force Composition

Consider the changing profile of workers in New York City. The fate of minority workers in the New York City economy has been closely tied to the "white flight," in which 2 million non-Hispanic whites left the city after World War II, and to the immigration of 80,000 persons each year between 1970 and 1980, most of them from the Caribbean, Latin America, and Asia. Samuel M. Ehrenhalt, regional commissioner of the U.S. Bureau of Labor Statistics, reports that, "as of 1987, minority workers comprised 1.6 million or 49.5 percent of the city's total resident work force of 3,225,000."[13] Differences in group predispositions, skills, education, language proficiency, and discrimination all have affected the disparate ways that minority workers have been integrated into the economy.

Utilizing New York City census data for 1970 and 1980 as our main resource, we can take stock of the changes in the composition of the clerical labor force in New York City during these 10 years. By exploring the distribution of clerical occupations, their gender composition, and the race and education configuration of women in them, we can offer a glimpse of the effects of the changing economy on the primarily female clerical workers of New York City.

The data used for this analysis is culled from the PUMS (Public Use Microdata Sample) files for 1970 and 1980 for the occupational grouping, "administrative support, including clerical," for New York City.[14]

There are many problems with this census data, not the least its age. Further obstacles arise from inconsistencies in classification of occupations and occupational groups as each census is carried out. Whole categories have been collapsed into others or partitioned. In 1970 secretaries were divided into "secretaries, legal," "secretaries, medical," and "secretaries, n.e.c." ("not elsewhere classified"); in 1980 all are classified under the singular "secretaries." In 1970 computer operators were categorized as "computer and peripheral equipment operators"; in 1980 they were divided into the two groups: "computer operators" and "peripheral equipment operators." In some cases entire categories were dropped or added.

Despite its flaws, the data is the best available. And although percentages produced should be viewed with a grain of salt, we believe they do reveal the changing tides of the New York City clerical employment between 1970 and 1980. For other data we rely on smaller studies which, although not comprehensive, give more recent figures. We also draw on interview material from a study by Epstein and Kai Erikson of communications workers in New York City and elsewhere (now in the process of analysis).

## Distribution

The most extreme changes in clerical occupation groups between 1970 and 1980 were recorded about those affected by new technology. Significant declines were recorded for such major categories as secretaries, stenographers, typists, and records processing, traditionally labor-intensive fields in which new technologies are replacing workers. These statistics form a pattern suggesting the varied ways in which technology affects the clerical labor force. In some areas technology creates jobs; new skills such as computer operators and technicians are needed to process information and to maintain new computer systems. In addition to demands for skilled workers, technology also tends to create new work needs. As Hartmann suggests,

> [t]he capabilities of microprocessors are ideally suited to many revisions, more personalized form letters, updated statistical reports, and more charts and graphs. . . .As a consequence, the production of a firm becomes more intensive in information content. . .and the decline in employment. . .is considerably less than if the new technology were used simply to produce the previous output.[15]

On the other hand, new technology has reduced employment in occupations in which productivity increases have outstripped the creation of new work needs. Communications work is a prime example; today messages and information are processed much more efficiently with new technology. For example, as one worker interviewed by Epstein described her work:

> What's different now [with the introduction of the computer in the office] is that you don't have to write as much. All you do is put the number in the computer and the information. . .automatically comes up on the screen. . .it's easier.

Of course, with diminished complexity, there is a need for fewer workers. Other communications workers interviewed in this study pointed out that their departments might soon be phased out. As one described the situation in his office:

> What's happening basically is that Representatives are going to take over the function that these Reviewers used to do. They're going to be able to sit right at their terminal and input orders without having to write up a piece of paper and sending [sic] it to somebody else to type it. So their jobs are being phased out.

And displacement may become more prevalent in the future, as Eli Ginzberg, an analyst of human resources, has commented:

Table 7.1   Distribution of Clerical Employment, Aggregate Categories: 1970–1980

| Occupation | 1970 % | 1980 % | Change % Pts. | Percent Increase |
|---|---|---|---|---|
| Computer Operator | 1.0 | 2.9 | 1.9 | 190.0 |
| Secretary, Steno, Typist | 39.5 | 35.3 | −4.2 | −10.6 |
| Information Clerk | 4.0 | 5.6 | 1.6 | 40.0 |
| Records Processing | 8.3 | 4.2 | −4.1 | −49.4 |
| Financial Records Processing | 16.0 | 15.4 | −0.6 | −3.8 |
| Office Machine Operator | 0.5 | 0.4 | −0.1 | −20.0 |
| Communications | 4.4 | 2.7 | −1.6 | −36.4 |
| Mail, Messenger, Delivery | 8.7 | 9.9 | 1.2 | 13.8 |
| Material Recording, Scheduling | 4.8 | 7.3 | 2.5 | 52.1 |
| Adjusters, Investigators | 3.0 | 3.5 | 0.5 | 16.7 |
| Miscellaneous Administative Support | 9.8 | 10.0 | 0.2 | 2.0 |
| Technician* | — | 2.8 | 2.8 | — |

Source: 1970 and 1980 Census Microdata Sample, adjusted for consistency.

*New category for 1980—includes Technicians n.e.c. and Computer Programmers.

Computer technology is now on a steeper curve; employers and employees are more willing and able to adapt to it since more than 70 percent of all jobs are in the service sector. Moreover, since U.S. management is striving to become and remain cost-competitive in the world marketplace, it must reduce its white-collar payrolls; wider reliance on the computer offers reasonable prospects for success in this effort.[16]

Yet Ginzberg, too, acknowledges that new technology creates new needs. If we look at specific job categories that were defined the same way in 1970 and 1980, we see no surprises in the patterns of change. Computer operators increased while the telephone operator and file clerk categories declined.[17] (See Table 7.1.) In the declining aggregate category of secretary, stenographer and typist, the secretary category has held steady, while the categories of stenographer and typist have decreased substantially.

These disparate findings may reflect qualitative distinctions between these suboccupations. Secretarial duties are varied and include interpersonal interaction with management, other departments, and the public; these skills may not be easily reducible by technology. The duties of typists and stenographers, however, have been decreased and at the same time made more productive through the use of increasingly efficient tools, such as word processors and sophisticated dictation equipment. In addi-

Table 7.2    Percent Distribution of Clerical Occupations,
Selected Categories: 1970–1980

| Occupation | 1970 % | 1980 % | Change % Pts. | Percent Change |
|---|---|---|---|---|
| Supervisor* | 1.1 | 9.6 | 8.5 | 772.7 |
| Computer Operator† | 1.0 | 2.7 | 1.7 | 170.0 |
| Secretary | 25.3 | 25.2 | −0.1 | −0.4 |
| Stenographer | 1.1 | 0.6 | −0.5 | −45.5 |
| Typist | 12.7 | 7.0 | −5.7 | −44.9 |
| Telephone Operator | 4.1 | 2.5 | −1.6 | −39.0 |
| File Clerk | 7.4 | 3.2 | −4.2 | −56.7 |

Source: See Table 7.1.

*Supervisor is an aggregate category for 1980.
†Computer Operator for 1980 includes Peripheral Machine Operator.

tion, the decrease in typists reflects the recategorization of many of their duties into the computer operator classification.

The occupation of supervisor showed a striking increase between 1970 and 1980, from 1.1 percent to 9.6 percent of the total clerical labor force. (See Table 7.2) Such a dramatic increase may reflect some classification changes, but is also consistent with the growth of "electronic sweatshops" composed of large pools of workers working at word and data processing.

National data shows similar trends. Hunt and Hunt state that

Between 1972 and 1982, when clerical employment rose by 28.8 per cent, employment of stenographers declined by 47.2 per cent. . . .Over the same 10-year period, the employment of computer and peripheral equipment operators increased 195.5 per cent.[18]

Hunt and Hunt go on to report that between 1950 and 1980, computer operators were by far the fastest growing occupation, and clerical supervisors were the fifth fastest. The number of typists grew rapidly between 1950 and 1970, but decreased dramatically in the next 10 years. The most rapid percentage declines over this 30-year span were in stenographers and telegraph operators, due mainly to technological advances.

## Sex Segregation

Although affirmative action programs have increased the percentage of minority women clerical workers, they have not significantly altered the

Table 7.3 Proportion of Women in Clerical Occupations,
Aggregate Categories: 1970–1980

| Occupation | 1970 % | 1980 % | Change % Pts. | Percent Change |
|---|---|---|---|---|
| Computer Operator | 20.2 | 51.0 | 30.8 | 152.5 |
| Secretary, Steno, Typist | 94.9 | 96.6 | 1.7 | 1.8 |
| Information Clerk | 77.5 | 83.4 | 5.9 | 7.6 |
| Records Processing | 71.7 | 70.7 | −1.0 | −1.4 |
| Financial Records Processing | 76.2 | 79.4 | 3.2 | 4.2 |
| Office Machine Operator | 46.8 | 41.6 | −5.2 | −11.1 |
| Communications | 91.9 | 88.5 | −3.4 | −3.7 |
| Mail, Messenger, Delivery | 16.6 | 17.9 | 1.3 | 7.8 |
| Material Recording, Scheduling | 16.9 | 25.4 | 8.5 | 50.3 |
| Adjusters, Investigators | 41.9 | 57.3 | 15.4 | 36.8 |
| Miscellaneous Administrative Support | 72.6 | 78.0 | 5.4 | 7.4 |
| Technician* | — | 39.8 | — | — |
| Total | 73.8 | 72.5 | −1.3 | −1.8 |

Source: See Table 7.1.

*New category for 1980—includes Technicians n.e.c. and Computer Programmers.

sex segregation of clerical work. Women may move out of clerical work into male-dominated work spheres, but few men have moved into clerical areas regarded as "women's work." In New York City, as in the rest of the country, women make up the vast majority of clerical workers, and male clerical workers tend to cluster in a small number of job titles. Just under three-quarters of the city's clerical workers are women, slightly less than the national average in 1980. The New York percentage remained relatively constant during the 1970s, while the national figure increased from 61 to 78 percent.[19]

Women white collar workers in New York City cluster in such traditional "women's work" as secretaries and telephone operators. The aggregate census category of secretary, stenographer, typist hovered at about 95 percent female in both 1970 and 1980, and the communications category was close to 90 percent. (See Tables 7.3 and 7.4.)

Women's participation is relatively low in some clerical occupation categories, however. In New York only about 20 percent of computer operators were women in 1970, and just under 17 percent were employed as mail, message, or delivery workers, or as material recording and scheduling workers. The percentages barely changed in the next 10-year period for mail, message, and delivery workers. Sex segregation lessened its

Table 7.4    Proportion of Women in Clerical Occupations,
Selected Categories: 1970–1980

| Occupation | 1970 % | 1980 % | Change % Pts. | Percent Change |
|---|---|---|---|---|
| Supervisor* | 51.5 | 45.6 | −5.9 | −11.5 |
| Computer Operator† | 20.2 | 51.0 | 30.8 | 152.5 |
| Secretary | 96.7 | 97.9 | 1.2 | 1.2 |
| Stenographer | 93.8 | 79.4 | −14.4 | −15.4 |
| Typist | 91.6 | 93.0 | 1.4 | 1.5 |
| Telephone Operator | 94.7 | 89.7 | −5.0 | −5.3 |
| File Clerk | 72.9 | 71.9 | −1.0 | −1.4 |

Source: 1970 and 1980 decennial census data, adjusted for consistency.
*Supervisor is an aggregate category for 1980.
†Computer Operator for 1980 includes Peripheral Machine Operator.

hold, however, in the other two occupational groups. Female computer operators increased to 51 percent of all operators in 1980. (This may, however, represent a transformation of typists into word processors.) Material recording and scheduling jobs, while still sex segregated in 1980 (25.4 percent female), reported more than a 50 percent increase in women in the 10-year period.

Rather than examine these sex distribution findings in isolation, we should compare work categories in which women have shown great strides or losses in the city between 1970 and 1980 with those occupations known to be expanding or decreasing. The occupations that reported the greatest increases in percentages of women employed during the 10 years were computer operator (where women rose from 20.2 to 51 percent of the total); material recording and scheduling (from 16.9 to 25.5 percent); and adjusters and investigators (from 41.9 to 57.3 percent). These occupational groups were among those showing the most significant increases in clerical job market share during the 10 years.

The percentages of women employed decreased somewhat over the decade in these broad categories: office machine operator (where women declined from 46.8 to 41.6 percent); communications (from 91.9 to 88.5 percent); records processing (from 71.7 to 70.7 percent). In contrast, in the secretary, steno, typist category women's share rose from 94.9 to 96.6 percent. These four occupational groups also showed the most substantive declines in share of the clerical labor force during the decade. This rather striking pattern suggests that women are constituting a larger share of expanding occupations and a lesser share of the declining ones. Why women would respond to opportunity is clear, but why women should retreat from shrinking fields faster than men is a bit more puzzling. Perhaps in these shrinking fields there has been a greater attempt to reduce sex segregation by management's encouragement of male employment. Specific job categories show contradictory patterns. Table 7.4 shows that the percentage of women employed increased dramatically in the occupation that best reflects the new technological work—computer operator. Where new technology has replaced workers, such as telephone operators and file clerks, women's participation has decreased. Yet, even though the percentage of supervisors rose sevenfold, women's share fell by 11.5 percent from 1970 to 1980. In the telephone company that Epstein and Erikson studied, for example, women supervisors were common in jobs sex-typed as female, such as operators and service representatives. However, as one worker reported, "Now they're hiring a lot of male reps so you'll see the supervisory force is [becoming] half and half." But even when women had jobs as supervisors they rarely were able to climb higher. This same worker spoke for many when she observed:

> The managers were the fellows they took out of college and they hired them off the street and they put them in charge of these women supervisors.

This may reflect continued barriers to employment of women in low-level management jobs. John Mollenkopf analyzed occupation by gender and race for New York City in 1980 and found that males were half again as likely as females to be managers, and whites half again as likely, compared to blacks or Latinos.[20] And as Cydney Pullman and Sharon Szymanski concluded in their 1986 study of the primarily female clerical work forces in New York's banking, insurance, and legal industries:

> Job mobility for clerical workers tends to be lateral, within the same occupation and the same industry, rather than vertical, within or outside their own companies. Clerical workers tend to stay clerical workers.[21]

Thus, the establishment of technologically demanding jobs and the decline of low-skilled work does not necessarily mean that new paths up and out of clerical work have been created. A 1984 Stanford University study on technology and the design of jobs in the insurance industry suggests that

> The gap between the skills of clerical workers and those of professionals has widened despite the elimination of unskilled clerical work such as coding and sorting mail and much filing, and reduction of routine keyboarding.

Skill requirements for clerical workers have increased at the same time that the jobs have become overwhelmingly dead-end.[22]

Among communications workers, whole classifications of jobs are being automated. Yet many people believe that training will affect their chances for employment in the new skills environment. This common view is expressed in the words of one communications worker Epstein interviewed who had taken some general courses:

> I fooled myself; I should have taken math along with Interpersonal Skills. I think I'm going to need that math more than I realized.

## Race and Ethnicity

Data on the racial and ethnic composition of the female clerical labor force in New York City shows that although white non-Hispanic women still make up more than 60 percent of the total number of women clerical workers, their numbers dropped precipitously between 1970 and 1980. The white share of female clerical employment declined from 78.2 percent in 1970 to 62.3 percent in 1980. (See Table 7.5.) White women's share has fallen *fastest* in the growing field of computer operator, dropping from 84.2 to 47.9 percent. The second greatest decline, however, occurred in the rapidly shrinking category of communications.

Several factors may explain the dramatic decrease in the white non-Hispanic female share of clerical labor in both expanding and shrinking job categories. First, the white exodus from the New York City labor market has reduced the pool of non-Hispanic white female workers. Second, because of continued racial and ethnic prejudice but relaxed sexual discrimination, white non-Hispanic women workers may be allowed to move up and out of clerical occupations or to start at higher levels—paths that may be denied for minority women. Third, as certain jobs become "more" black and Hispanic, white women may become more reluctant to work in them.

Turning to specific clerical job categories, Table 7.6 shows that the percentages of white non-Hispanic women declined substantially in all of them between 1970 and 1980, whether they expanded or contracted. The percentage of white non-Hispanic female computer operators declined from 84.2 to 47.9 percent; for typists the drop was from 75.7 to 49.9 percent. Interestingly, white women showed the smallest declines in supervisors (from 78.8 to 60 percent), and secretaries (from 86.2 to 72.2

Table 7.5 Proportion of Women in Clerical Occupations
Who Are Non-Hispanic White, Aggregate Categories: 1970–1980

| Occupation | 1970 % | 1980 % | Change % Pts. | Percent Change |
|---|---|---|---|---|
| Computer Operator | 84.2 | 47.9 | −36.3 | −43.1 |
| Secretary, Steno, Typist | 82.7 | 67.8 | −14.9 | −18.0 |
| Information Clerk | 76.7 | 61.0 | −15.7 | −20.5 |
| Records Processing | 70.5 | 47.0 | −23.5 | −33.3 |
| Financial Records Processing | 85.1 | 69.2 | −15.9 | −18.7 |
| Office Machine Operators | 54.6 | 38.5 | −16.1 | −29.5 |
| Communications | 71.7 | 45.2 | −26.5 | −37.0 |
| Mail, Messenger, Delivery | 52.3 | 33.3 | −19.0 | −36.3 |
| Material Recording, Scheduling | 60.8 | 55.1 | −5.7 | −9.4 |
| Adjusters, Investigators | 83.2 | 59.8 | −23.4 | −28.1 |
| Miscellaneous Administrative Support | 60.8 | 49.4 | −11.4 | −18.8 |
| Technician* | — | 78.5 | — | — |
| Total | 78.2 | 62.3 | −15.9 | −20.3 |

Source: See Table 7.1.

*New category for 1980—includes Technicians n.e.c. and Computer Programmers.

percent). These were the only selected occupations in which white non-Hispanic women retained clear majority status in 1980. As noted, for supervisors, this may reflect the relative privilege conferred on white non-Hispanic women by continued racial and ethnic discrimination, a situation not unnoticed by minority women such as the one who remarked to Epstein:

If you're [a] white [woman] you have to prove yourself to two people; if you're black, you have to prove yourself to a hundred. . .advancement for white females; they're going, but with blacks, there's no change.

Thierry J. Noyelle's study of shifting employment distribution in twelve industries nationwide between 1970 and 1980 found that white non-Hispanic women did make significant advances into professional positions during the 10-year span.[23] In the case of secretaries, white non-Hispanic women's "cultural capital" is thought necessary for front office work and the personal contact with executives who are primarily white and non-Hispanic.

The corollary of the substantial decrease in percentages of white non-Hispanic women in the city's clerical work force has been the dramatic

**Table 7.6    Proportion of Women in Clerical Occupations**
**Who Are Non-Hispanic White, Selected Categories: 1970–1980**

| Occupation | 1970 % | 1980 % | Change % Pts. | Percent Change |
|---|---|---|---|---|
| Supervisor* | 78.8 | 60.0 | −18.8 | −23.9 |
| Computer Operator† | 84.2 | 47.9 | −36.3 | −43.1 |
| Secretary | 86.2 | 72.2 | −14.0 | −16.2 |
| Stenographer | 76.8 | 54.7 | −22.1 | −28.8 |
| Typist | 75.7 | 49.9 | −25.8 | −34.1 |
| Telephone Operator | 71.2 | 45.3 | −25.9 | −36.4 |
| File Clerk | 70.4 | 44.9 | −25.5 | −36.2 |

*Source:* 1970 and 1980 decennial census data, adjusted for consistency.

*Supervisor is an aggregate category for 1980.
†Computer Operator for 1980 includes Peripheral Machine Operator.

rise in percentages of black, Latina, Asian, and other minority females, as Tables 7.7, 7.8, and 7.9 show. Black female representation in the clerical labor force almost doubled from 13.6 percent in 1970 to 23.2 percent 10 years later. Latina women clerical workers rose from 7.5 to 11.8 percent, while Asian and "other" women clerical workers rose from .7 to 2.7 percent, a small absolute increase but a relative increase of over 280 percent. (This matches the growth in the city's Asian work force as a whole during this time; from only 31,000 in 1970 to three times this number in 1980.)[24]

Minority women increased their shares in virtually all of the aggregate occupational categories, whether expanding or contracting. Black women increased their representation among computer operators from 10.5 percent of the women in 1970 to 36.2 percent in 1980; Latina women increased from 5.3 to 11.4 percent, and Asian women increased from 0 to 4.5 percent. But even faltering occupations, such as records processing and financial records processing, reported increases in minority women, although less uniformly. Similar gains by minority women in the clerical labor force during this 10-year span have been reported in national studies as well.[25]

The increase of minority women in the city's clerical labor force is a result not only of the diminished pool of white non-Hispanics, but of affirmative action, the influx of minority immigrants, and the changing ethnic and racial population of New York City.

However, limitations persist on opportunities for minority women. Even in public employment, traditionally more open to minorities,[26] minority women tend to be situated in lower-level jobs without direct pro-

Table 7.7   Proportion of Women in Clerical Occupations
Who Are Non-Hispanic Black, Aggregate Categories: 1970–1980

| Occupation | 1970 % | 1980 % | Change % Pts. | Percent Change |
|---|---|---|---|---|
| Computer Operator | 10.5 | 36.2 | 25.7 | 244.8 |
| Secretary, Steno, Typist | 9.8 | 18.2 | 8.4 | 85.7 |
| Information Clerk | 11.3 | 23.0 | 11.7 | 103.5 |
| Records Processing | 19.0 | 38.5 | 19.5 | 102.6 |
| Financial Records Processing | 9.0 | 16.9 | 7.9 | 87.8 |
| Office Machine Operator | 22.7 | 36.5 | 13.8 | 60.8 |
| Communications | 23.1 | 46.6 | 23.5 | 101.7 |
| Mail, Messenger, Delivery | 37.9 | 51.7 | 13.8 | 36.4 |
| Material Recording, Scheduling | 13.5 | 27.0 | 13.5 | 100.0 |
| Adjusters, Investigators | 11.5 | 26.9 | 15.4 | 133.9 |
| Miscellaneous Administrative Support | 25.7 | 32.1 | 6.4 | 24.9 |
| Technician* | — | 11.40 | — | — |
| Total | 13.6 | 23.2 | 9.6 | 70.6 |

Source: See Table 7.1.

*New category for 1980—includes Technicians n.e.c. and Computer Programmers.

motional tracks. A recent study of the New York City municipal work force by the Urban Research Center of New York University reports that,

> Of the predominantly female and/or predominantly minority jobs, approximately one-third are entry level. Of this third, three in ten, mostly minority, have no direct line of promotion.[27]

As we saw earlier, in the study of communications workers, minority women expressed a sense of defeat with regard to promotion possibilities.

Nationally, minorities have improved their representation in clerical occupations, but not nearly as impressively as in New York City; Current Population Survey data from 1972 to 1982 show an increase from 8.7 to 11.8 percent.[28] In 1985 nearly 30 percent of all employed minority women were clerical workers.[29] Minority workers are expected to become an even larger part of the labor force in the future; their birthrates tend to be high, their current populations young, and it is likely that high rates of immigration will continue for working-age minority people.[30]

Members of certain minority groups cluster in particular occupations. In New York, black women's representation in communications rose from 23.1 percent in 1970 to 46.6 percent in 1980; neither Hispanic nor Asian

Table 7.8  Proportion of Women in Clerical Occupations
Who Are Hispanic, Aggregate Categories: 1970–1980

| Occupation | 1970 % | 1980 % | Change % Pts. | Percent Change |
|---|---|---|---|---|
| Computer Operator | 5.3 | 11.4 | 6.1 | 115.1 |
| Secretary, Steno, Typist | 6.8 | 11.9 | 5.1 | 75.0 |
| Information Clerk | 11.3 | 13.4 | 2.1 | 18.6 |
| Records Processing | 10.0 | 12.6 | 2.6 | 26.0 |
| Financial Records Processing | 5.2 | 9.7 | 4.5 | 86.5 |
| Office Machine Operator | 22.7 | 19.2 | −3.5 | −15.4 |
| Communications | 4.4 | 6.9 | 2.5 | 56.8 |
| Mail, Messenger, Delivery | 8.3 | 13.8 | 5.5 | 66.3 |
| Material Recording Scheduling | 21.6 | 16.2 | −5.4 | −25.0 |
| Adjusters, Investigators | 4.4 | 10.2 | 5.8 | 131.8 |
| Miscellaneous Administrative Support | 10.9 | 15.0 | 4.1 | 37.6 |
| Technician* | — | 11.4 | — | — |
| Total | 7.5 | 11.8 | 4.3 | 57.3 |

*Source:* See Table 7.1.

*New category for 1980—includes Technicians n.e.c. and Computer Programmers.

women increased their presence in the field to this extent. (Compare Tables 7.7, 7.8, and 7.9.) The percentage rise of Hispanic women among mail, message, and delivery workers was more pronounced (37.9 to 51.7 percent) than for the other minority groups (the percentage of Asian females in this classification actually fell during the decade). And the percentage rise for Asians employed as office machine operators (0 to 5.8 percent) was greater than for black or Hispanic women.

The New York data on minority women in selected clerical occupations show clearly that minority females gained representation in all occupations. Again, black women comprise the largest minority in each occupation and, with the exception of the supervisor category, they recorded the largest absolute gains in percentage in all occupations between 1970 and 1980. Black women showed particularly substantial increases as telephone operators and file clerks, while Latina and Asian women enjoyed their largest proportional increases as supervisors and typists.

The varied increases shown by minority groups in different occupations may reflect their degree of underrepresentation in these fields in 1970. For example, the considerable percentage increase in Latina and Asian supervisors stems from a minuscule or nonexistent base in 1970: only 1.9 percent of women supervisors were Latina, while none were

Table 7.9    Women in Clerical Occupations Who Are Asian
and Other Non-Hispanic, Aggregate Categories: 1970-1980

| Occupation | 1970 % | 1980 % | Change % Pts. | Percent Change |
|---|---|---|---|---|
| Computer Operator | 0.0 | 4.5 | 4.5 | — |
| Secretary, Steno, Typist | 0.7 | 2.1 | 1.4 | 200.0 |
| Information Clerk | 0.7 | 2.6 | 1.9 | 271.4 |
| Records Processing | 0.6 | 2.0 | 1.4 | 233.3 |
| Financial Records Processing | 0.6 | 3.9 | 3.3 | 550.0 |
| Office Machine Operator | 0.0 | 5.8 | 5.8 | — |
| Communications | 0.8 | 1.3 | 0.5 | 62.5 |
| Mail, Messenger, Delivery | 1.5 | 1.2 | -0.3 | -20.0 |
| Material Recording, Scheduling | 1.4 | 2.8 | 1.4 | 100.0 |
| Adjusters, Investigators | 0.0 | 3.1 | 3.1 | — |
| Miscellaneous Administrative Support | 1.0 | 3.5 | 2.5 | 250.0 |
| Technician* | — | 22.8 | — | — |
| Total | 0.7 | 2.7 | 2.0 | 285.7 |

Source: See Table 7.1.

*New category for 1980—includes Technicians n.e.c. and Computer Programmers.

Asian. The rise in participation of black women in communications, and particularly as telephone operators, reflects a need for English language skills which Hispanic and Asian women may not possess.

Although the growth of minority women in the clerical work force is encouraging, they are often entering dead-end jobs. As the U.S Department of Labor reports,

> Like women generally, [minority women] are underrepresented in the middle and top level professional and technical computing jobs. . . .Bureau of Labor Statistics suggest that black and Hispanic women occupy only about 3 percent of the professional and technical level computer jobs but five times as many (16 percent) of the lower level data entry and computer operator jobs.[31]

The report goes on to give the example of the high-tech office and computing machine industry itself, where minority women make up 2.4 percent of professional workers and less than 1.5 percent of sales workers. Minority women, however, hold 11 percent of the office and clerical jobs, and nearly 20 percent of the lower-level operative and laborer jobs in the industry.[32]

In the legal office and clerical work force, an area of growth marked by use of computer technology, minority women are finding increased employment; 27.9 percent in 1982, up from 17.5 percent in 1975.[33] Minorities are not likely, however, to have access to jobs as legal secretaries, the "clerical brahmins," according to Mary Murphree, who has studied clerical workers in New York law firms.[34] (Legal secretaries, however, are a diminishing breed whose functions have been taken over by paralegal personnel and word processing pools.) Of course, minority workers are relative newcomers to the legal sector. This is an occupation rooted in tradition, especially with regard to employment in the large Wall Street firms, which represent the sector of highest growth. Many of these firms still had white non-Hispanic men working as secretaries until World War II and only reluctantly began to hire women when the pool of male workers diminished.[35]

## Education and Its Consequences

A steady theme in the analysis of workplace opportunity is that of the fit between worker and job. New technology is said to require a more educated worker than before, and it seems to be widely believed that the preparation of the worker lags behind the economy's needs. A complete analysis requires more detailed data than are provided by the census, but the census data nevertheless hold some surprises. In spite of the perception that New York City suffers from an ill-prepared pool of workers, census figures indicate they were better educated in 1980 than in 1970, an indication true for all workers across the United States.[36] There was a decrease in the percentage of women clerical workers in New York City with grade school or high school educations (years 1–8 and 9–12), a smaller decrease in those with only a college or trade school education (years 13–16), and an increase in those with post-college (graduate school or post-college trade school) education (years 17+). This shift is due to the rather large decline in the percentage of women with only primary education and a slight decline in the percentage with secondary education.

Although this is a trend common to all the occupations we have examined, Table 7.10 shows that it is more pronounced in the expanding occupations of supervisor and computer operator and less so for shrinking occupations like telephone operator. For 1980, 7.3 percent of supervisors (down from 14.9 percent in 1970) and 5.5 percent of computer operators (down from 12.8 percent) had attended only grade or high school, while 26.9 percent of supervisors (up from 13.9 percent) and 19.8 percent of computer operators (up from 9.6 percent) had at least some postsecondary

Table 7.10   Education of Women in Clerical Occupations,
Selected Categories: 1970–1980

| Occupation | | Years of Education | | | |
| --- | --- | --- | --- | --- | --- |
| | | 1–8 % | 9–12 % | 13–16 % | 17 or More, % |
| Supervisor* | 1970 | 0.0% | 14.9 | 71.3 | 13.9 |
| | 1980 | 1.1 | 6.2 | 65.8 | 26.9 |
| Computer | 1970 | 1.1 | 11.7 | 77.7 | 9.6 |
| Operator† | 1980 | 0.8 | 4.7 | 74.7 | 19.8 |
| Secretary | 1970 | 0.9 | 7.4 | 80.3 | 11.4 |
| | 1980 | 0.6 | 2.6 | 79.1 | 17.6 |
| Stenographer | 1970 | 1.0 | 7.3 | 86.5 | 5.2 |
| | 1980 | 1.7 | 5.7 | 78.3 | 14.3 |
| Typist | 1970 | 1.3 | 11.7 | 80.1 | 6.9 |
| | 1980 | 0.7 | 5.7 | 82.8 | 10.8 |
| Telephone | 1970 | 1.3 | 33.4 | 61.3 | 4.0 |
| Operator | 1980 | 1.3 | 14.0 | 77.3 | 7.4 |
| File Clerk | 1970 | 1.8 | 22.9 | 67.5 | 7.8 |
| | 1980 | 1.7 | 12.6 | 71.4 | 14.4 |

Source: 1970 and 1980 decennial census data, adjusted for consistency.

*Supervisor is an aggregate category for 1980.
†Computer Operator for 1980 includes Peripheral Machine Operator.

education. Fifteen and one-third percent of telephone operators in 1980, on the other hand, had only a grade or high school education (although this is down from 34.7 percent in 1970), while 7.4 percent had postsecondary schooling (this, too, however, is up from 4 percent).

In the sample of clerical workers in the financial, insurance, and legal sectors studied by Pullman and Szymanski, only 1.4 percent had less than a high school degree, while over 64 percent had some college or more education. The legal field had a greater percentage of people educated at higher college levels. Banking and insurance employed a sizeable number of those holding no more than high school diplomas.[37]

This increase in employment of workers with postsecondary education may be a response to the demand for a higher degree of skill necessary to operate the new technology in the marketplace, or it may reflect a rise in demand for credentials. Many employers in New York City claim that the quality of education has gone down and that employers must seek college-educated employees for what used to be characterized as jobs that called for no more than a high school education. Some, however, admit that because of high unemployment, they now have the luxury of choosing from among college-educated applicants. John Kasarda, in his analysis of job creation in nine major U.S. cities between 1970 and 1980, suggests an occupational shift toward knowledge-intensive jobs. This pattern is most pronounced for New York City.[38] Steven Vallas notes that the need for enhanced worker skills is not clear in clerical and communications work, and there is considerable variation in the need for prior training.[39] Indeed, because technology may produce atomization of tasks, many jobs might be quite simple to learn and for many clerical jobs training takes place on the job. Higher educational levels therefore may be sought by employers to insure that recruits possess social qualifications such as middle class comportment, demeanor, and a receptivity to training.[40]

Although the census data we have analyzed show that the clerical work force is better educated (presumably a good thing), it also means that many prospective workers will find it difficult to find employment when their educational level is not as high.

A study by the Regional Plan Association estimates that

> Since 1970. . .New York City lost almost one half million jobs requiring less than a high school education, and gained over one quarter million jobs requiring some college. By 1984, more than one million positions were filled by college-level workers, while less than one million were held by workers without a high school diploma. These changes, and the future direction of New York's economy, are *incompatible* with high levels of high school dropout rates (35 percent) and the failure of a large proportion of the adult population to complete a high school diploma (40 percent in New York over age 25).[41] [emphasis added]

The relatively high level of educational attainment in the current clerical labor force, a quality likely to be even greater in the future, will shut out a significant part of New York City's population from the labor market. This is especially true for the city's minority population, which tends to have a relatively high dropout rate and low educational attainment levels compared to white non-Hispanics.[42] As Ehrenhalt states, "Many of the better jobs may be well beyond reach for these groups."[43]

Education is also used as a gatekeeping factor. Although internal promotion ladders traditionally allowed some individuals who started at entry-level positions to work their way up in a company, this is a diminishing possibility. Professional and managerial personnel now are usually being recruited by companies directly from college. As Noyelle states:

> No longer could a sales clerk expect to become a buyer for a major retail organization, or a messenger expect to become an insurance executive by simply moving through the ranks.[44]

A higher education level does not necessarily lead to opportunity for the average worker beyond that of obtaining employment. One communications worker in the Epstein-Erikson study recalled that:

> I came into this job with a college degree and thought I would move up in a couple of years. But I'm still where I started and there are people in this office who have been here for years: 7, 8, 9, 12 years doing the same job.

Furthermore, education does not necessarily translate into a substantial differential in pay. A survey by Professional Secretaries International, cited by the U.S Department of Labor, recorded that for secretaries, like other clerical workers, the lack of a high school diploma costs $2,500 a year, while a master's degree adds only $1,500 to the average annual salary.[45]

Pullman and Szymanski's study shows that annual salaries for clericals span a wide range, with 25 percent earning between $6,000 to $9,000 a year, almost another 25 percent clustering in the $15,000 to $18,000 range, and those remaining earning between $18,000 to $24,000. In both insurance and banking, in which the majority of black women sampled (85 percent) work, the largest percentage of the sample was clustered in the $15,000 to $18,000 range. Although this was in the midrange of the salary scale, the direction of automation is to eliminate the type of jobs which black women have only recently entered.

Although white collar workers may make more money in New York City than elsewhere in the country, they do not make much more and it is harder to live in the city. Furthermore, minority women endure greater difficulties in organizing their lives to include continuous work because they are more likely than white women to be single mothers. In the Pullman and Szymanski study, 42 percent were the heads of households.[46] In New York City as elsewhere, women suffer from the double burden of home work as well as work in the office, factory, and retail store. This also has consequence for their ability to obtain further education. A communications worker interviewed by Epstein and Erikson indicated motivation but lack of time in seeking more training:

I think basically you need to get back into school, but it's very hard especially for the working mother. . .men have the advantage; take my husband, he finished his degree in accounting. . .I have to come home from work and cook and make sure his dinner is ready when he comes home from school. It's harder for the woman.

Although there is a large immigrant work force that provides some child-care support for women who can afford it, most women workers must rely on family members or other private arrangements. Clerical workers are typically locked into inflexible schedules that do not recognize family needs, and little or no private or public help exists.[47]

Office automation technology has enabled some firms to restructure their work force so that they can avoid hiring full-time workers. Part-time or temporary work often pays less per hour than similar full-time work. Furthermore, the employment of these workers allows firms to avoid providing the benefits required by law for full-time workers. We do not have figures for New York City, but part-time or temporary workers are said to make up 27 percent of the work force.[48] It is reported that two-thirds of the 26.8 million part-time workers in the United States are women. Women make up 62 percent of all temporary workers, employed primarily as clerical workers.

## Job Content

The numbers and trends tell only a part of the story of white collar workers. How do women clerical workers regard their jobs? A number of writers predict a growing alienation of clerical workers as deskilling becomes common alienation in the workplace. Barbara Garson's recent book, *The Electronic Sweatshop* (1988), includes professionals as well as clerical workers among those who must face a deskilled work situation. Others, however, see far more variation. Shoshana Zuboff, for example, writes that the introduction of information technologies brings about a shift in the roles of the worker's body and mind in the process of production. "Intellective skills" can replace the drudgery of work, according to Zuboff, who studied the effects of computerization in manufacturing and clerical work settings. She found that physical tasks were replaced by mental ones in many instances in the paper mill at which she did research. But for groups of clerical workers in an insurance firm and a telephone company, she found that management employed information systems to set quotas and monitor each worker's performance with little or no concern for their skills or commitment to the firm.[49]

Yet there has been a transformation of skills in the clerical workplace and new jobs have been created. Pullman and Szymanski found that clusters of many lower-skilled jobs were amalgamated into fewer higher-skilled positions, professional work was clericalized, and routine tasks were automated to control and verify data. In the Epstein-Erikson study many workers found their jobs "easier" with the introduction of computers and did not complain of deskilling. There was even an "evolution of 'lower-skilled' jobs into 'higher-skilled'" jobs due to increased technical skills in the Pullman-Szymanski study. In their findings, some 87 percent of clerical workers perceived that their skills were increased by technology. Yet they claimed that managers often failed to reward these changed jobs with promotion and additional pay. When asked if people were promoted as a result of working with computers, only 17 percent said it was "quite likely," and 12 percent said that raises in pay were "likely"; the vast majority of respondents claimed that people did not get raises in pay for this activity.[50] Managers pointed out that many clerical workers do not want administrative jobs, but this may be because they are not prepared for or oriented toward such jobs. Clerical workers are often not allowed to make small decisions about their immediate work environments or the design of their work; it is thus possible that administrative work seems out of reach to them.

Nonetheless, office workers show a high level of motivation when it comes to learning more about computers and upgrading their skills. Three-quarters of them report interest in pursuing company-subsidized computer training at the workplace, and nearly as many would take courses outside.

## Work Organization

The structure of work has many consequences for workers' satisfaction. There has been concern that growing numbers of office workers will be working in large typing-pool-like environments. Mary Murphree's investigation of secretarial work in a large Wall Street law firm has showed that much of the work formerly done by private secretaries has been relegated to typing (now word processing) pools, where typists do not have personal contact with their bosses and have suffered a decrease in job diversity. In the Pullman-Szymanski study, only about 16 percent of the workers worked in a pool environment, although many were in settings where they were arranged in clusters and still did pool-type functions. Boredom seemed endemic and the level of turnover was high. Seventy-nine percent of the respondents said that they did the same things over and over again. Such work settings recall Taylorism, a questionable policy on the contemporary work scene, where decentralized, nonhierarchical forms of organization may be more efficient for management and more satisfying for the worker.

## Conclusion

The trends and issues facing women clerical workers in New York City present a mixed picture. Certainly, the office worker faces a transforming work environment, but change is not new to the clerical workplace. The introduction of the typewriter, the Xerox copier, and other technology also resulted in changes in the status of personnel and the quality of work life. The pace and control of work may have accelerated, but office workers have always had to face control and quotas. Computer technology has offered the worker a possibility of diminished drudgery and that has happened in some sectors, in others, however, deskilling has occurred.

Advantages and disadvantages have been variously distributed. Although the deskilling of certain jobs diminished the satisfaction and autonomy of the workers who performed them, the growth of such jobs may have created opportunities for people who did not have the preparation or competence to gain employment in the past. Certainly the movement of black women workers from domestic employment to clerical and other white collar work over the past 25 years has given them a net gain in income, job security, and health and other fringe benefits. This may also be so for those women who once worked in factories at female sex-labeled jobs—those in sweatshops, for example.

Yet, according to Patricia Sparks, minority women are locked into the lower echelons of such clerical occupations as data entry and other jobs from which vertical mobility is virtually impossible.[51] According to Norman Fainstein this is not due to their lack of human capital but because of racial discrimination.[52] In addition, the technology that enabled minority women to gain access to lower-level jobs in the clerical world may in the long run deskill and eliminate these jobs. Managers may no longer know the worker but rely on numerical indices or computer keystrokes to gauge performance.

These transformations in the clerical work force are not inevitable developments of technology. All change is introduced and applied by managers of businesses and government agencies who by their choices express their values and assumptions about production, efficiency, working conditions, and preferences for employees with certain backgrounds. Workers also express their interests and preferences through union activity or lack of it, commitment to employers, and their own productivity. Both face external constraints imposed by their economic needs and by the attitudes of their communities and the society. Technology, as we know, does hold promise for maximizing the interests of both groups. It remains to be seen how it will further affect the clerical workplace when the changes now taking place have become institutionalized. The ghetto-ization of work, whether by sex or race or ethnic designation, usually creates new barriers to opportunity, autonomy, and integrity for the workers confined within them. It also remains to be seen whether the prejudices of the past will be altered by the participation of minorities who have entered the clerical work force in the past two decades. Deep-seated views that reinforce the female sex-typing of clerical employment seem virtually unchanged, with all the restrictive consequences that follow.

## Notes

The research on which this chapter is based was funded by grants from the Robert F. Wagner, Sr. Institute of Urban Public Policy and the Russell Sage Foundation. We also wish to acknowledge the assistance of Mitu Hirshmann and Kim Reed.

1. Hunt, Allen H., and Timothy L. Hunt, "Recent Trends in Clerical Employment: The Impact of Technological Change," *Computer Chips and Paper Clips, Vol. II*, Hartmann, Heidi I., ed. (Washington, DC: National Academy Press, 1987), pp. 223–224.

2. In the insurance industry, where 70 percent of the 1 million female employees are clerical workers, approximately one-fifth of the female work force in 1980 were minorities. Baran, Barbara, "The Technological Transformation of White Collar Work," Hartmann, *Computer Chips, Vol. II*, p. 53.

3. Waldinger, Roger, "Changing Ladders and Musical Chairs: Ethnicity and Opportunity in Post-Industrial New York, *Politics & Society* 15:4 (1986–7): 369–401; and Lieberson, Stanley, *A Piece of the Pie* (Berkeley: University of California Press, 1980).

4. There recently has been some stagnation in the percentage of clerical workers in the U.S. economy—hovering close to 17 percent in the early eighties and then dropping to about 16 percent in 1984. For example, increased automatic banking will probably cut into the future employment of clerical workers in banking and insurance, and a decrease in the rate of employment is forecast. Legal services, however, are expected to grow at the average rate. Pullman, Cydney, and Sharon Szymanski, "The Impact of Office Technology on Clerical Worker Skills in the Banking, Insurance and Legal Industries in New York

City: Implications for Training." A Study for the Private Industry Council of New York City (New York: The Labor Institute, August 1986), pp. 12,16.

5. Hartmann, Heidi I., Robert E. Kraut, and Louise A. Tilly, eds., *Computer Chips and Paper Clips: Technology and Women's Employment, Vol. I* (Washington, DC: National Academy Press, 1986), p. xi.

6. U.S. Department of Labor, Women's Bureau, *Women and Office Automation: Issues for the Decade Ahead* (Washington, DC, 1985), p. 1.

7. Sparks, Patricia, "The Impact of Office Automation on Working Women." Testimony before The Committee on Women (New York: The Council of the City of New York, 20 May 1986), p. 4.

8. Garson, Barbara, *The Electronic Sweatshop: How Computers are Transforming the Office of the Future into the Factory of the Past* (New York: Simon & Schuster, 1988), p.10.

9. Zuboff, Shoshana, *In the Age of the Smart Machine: The Future of Work and Power* (New York: Basic Books, 1988).

10. Ehrenhalt, Samuel M., "The Service Economy and Job Quality: The New York Experience," (New York: Bureau of Labor Statistics, U.S. Dept. of Labor, 1986a); Hartmann, *Computer Chips Vol. II*; Pullman and Szymanski, "The Impact of Office Technology on Clerical Worker Skills"; and U.S. Dept. of Labor, *Women*.

11. Ehrenhalt, Samuel M., "The Service Economy"; Ehrenhalt, Samuel M., "The New York Experience as a Service Economy" (New York: Bureau of Labor Statistics, U.S. Dept. of Labor, 1986).

12. New York State Department of Labor, Bureau of Statistics, "Occupational Needs in the 1980's" (Albany: N.Y. State Department of Labor, 1986).

13. Ehrenhalt, Samuel M., "After the Crash: New York Prospects" (New York: Bureau of Labor Statistics, U.S. Department of Labor, July 1988).

14. These data were initially organized by Roger Waldinger of the City College of New York and the Graduate Center of the City University of New York.

15. Hartmann, *Computer Chips, Vol. II*, p. 82.

16. Ginzberg, Eli, "Technology, Women, and Work: Policy Perspectives," in Hartmann, *Computer Chips, Vol. II*, p. 9.

17. The 1970 categories of "telegraph messenger" and "telegraph operators" do not appear in 1980, although in this case it represents the almost complete disappearance of the occupation. Heidi Hartmann et al. point out how "the census is revised. . .without systematic attention to the way technological changes have redefined the task content of jobs." For example, word processors were formerly classified as "typists" in census data, but in 1980 were considered "computer operators" (Hartmann, Kraut, and Tilly, *Computer Chips*, p. 66). Thus, to some extent, when trying to assess trends and changes, it is difficult to know which categories to aggregate and which to include when investigating the meaning of changes. However difficult, it is not a futile task. In this chapter, we divide the entire clerical occupational field into

twelve common aggregate categories, attempting to take into account the changes that have occurred in the census. In addition, we have chosen as examples seven relatively discrete and consistent occupational categories, each of which reveals interesting shifts in the work force between 1970 and 1980: "computer operators," the fastest growing occupation during this time period and one which is obviously positively influenced by the growth in technology; "telephone operator" and "file clerk," the most rapidly shrinking occupations and most negatively influenced by technological growth; "secretary," "stenographer," and "typist," the "traditional" clerical occupations of women and composed of the largest share of female clerical workers; and "supervisor," a low-level management position which may reveal trends concerning bars to advancement contingent on sex, race, ethnicity, and education.

18. Hunt, Allen H., and Timothy L. Hunt, "Clerical Employment and Technological Change: A Review of Recent Trends and Projections." Paper prepared for The Panel on Technology and Women's Employment and Related Social Issues (Washington, DC: National Research Council, 1985).

19. Hartmann, Kraut, and Tilly, *Computer Chips, Vol. I*, p. 3.

20. Mollenkopf, John, "The Postindustrial Transformation of the Political Order in New York City," in J. Mollenkopf, ed., *Power, Culture and Place* (New York: Russell Sage Foundation, 1989), pp. 235–237.

21. Pullman and Szymanski, "The Impact of Office Technology," p. 7.

22. U.S. Dept. of Labor, *Women*, p. 12.

23. Noyelle, Thierry J., "The New Technology and the New Economy: Some Implications for Equal Opportunity Employment," in Hartmann, *Computer Chips, Vol. II*, p. 379.

24. See Chapter 2, Bailey and Waldinger.

25. Noyelle, "The New Technology," pp. 376–377.

26. See Chapter 2, Bailey and Waldinger.

27. Urban Research Center, New York University, *Wage Discrimination and Occupational Segregation in New York City's Municipal Workforce: Time for a Change* (New York: August 1987), p. II.

28. Hunt and Hunt, "Clerical Employment."

29. U.S. Dept. of Labor, *Women*, p. 20.

30. Ehrenhalt, "After the Crash," p. 7; Hartmann, Kraut, and Tilly, *Computer Chips, Vol. I* , p. 80.

31. U.S. Dept. of Labor, *Women*, p. 20.

32. U.S. Dept. of Labor, *Women*, pp. 20–21.

33. Mollenkopf, John, "The Corporate Legal Services Industry in New York," *New York Affairs* (January 1983).

34. Murphree, Mary C., "Rationalization and Satisfaction in Clerical Work: A Case Study of Wall Street Legal Secretaries." Ph.D. Diss., Department of Sociology, Columbia University, 1981.

35. Epstein, Cynthia Fuchs, *Women in Law* (New York: Basic Books, 1981).

36. Ehrenhalt, Samuel M., "The New York Experience," p. 24.

37. Pullman and Szymanski, "The Impact of Office Technology," p. 97.

38. Cited in Castells, Manuel, *The Informational City* (London: Basil Blackwell Press, 1989), p. 392.

39. Vallas, Steven Peter, "Computers, Managers and Control at Work," *Sociological Forum* 4:2 (June 1989): 291–303.

40. Pullman and Szymanski, "The Impact of Office Technology," p. 143.

41. Regional Plan Association of New York, "New York in the Global Economy: Studying the Facts and the Issues." Presented to World Association of Major Metropolises meeting, Mexico City, April 1987, p. 54.

42. Ehrenhalt, "After the Crash," p. 39.

43. Ehrenhalt, "The New York Experience," p. 8.

44. Noyelle, "The New Technology," p. 366.

45. Noyelle, "The New Technology," in Hartmann, *Computer Chips, Vol. II*, p. 367.

46. Pullman and Szymanski, "The Impact of Office Technology," p. 184.

47. For the first time some of these problems have been addressed in a new contract negotiated between the Communications Workers of America and AT&T.

48. Pullman and Szymanski, "The Impact of Office Technology," p. 166.

49. Zuboff, *In the Age*.

50. Pullman and Szymanski, "The Impact of Office Technology," pp. 132, 160.

51. Sparks, "The Impact of Office Automation."

52. Fainstein, Norman, "The Underclass/Mismatch Hypothesis as an Explanation for Black Economic Deprivation," *Politics and Society* 15:4 (1986–7): 403.

# PART IV

# Trends
# in Social Organization

# 8

# The Separation of Mothers and Children

## Ida Susser

The relationships between work, child rearing, and household formation highlight some of the contradictory consequences of recent changes in New York City's class structure. The increasing social and economic polarization in recent decades has been accompanied by growing interdependence among different kinds of households. The household is the linchpin that connects changing relations of labor, social reproduction, and biological reproduction.[1] Historically, women have performed most of the tasks associated with the creation of "home" and family, in the ideological sense. The processes of home creation and family formation are constantly changing and involve interdependencies of both class and gender. The changes of recent decades in New York City have led households to employ a wide variety of strategies to maintain home and family, most of which rely primarily on women. The following discussion focuses on the contrasting opportunities open to women of different groups and how their new strategies for organizing biological and social reproduction have shaped the interconnections among different kinds of women. The restructuring of households varies by class, and this ultimately determines the rearing and socialization of children for different class positions.

The growing female work force spans the labor market from the lowest paid wage earners to the highest paid lawyers, doctors, and corporate investors. As the 1980 census indicated, 27.9 percent of all children under six in New York City had mothers who were working, and another 3.8 percent had mothers who were in the labor force but unemployed.[2] The increasing incorporation of women into the labor market has led to far-reaching changes in household structure that vary with the education of women and their changing economic resources.

As more women work, children are being reared in increasingly various conditions that do, however, share at least one element. It appears to be progressively less common that children are being reared solely by the "mother." Although the concept of the biological mother as full-time caretaker has been an element of the ideology of the family since the nineteenth century, current conditions for households in New York City render this progressively less common among both poor and professional women.

Two processes in particular have transformed social reproduction in New York City: (1) the increase in poverty since the 1970s along with the growth of the uncounted unemployed, marginal employment, the imposition of "workfare policies," and increased homelessness; and (2) the professionalization of educated women and their dependence on hired domestic workers. Each has contributed to interdependency among women workers and the separation of biological mothers from the care of their children. The circumstances of child rearing differ strongly according to class. In professional families, many children are reared by housekeepers and trained nursery school teachers. In poor families, children are often reared by overworked baby sitters, in overcrowded daycare centers staffed by untrained low-paid caretakers, or are left in the charge of other children. Among homeless families, children are frequently removed from the "home" by social workers or caseworkers and put into foster care.

This analysis draws cases from the extremes of the economic spectrum—the poor and the homeless, in contrast with highly paid professionally employed women—to illustrate trends that are quite likely to have influenced a wide range of households between these extremes. It focuses on the years between 1965 and 1985 for two reasons. First, this period includes the 10 years leading up to the pivotal fiscal crisis of 1975 and the 10 years following. Second, 1965 was a turning point in immigration policy. Migrant workers comprise a growing proportion of young households in New York City and probably the majority of domestic workers.[3] Control of migrant entries in turn affects the cost of domestic service and the availability of women to replace those who find well-paid work. The period described here was shaped by the immigration legislation in place between 1965 and 1986.[4]

## Poverty, Homelessness, Welfare Regulations, and Household Structure

In 1985, nearly one-quarter of the children under 6 years of age in the United States were growing up in households with incomes below the poverty level.[5] More than half the families living below poverty level were supported by women alone.[6] In the period under review the number of children living in poverty and the number of households "headed" by women in New York City have also been increasing. In 1950, the poverty rate for New York City was below the national rate, 16 percent in contrast to a national figure of 22 percent. Since 1969, however, the poverty rate has consistently exceeded U.S. national rates, and in recent years the margin appears to have widened. By 1989, 23.2 percent of New York City families were living below the poverty line as opposed to a national rate of 13.5 percent.[7] The poverty rate for female-headed households in New York City increased from 41 percent in 1969 and 55 percent in 1979 to 63 percent in 1987. In addition, while one out of five New York City children lived in poverty in 1969, by 1987 almost two out of five children were being reared in poverty, a rate which exceeded the national average.[8] While the numbers of poor children and poor adults have been increasing in New York City since 1969, the number of people in poverty who have been able to obtain public assistance in the form of Aid to Families with Dependent Children (the main source of public assistance in New York City) has been decreasing.[9] Along with the restructuring of the New York City economy and decline in manufacturing and unskilled jobs, expenditures on the social reproduction of the poorer segments of the labor force appear to have decreased.

A 1988 survey reported that 45 percent of the adult population of New York City (aged 16 to 64) did not hold a job.[10] As the unemployment rate at that time was 4.5 percent, this suggests that approximately 40 percent of the adult population was not in the labor force. Since 1977, there have been increases in jobs available in white collar occupations in the public sector, financing, and insurance. However, the retail and manufacturing jobs generally available to the poor have decreased since the 1970s.[11] Thus, poor children growing up with inadequate resources, under the supervision of women working for incomes below poverty level, have, in fact, poor prospects in the labor market. Let us now examine the household organization and conditions for child rearing engendered by these circumstances.

Since 1975, the problems of poverty in New York City have been manifested most obviously in the increasing numbers of homeless people and the renewed phenomenon (not seen since the 1930s Depression) of homeless families. However, homelessness is only one extreme example of how poverty and reduced government support for the unskilled labor force have undermined households. Unemployment, underemployment, and poverty are the first assaults on household structure; homelessness is the second.

The provision of public assistance benefits increased between 1965 and 1972 in New York City.[12] In the 1960s new public housing was built, both in the form of low-income New York City Housing Authority projects and moderate-income Mitchell-Lama construction. In contrast, between 1975 and 1985, low-income housing production declined, low and moderate rent apartments were destroyed by abandonment, and the gap between the cost of living and public assistance benefits increased.[13] These trends had a major impact on household organization and the rearing of children.

Inadequate public assistance payments in New York City in the 1970s led to poor housing conditions. Poor mothers who stayed home to care for children did not have sufficient funds to feed and clothe their households.[14] The gap between the cost of living and public assistance payments increased and many people who were eligible for public assistance did not receive it.[15]

Families were forced into the informal if not the illegal economy to supplement household income. Since the budget required to maintain a family was almost double that allotted by public assistance in New York City, poor families were drawn into multiple forms of "hustling," including drug dealing and the sale of sexual services.[16] Hustling tended to be differentiated by gender. Boys got involved in the hazardous narcotics business while girls were more likely to juggle welfare regulations and engage in prostitution.[17] Under such conditions many poor children grew up with little chance of completing school or finding well-paying jobs.[18] However, homelessness and the disintegration of the family which accompanies loss of shelter remained relatively infrequent in the 1970s.

Whether unemployment or public assistance regulations led to the high proportion of female-headed households, it is clear that the burden of household maintenance and child rearing falls upon poor women to an even greater extent than it does on women of higher incomes.[19] Yet poor women and women on public assistance have always worked. Women on public assistance often work "off the books" or in the informal economy, cleaning houses or minding children or in various forms of hustling. Since changes in federal regulations implemented in the early 1980s, households that were previously eligible for public assistance over and above their low earned wages were no longer entitled to supplemental assistance. Such supplements had taken into account the costs of daycare which allowed women to work.[20] Reduced supplemental assistance forced women either to stop working or to cut costs possibly through finding less expensive ways of taking care of their children.

In the late 1980s, new federally mandated workfare provisions required women with young children to work in order to qualify for public assistance.[21] As a result of workfare women may seek to place their children in publicly certified and subsidized forms of daycare. If they fail to find daycare and leave children alone or arrive late to pick them up, children may be removed from their families by the Child Welfare Administration, an agency of the Human Resources Administration.

While the federal government and New York State mandate that the "welfare mother" go out to work, they do not provide care for her children commensurate to newly created needs. In 1980, New York City provided places for only 22 percent of the 144,000 children under six who were financially eligible for publicly funded daycare and in need of the service because their mothers worked. Of the 72,000 children under two in need of publicly funded daycare, only 6 percent were able to find spaces.[22] Other children were placed in daycare situations that were often overcrowded, sometimes dangerous, and conducted in poor housing with poor supervision and no state certification. Since they are not licensed, there is no way to count the actual number of children in such situations. In 1985, only 16 percent of all children in need of "substitute care" (care other than the mother), were cared for by licensed childcare providers in New York State.[23] As Governor Mario Cuomo's Report on the *State of the Child in New York State* notes, "The low proportion of estimated need that is accommodated by licensed care is one indication that the majority of childcare in New York State is unregulated."[24] Care given in a child's own home or by a relative other than a mother has also declined. Thus, it is probable that most children being cared for outside licensed facilities are under the care of women who are paid to watch a number of children but fail to meet licensing requirements.[25]

According to the 1980 U.S. Census figures provided in Table 8.1, most children under six years old, regardless of family type or whether the mother was working, were not enrolled in public, church, or other private schools. (Approximately 26 percent of these children were in some form of school.) Only within female-headed households where the mother worked does this proportion rise to 40 percent, and this accounts for only a small fraction of the children under six. The census does not tell us who cared for the great majority of children under six who were not in school. The great bulk of them (almost 285,000 children) had mothers who were not working and who could presumably care for them, but over one out of four (94,520) neither were in school nor had a mother not working. In households where the mother worked, only 34 percent of the children under six were in any form of school or nursery school, leaving 66 percent without an obvious source of care. Even among female-headed households with working mothers, 60 percent of the children under six were not in nursery school or kindergarten. Presumably, while the mother was

Table 8.1    New York City Children Aged 0–5 Not in School,
by Family Type and Mother's Labor Force Status: 1980

| | Percent Not in School | Number |
|---|---|---|
| Total Children Aged 0–5 N=513,160 | 73.8 | 378,580 |
| Mother not in Labor Force | | |
| In all-family households N=350,380 | 68.3 | 269,160 |
| In married-couple families N=233,300 | 66.6 | 176,540 |
| In female-headed households N=110,780 | 74.5 | 88,270 |
| Mother Unemployed | | |
| In all-family households N=19,740 | 75.5 | 14,900 |
| In married-couple families N=12,020 | 74.9 | 9,000 |
| In female-headed households N=7,480 | 77.0 | 5,760 |
| Mother Employed | | |
| In all-family households N=143,040 | 66.1 | 94,520 |
| In married-couple families N=107,380 | 67.3 | 72,280 |
| In female-headed households N=30,500 | 60.0 | 18,300 |

Source: 1980 Public Use Microdata Sample for New York City.

working many of these children were cared for by relatives and unlicensed providers.

Mothers staying at home was doubtless the predominant mode of rearing small children in New York City in 1980, but this accounted for only slightly more than half of these children, a fraction that is probably declining. The fraction of small children, especially poor children, who have been removed from the supervision of their parents is doubtless increasing. Although some are cared for in school or certified programs, it is clear that most have been given inadequate or no resources in place of their mothers.

The economic boom of the 1980s led to widespread renovation of apartments for sale, rising cost of rents, and the reduction of low-income housing. This has made it even more difficult for poor families to house themselves than was the case a decade earlier.[26] There are currently 200,000 names on the waiting list for apartments in New York City housing projects.[27] More than 300,000 people may be doubled up in apartments, living with friends or relatives. In 1988, 15,600 people, including 10,000 children, lived in 82 hotels for homeless families citywide.[28] The number of homeless families increased from 30 to over 5,000 between 1969 and 1987.[29] Since the homeless population is constantly shifting, as people find and lose housing, the figures consistently underestimate the number of people who have experienced homelessness in any one year.

It is significant that we talk of homeless and not "houseless" or "shelterless" people. Just as a person or family creates a "home" out of a household, the process of homelessness involves "de-domestication," the loss not simply of a house but the destruction of a home. People need a "home" in order to create the emotional and organizational elements of a "family." The 300,000 families "doubling up" in apartments might also be viewed as lacking a home by these criteria. Let us now examine the progressive destruction of family that accompanies the process of becoming homeless.

As mentioned above, the number of female-headed households with children increased 72 percent in New York City between 1969 and 1979. Some of these households were created through divorce and others represent mothers who never married. It has long been argued that unemployment leaves men unable to contribute to household income and thus exaggerates family conflicts through increased alcoholism, child and wife abuse, and depression among all household members.[30] Male unemployment may be the first step in the destruction of family ties. The impact of female unemployment on families has rarely been studied.

In New York City, home relief programs will fund families where an unemployed father is present. However, the federal program, AFDC, primarily funds women and their children.[31] When a woman applies for public assistance, those for whom the woman is financially responsible and who meet the Department of Social Services criteria are placed on the woman's "budget." In other words, her biweekly check is calculated to include some funds for each of these dependent individuals. For a variety of reasons, older male children (who unlike girls cannot claim public assistance for children of their own) and fathers are not generally listed on a woman's budget with public assistance.[32] This step in the disintegration of the family becomes more significant when people lose housing.

Families who cannot find rental housing or who lose their homes through inability to pay rent, landlord harassment, or fires are eventually referred to offices recently created to deal with the new demand known as Emergency Assistance Units (EAUs). Approximately 48 percent of the people referred to such EAUs every night are children.[33]

The EAUs continue the institutional assault on the household begun by unemployment, poverty, and public assistance. To quote one mother waiting with her pre-school daughter for a night's shelter, "He's not on my budget, but he's their father. He's taking care of our baby son right now. I also lost my other child to foster care, and if I didn't know how to fight, she'd still be there."[34] Her case illustrates how the EAUs reinforce both the separation of the father through regulations concerning public assistance budgets and the removal of children through recommendation for foster care.

If public assistance has not accepted the father on a woman's AFDC budget, he is not entitled to share her shelter should they lose their home. As one helpful caseworker said to a client at an EAU: "Is he on your budget? If he's not, you may have to try to sneak him in. If there's a hotel where they accept families, they'll accept couples, but don't tell me, we're not supposed to know."[35] Fifty-two percent of the families arriving at the EAUs had only one parent (mostly mothers with children). The process of finding shelter after first entering the EAU is long and arduous and the likelihood for both parents and children to be separated increases with time.[36]

A high proportion of the people who enter the EAUs have already been separated from their children. It has been reported that 25 percent of the children of families entering the EAU were living away from them. Among these, the highest proportion (45 percent) were living with grandmothers. The next highest proportion (23 percent) had been placed in foster care. Nine percent were living with their fathers and 4 percent were adopted by other families.[37] Thus, about one in eight of children whose parents are seeking shelter have already been removed from the care of their parents by legal mechanisms.

The institutional procedures in the EAUs and the shelters lead to further separation. One mother with a four-year-old son and a three-month-old daughter waiting in the EAU for shelter assignment said: "She was only a day old and I was sitting in this place right here. . . .My worker said why don't you put your kids in foster care so I can put you in a shelter."[38] Parents are frequently informed that if they place their children in foster care, shelter can be found for them.[39] However, such shelters are temporary. Until parents can prove they have found a permanent home for their family, they will not find it easy to extract their children from the foster care system.[40]

Those classified as single men and women and housed in adult shelters still see themselves as responsible for their disintegrated households. As one father whose three children had been placed in foster care until he could find a place to live said, "We're still a family even though our children are not with us."[41] City officials estimate that over 1,200 women in city shelters for single women could be reunited with their families if housing were available.[42]

The pressures toward separation of parents and children do not end once families have been placed in hotels for the homeless. If they are "fortunate," families waiting in EAUs will be referred to one of the hotels for homeless families. One or two rooms with nonfunctional bathrooms, no kitchen, and often hazardous stairways and elevators are common. However, families not assigned such rooms (at a cost of approximately $3,000 per month to the city, state, and federal governments) may end up in the streets. At that point, they are almost certain to lose their children to foster care. Families in hotels for the homeless are also liable to find themselves designated as unfit parents by New York State and their children placed in foster care or temporary group homes. In 1988 there were 20,553 children in foster care in New York State and 3,472 children being cared for by relatives paid foster care stipends; these numbers have subsequently increased. A 1987 survey by the Council of Family and Child Caring Agencies, a group representing foster care agencies, found that approximately one-half of children in foster care in New York City "could be returned home immediately if their parents found permanent housing."[43]

Children are referred to the foster care system through the Child Welfare Administration, an agency of the Human Resources Administration responsible for identifying children at risk. Placements may be made in response to referrals of child abuse and neglect by hospitals, schools, and other agencies. In addition, evidence of use of illegal narcotics by the mother (in hospital urine samples, for example) can also precipitate the removal of children. A recent study found evidence of illegal drug use among 11 percent of pregnant mothers in hospitals around the country; numerous New York City children could possibly be removed from their families.[44] Since the rates of drug use among pregnant women are much higher than the rates of foster care, certain selection factors not clearly delineated are implicated. Most significant among these are probably the mother's poverty, homelessness, and lack of prenatal care.

Thus, if the lives of the poor in New York City are examined since 1965, several factors have converged to increase the separation of social reproduction from familial ties. Most mothers must work to support their children. Among the marginally poor but not yet homeless, new public assistance regulations require women with young children to work in order to qualify for public assistance. While the image of the "welfare mother" may be changing as she is required to go out to work, adequate publicly subsidized daycare facilities do not yet exist. Such a mother must, however, place her children in daycare situations, whether licensed or unlicensed. Among the homeless, a combination of unemployment, poverty, and public assistance regulations frequently leads to the removal of children from their parents and their placement in foster care.

## The Interdependence Between Professional Households and Poor Women

Major economic shifts have also affected the domestic division of labor and the experience of family life in the corporate and professional strata. For the educated elite, new jobs have been created in information processing, management, the financial sector, and the legal and medical fields. Although variations within this group must be recognized, certain common characteristics affect modes of social reproduction.

First, as a consequence of the women's movement and federal requirements for affirmative action, women have been hired in highly paid professional and corporate employment from which they were previously excluded. In the 1970s the Equal Employment Opportunities Commission (EEOC) was strengthened and became particularly active in investigating discriminatory hiring with respect to women. As a result, large corporations, professional schools, and universities were pressured to employ women in higher paying, higher status jobs from which they had previously been excluded.[45] As financial services expanded rapidly in New York City over the last 10 years, so too did the number of women managers and professionals employed in that sector. This was in marked contrast to the 1950s and 1960s, when women were entering the labor market in large numbers but were confined to the lower-paying rungs of the service sector. Although women are still highly underrepresented in the upper echelons of the corporate world, many more women are earning higher salaries in this arena than before the impact of federal legislation and the woman's movement.[46]

Second, since the mid 1970s and more obviously in the 1980s, families have required two incomes in order to maintain their standard of living. In 1987, a middle class family required two incomes to maintain the living conditions a husband's income alone would have covered in 1967. The rising cost of living, particularly manifest in New York City real estate and rental costs, has been paid for through extra work performed by women at a paid job outside the home, while they nevertheless remain primarily responsible for household services. Some men have increased the amount of work they do in the household, but this has seldom replaced the work carried out by women in many tasks associated with creating a home. In addition, the proportion of female-headed households has increased for high-income families as well as among poor households, and many professional women are rearing children alone.

Thus, educated women in New York City are increasingly employed in high-paying professional jobs, which require extensive time commitments. At the same time, many of these women are also primarily responsible for the maintenance of home and family. The impact of these dual and contradictory commitments is being reflected in current discussion of the "mommy track" and the career compromises highly paid professional women are making in order to provide for children.

The popular advice literature oriented towards middle class women with children is beginning to reflect changes in women and men's roles. To quote the revised edition of T. Berry Brazelton's *Infants and Mothers*, one of the most widely read publications, "When this book first appeared I hoped it would demonstrate the vital importance of nurturing a baby in the first year. . . . Inadvertently, I may have added to mothers' feelings of guilt when they were not able to stay at home throughout the first year."[47] The literature of the 1980s reflects women's guilt and sense of incompetence about their lack of full-time child rearing and the same problems with relation to career. There is lip service paid to the need for "quality" childcare at the same time pediatricians and psychologists are emphasizing bonding and the importance of the parents' involvement with the child.

Middle class women rearing children are thus caught between the need to be available to children and the demands of a professional career.[48] In New York City, this contradiction is partially mediated by the poor and immigrant women who serve as householders, baby sitters, and combining these tasks, as full-time housekeepers. Frequently, housekeepers cook, do the laundry, and clean the house/apartment, as well as care for babies and meet older children at the school bus. Sometimes, they also do the shopping and chores. Some live-in housekeepers may even be responsible for picking up crying babies at night, in addition to full daycare, cooking, and tidying up.[49]

Domestic work in New York City today pays higher than the minimum wage paid for home health aides and higher than the $5 or $6 an hour earned by temporary sales help. In Manhattan in 1988, daytime baby sitters may earn $6 to $10 an hour in middle class households, and weekly house cleaners may earn more for less time. Immigrant women may seek domestic work to obtain migration papers. For most poor women, domestic employment is a reasonably flexible alternative to other low-paying service work. For immigrant women with problems of language, education, and possibly a lack of working papers, domestic service may be one of the few forms of employment available, other than garment work in a sweatshop.

In spite of all the paid assistance, mothers still act in a capacity similar to air-traffic controllers—they arrange baby sitting, play dates, transportation, and coordinate family interactions such as meals, excursions, and visits to relatives and friends. The mother's role may not in fact involve many hours actually spent with family members. It is the poor woman in the middle class household who is hired to spend time with the children.

Not only is the domestic worker expected to do household chores, but she is expected to stand in for the constant care provider and thus to provide, in many instances, unconditional time as a corollary of the "unconditional" love expected of parents. Her time is the child's and if the parents are home late or miss an appointment, she must fill in. Thus, the hours of the domestic worker are many times subordinated to the needs of the household she serves. Her own household and children must adapt to these demands.[50] This is a negotiated settlement which is continually being worked out between two women, each with conflicting household and work responsibilities.[51] However, since the middle class woman has the higher income and is in the controlling position (in her household if not at her own job), in most instances, circumstances probably bend in favor of her household and professional needs.

This is not the only adaptation to middle class needs for social reproduction. Privately run daycare centers have also increased. However, New York State and City regulations concerning bathroom facilities, size, number of care providers, and fire hazards have made these difficult to operate legally in New York City. Nursery schools are available, at a high price (between $600 and $1000 per month from around 8:30 to 5:30, five days a week). As with publicly funded daycare, the demand for private daycare far exceeds supply, in spite of exorbitant costs. There are spaces for only one-third of the children under six who need care in full-day licensed programs, public or private. For infants under 2, the situation is even worse. Licensed childcare programs, public or private, have space for only 7 percent of this population who need full daycare.[52] For many full-time working parents even daycare hours are not sufficient, and a combination of domestic worker and nursery school care is worked out.

In sum, the rearing of young children among the managerial and professional classes in New York City is largely a private enterprise. High-income working women hire low-income women to replace them in the household or to look after their children in nursery school. Federal regulations allow visas for domestic workers, and New York State attempts to certify daycare centers. By law, domestic workers are supposed to be registered for social security and pay taxes on their income. In practice many do not. Although an estimate of numbers in this case is difficult, many domestic workers do not want to jeopardize possible access to public assistance or pay taxes, and most domestic employers do not want to be liable for payment of social security and other expenses. In such cases, no official record is made of the relationship, by mutual agreement. On the other hand, immigrants who come specifically to work in a household must pay social security or they lose their status with the immigration authorities. In these cases, official records exist of the arrangements.

Although a middle class child may see his or her parents little more frequently than the immigrant or poor children, he or she is provided with a parental substitute. In fact, the first language of many middle class U.S. children looked after by baby sitters may be Spanish. Thus, the definition of "mother" among upper income families comes to rely more on biological and economic factors as other aspects of the relationship between parents and children are eroded.

## Conclusion

As most women, including most mothers of small children, are beginning to work outside their own homes, the jobs they find in New York City are becoming more differentiated. The data and examples presented here suggest a growing polarization among women workers, as some join the professional and corporate elite and, at the other extreme, poor women find themselves working for below poverty-level wages. Childbearing and rearing patterns reflect this polarization, starting with the age and education of the mother and followed by access to different childcare facilities and schooling opportunities.

Among both groups of women examined here, mothers are increasingly separated from their children and dependent on others to rear them, almost from birth. This may indicate changes that more households in New York City will face over the next decade.

The increasing separation of mothers from their children has created interdependencies among women in caring for children. Poor women may leave children with older siblings, other relatives, neighbors, or alone while a fortunate few will find publicly subsidized daycare, frequently overcrowded and staffed largely by poorly paid, untrained women workers. Others may lose their homes altogether and then lose their children to be looked after by other women in foster care programs.

Among the professional, educated households of New York City there has also been a progressive separation of children from maternal supervision. In contrast to the poorer groups, children may stay in their own households. Fathers, if present, may increase their input. However, in general, highly educated, well-paid mothers hire poor women to replace themselves in the household. Alternatively, or, in addition, children are sent to nursery schools with small classes, staffed increasingly by women trained in early childhood education.

Thus, shifts in New York City's employment and housing structure have led to major changes over the last two decades in how homes and families are created. These examples suggest an emerging trend toward the separation of young children from their parents.

By viewing women as the source of social reproduction, whether paid or unpaid, we can begin to disentangle the changing relations between work, family, and household and the construction of gender roles in New York City of the 1990s. The need for women workers and the need of women to earn money have created a crisis in how society provides for its children. Professional women have partially solved the problem by hiring other women to be daycare workers, housekeepers, and substitute parents. This privately financed solution relies upon the low-paid female workers. Poor women simply have no truly acceptable response. In the absence of adequate public programs to care for children, the current situation in New York City not only perpetuates gender stereotypes about the responsibilities of both poor and professional women, it reinforces the polarization among both groups of women and the life chances of their children.

# Notes

1. Edholm, F., O. Harris, and K. Young, "Conceptualising Women," *Critique of Anthropology*, vol. 3, issues 9, 10 (1977); Sacks, K., "Toward a Unified Theory of Class, Race and Gender," *American Ethnologist* 16, 3 (1989): 534–551; Rapp, R., "Urban Kinship in Contemporary America: Families, Classes and Ideology," in Mullings, L., ed., *Cities of the United States* (New York: Columbia University Press, 1987); Sacks, K., *My Troubles Are Going to Have Trouble with Me* (New Brunswick: Rutgers University Press, 1984), Introduction; Lamphere, L., *From Working Daughters to Working Mothers: Immigrant Women in a New England Industrial Community* (Ithaca: Cornell University Press, 1987), Introduction; Susser, I., "Gender in the Anthropology of the U.S.," in Morgen, Sandra, ed., *Gender in the Anthropology Curriculum* (Washington, DC: American Anthropological Association, 1989).

2. As calculated by the CUNY Data Services from the 5 percent 1980 Public Use Microdata Sample for New York City.

3. Colen, S., "Just a Little Respect: West Indian Domestic Workers in New York City," in Chaney, Elsa M., and Mary Garcia Castro, *Muchachas No More: Household Workers in Latin America and the Caribbean* (Philadelphia: Temple University Press, 1989); Pessar, P., "The Linkage Between the Household and Workplace of Dominican Women in the U.S.," in Sutton, C., and E. Chaney, eds., *Caribbean Life in New York City* (New York: Center for Migration Studies, 1987), pp. 255–278.

4. For an overview, see Waldinger, R., "Immigration and Urban Change," *Annual Review of Sociology* 15 (1989): 211–232.

5. Pear, R., "U.S. Poverty Rate Dropped to 14.4% in '84, Bureau says," *New York Times* (August 28, 1985).

6. U.S. Department of Commerce, Bureau of the Census, *Money, Income and Poverty Status of Families and Persons in the U.S.: 1984*, Current Population Reports, Series P 60, No. 149 (Washington, DC: U.S. Government Printing Office, 1985), pp. 26–29. See also Sidel, R., *Women and Children Last* (New York: Viking, 1986).

7. Rosenberg, Terry J., *Poverty in New York: The Crisis Continues* (New York: Community Service Society, 1989), Appendix Table 2. See also Tobier, E., *The Changing Face of Poverty: Trends in New York City's Population in Poverty 1960–1990* (New York: Community Service Society, 1984).

8. Rosenberg, *Poverty*, Chapter 6; Tobier, *The Changing Face of Poverty*, p. 8.

9. City of New York, Human Resources Administration, Office of Policy and Program Development, *Dependency: Economic and Social Data for New York City, June, 1988*, vol. 5 (1989), Table 13; Rosenberg, *Poverty*, Chapter 5; Tobier, *Changing Face of Poverty*, p. 9; Susser, I., and J. Kreniske, "The Welfare Trap: A Public Policy for Deprivation," in Mullings, ed., *Cities of the United States*, pp. 51–71.

10. *New York Times* (August 3, 1988), p. 1.

11. Tobier, *Changing Face of Poverty*. See also Chapters 2 and 3 in this book.

12. Piven, F., and R. Cloward, *Regulating the Poor* (New York: Vintage, 1971); Susser and Kreniske, "Welfare Trap"; Tobier, "Changing Face of Poverty."

13. Marcuse, P., "Gentrification, Abandonment and Displacement: Connections, Causes and Policy Responses in New York City," *Journal of Urban and Contemporary Law* 28 (1985): 193–240; Center on Budget and Policies Priorities, *Smaller Slices of the Pie: The Growing Economic Vulnerability of Poor and Moderate Income Americans* (Washington, DC: Center on Budget Policies Priorities, November 1985); Abramowitz, M., *Regulating the Lives of Women: Social Welfare Policy from Colonial Times to the Present* (Boston: South End Press, 1988).

14. Susser, I., *Norman Street: Poverty and Politics in an Urban Neighborhood* (New York: Oxford, 1982).

15. Baxter, E., and K. Hopper, *Public Places, Private Spaces* (New York: Community Service Society, 1981); Susser and Kreniske, "Welfare Trap"; Hopper, K., E. Susser, and S. Conover, "Economics of Makeshift: Deindustrialization and Homelessness in New York City" *Urban Anthropology* 14, 1–3 (1986): 183–236.

16. In addition to Chapter 9 in this book, see Sharff, J., "The Underground Economy of a Poor Neighborhood," in Mullings, ed., *Cities of the United States*, pp. 19–51, and Valentine, B., *Hustling and Other Hard Work* (New York: Free Press, 1978).

17. Sharff, J., "Free Enterprise and the Ghetto Family," *Psychology Today* (March 1981).

18. Sharff J., "Families with Dead Sons," *Amsterdams Sociologish Tijdschrift* (December 1979).

19. For discussion of opposing views on the issues concerning female-headed households, class, and race, see Wilson, W. J., *The Truly Disadvantaged* (Chicago: University of Chicago Press, 1986) and Mullings, L., "Gender in Applied Anthropology of the U.S.," in Morgen, ed., *Gender in the Anthropology Curriculum*.

20. Foundation for Child Development, *Public Expenditures for Children, 1980–1983: The Impact of Federal Changes* (New York: Foundation for Child Development, 1985), "Key Findings," p. 1.

21. Tolchin, M., "Congress Leaders and White House Agree on Welfare," *New York Times* (September 27, 1988), p. A1.

22. Childcare Inc., *Basic Facts About Child Care in New York City* (New York, July 1987), p. 17.

23. New York State Council on Children and Families, *State of the Child in New York State* (Albany, NY, 1988), p. 83.

24. New York State Council on Children and Families, *State of the Child*, p. 83.

25. Ibid., p. 85.

26. For an analysis of the dimensions of this problem, see Chapter 11 in this book as well as Stegman, Michael, *Housing and Vacancy Report, New York City 1987* (New York: Department of Housing Preservation and Development, April 1988). See also Daley, D., and R. Meislin, "New York City, The Landlord: A Decade of Housing Decay," *New York Times* (February 8, 1988), p. 1; Berger, J., "Failure of Plan for Homeless Reflects City Housing Crisis," *New York Times* (Feb. 19, 1985), p. A1.

27. Barbanel, J., "Hotel Shelters to End By '90 Koch Says: Families Move to Top of Housing Projects List," *New York Times* (August 2, 1988), p. B1.

28. Murphy, K. M., Deputy Commissioner, Human Resources Administration, Adult Services Agency, Crisis Intervention Services, Memorandum, January 18, 1989. At the end of 1988, the Koch administration agreed to build better temporary and permanent facilities for all families housed in the "welfare

hotels." But by the early Dinkins administration, these goals had not yet been fully achieved.

29. New York State Department of Social Services, *Annual Report to the Government and the Legislature. Homeless Housing and Assistance Program* (Albany, NY, 1988).

30. Susser, M., W. Watson, and K. Hopper, *Sociology in Medicine* (New York: Oxford University Press, 1985).

31. Susser, *Norman Street*; Stack, C., *All Our Kin* (New York: Harper & Row, 1974); Abramowitz, *Regulating the Lives of Women.*

32. Susser, *Norman Street.*

33. Dehavenon, A., *Toward a Policy for the Amelioration and Prevention of Family Homelessness and Dissolution: New York City's After-hours Emergency Assistance Units in 1986–1987* (The East Harlem Interfaith Welfare Committee, May 1987).

34. Dehavenon, p. 28.

35. Ibid., p. 26.

36. Ibid., p. 25; Kozol, J., *Rachel and Her Children* (New York: Crown, 1988).

37. Dehavenon, p. 33.

38. Ibid., p. 29.

39. Kozol, *Rachel and Her Children.*

40. Barbanel, J., "Rent Aid is Enacted for Families with Children in Foster Care," *New York Times* (August 18, 1988), p. B1.

41. Dehavenon, p. 33.

42. Barbanel, "Rent Aid."

43. Ibid.

44. *New York Times* (August 30, 1988), p. 1.

45. Gelb, J., *Feminism and Politics* (Berkeley: University of California Press, 1989); U.S. Department of Labor, *Workforce 2000: Work and Workers for the 21st Century,* Study by the Hudson Institute for the U.S. Department of Labor (Washington, DC, 1987); Herzlinger, R., "Dancing on the Glass Ceiling," *Wall Street Journal* (February 17, 1988), p. 28.

46. Herzlinger, "Dancing on Glass."

47. Brazelton, B., *Infants and Mothers,* revised edition (New York: Dell, 1983), p. xxviii. See also Brooks, A., "1 Woman, 2 Roles and Stress," *New York Times* (March 23, 1987), p. C12.

48. Gerson, K., *Hard Choices: How Women Choose Between Work, Career, and Motherhood* (Berkeley: University of California Press, 1985); Hewlett, S., *A Lesser Life* (New York: William Morrow and Co., 1986); Kammerman, S., and Hayes, C., eds., *Families That Work: Children in a Changing World* (Washington, DC: National Academy Press, 1982).

49. Colen, "Just a Little Respect"; Pessar, P., "The Dominicans: Women in the Household and the Garment Industry," in Foner, N., ed., *New Immigrants in New York* (New York: Columbia University Press, 1987), pp. 103–130.

50. Colen, "Just a Little Respect."

51. Rollins, J., *Between Women* (Philadelphia: Temple University Press, 1984).

52. Childcare, Inc., *Basic Facts About Child Care*, p. 16.

# 9

# Crime and the Social Fabric

## Mercer Sullivan

## Introduction

A few years ago, a Paris newspaper published a map of Manhattan showing areas where it was not safe to walk. The resulting indignation in New York City produced a spate of denials and protests, including a map of the dangerous areas of Paris. Injured municipal pride aside, the incident dramatized New York City's longstanding and international reputation for street crime.

In the late 1980s, New York City was the locus of highly publicized crimes in many sectors. Political crimes resulted in the jailing of one borough president and the suicide of another. Massive conspiracy trials resulted in the convictions of some of the nation's best known and most powerful traditional organized crime figures. And insider trading scandals on Wall Street focused public attention on white collar crime. Yet, despite New York City's prominence in so many fields of criminal endeavor, it is street crime that most profoundly affects the daily lives of most residents—their interactions, their perceptions of one another, their patterns of residence, and their politics.

Street crime is at once the cause, the result, and the symbol of the dual city. New York City's status as the capital of capital and the exemplar of dualism is reflected in its extraordinary reputation for street crime. The concentration of wealth and poverty in the same geographical area constitutes the precondition for street crime in the city. The causal direction of the relationship between crime and other aspects of dualism, however, is controversial. Does inequality cause crime, or does crime increase the stark contrasts of wealth and poverty by driving away middle class residents and economic activity which might provide jobs, while further stigmatizing and disempowering poor neighborhoods?

Both processes are evident. This chapter attempts to raise and provide some answers to a more detailed set of questions about the social processes which give rise to both crime and responses to crime in New York City, particularly the ways in which these processes contribute to the dualization of neighborhoods, consciousness, and politics. Much of the discussion is based on ethnographic data collected in field studies of Brooklyn neighborhoods and their residents, particularly young males involved in crime.

This case material compares the genesis and control of criminality as they occur in residential neighborhoods and contrasts the social processes that occur in two poor, minority neighborhoods with those that occur in a working class, white neighborhood. This approach helps to explain two of the salient facts about street crime in New York City: that the city leads the nation in street muggings and that so many of these muggings are committed by young minority males.

Reported crime in New York City rose steadily between 1960 and the early 1980s, from 108,491 felonies in 1960 to an all-time high of 637,451 in 1981.[1] Beginning in 1982, crime rates began to decline consistently for the first time in more than 20 years. This decline may or may not have had something to do with changes in the operation of the criminal justice system, particularly its harsher sentencing policies, but it very probably was related to demographic change. A declining proportion of the population consists of males in the crime-prone ages of the late teens and early twenties. In 1986, however, crime began to increase once again. This rise has been widely attributed not to demographic trends in age distribution but to the crack epidemic.[2]

As other chapters in this book show, the historical period in which crime has risen so dramatically in the city is the same period in which there have been pronounced changes in population and in economic activity. Blacks and Latinos have replaced non-Hispanic whites at the same time that the employment base has been radically transformed, leaving large proportions of minority immigrants to the city in poverty, either welfare-dependent or marginally employed in unstable, low-wage jobs.

The minority population of the city is also much younger than the nonminority population, and it is young, minority males who most often commit and are arrested for street crimes. In 1979, for example, in Brooklyn, where the case material to be discussed was collected, blacks and Latinos accounted for 84 percent of all male arrestees but only 48 percent of the borough's overall population. Although the median age of the borough's population was 31, 60 percent of these arrestees were under the age of 25 and 35 percent were 19 or younger.[3] (Approximately 85 percent of all arrestees nationwide are male.)[4]

While New York City is similar to other large U.S. cities in the rise of crime rates since the 1960s and the disproportionate representation of young, minority males in arrest figures, it is quite distinctive in the quality of its criminal activity, particularly the prominence of robbery. Among the 10 largest cities in the country in 1981, New York City ranked only third in overall crime and as low as seventh for murder. The likelihood of being murdered or burglarized was higher in economically depressed Detroit or in the Sunbelt cities of Texas which have experienced rapid and unchanneled growth. New York City, however, ranked first for robbery,[5] primarily street robbery. The city's reputation for crime stems from its preeminence as the mugging capital of the country.

New York is a city with an uncommonly rich street life, including street crime as well as other, more benign sorts of interactions. New Yorkers use automobiles less and walk the streets and ride the subways more than people in other U.S. cities. It is the image and the reality of young, male, drug-using, black and Latino muggers on the streets and subways which haunt French tourists as well as New Yorkers of all ages and racial and ethnic backgrounds.

The following sections of this chapter discuss ethnographic data on different types of crime, including muggings and other forms of theft; arson; and drug use and sales. Throughout these discussions, the emphasis is on the relationships between crime and processes of social polarization. Ethnographic data are particularly useful for such discussions since they place crime and the responses to crime in a holistic context. By grounding questions about crime in space and in community context, ethnographic data make it possible to avoid some of the difficulties in the criminological literature which have resulted from the neglect of social ecology. This has frequently led to attempts to repudiate poverty, discrimination, and other social factors in the etiology of crime in favor of biological, psychological, and even cultural explanations, as if these dimensions of behavior could be separated.[6]

The ethnographic data discussed below were collected in three neighborhoods of Brooklyn between 1979 and 1987, and most of the data focused on crime were collected in the early 1980s.[7] The three neighborhoods were all relatively low-income and predominantly black, Latino, and white, respectively. Because of promises of confidentiality made during the fieldwork, it is necessary to use pseudonyms in referring to the neighborhoods. The predominantly black neighborhood is referred to as Projectville, the predominantly Latino neighborhood as La Barriada, and the predominantly white neighborhood as Hamilton Park. The white neighborhood, though low-income in relation to the city as a whole, was nonetheless much better off than the two minority neighborhoods in family income and employment levels, welfare dependency levels, and levels of two-parent families.[8] It is the difference in the crime career patterns between these white working-class youths and their minority peers which is of paramount interest for understanding the roles of crime and the responses to crime in processes of dualization.

It must be stressed that these youths do not necessarily represent all black, Latino, and white youth in the city; they were sought out *because* they were criminally involved. Nonetheless, the social processes involved in both the genesis and the control of criminality among these particular youths are processes which must be confronted when interpreting the disproportionate numbers of young, minority males who commit and are arrested for crimes in the city and who have provoked such a drastic alteration of the fabric of daily life in the city since the 1960s. The crime patterns described below also vary among these neighborhoods in official arrest statistics in the same ways in which they vary in the ethnographic data.[9]

# The Ethnography of Crime

## Theft

In all three neighborhoods, many families were unable to provide much more than basic food and shelter for their children. In addition, adolescents, particularly boys, were largely unsupervised by adults for much of the day, unless they were in school (and they frequently were not). This combination of low income levels and large amounts of unsupervised time for adolescents led to essentially similar patterns of early delinquency in all three neighborhoods.

Most of the youths we studied in each place had been involved in street fighting and petty theft by their early teens. Organized youth gangs existed only in La Barriada, but the practice of local boys defending their turf against outsiders was similar in all three places.

Similarly, episodic experiences of nonviolent stealing were common in the early adolescent careers of most of those we studied. La Barriada and Hamilton Park are near large concentrations of factories and warehouses, and most of those we studied in these two neighborhoods had broken into these facilities and stolen merchandise or office equipment. Projectville consists mostly of public housing and is far from major commercial and industrial centers. Early experiences with theft among those youths were with shoplifting or picking pockets.

In contrast to these essentially similar early delinquent experiences of fighting and stealing, youthful careers diverged sharply among the different local cliques by their mid-teens, as the youths from the minority neighborhoods became much more heavily involved in crime as a regular source of income and they turned to more violent types of crime. This divergence in crime patterns among the neighborhood groups resulted from differences in economic opportunity and also from different local patterns of social control, which were themselves the results of differences in economic opportunity at the neighborhood level.

One reason that the Hamilton Park youths did not become as heavily involved in stealing as did their minority peers was that they had better economic opportunities. Their families were less poor and more likely to contain an employed adult male. As they entered their middle teens, they began to find employment in local businesses through family and neighborhood-based personal networks. They did suffer periods of joblessness and they did not altogether abandon stealing as a source of income, but they had access to far more jobs than did their minority peers. These jobs were usually off-the-books and lasted only a few days to a few months, but they usually paid better than minimum wage. As these youths reached their late teens and early twenties, some of them began to find their way into the well-paying, unionized, blue collar jobs which had traditionally sustained this neighborhood. These jobs are disappearing from the regional economy, however, and some of these youths began leaving the area for the suburbs or other parts of the country. Despite their own difficulties in the labor market, they held a relative advantage over their minority peers, an advantage based on personal networks, not on superior human capital. Indeed, they stayed in school even less than did those in Projectville.

In contrast, although most of the youths from the two minority neighborhoods actively sought work beginning in their middle teens, they were more often jobless, usually earning minimum wage when they did manage to find work. During their middle teens, the youths from La Barriada found occasional days of off-the-books, temporary work in the factories or for small local landlords. They also got some work through local youth programs. The Projectville youths reported virtually no employment during their mid-teens other than in government-sponsored summer youth programs. As they got older, those from La Barriada began to find more work in the factories and also, for those who had done better in school and were more proficient in English, in clerical and service-sector jobs outside the neighborhood. The Projectville youths stayed involved in schooling and training programs longer than their peers did in either of the other two neighborhoods, which also kept them out of the labor market longer. In their late teens, they began to enter low-wage clerical and service sector jobs.

Poorer and more jobless than their peers in Hamilton Park, more of the minority youths progressed from exploratory involvement in petty theft to more systematic involvement in crime, including much greater amounts of violent street crime. Some from La Barriada participated regularly in factory burglaries, auto theft, and knife-point robberies near subway stations and in more distant neighborhoods. Some from Projectville became involved in snatching gold chains on the subways and in various levels of the street drug trade, which also carried much potential for violent confrontations.

Although the effects of local structures of economic opportunity on different rates of involvement in street crime were substantial, the divergence in youthful careers between the white working-class youths and their minority peers was a result not just of the prompting of economic need but also of local patterns of social control. These differing patterns of social control were themselves related to economic disparities among the neighborhoods, but they also were highly neighborhood-specific. These patterns of internal social control were quite complex and illustrate the ways in which processes of dualization have transformed the social fabric not just of poor, inner-city neighborhoods but of the entire city.

Young criminal entrepreneurs usually begin their criminal activities on their own turf. Their neighbors are their first victims. No neighborhood readily submits to victimization, but resources and strategies for responding vary. The criminal justice system was not always or even primarily the major social resource for dealing with violent, predatory youths in these neighborhoods. In each neighborhood, there were direct responses to youthful predators, particularly when they committed violent crimes. Some youths in each place had to flee adult men who had come to retaliate against them. The youths had then fled to the homes of relatives or friends either in other neighborhoods of the city or to Puerto Rico, the southern United States, or, in one case in Hamilton Park, to Europe. A major difference among the neighborhoods was in the presence of employed, adult men attached to households who could perform this informal social control function. Young men were much more able to commit crimes with impunity in the two minority neighborhoods in which adult men attached to households were fewer and the median age of the population much younger.[10] Hamilton Park's residents were much more able to mobilize both formal and informal controls. Besides the informal control activities of adult males, Hamilton Park's residents also used their local precinct much more readily. Their use of the police, like their access to the labor market, was related to personal networks, since many of them had relatives in the police department.

Differences also existed between the two minority neighborhoods in their use of the criminal justice system. La Barriada's residents were the most alienated from the police and courts. Some Projectville residents did participate in citizen patrols, generally with little effect, and they also were subject to social control efforts coordinated between public housing authorities and the housing police. The sheer concentration of poor, young males in the anomic environment of the projects often defeated these efforts, however.

Though unable adequately to control localized predation by local youths or to provide job networks which might offer other sources of income, the social control processes in the two minority neighborhoods did succeed to some extent, primarily by forcing systematic offenders to direct their activities outside the neighborhood. Especially as they became more involved in muggings, these young men realized that they were better off working the subways and the streets of business districts and middle class neighborhoods. By going outside their own neighborhoods, they increased their chances for more lucrative profits and decreased their chances of being recognized by someone who knew them and might retaliate by formal or informal means.

Going outside their local neighborhoods also brought into play another set of forces in their local neighborhoods which reinforced their participation in crime. Certain crime patterns actually redistribute resources into a neighborhood from outside. These are not the crimes of the youngest and most inexperienced who prey on their immediate neighbors but rather the crimes of the older and more experienced who victimize at some distance and then spend the proceeds closer to home, in some cases explicitly to buy protection. The clearest example we witnessed involved a group of auto thieves in La Barriada who paid little children to watch for the police while they stripped cars in the middle of the street or in empty lots. Other examples include the many cases in which youths reported to us the selling of stolen goods to local adults.

The implications of the redistributive aspects of crime for local social control patterns were also apparent in the relationships between youths who stole and their parents. Even though their parents disapproved of crime and warned them of the consequences, they appeared to turn their heads at evidence of criminal activity, such as new clothing worn by their unemployed sons. Despite generalized disapproval of crime by many citizens in these neighborhoods, their actual responses to crime depended not only on their resources and strategies for protecting themselves but also on their perceptions of whether particular crimes or crime patterns were endangering them or, conversely, bringing cash and cheap merchandise into their households and neighborhoods.

The combined effects of the spurs of poverty, the lack of jobs, the lack of neighborhood resources for social control, and the undercutting of neighborhood social control by the redistributive aspects of youth crime all led to the intensification of criminal activity for many of the youths we studied in the minority neighborhoods, leading to a peak of involvement in the late teens. The costs of systematic involvement in street crime eventually began to mount, at about the same period as their access to the labor market, though still impaired, began nonetheless to improve over the situation they faced in their mid-teens. For many, criminal involvement then began to wane. As the dangers of sustained involvement in street crime became apparent, many of these youths began to age out of crime and to accept low-wage jobs. Those who persisted faced early death or extended periods of incarceration. Even many of those who eventually decreased their criminal activity suffered in their personal careers from the stigmatization of criminal records. This peaking of crime involvement in the late teens is apparent in many data sets and accounts for the disproportionate fear of young males felt by many New Yorkers and other urban residents. The causes of this age pattern of criminality have been the subject of recent lively debate. Hirschi and Gottfredson have proposed that the pattern is so prevalent in different social milieus that social factors must not be responsible, thus implying biological causality. Greenberg and the analyses offered here point instead to the social rather than the biological aspects of aging which appear to account for these patterns.[11]

In this way, street crime began in the poverty and social and economic isolation of these neighborhoods and then was exported to the rest of the city. This process led in turn to the further isolation of these neighborhoods. Even during the fieldwork period, the progressive emiseration of these areas was visible. Besides suffering the destructive effects of crime on their own careers, these young men also brought about a deterioration in the quality of life at the neighborhood level: many people do not venture out at night; small businesses have left. Fires, many of them the result of arson, destroyed many businesses in Projectville during our observations as well as much of the viable housing on the block where we conducted our observations in La Barriada. The crack epidemic beginning in the mid 1980s has led to an increase in the control by violent, young men over daily life in these areas.

Both arson and the drug trade, however, involve adults more than the patterns of youthful stealing just described. Most youthful theft grows spontaneously out of the activities of adolescent peer groups. Arson and drug trafficking frequently involve adults who are consciously preying on ghetto neighborhoods as sources of profit. These processes represent another aspect of the polarization processes associated with crime and are discussed further below.

## Arson

Arson is motivated by various factors, including individual psychopathology, political protest, personal revenge, and profit. It is extremely difficult to document its extent and causes. The origin of most fires remains undetermined and, even when arson is established, the identity and motives of the arsonist usually remain unknown. During the 1970s, however, large areas of New York City burned, especially poor neighborhoods in which disinvestment in housing took many forms. The historical pattern of fires in the city shows quite dramatic rises from about 60,000 reported fires in 1960 to rates of over 120,000 per year throughout most of the 1970s, peaking in 1980. In 1981, fires began to decrease again and declined to a level of about 90,000 in 1987.[12] This decrease began at the same time that real estate values began to skyrocket. Unfortunately, consistent statistics on arson over this time period are not available, but it is probable that arson was responsible for much of the burning in the South Bronx, the Lower East Side, and Bushwick. Arson represented the most extreme and criminal form of disinvestment in these areas.

Despite the lack of good statistics on arson during the 1970s, journalists and community activists identified several patterns of arson. One analysis pointed to three distinctive patterns: arson at branches of particular businesses, on certain blocks, and in buildings owned by particular landlords.[13] Our case material concerns a block pattern, combined with implications of landlord patterns.

During our observations in La Barriada, we saw much of the block we studied burn down. In the fall of 1979, there were fourteen occupied residential buildings on the block. One year later, only eight of these buildings remained occupied. The other six had burned and had either been demolished or remained standing and officially unoccupied. Examination of our field notes and of fire and real estate records reveals some of the complexity of the arson in poor neighborhoods that literally redrew much of the map of New York City during the 1970s.

The youths we studied generally reported that they conceived and executed their burglaries and robberies themselves. When asked about other illegal ways of making money, however, some of them mentioned knowing of landlords who paid people to burn down their buildings:

> A guy'll give you $500 to burn down a building you know. You got landlords around here, they don't want their buildings any more and they got a lot of insurance on the house. So they tell you, "do me a favor" . . .they give you a week to do it. It's easy to do it too, real easy. All those houses are old, they burn quick. I got burned out before. Now it's happening around here.

Though none of those we interviewed reported undertaking arson themselves, the people on this block were quite aware that the fires they were experiencing were not merely accidental. In one 3-week period, a row of three buildings burned, one after the other. Between the time that the second and third of these buildings were emptied by fires, we recorded the following behavior of the residents of the next building in line:

> Today I saw the people in the building next to the ones that burned packing up their things. I asked them, why they were moving. They said, "We're next."

After this building burned, some people reported to us that they had actually seen the landlord running away from the building with a can, although, as usual, they refrained from going to the police.

Although most residents were firmly convinced that the landlords were involved, they did not attribute all the arson to the landlords. At this same time, a group of heroin addicts had begun to move into the block. The addicts were older than the youths we studied and did not live in family households. They bought heroin from a supplier who had established residence on the block, and they lived together in abandoned buildings. They made money by systematic theft that was even more intensive than that of the local youths and also by stripping the plumbing fixtures out of buildings that had burned. Some fires were attributed to them. In some cases, the suspicion was that they had been paid by landlords; in others, the addicts appeared to be acting on their own. In another case, two fires in one building were attributed by residents of the building to troubled children who may have been acting out their inner conflicts regarding what they were seeing all around them.

In an effort to find out more about this pattern of fires, we subsequently located real estate and fire records. These records and our field notes show quite distinctive patterns accounting for which buildings burned and were vacated and which survived during this period. Of the eight buildings that remained occupied, four had no fires during this period. Four others experienced fires but survived. Five of these buildings were owned by local landlords whose identity was well known in the neighborhood and who had a demonstrated stake in maintaining their buildings.

One landlord, who owned two of the buildings that survived, was an elderly man who did not live in the neighborhood but who came to maintain his buildings almost every day. We frequently observed him sweeping the sidewalk, even as the local youths could be seen stripping cars in the middle of the street. In conversations with us, he said that he had owned the buildings for a long time and had paid off the mortgages. He did not see how these buildings could be profitable for someone who had recently taken out a mortgage. He said that many of his tenants were poor and on welfare, but that he took care of the building and they were good about paying their rent.

Three other buildings that survived were owned by the pentecostal church on the corner and housed many members of the church. Although there were some fires in these buildings, fire records classified most of the causes as either "mechanical" or "unknown." The two fires reportedly set by young children were in one of the elderly landlord's buildings. The only fire classified as incendiary in any of the surviving buildings occurred in one of the church-owned buildings. Despite these fires, however, all these buildings survived and were repaired and subsequently maintained by their owners. Although we know less about the other three surviving buildings, real estate records list named individuals, rather than realty corporations, as the owners.

In contrast to these patterns of ownership and fire history, the buildings that did not survive had all experienced fires that were classified as either "suspicious" or "incendiary" in fire reports. All of them were owned by anonymous realty corporations. Two such corporations owned two of these buildings apiece. These corporations all acquired the buildings during a period of from two years to a few weeks before the buildings burned. People who lived in these buildings reported to us that essential services, such as garbage collection, heat, and hot water, began to be withheld during the period before the fires began.[14]

This block was also part of a larger area in which fires raged during that year. An executive in a local community development organization told us that nearly ten thousand families were displaced from this area in the course of a year. At the present, there is talk in the neighborhood that developers are planning to build luxury condominiums in this area.

As noted, fire and arson rates have fallen dramatically since the early 1980s. Arson is highly responsive to real estate conditions: it is a crime pattern that produces profits from poverty. Although the immediate agents may be poor youths or desperate addicts, the instigators are generally unscrupulous real estate interests for whom poor neighborhoods can be highly profitable, either in decline or as potential areas for gentrification. Arson, along with more legal forms of disinvestment, has severely depleted the stock of low-income housing in the city, contributing to one of the most notable transformations of the social fabric in the late 1980s, that of the burgeoning homeless population.

## Drugs

The effects of drug use and drug traffic on the social fabric are many and complicated. New York City is a major international center of drug activity, particularly hard drug use and traffic. It has been the major national center of heroin use and traffic since the 1960s. In the late 1980s, the crack epidemic became a major political issue nationwide. As is so often the case, New York City was one of the first places to experience this new crime problem and has one of the largest problems to deal with.

The relationship between crime and inequality is very much at issue in competing perceptions of the drug problem. For conservatives, drug use among the poor is a symptom of the same moral turpitude that they see as the ultimate cause of poverty and its other associated problems. For residents of poor neighborhoods, drug use and traffic are more often seen as responses to the hopelessness they feel in the face of poverty and discrimination. In more extreme formulations, some poor people and their spokespersons see drugs as part of a genocidal conspiracy against them. Alternatively, drugs are sometimes seen by both conservatives and spokespersons for the disadvantaged as symptoms of general moral decay. In this formulation, the drug menace appears as a problem entirely exogenous to processes of polarization.

Some ethnographic case material is presented here in an attempt to raise questions about how drug use and drug traffic affect the social fabric of the city. Specifically, the following discussion raises questions concerning the relationship of drug use and drug trafficking patterns to processes of social polarization. The ethnographic material points once again to a set of extremely complicated relationships within poor neighborhoods and between poor neighborhoods and the rest of the city and region. Drug use and traffic are not phenomena merely of these poor neighborhoods but both increase the social isolation of inner-city areas and make them suppliers of vice to residents of more affluent areas.

Two aspects of drug use and traffic are discussed here. The first concerns the secular progression of drug use patterns and associated marketing patterns. The second concerns the variety of ways in which these patterns of drug use and marketing have affected the social fabric in different neighborhood environments.

Some of the complicated relationships between illegal drugs and processes of polarization can be illustrated by comparing field data from different times and places. Use of illegal drugs was common in all three neighborhoods throughout the 1980s. There was considerable variation, however, in drug use patterns between the neighborhoods, between different age cohorts within the neighborhoods, and over time.

The drug of choice for youths in their teens and early twenties in the early 1980s was marijuana. Most of those we interviewed used marijuana and spent some of the proceeds of their legal and illegal earnings to purchase it, although their first consumption priority was usually clothing. Marijuana was an important part of their recreational lifestyle, but they were not primarily stealing for a fix. The chief variation between the neighborhoods for teenagers during the early 1980s was the greater variety of drugs consumed by the youths in Hamilton Park. They consumed marijuana primarily but also consumed PCPs, hallucinogens, and a wide variety of pills to a greater extent than their minority peers did. This pattern of greater drug use among white delinquents has also been found in a number of other studies across the country.[15] For one thing, whites tend to be more affluent and thus have more money to purchase drugs. That was certainly apparent in our studies. Another set of factors appears to be subcultural, a difference in tastes among different groups.

Despite this difference, however, the preference of most of these youths most of the time was for marijuana. Hard drug use was also visible in all three neighborhoods, but primarily among older people in their twenties and thirties. The enormously destructive lifestyle of heroin addicts in La Barriada was described in the previous discussion of drugs. These men, and some women, were very much stealing for a fix, on a massive scale that rapidly destroyed their own lives and their neighborhood. Most of the younger people we studied did not use heroin and offered explicit reasons: they had seen the effects of heroin addiction among their older siblings and relatives when they were young children and had grown up wary of the drug.

In addition to this age cohort variation in drug use, there was also a striking contrast between the lifestyles of heroin addicts in the two minority neighborhoods and those in Hamilton Park. In contrast to the lifestyles of the addicts in La Barriada, who lived outside of family households, were usually jobless, and depended on intensive theft for income, many of the Hamilton Park addicts lived in family households and were employed. Many of these men were Vietnam veterans who worked at relatively high-paying jobs in local establishments, had daily heroin habits, and hung out in the evenings in local bars. Although their addiction was a serious problem for them and their families and also led some of them into crime and incarceration, it was not associated with theft, violence, and social disruption to nearly the same extent as in the two poorer, minority neighborhoods.

Patterns of drug use in the city have altered considerably since the early 1980s with the advent of cheap cocaine and its consumption in the highly addictive, smokable form known as crack. In 1983, the wholesale price of cocaine on the world market was cut in half. Although these lower costs were not immediately passed on to consumers, by 1985 low-cost, smokable cocaine had become commonplace. Although crack use is by no means confined to poor neighborhoods, it is particularly prominent in those areas. Crack use is also socially differentiated by age. Crack users and sellers tend to be younger than those involved in the use and sales of both heroin and powdered cocaine.[16]

As noted earlier, crack has been associated with a rise in crime rates after 5 years of steady decline in crime rates—the first such declines in a generation. Crack-related crime includes the crimes of crack smokers committing crimes for money to buy crack; as a result of the effects of crack; and the crimes of crack dealers engaged in violent competition.

Comparison of patterns of drug trafficking in the ethnographic study neighborhoods reveals other complex processes arising out of and reinforcing processes of dualization. In the two minority neighborhoods in the early 1980s, marijuana was sold on the streets as well as in specialized establishments, including apartments, abandoned buildings, and storefronts with covers as variety or candy stores. Hamilton Park's residents and police would not tolerate such drug "stores," although teenagers actively sold marijuana and other drugs in the parks. In all three neighborhoods, teenagers played a prominent role in the marketing of marijuana and pills. Entry into the trade was easy and the conduct of the trade fairly open. The heroin trade, in contrast, was much more tightly controlled: sheltered behind closed doors to a greater extent and managed by older people who were heavily armed and extremely prone to violence. The higher profits and more extreme risks of hard drug traffic led to much more tightly defined selling territories and more tightly controlled selling organizations along with more violent defense of selling territories.[17]

There was another striking difference among the neighborhoods in the marijuana-selling patterns of the early 1980s. Although several youths in each of the groups we studied had been involved in this activity, the traffic itself was more internal to the neighborhood in Hamilton Park and to some extent in La Barriada, than in Projectville. Many of the Hamilton

Park youths who sold had jobs and sold marijuana on the side. The Projectville youths, in contrast, were more likely to become involved as full-time drug sellers. Several of those we studied became more heavily involved as they began going into the downtown business districts and selling "loose joints" and also cocaine to office workers. Two young men in their early twenties whose activities we followed had a regular selling schedule. During the weekdays they concentrated on selling to office workers in Manhattan. In the evenings and on weekends, they worked the avenues of Brooklyn, selling to working people in their own neighborhoods for weekend recreation.

In the period since the early 1980s, some of the patterns observed earlier continue. Drug traffic remains more concealed in Hamilton Park and more internal to the neighborhood. Heroin use is even more prominent in Hamilton Park than previously, but users of all types of drugs there are more often employed. Although working people in the other two neighborhoods also constitute an important part of the clientele for drug sellers, drug consumers there are more often involved in illegal activities in order to obtain money for drugs. In La Barriada, heroin use remains prominent, though cocaine use and traffic have increased tremendously.

Life in Projectville has been substantially transformed by crack. Crack sellers have taken over apartments and buildings; violence associated with crack use and sales has escalated steadily. Crack-related prostitution by very young female users has become common. The level of violence associated with crack traffic is especially striking and is associated both with the extreme youth of those involved as well as with the high profits and associated intense competition. The dichotomy between the marijuana and heroin distribution systems of the earlier period has broken down. Crack is distributed by very young people who are heavily armed. The necessity for violent defense of drug-selling territories combined with the relative lack of judgment and restraint among younger sellers has proved a lethal combination.

Two points should be emphasized in relation to these patterns. First, the enormous profits of the drug trade could not be sustained without a broadly based clientele, including many working people, both white collar and blue collar. Most of the income of drug traffickers derives from wages and not from the full-time thefts of users, such as the heroin addicts in La Barriada, despite the admittedly intensive rates of theft among that class of users. In this sense the drug problem spans society.

Second, although drug use and drug trafficking are found in all social strata, they have a disproportionate effect on life in poor, inner-city neighborhoods. Hard drug use is more concentrated in these areas, and the selling of drugs occupies a more prominent role in the local economy.[18] Violent criminal entrepreneurs from these neighborhoods take prominent roles in distributing drugs both within their own neighborhoods as well as to middle class consumers. In the past few years, some neighborhoods have functioned as retail drug markets serving a metropolitan clientele. Harlem and the Lower East Side have been centers of heroin distribution. Washington Heights has played this role in cocaine and crack distribution.

## Conclusions

The scraps of ethnographic data and official statistics contained in this chapter cannot possibly add up to an adequate description of the enormous complexities of crime and criminal justice in New York City and how they affect the social fabric. Our more limited aim has been to point out some general features of crime and crime control and how these activities grow out of, reinforce, and symbolize processes of social polarization.

High levels of street crime in the city are produced by the severe segmentation of the local labor market, which produces great wealth along with locally concentrated poverty.[19] This poverty results not just from low-wage jobs but from widespread exclusion from the labor force and the disruption of family and neighborhood life produced by the combined effects of the labor market and the welfare system. The ghettos produce many idle young men for whom crime, despite its considerable risks, is preferable to total invisibility and uselessness. At the same time, the ghettos attract the attention of another class of criminals, the arsonist landlords and high-level drug traffickers to whom poor people and their neighborhoods represent a source of obscene profits.

The effects of crime on the weaving of the city's social fabric are extremely complex. This chapter has shown some of the ways in which crime affects the internal organization of poor neighborhoods, the quality of public life in non-poor areas of the city, and the relationships between poor neighborhoods and the rest of the city. They may be summed up as follows:

INTERNAL DISRUPTION OF POOR NEIGHBORHOODS  The inability of adult men to earn family wages in poor, minority neighborhoods results in their separation from households and in high proportions of poor, welfare-dependent, officially female-headed households. Poverty, erratic school attendance, low labor force participation, and high unemployment among youths in these neighborhoods produce a large population of young, poor, and idle young men who are prone to involvement in intensive drug use and crime. These young men dominate their environments to a much greater degree than they would in more affluent neighborhoods. Although the operative social control processes tend to deflect some predatory street crime outside the local area, the social control resources locally available are not sufficient for the task of adequately controlling crime in the local area. Inner-city criminals prey first and most often on their own neighbors. Criminals and victims are concentrated in the same areas. Indeed, they are sometimes the same people, exchanging roles from situation to situation.[20] Much street crime simply circulates resources within poor neighborhoods.

REDISTRIBUTION OF RESOURCES INTO POOR NEIGHBORHOODS    The development of street crime careers among inner-city males, however, is not just the result of the stresses of poverty and enforced leisure. Some patterns of street crime actually bring extra resources into a neighborhood from outside. The market for stolen goods is an important source of cheap merchandise in inner-city neighborhoods.[21] To the extent that this merchandise emanates from outside a local community, the community as a whole has a stake in the crime pattern that is bringing in these resources. Many local residents may still normatively disapprove of crime, but, practically, they are unwilling to devote their scarce social control resources to controlling crimes that are not hurting them directly and which are bringing in merchandise and cash from outside the local area.

Both the market for stolen goods and the drug trade generate a great deal of economic activity in poor neighborhoods. Such economic activity also occurs in non-poor neighborhoods, but the proportion of all economic activity that is underground and/or illegal is simply much greater in poor neighborhoods because other kinds of economic activity are so restricted as a result of the exclusion of local residents from the labor market.

EXPORT OF CRIME FROM POOR TO NON-POOR AREAS    Because inner-city residents devote their scarce social control resources to protecting their own local areas, local criminal entrepreneurs are deflected into the subways, business areas, and other residential areas of the city. In this way, street crime is exported from poor neighborhoods to the rest of the city. This process has transformed the entire fabric of urban life in New York City and other large U.S. cities in the period since the 1960s.

EXPLOITATION OF POOR NEIGHBORHOODS BY NON-POOR PROFITEERS    The increasing social isolation and political vulnerability of poor neighborhoods have made them subject to a variety of forms of financial manipulation.

Although average income levels in poor neighborhoods are low, the density of population is such that there is still a great deal of money in these areas. The arsonist landlords and high-level drug traffickers alluded to in this chapter represent the criminal element among these exploiters of urban poverty, although many of the real estate and other practices which drain money from poor neighborhoods are perfectly legal.

STIGMATIZATION OF INNER-CITY NEIGHBORHOODS AND THEIR RESIDENTS Over time, the processes described above reinforce the social isolation of poor neighborhoods. Those inner-city residents who do manage to obtain education and jobs move away, leaving increasingly concentrated poverty and social pathology behind them.[22] The concentration of pathology in these areas stigmatizes the areas and their residents. Businesses refrain from locating there. Social services deteriorate as service providers begin to feel overwhelmed by the problems they have to deal with; they become cynical about the missions of the schools, the welfare system, and other agencies. Inner-city residents are also stigmatized as individuals, particularly young, poor, black, and Latino men who encounter constant suspicion and harassment which further alienate them from the schools, lock them out of the job market, and convey to them that they are expected to assume deviant lifestyles.

# Notes

1. New York City Police Department, Crime Analysis Section, *Arrests and Complaints* (1960–1982).

2. *New York Times* (October 27, 1988), p. B8.

3. Arrest statistics taken from Sviridoff, Michele, with Jerome E. McElroy, *Employment and Crime: A Summary Report*. A Report to the National Institute of Justice (New York: Vera Institute of Justice, mimeo, 1984), p. 28; borough population statistics from U.S. Bureau of the Census, *Census Tracts: New York New Jersey SMSA 1980*.

4. Simon, R. J., and N. Sharma, "Women and Crime: Does the U.S. Experience Generalize?" in Simon, R. J., and N. Sharma, eds., *Criminology of Deviant Women* (Boston: Houghton Mifflin, 1979), p. 394.

5. McGahey, Richard, "Economic Development and the Perception of Crime," *New York Affairs* 8, 1 (1983): 19.

6. A recent and influential book (Wilson, James Q., and Richard Herrnstein, *Crime and Human Nature* (New York: Simon & Schuster, 1985)) has culminated a trend in the criminology of the past two decades to move away from social explanations of crime to individualistic explanations. A revival of inter-

est in the social ecology of crime, however, is evident in the work reported here as well as in several other recent groups of studies, including Reiss, Albert J., and Michael Tonry, eds., *Crime and Justice, A Review of Research, Volume 8: Communities and Crime* (Chicago: University of Chicago Press, 1986); Byrne, J. M., and R. J. Sampson, *The Social Ecology of Crime* (New York: Springer Verlag, 1986); and Shannon, Lyle W., "Ecological Evidence of the Hardening of the Inner City," in Figlio, Robert M., Simon Hakim, and George F. Rengert, eds., *Metropolitan Crime Patterns* (Monsey, NY: Criminal Justice Press, 1986), pp. 27–53.

7. Reports on this research include: Sullivan, Mercer L., *Getting Paid: Youth Crime and Work in the Inner City* (New York: Cornell University Press, 1989); Sullivan, Mercer L., "Youth Crime: New York's Two Varieties," *New York Affairs* 8:1 (Fall 1983); "Absent Fathers in the Inner City," *The Annals of the Academy* (special issue on the underclass, William Julius Wilson, ed., vol. 501, January 1989); "Teen Fathers," *Exploratory Ethnographic Study* (A Report to the Ford Foundation, Vera Institute of Justice, mimeo, April 1985).

8. About half of the households in the two minority neighborhoods received public assistance and fell below the poverty line, in comparison to about 10 percent of the households in Hamilton Park. Female-headed households accounted for half or more of all households in the minority neighborhoods, compared to only 20 percent of households in Hamilton Park.

9. See Sullivan, *Getting Paid*, for comparisons of ethnographic and census data.

10. The census shows a mean median age of about 20 for the two minority neighborhoods and about 36 for Hamilton Park. Some caution must be exercised in interpreting census figures on median age and household composition, since the census substantially undercounts adult men, as much as 30 percent for minority men in their twenties (see Hanier, Peter, Catherine Hines, Elizabeth Martin, and Gary Shapiro, "Research on Improving Coverage in Household Surveys." Paper presented to Bureau of the Census, Fourth Annual Research Conference, Arlington, VA, March 20–23, 1988). Still, the undercount is not severe enough to account for such skewed age distributions between these neighborhoods. Our ethnographic observations, while revealing perhaps more present adult males than discovered by the census, also showed a relative difference between the neighborhoods and a shifting attachment, related to their marginal labor force status, among many of the men who were present in the households of the minority neighborhoods.

11. The causes of this age pattern of criminality have been the subject of recent lively debate. Hirschi, Travis, and Michael Gottfredson, "Age and the Explanation of Crime," *American Journal of Sociology* 89,3 (1983): 552–584, have proposed that the pattern is so prevalent in different social milieus that social factors must not be responsible, thus implying biological causality. Greenberg, David F., "Delinquency and the Age Structure of Society," *Contemporary Crises* (April 1977): 189–223; Greenberg, David F., "Age, Crime, and Social Explanation," *American Journal of Sociology* 91,1 (1985): 121; and the

analyses offered here point instead to the social rather than biological aspects of aging which appear to account for these patterns.

12. City of New York, Fire Department, *Annual Report and Statistics* (1960–1987).

13. "Patterns of Suspicious Fires Involve Types of Businesses, Blocks, and Landlords," *New York Times* (November 11, 1980), p. B1.

14. I am indebted to Nicole Gueron for her assistance in locating and analyzing these fire and ownership records.

15. Elliot, D. S., S. S. Ageton, S. S. Huizinga, B. A. Knowles, and R. Canter, *The Prevalence and Incidence of Delinquent Behavior: 1976–1980* (Boulder, CO.: Behavioral Research Institute, 1983); Tucker, M. B., "U.S. Ethnic Minorities and Drug Abuse: An Assessment of the Science and Practice," *International Journal of the Addictions* 20 (1985): 1021–1047.

16. City of New York, Police Department, "Narcotics and Drug Arrests, 1/87–12/87," *Arrests and Complaints* (1987).

17. Soref, Michael J., "The Structure of Illegal Drug Markets: An Organizational Approach," *Urban Life* 10,3 (October 1981): 329–352.

18. Detailed estimates of the economic activity associated with heroin traffic in Harlem and on the Lower East Side are contained in Johnson, Bruce D., et al., *Taking Care of Business: The Economics of Crime by Heroin Abusers* (Lexington, MA: Lexington Books, D.C. Heath, 1985).

19. See Gordon, David M., Richard Edwards, and Michael Reich, *Segmented Work, Divided Workers: The Historical Transformation of Labor in the United States* (Cambridge: Cambridge University Press, 1982) for a broad historical overview of labor market segmentation in the United States; and Stafford, Walter, *Closed Labor Markets: Underrepresentation of Blacks, Hispanics and Women in New York City's Core Industries and Jobs* (New York: Community Service Society, 1985) for an analysis of segmentation within the New York City labor market.

20. Fagan, Jeffrey, Elizabeth S. Piper, and Yu-Teh Cheng, "Contributions of Victimization to Delinquency in Inner Cities," *Journal of Criminal Law and Criminology* 78,13 (1987): 408–428.

21. See Preble, Edward, and John J. Casey, "Taking Care of Business—The Heroin User's Life on the Street," *International Journal of the Addictions* 4 (1969): 1–24, for seminal insights into the redistributive aspects of street crime, along with the work of Johnson et al. (see Note 18).

22. See Wilson, William Julius, *The Truly Disadvantaged: The Inner City, the Underclass and Public Policy* (Chicago: University of Chicago Press, 1987) for national-level analyses of the increasing concentrations of poverty in the inner cities; and Tobier, Emanuel, *The Changing Face of Poverty: Trends in New York City's Population in Poverty: 1960–1990* (New York: Community Service Society, 1984) for similar analyses of poverty in New York City.

# 10

# The Structure of the Media

## Mitchell Moss / Sarah Ludwig

Two of the major symbols of the information age are electronic media and world cities. Both reflect the centralizing tendencies of telecommunications technologies on urban economic and social systems. New York City is widely known as the media capital of the United States, where the nation's largest publishing firms, television networks, and advertising agencies are located. These corporations produce the information and images that are communicated across the country and the world, in the form of newspapers, magazines, books, and radio and television programs. The presence of information-intensive firms in New York City contributes to the economic well-being of the city, but these corporate communication giants do little to add to the information that citizens rely upon in their daily lives. Indeed, even the major daily newspapers and television stations based in New York City have a remarkably limited orientation towards events within the city itself; and due to market constraints, they increasingly serve the larger metropolitan region surrounding the city itself. The media in New York City can be characterized as consisting of three types: (a) the mass, citywide media which also serve the surrounding metropolitan area; (b) the local community or neighborhood media which serve distinct geographic areas within New York City; and (c) media designed to serve specific racial, ethnic, and cultural groups.

The city's ethnically and culturally diverse population has fostered a complex structure of print, radio, and television media which provides a powerful alternative to that provided by the dominant citywide media. Since individuals rely on the media for information and the clarification of events, it is essential to understand the different images of New York that are provided by media within New York City. Moreover, different population groups are served by different kinds of media. Despite the trend towards the centralization of media, New York City has developed a robust local communications infrastructure which presents a countervailing trend to the consolidation of news operations in advanced industrial countries.

Individuals rely on a multiplicity of information sources to learn about the community in which they live, their own experiences, that of friends and neighbors as well as on formal sources such as newspapers, television, and radio. In New York City, the dominant newspapers and television and radio stations have only a limited role as an information source for much of the city's population. This chapter examines the structure of media in New York City and highlights the way in which two media systems have evolved: one that serves the larger metropolitan region and is targeted towards white, middle class groups, and another that is aimed at black, Hispanic and foreign-born residents, and the local communities within the city.

## Citywide Media

New York City, with four citywide daily newspapers, is one of the few cities in the United States where newspapers compete. It has a century-long tradition of multiple newspapers. In the 1890s, paid advertising began to absorb the printing costs of newspapers, resulting in the penny paper. At that time New York City had 29 papers, with an average circulation of 92,000. Hearst's *Journal* and Pulitzer's *World* each claimed circulations exceeding one million. Yet the pre-tabloidesque *World* and *Journal* did not reflect the interests of the influx of immigrants who barely spoke, much less read, English. Consequently, many foreign language publications were established, some of which continue today, such as the *Jewish Forward* and *Il Progresso*.

### The Major Daily Newspapers

The four major daily newspapers in New York City have an aggregate circulation in the metropolitan region of approximately 4.6 million; however, they differ considerably in the share of their circulation that is based in New York City (see Table 10.1). More than two-thirds of the *New York Post*'s sales occur in New York City, but only 56 percent of the *New York Daily News*, 34 percent of the *New York Times*, and 15 percent of *Newsday* sales occur in New York City. These figures, which are inflated due to the

Table 10.1    Circulation of Major Daily Newspapers (1988)

| Newspaper | Total Circulation | NYC Circulation | NYC as Percentage of Total |
|---|---|---|---|
| Daily News | 1,500,000 | 844,000 | 56 |
| New York Newsday | 1,218,000 | 178,000 | 15 |
| New York Post | 644,057 | 453,377 | 70 |
| New York Times | 1,235,636 | 423,384 | 34 |

Source: Telephone surveys with newspapers.

Note: Total circulation includes entire twenty-four-county area of dominant influence (ADI). Total metropolitan circulation for New York Newsday includes the Long Island Newsday edition.

inclusion of newspapers bought by suburban commuters, indicate that the so-called dominant daily newspapers serve markets not limited to the city and must adapt their news coverage accordingly, often resulting in diminished reporting of local events.

Each of the daily newspapers has a distinctive approach to the news, reflecting the socioeconomic characteristics and geographic location of its readers (see Table 10.2). The New York Times is oriented towards a college-educated, white, upper middle and upper-income readership. The newspaper's front page emphasizes national and international events, as well as scientific breakthroughs, economic trends, or significant local events. New York City and regional news are concentrated in the "Metropolitan Section," which is oriented towards the city and the surrounding metropolitan region. The coverage of international and national news at the New York Times has long superseded local news. More than 25 years ago, Arthur Sulzberger, in the introduction to A. M. Rosenthal's book, Thirty-Eight Witnesses, observed:

It is often forgotten—I think sometimes by ourselves [at The New York Times]—that we are above all a community newspaper. We are The New York Times, not the Times of London or of Los Angeles or of Washington. . . .Sometimes we suffer from Afghanistanitis—the theory that what happens in exotic places is somehow more important than what happens in Queens.[1]

Many New Yorkers read more than one newspaper, with one-fourth of the New York Times readers also reading the New York Post, and almost one-third of the Post's readers also reading the Daily News.[2]

The New York Post, once the premier liberal newspaper in New York City, has undergone two ownership changes in the past two decades.

**Table 10.2    Reader Profile (1988)**

|  | White | Black | Other* |
|---|---|---|---|
| A. Race of Readers, by Newspaper (%) |  |  |  |
| New York Times | 77.2 | 18.2 | 4.6 |
| New York Newsday | 67.9 | 27.3 | 4.8 |
| New York Post | 66.9 | 28.7 | 4.4 |
| Daily News | 63.9 | 31.4 | 4.6 |

| B. Median Household Income of Newspaper Readers, by Newspaper |  |
|---|---|
| New York Times | $40,500 |
| New York Newsday | $37,200 |
| New York Post | $35,000 |
| Daily News | $30,900 |

Source: Scarborough Research.

*No further breakdown available.

According to journalist James Ledbetter, former *Post* owner Rupert Murdoch "successfully created a right-wing mouthpiece out of the traditionally liberal tab."[3] The *Post*, with a circulation of about 453,000, has had difficulty in generating a strong advertising base (see Figure 10.1). Under the recent ownership of realtor Peter Kalikow, the *Post* has brought in new editors and has expanded its real estate and local coverage. The *Daily News* is the "only [New York City] tabloid in the black."[4] Owned by the Chicago-based Tribune Company, the *News'* profits in 1987 reached $12 million, far less than the *New York Times'* $196 million profit. The *Daily News* makes an effort to cover community news with some emphasis on blacks and Hispanics, since many of its white ethnic readers have moved to the suburbs. It includes an insert with local news for each borough, as well as a Sunday magazine, *Vista*, written in English but geared to and distributed in targeted Hispanic communities throughout New York City (with the exception of Staten Island). The *Daily News* has the most black and Hispanic reporters.

New York Newsday, owned by The Times-Mirror Corporation, entered into the city's tabloid competition in 1985 as an extension of its parent paper, which has a circulation exceeding one million on Long Island. *New York Newsday* has attracted nearly one-third of the city's total newspaper advertising dollars and its circulation has increased steadily. Most copies are sold in Queens (110,000), while the paper's circulation is less than 70,000 in Brooklyn and Manhattan combined. The readership of *New York Newsday* is predominantly white and middle class, second to the *New York Times* in median income.[5] *Newsday* has built a strong local staff

**Figure 10.1  Percentage of Advertising Dollars, by NYC Major Daily Newspaper (1987)**

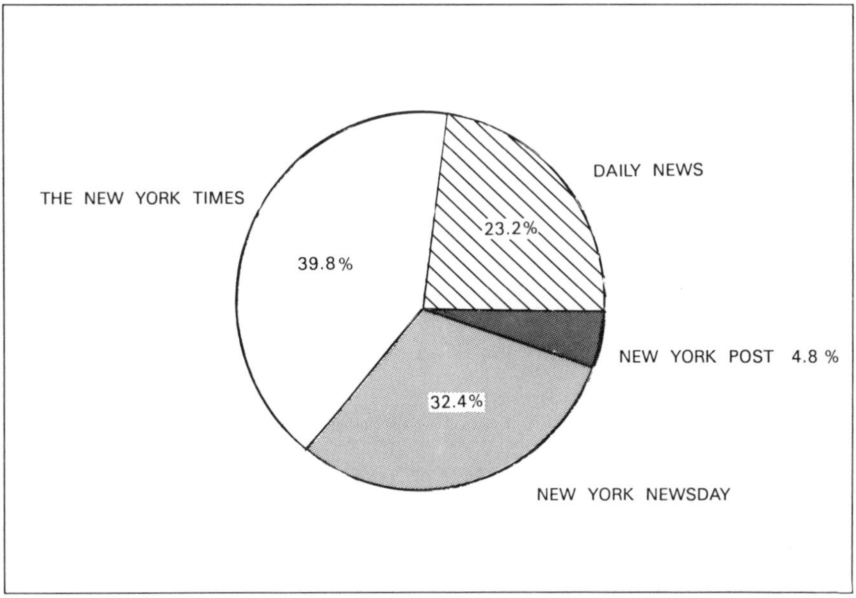

*Source:* Media Records 1988.

which covers state and municipal news in depth, filling a gap left by the other daily newspapers.

## Citywide Television and Radio

Just as New York City has a relative abundance of daily newspapers, it also has a considerable number of broadcast television stations. City residents can receive fifteen, and in some cases, sixteen television stations without subscribing to cable television. There are four network-owned stations: WCBS, Channel 2; WNBC, Channel 4; WNYW, Channel 5; and WABC, Channel 7. There are three independent channels: Channels 9 and 11, WWOR and WPIX, respectively plus Channel 55, broadcast from Long Island; and six public television stations, five of which are broadcast on UHF, including one based on Long Island and one in New Jersey. In addition, there are two New Jersey-based Spanish language television stations, Channels 41 and 47. Finally, there is a low-power television station, LPTV-44, with "alternative programming," which can be received in a few areas of the city.

One reason for the plethora of broadcast television stations is that New

York City is located within the nation's largest "area of dominant influence" (ADI), the technical name for a regional television market. While the New York ADI has 6.8 million ADI TV households, the city accounts for only 42 percent of the television households within the region, causing the television stations to balance city and suburban news and editorial coverage. In fact, organizations in northern New Jersey and on Long Island have protested the lack of adequate news coverage of their suburban counties, leading to the creation of suburban news bureaus by some of the major television stations.

New York City is served by 38 radio stations, 15 AM and 23 FM, including stations licensed in the nearby New Jersey communities of Secaucus and Newark. The capacity of radio to reach highly targeted audiences is demonstrated by the presence of eight stations with a virtually all-black listenership (encompassing a variety of formats), four Spanish stations, and one sports station. Moreover, several stations provide foreign language programming, which will be discussed later in this chapter.

### Foreign Language and Ethnic Media in New York City

In New York minorities constitute a majority of the population; but unlike Philadelphia, Detroit, or Washington, D.C., no single minority group is numerically predominant. Tobier notes that one-fourth of New Yorkers are foreign-born, and that figure is expected to increase by the year 2000, with an estimated 100,000 immigrants locating within the city annually. The mainstream media have made little attempt to gain readers among New York City's immigrant population, and an extensive foreign language media has developed to serve these immigrants.

This study identified 80 foreign language newspapers in the five boroughs. Most of the papers operate on a weekly basis, with the notable exception of the Korean papers, which are all dailies. Many of the non-English papers that traditionally served the Eastern and Southern European immigrant population are no longer published. Still, four Lithuanian papers continue to be published, along with two Russian and five Yiddish/Jewish newspapers.

Economic, demographic, and cultural factors influence the number and type of newspapers produced for each ethnic group. In the Korean community, some of the local Korean papers receive funds from the homeland. Although language itself is a factor for all non-English-speaking people in New York City, it is especially significant for those groups, such as the Chinese, whose alphabet and native tongue differ fundamentally from Romance languages. Moreover, Chinese papers are split into pro-Taiwan and pro-Mainland, as well as by progressive or traditional orientations. Yet language is only one factor, for cultural and ethnic identity influence the strength of the four Irish papers (three weeklies and one published three days per week), with a combined weekly circulation of 156,000.

The foreign language press acts as a "facilitator" for the tens of thousands of immigrants who settle in the city annually, providing useful information about employment, immigration laws, housing, and English language instruction. The Korean press, for example, assists Korean small businesses by furnishing information on tax guidelines, accounting, and other commercial issues. And Korean examples of Horatio Alger success stories help to reinforce the entrepreneurial spirit.[6]

Most of the Korean newspapers are flown daily to Kennedy Airport from Kimpo International Airport in South Korea. The New York offices then add local news and advertisements; many are distributed on a subscription basis only.[7] A large proportion of Korean immigrants are college-educated and highly literate. By contrast, the Haitian population is less literate, and therefore the handful of weekly Creole newspapers are less important than Creole radio programs as an integrative force for immigrants.[8]

New York City's Latino population, estimated at 25 percent of the total, has two daily newspapers, *El Diario-La Prensa* and *Noticias del Mundo*. *El Diario* was owned by The Gannett Company (whose 93 newspapers yield a total circulation of six million) until recently, when a minority-dominated management group bought the paper.[9] News World Communications, the publishing arm of Reverend Sun Myung Moon, owns *Noticias*.[10] In addition to the two major Latino dailies, several Spanish weeklies are published in New York City, and an array of imported papers are available at newsstands.

There are 22 daily foreign language publications, only two of which include sections in English (see Table 10.3). Fourteen dailies were established after 1970, and ten of these are foreign language publications, along with one Korean paper entirely in English. There are seven Korean daily papers, and seven Chinese. Certain foreign language dailies serve the entire United States, such as the Chinese *Sing Tao Newspapers*. Despite this, the readership of such dailies is predominantly New York City-based.

The organization of ethnic and immigrant groups influences the number, format, and content of media, as do financial considerations. Some papers offer world news combined with local advertising; others include news of the homeland, perhaps combined with local news; while still others contain local content only.

Table 10.3    Daily Newspapers in New York City (1988)

| Description | Newspaper | Year Established | Circulation |
|---|---|---|---|
| Black | Daily Challenge* | 1972 | 46,300 |
| Business | Brooklyn Daily Bulletin† | 1954 | 5,250 |
| | Journal of Commerce & Commercial† | 1827 | 20,838 |
| | Wall Street Journal | 1889 | 168,365 |
| Chinese | Centre Daily News | 1982 | 30,000 |
| | China Daily News* | 1940 | 25,000 |
| | China Tribune | 1943 | 10,000 |
| | International Daily News | 1982 | 10,000 |
| | Sing Tao Newspapers | 1965 | 36,000 |
| | United Journal† | 1952 | 32,000 |
| | World Journal | 1976 | 30,000 |
| General | New York City Tribune | 1983 | 1,500 |
| | New York Daily News | 1919 | 1,500,000 |
| | | | 844,000 |
| | New York Newsday | 1985 | 178,000 |
| | New York Post | 1801 | 644,057 |
| | | | 453,377 |
| | New York Times | 1851 | 1,235,636 |
| | | | 423,384 |
| | Staten Island Advance | 1886 | 74,867 |
| | Wall Street Journal | 1889 | 112,920 |
| Greek | Ethnekos Kerix (National Herald) | 1915 | 35,000 |
| | Proini (Morning)* | 1976 | 37,000 |
| Hispanic | El Diario-La Prensa† | 1961 | 64,000 |
| | Noticias del Mundo† | 1980 | 52,000 |
| Italian | Il Progresso | 1880 | 33,500 |
| | La Voce Italiana | 1926 | 40,000 |
| Korean | Dong-A Ilbo | 1972 | 10,000 |
| | Korea Central Daily News | 1975 | 13,000 |
| | Korea Chosun | 1981 | 50,000 |
| | The Korea Herald/USA* | 1953 | 5,000 |
| | Korea News* | 1967 | 15,000 |
| | Korean American Daily News | 1986 | 7,000 |
| | Sae Gai Times | 1982 | 12,000 |
| Polish | Nowy Dziennik (Polish Daily News) | 1971 | 20,000 |
| Political | People's Daily World | 1986 | 10,000 |
| Russian | Novoye Russkoye Slovo* | 1910 | 40,931 |

Sources: Urban Research Center.

*Editor & Publisher Int'l Yrbook 1987.
†Working Press of the Nation 1988.

**Table 10.3** (*continued*)

| Site | Owner | Other Information |
|------|-------|-------------------|
| Brooklyn | Daily Challenge Corp. | 110,000—weekend |
| Brooklyn | Brooklyn Bulletin | Subscription Basis only |
| Manhattan | Knight-Ridder Newspapers | |
| | | |
| Manhattan | Dow Jones & Co. | NY statewide circulation |
| Queens | | local with US nat'l/int'l |
| Manhattan | | pro-Mainland |
| Manhattan | | 100—free |
| Manhattan | | San Francisco-based |
| Manhattan | | international paper |
| Manhattan | | |
| Queens | | Pro-Taiwan/party paper |
| Manhattan | News World Communications | Rev. Moon |
| Manhattan | Chicago Tribune Co. | 1.6 million on Sundays |
| | | City circulation |
| Manhattan | Times Mirror Corp. | |
| Manhattan | New York Post Corp. | SMSA circulation |
| | | City circulation |
| Manhattan | The New York Times Co. | 1.6 million on Sunday |
| | | City circulation |
| Staten Island | Advance Publishing | 84,503 on Sunday |
| Manhattan | | |
| Queens | Anthony H. Diamataris | |
| | | |
| Queens | | 5,000—free |
| Manhattan | Gannett | 55,000 on Sunday |
| Manhattan | News World Communications | Rev. Moon |
| Emerson, NJ | Italo-Americano | |
| Manhattan | | |
| Manhattan | | Published in S. Korea |
| Queens | | |
| Manhattan | | Published in S. Korea |
| Manhattan | | Tu-Su; English |
| Queens | | |
| Queens | | |
| Manhattan | | |
| Manhattan | | |
| | | |
| Manhattan | Long View Publishing Co. | National circulation figure |
| Manhattan | | |

## The Black Press

The principal medium explicitly serving blacks in New York City is radio, not television or newspapers. Newspapers rank second in impact and prominence for the black community, and television and cable stations present almost no local black programming. Limited financial resources in a television media market dominated by national broadcasting firms have limited black entry into television ownership in New York.

There are five black weekly newspapers in New York City, plus one black daily, the *Daily Challenge*, which is published in Brooklyn and claims a circulation exceeding 40,000. The combined circulation of the black weeklies is just over 200,000. The *Amsterdam News* and the *City Sun* are the most influential of the group. Though the smaller black newspapers emphasize local news, the *Amsterdam News, City Sun,* and the *Daily Challenge* cover local as well as national and international, primarily black, news.

A *New York Newsday* survey of black New Yorkers showed that 23.5 percent felt that black-generated media were their most important sources of news and information. Almost half (47 percent) indicated that black media provided one of the news sources on which they relied.[11] In addition, there are community papers that may not fall directly into a black classification, yet whose local basis and readership are predominantly black. This is not to suggest, however, that the readership of black papers is uniquely Afro-American. The major daily newspapers have been criticized for their poor representation of blacks and other minorities on their news staff, although efforts are underway at several newspapers to ameliorate the situation. There are black and Latino newscasters on local television news programs, but the stories they cover often reinforce stereotypes of blacks as criminals, drug addicts, and sports luminaries. In *Minorities and Media,* Wilson and Gutierrez note that the development of the mass media in the United States, which directed programming to the broadest population possible, ruled out the formation of small media outlets that would serve specific groups:

> As media strove to accumulate large audiences, they developed content that would attract the widest audience possible and offend the fewest people. Rather than including a variety of small outlets, each addressing the needs of segments of the society, media in the United States became synonymous with the mass audience. . . . [Since] news people think of minorities as outside the American system, the actions of minorities must be reported as adversarial because they are seen as threats to the social order.[12]

*Spanish, Black, and Foreign Language Radio*

Commercial radio in New York City serves as a vital communications outlet for blacks and Latinos. One official at a Latino radio station stated, "This is only a foreign language station if you still consider Spanish a foreign language in New York. We do not." Only one of the four Latino radio stations has even partial ownership by Latinos, and the three others are owned entirely by non-Latino companies.[13] *Daily News* reporter Juan Gonzalez explains that

> [Some Latino political leaders feel that] the Latino community, which in our information age desperately needs education geared to lifting it out of its economic quagmire, is instead being milked by farmers who couldn't give a damn about the cow.[14]

The *New York Times* reports that black talk radio is emerging as an important new medium for blacks throughout the nation and provides a "kind of regular town meeting of the air."[15] Acting as a "facilitator" for political and community organization, some black talk radio programs

> . . .have an ability to penetrate black neighborhoods and elicit instant response in a way that evokes comparisons with the historic roles of the black church as a kind of communications switchboard and forum for community action.[16]

In New York City, WLIB (AM), owned by Inner City Broadcasting, is the foremost black talk radio station. All programs are geared specifically towards black, Caribbean, and Latino communities. WLIB, which calls itself "The Nation's First Black Superstation," runs talk and news shows Monday through Thursday. These range from news programs and interviews to the reporting of West Indian cricket scores. From Friday until Sunday evening, the station metamorphoses, carrying Caribbean music and information, primarily Jamaican, in addition to several hours of Haitian music on Saturday mornings.

The *New York Times* has described WLIB as "an important vehicle for reaching blacks." In fact, many public figures seek access to the black community through WLIB, due to its overwhelmingly black listenership. *New York Newsday* suggested that, "Its format is so attuned to the mood of black New York that last year the Police Department secretly monitored the station as a means of collecting information on black activists."[17] WLIB runs counter to the mainstream media, treating blacks seriously in its coverage. As David Lampel, senior vice-president of Inner City Broadcasting, told a *Newsday* reporter, "The black community is covered [by the mainstream media] as though you were covering a foreign country."[18]

The timeliness of radio enhances WLIB as a daily source for news and information, since the two major black newspapers, *City Sun* and *Amsterdam News*, circulate on a weekly basis.[19] Lampel commented that WLIB allows "blacks to communicate with one another without going through the filter of someone else. [The station] acts as an electronic marketplace of African and African-American ideas."[20] Yet WLIB's listenership is equivalent to just 20 percent of that of New York's top news station, WINS.

A handful of public and not-for-profit radio stations transmit foreign language programming. Most foreign language radio time falls into what *The Broadcasting/Cablecasting Yearbook* calls "special programming" (i.e., runs under 20 hours per week).[21] This study found only one for-profit radio station, WEVD, with regularly scheduled "special programming." FM college radio stations in New York City also carry non-English and ethnic radio shows, especially WFUV of Fordham University, the Medgar Evers College Radio Project, WNYE, and Columbia University's WKCR.

Fordham University's WFUV, with the largest wattage of the three college stations, reaches the greatest potential number of listeners with more than 23 hours of special programming each week. Columbia University's radio station, WKCR, broadcasts 22.5 hours of special programming per week, including 7.5 hours of Latin shows, Caribbean/West Indian music, both Cantonese and Mandarin content, (East) Indian selections, and several hours of African music. Medgar Evers College Radio Project, WNYE, under the jurisdiction of the New York City Board of Education, is geared to the neighboring Hispanic, black American, and West Indian populations; its programs include 8 hours of Caribbean, 6 hours of Spanish, music and talk, and roughly 6 hours entirely in Creole. WEVD(FM) is the only for-profit radio station with a substantial number of hours per week devoted to ethnic and foreign language programming. WEVD complements its usual Oldies/Big Band format with almost 40 hours of non-English programming, in addition to one half hour of Irish and several hours of "Anglo-Jewish" content. When WEVD does not broadcast its own programs, it allows broadcasters to purchase time, the bulk of which is taken up by Greek and Jewish spots (21 hours combined).

WNWK-FM, a noteworthy New York City radio station, claims to be "the only multiethnic station in the tri-state area." The station transmits in 27 different languages, ranging from 34.5 and 22.5 hours per week in Greek and Italian, respectively, to one hour or less segments in Arabic, Armenian, Bengali, Farsi, Macedonian, Serbian, Slovak, and Urdu. The WNWK program guide explicitly differentiates among Latinos. Rather

**Figure 10.2    Radio Stations in New York City**

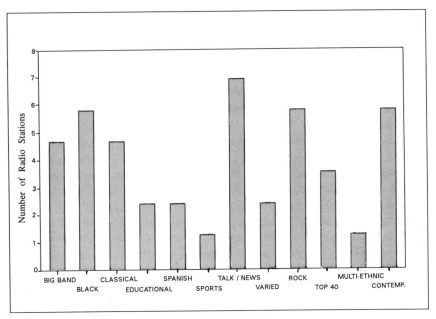

*Source:* Broadcasting/Cablecasting Yearbook 1988: Urban Research Center, NYU.

*Note:* Stations that can be included in more than one category are indicated twice.

than treating Latinos as a homogeneous group, WNWK distinguishes among varied Hispanic groups, such as Argentine, Chilean, Dominican, Ecuadorian, and Peruvian.

A relatively new technological innovation, the "subsidiary communications carrier," or SCA, provides several ethnic and foreign language broadcasting companies with access to the radio. These subcarrier radio systems are linked to the FM transmitters of noncommercial stations. Only not-for-profit stations may lease the FM transmitters. The Federal Communications Commission authorizes SCA subcarriers. They operate on a full-time basis, and in much the same way that Muzak has been piped into doctors' offices and shopping malls for years. There are several Chinese (Mandarin and Cantonese), one West Indian, and two Italian subcarriers in New York. To receive the SCA frequency, customers must purchase a receiver that picks up the subcarrier frequency only—a one-time expense, ranging from $100 to $140 per unit. One Chinese broadcasting company, transmitted through the SCA, reported that it has sold over 10,000 receivers in the New York metropolitan area.

## UHF Television: Programming for Blacks, Latinos, and Immigrants

Five UHF television stations also broadcast programming that serves the city's diverse ethnic and racial groups; WNYC, Channel 31; WNYE, Channel 25; WNJU, Channel 47; WXTV, Channel 41; and LPTV, Channel 44, New York's only operating low-power television station (see Table 10.4). WNYC, Channel 31, a public broadcasting station, operated under the auspices of the City of New York, programs 40 hours of ethnic and foreign language programming each week. An additional 16 leased hours are devoted to Italian, and 12 to Japanese. The Italian shows include local and Italian news, films, and live soccer matches transmitted from Europe. WNYC's Japanese programming consists of news, entertainment, and Japanese language instruction. The 4 hours of Chinese programming at Channel 31 are broadcast in either Cantonese with Mandarin subtitles, or vice versa, which is common in all Chinese television in the city. The news is both local and Taiwan-related. In fact, 60 percent of the programming is produced in Taiwan. Channel 31 also carries programs geared to East Indian, Greek, Polish, and Brazilian (in both English and Portuguese) groups in New York. Channel 25 of the New York City Board of Education, WNYE, broadcasts black television programs produced for a national audience, which rarely address issues specific to New York City.

Although Channel 47, WNJU, is located in northern New Jersey, it joins Channel 41, WXTV, in serving the New York Hispanic community. Channel 41 is owned by Spanish International Television (SIN), which broadcasts in metropolitan regions with substantial Spanish-speaking concentrations throughout the country. SIN broadcasts 133.5 hours per week, entirely in Spanish. WXTV, though predominantly Hispanic, also transmits in seven other languages, including Tagalog (Filipino), Chinese, Korean, and Serbo-Croatian.

One UHF station that functions differently from the above public and Hispanic stations is LPTV, Channel 44, the only low-power television station currently operating in New York City. The station performs the unique function of providing a sort of public access not achieved through cable television. At $120 per airtime hour, Channel 44 is open to broadcasters 60 hours each week. Programming includes Farsi, Bengali, and Caribbean Indian, in addition to Hebrew, Greek, Russian, English, and religious-oriented content. Its 16 Spanish hours are predominantly Argentine, Columbian, and Dominican. According to one station official:

> We . . . found there was a lot of interest [in LPTV] from Latino groups. That surprises some people—they think New York's Hispanics are served by Channels 41 and 47, until you tell them that there are Spanish-speaking

Table 10.4   UHF Television: Foreign Language and Ethnic Programming
in New York (hours per week)

| | CH31 WNYC | CH25 WNYE | CH47 WNJU | CH41 WXTV | CH44 LPTV | Total Hours/ Week |
|---|---|---|---|---|---|---|
| Asian | | | 3.5 | | | 3.5 |
| Bangli | | | | | 1.0 | 1.0 |
| Brazilian | 0.5 | | | | | 0.5 |
| Caribbean Indian | | | | | 1.0 | 1.0 |
| Chinese | 4.0 | 7.0 | | | | 11.0 |
| East Indian | 1.0 | | | | | 1.0 |
| Farsi | | | | | 1.0 | 1.0 |
| Filipino | | | 0.5 | | 1.0 | 1.5 |
| Greek | 4.0 | | 2.5 | | 1.0 | 7.5 |
| Haitian | | | 2.0 | | | 2.0 |
| Hebrew | | | | | 4.0 | 4.0 |
| Italian | 16.0 | | | | | 16.0 |
| Japanese | 12.0 | | 3.0 | | | 15.0 |
| Korean | | 5.0 | 1.5 | | | 6.5 |
| Polish | 2.5 | | | | | 2.5 |
| Russian | | | | | 1.5 | 1.5 |
| Spanish | | | 89.5 | 133.5 | 16.0 | 239.0 |
| Yugoslav | | | 0.5 | | | 0.5 |
| Total Hours | 40.0 | 12.0 | 103.0 | 133.5 | 26.5 | 305.0 |

Source: Urban Research Center, NYU.

people in New York from a dozen countries and every kind of social and political background.[22]

LPTV-44 also serves the homosexual community with a program, *Out in the '80s*, the city's "only regularly scheduled over-the-air program aimed at the gay community."[23]

## The Local Community Press

The local community press provides coverage of the events in New York's neighborhoods that are not available in the major dailies or on the dominant radio and television stations. As Bagdikian argues, given the pressures of advertising to appeal to the wealthiest and broadest-based audience possible, "without being deliberately racist or class-prejudiced, newspapers, magazines, and broadcasters de-emphasize the content that

will be relevant or interesting to the less affluent and the older population."[24] Given the sheer size of New York City, the city's dominant print
and television cannot regularly cover all areas and population groups located within the city. Even when local television news programs have
been expanded, there is a tendency to carry entertainment and feature
stories that are of interest to the broadest possible audience within the
metropolitan region. Further, the major newspapers and television stations are headquartered in Manhattan, and unless a winning lottery ticket
is purchased, a highway collapses, or a vicious crime occurs in the other
four boroughs, relatively few news stories originate outside of Manhattan.

Staten Island is the only borough that has its own daily newspaper, the
*Staten Island Advance*, owned by the Newhouse chain. The other boroughs have numerous weekly community papers that explicitly cover
specific neighborhoods. It should be noted, though, that both the *Daily
News* and *New York Newsday* include borough-oriented inserts in the editions circulated in Brooklyn and Queens. Within the past two decades,
there has been a resurgence in grassroots print media in New York City.
Excluding the countless weekly shoppers, there are more than sixteen
community weeklies in the five boroughs, along with two monthlies and
one biweekly publication established after 1970, whose combined circulation exceeds 700,000 (see Table 10.5).

Community weeklies also adapt rapidly to changes in their environment. For example, *Battery News*, a community newspaper originally
created for residents of Battery Park City, has enlarged its market and
circulation area to cover all of lower Manhattan below Canal Street as a
result of the growing residential and commercial life in that part of the
city. Most of New York's community newspapers provide readers with
stories about events within their neighborhoods and such local issues as
crime and land use. New York City's four major dailies can give only
limited coverage of the city's diverse neighborhoods and usually on issues
of citywide importance, such as a local school board scandal, choosing a
site for a prison or waste disposal plant, or high-rise development amidst
a low-rise community.

Neighborhood weeklies include articles about local residents, calendars
of community meetings and events, and other local interest stories. Such
weeklies are also filled with advertisements by local merchants who can
reach their customers without having to buy space in the citywide dailies.
In fact, advertising revenues from local businesses are vital to the economic health of local newspapers. Indeed, "the great majority of local
weeklies are marginal financial operations."[25] Of course, the major daily
newspapers also face advertising pressures, and supplements in education, real estate, and travel are designed to attract advertisers.

**Table 10.5    Community Weekly Newspapers, by Borough**

| Borough | Newspaper | Year Established | Circulation |
|---|---|---|---|
| Bronx | Bronx News | 1973 | 20,000 |
| | Bronx Press-Review | 1939 | 16,000 |
| | Co-op City News | 1968 | 15,000 |
| | Co-Op City Times | 1969 | 20,000 |
| | Parkchester News | 1971 | 14,000 |
| | The Riverdale Press | 1950 | 14,500 |
| | Total Weekly Circulation | | 99,500 |
| Brooklyn | Bay News | 1945 | 20,700 |
| | Bay Ridge Courier | 1978 | 10,300 |
| | Bensonhurst News | 1955 | ‡ |
| | Brooklyn Graphic | 1958 | 20,000 |
| | Brooklyn Heights Press | 1937 | 18,500 |
| | Brooklyn Home Reporter & Sunset News | 1955 | ‡ |
| | Brooklyn Papers | 1978 | ‡ |
| | Brooklyn Phoenix | 1973 | 18,000 |
| | Brooklyn Record | 1937 | 8,500 |
| | Brooklyn Spectator | 1933 | ‡ |
| | Canarsie Courier, Inc. | 1921 | 13,700 |
| | Canarsie Digest | 1959 | 13,800 |
| | Flatbush Life | 1956 | 13,800 |
| | Greenpoint Gazette Advertiser | 1928 | 8,000 |
| | Kings Courier | 1951 | 19,200 |
| | Total Weekly Circulation | | 181,300 |
| Manhattan | Battery News* | 1987 | 19,000 |
| | Chelsea Clinton News | 1940 | 12,000 |
| | East Side Express | 1976 | 23,500 |
| | New York Heights Inwood | 1972 | 5,800 |
| | Our Town Newspaper | 1974 | 131,000 |
| | Town & Village | 1947 | 9,000 |
| | Villager | 1933 | 14,000 |
| | Westsider | 1972 | 15,000 |
| | Total Weekly Circulation | | 210,300 |

*Source:* Urban Research Center, NYU.

*Biweekly
†Monthly
‡Information unavailable

**Table 10.5** *(continued)*

| Borough | Newspaper | Year Established | Circulation |
|---|---|---|---|
| Queens | *Bayside Times* | 1935 | 16,500 |
| | *Forum of South Queens* | 1977 | 15,000 |
| | *Glendale Register* | 1935 | 10,000 |
| | *Leader Observer* | 1909 | 8,000 |
| | *Little Neck/Glen Oaks Glen Oaks Ledger* | 1918 | 7,000 |
| | *Long Island City Journal* | 1987 | 10,000 |
| | *North Shore News* | 1979 | 12,000 |
| | *Queens Chronicle* | 1980 | 70,000 |
| | *Queens Ledger* | 1873 | 15,000 |
| | *Queens Tribune* | 1970 | 100,000 |
| | *Ridgewood Times* | 1908 | 20,000 |
| | *Rockaway Press* | 1985 | 10,000 |
| | *Western Queens Gazette* | 1982 | 35,000 |
| | *Woodside Herald* | 1936 | 14,000 |
| | Total Weekly Circulation | | 342,500 |
| Staten Island | *Star Reporter* | 1965 | ‡ |
| | *Staten Island Eagle†* | 1987 | 131,000 |
| | *Staten Island Register†* | 1975 | 95,000 |
| | Total Weekly Circulation | | 226,000 |

Although the local weeklies fill the news vacuum created by the lack of systematic community coverage in New York City's predominant newspapers, there is often a considerable gap in the quality of journalism. Many communities must rely on neighborhood publications for coverage of their communities. Frank Griffin, owner of Brooklyn's *Home Reporter and Sunset News*, states that "Brooklyn is virtually ignored by the dailies," and that the *Daily News'* borough inserts exist "merely for advertising reasons," hardly providing an effective local news medium.[26]

No discussion of New York City's grass-roots media would be complete without a description of the *Village Voice*, a weekly newspaper formed in the 1950s that addresses citywide and national issues. The *Voice's* coverage of municipal corruption and cultural trends provides a powerful alternative to the dominant media. In recent years, a new citywide weekly newspaper, the *New York Observer*, began publication. It focuses principally on Manhattan-based events and personalities.

Besides defining the community and filling the news vacuum with local coverage, community newspapers serve other social and political functions as well. The neighborhood paper is a "facilitating mechanism,"
which helps the urban dweller to make sense out of a complex and often
confusing environment.[27] Not all communities have their own newspapers. The presence of a community weekly can be attributed to the willingness of local merchants to invest advertising dollars to reach local
readers, the sense of community cohesiveness possessed by local residents, and the fact that the citywide media are too big to cover the diversity of small-scale communities within New York City.

## Cable Television in New York City

New York City was one of the first large cities in the United States to have
cable franchises. In 1971, the Lindsay Administration granted two cable
television franchises for Manhattan; it took more than 15 years to grant
cable franchises in the other four boroughs of New York City. Four major
cable television franchises are discussed here: Manhattan Cable TV and
Paragon Cable, which serve lower and upper Manhattan, respectively;
American Cablevision of Queens (ACQ); and Brooklyn-Queens Cable
(BQ), which services both Brooklyn and Queens. The Manhattan franchises have a combined subscribership in excess of 300,000 households
and can provide up to 36 channels over the existing—and technologically
outmoded—cable plant. The cable systems in the other four boroughs
have been installed over the last several years and have the technological
capability to provide up to 99 channels of programming, although they
now utilize approximately 70 channels. As Table 10.6 shows, all four cable companies offer some ethnic and foreign language programming, but
the public and leased access stations do not serve as a full-fledged means
of local community communications.

Cable television, with significantly greater channel capacity than
broadcast television, does have the potential to provide population groups
within cities with their own electronic channels of communication.[28] Cable television could be used to strengthen local communities within cities,
by publicizing local events, providing an electronic forum to discuss
neighborhood issues, serving as an advertising vehicle for local merchants, and by allowing elected officials to communicate with their local
constituents.

All of the cable television systems include VHF and UHF channels as
part of their basic service, and the improved UHF television reception
with cable is important for the foreign language and public UHF stations.
Black Entertainment Television (BET) is included in basic cable service,

**Table 10.6** **Foreign Language and Ethnic Cable TV Programming in New York City (hours per week)**

| | BET* | Chinese | Greek | Indian | Jewish | Korean | Spanish |
|---|---|---|---|---|---|---|---|
| Manhattan Cable | 168 | 28 | | | 3 | | 2 |
| Paragon Cable | 168 | | | | | | |
| American Cablevision of Queens (ACQ) | 168 | 84 | 70 | 56 | 3 | 84 | 168 |
| Brooklyn-Queens Cable (BQ) | 168 | 84 | 70 | 56 | 3 | 84 | 168 |

*Source:* Urban Research Center, NYU.

*Black Entertainment Television.

yet cable franchises report that many viewers have complained that BET does not offer enough specifically black programming. Manhattan Cable broadcasts 31 hours of locally originated ethnic and foreign language programming per week. Ninety percent of this time (28 hours) is devoted to Apple Television (ATV), a Chinese broadcasting company that can be received only by an additional monthly charge from ACQ and BQ Cable. More than one-third of Paragon's public and leased access is used by blacks, and 35.1 percent by Latinos.

American Cablevision of Queens (ACQ) is situated in an area of Queens where over half of the residents are minorities; 39 percent are foreign-born, 49 percent speak a foreign language, and 19 percent do not speak English at all. By adding the five pay channels—The Korean Channel, Apple Television, Indian TV, The Greek Channel, and Galavision[29]— ACQ and BQ have increased cable subscriptions, since basic cable is required to receive a pay channel. Clearly, cable has been able to respond to the growing foreign-born population, especially in the outer boroughs.

## Conclusion

This chapter highlights the dual structure of the media in New York City. On the one hand, the so-called dominant media are geared to the broadest possible audience and consolidated so that a small number of firms control the major television channels, radio syndicates, and major daily newspapers. On the other hand, a multiplicity of grassroots media outlets in New York City have emerged to counter the inadequate coverage and appeal of the mainstream, and often national, media. The duality of the city's media is especially apparent in the hundreds of foreign language, ethnic, and community-based newspapers, and in the extensive special radio and cable television programming.

There is a growing disparity between the traditional television and print media that serve New York City and its surrounding counties and the groups that make up the majority of New York City's population. The major daily newspapers and broadcast television and radio stations have a limited capability to serve New York City's diverse ethnic and minority groups, and, as a result, there has been a remarkable growth in new media, encompassing print, radio, and television. Despite the trends towards the centralization of news and media sources, a diversity of information sources in New York City serve the various population groups within the city. The evidence presented here indicates that Hispanic and Asian groups have been far more able than have black groups to utilize new television channels and print media. Moreover, there is a growing bifurcation of the media, with the citywide print and television increasingly serving the affluent middle class within the city and surrounding region, while radio and community newspapers serve specific ethnic and minority groups. Certainly, no single media source conveys an image of New York that includes all elements of the political and social community within which New Yorkers live. This arena offers a strong example of how elites are able to organize their mass communications coherently while those of peripheral groups have become increasingly fragmented.

# Notes

1. Rosenthal, A.M., *Thirty-Eight Witnesses* (New York: New York Times, 1964), p. 8.
2. Diamond, Edwin, and Piera Pine, "The Media in the Game of Politics," in Bellush, Jewel, and Dick Netzer, eds., *Urban Politics, New York Style* (Armonk, NY: M. E. Sharpe, 1990), pp. 339–358.
3. Ledbetter, James, "Tab Wars," *7 Days* (June 1, 1988), p. 6.
4. Ibid.
5. Katz, Jon, "It Came from Queens," *7 Days* (June 1, 1988), p. 8.
6. Kim, Ilsoo, "The Koreans: Small Business in an Urban Frontier," *New Immigrants in New York*, Foner, Nancy, ed. (New York: Columbia University Press, 1987), p. 227.

7. Ibid, p. 236.

8. Stafford, Susan Buchanan, "The Haitians: The Cultural Meaning of Race and Ethnicity," in Foner, ed., *New Immigrants in New York*, p. 140.

9. Bagdikian, Ben, *Media Monopoly* (Boston: Beacon Press, 1987), p. 19.

10. Gonzalez, Juan, "Not Masters of Our Media Fate," *Daily News* (July 24, 1988), p. 14.

11. Meier, Barry, "A Primary Source Outside Mainstream," *New York Newsday* (April 13, 1988), p. 26.

12. Wilson, Eliot, and Felix Gutierrez, *Minorities and Media: The End of Mass Communication* (Beverly Hills, CA: Sage, 1985). p. 38.

13. Gonzalez, 1988, p. 14.

14. Ibid.

15. Schmidt, William E., "Black Talk Radio: A Vital Force Is Emerging to Mobilize Opinion," *New York Times* (March 31, 1989), p. A1.

16. Ibid., p. A12.

17. Meier, p. 9.

18. Ibid.

19. Shipp, E. R., "WLIB: Radio 'Heartbeat' of Black Life," *New York Times* (Jan. 22, 1988), p. B3.

20. Ibid.

21. *Broadcasting/Cablecasting Yearbook* (1988).

22. Eder, Bruce, "Channel 44: The Little Station That Could," *Village Voice* (May 24, 1988), p. 57.

23. Ibid., p. 58.

24. Bagdikian, *Media Monopoly*, p. 109.

25. Deacy, Jack, "What the Big Dailies Don't Tell You About What's Going On in the City," *New York* (May 24, 1971), p. 41.

26. Ibid., p. 43.

27. Stamm, Keith R., *Newspaper Use and Community Ties: Toward A Dynamic Theory* (Norwood, NJ: Ablex Publishing Corp., 1985), p. 5.

28. White, Stephen, "Toward a Modest Experiment in Cable Television," *The Public Interest* (Spring 1967).

29. Moss, Brian, "Foreign, but Familiar," *Daily News* (Feb. 14, 1988), p. 11.

# 11

## Patterns of Neighborhood Change

### Frank F. DeGiovanni / Lorraine C. Minnite

## Introduction

New York City has experienced a number of major economic and demographic changes in recent decades. The city's population declined precipitously during the 1970s before rising somewhat during the 1980s: while the overall population was shrinking, the minority population increased to become a majority by 1987.[1] Resident employment levels followed a similar pattern: dropping from 3.2 million in 1969 to 2.5 million in 1976, then increasing to 3 million in 1987.[2] The employment upswing over the last decade was accompanied by a marked shift in the industry and occupational mix.[3]

These broad social and economic trends fueled parallel changes in New York City's housing stock during the 1970s and 1980s. The number of occupied dwelling units fell from 2,839,000 in 1975 to 2,792,000 in 1981 before rebounding to 2,840,000 in 1987.[4] The city lost a net of approximately 360,000 units between 1970 and 1984 as the housing market reacted to the substantial downturn in population and employment.[5] Similarly, the population growth and economic recovery during the 1980s generated the upturn in the city's housing market after 1981.

This chapter examines the overall changes in New York City's housing stock and selected demographic and socioeconomic changes in the households occupying these units between 1981 and 1987, a period when the city's housing market began to recover from the long decline of the previous 11 years. The changes observed during this 6-year period reveal a marked improvement in the overall strength of the city's housing market.

But a closer examination of these trends also reveals that many New York did not share in the overall improvement in housing and economic conditions that occurred in the city during the 1980s.

The first section describes aggregate changes in selected aspects of New York City's housing stock and population between 1981 and 1987, relying on the Housing and Vacancy Survey conducted every three years in New York City (see Appendix 11.I for a description of this data source and the study methodology). The second section uses the longitudinal file of the Housing and Vacancy Survey to explore the dynamics of the changes underlying the aggregate trends described in the first section. It also examines racial and income differences in these trends. The third section examines the spatial distribution of these housing and population trends over New York City's geography, and the final section presents the conclusions drawn from the analysis.

# Overall Trends in Housing and Socioeconomic Characteristics

Housing analysts generally use three major dimensions to investigate housing needs or problems—availability, adequacy, and affordability. *Availability* indicates whether a particular geographic area contains a sufficient supply of housing, regardless of quality, for the population. The quality of the available housing indicates whether the existing supply is *adequate*. Finally, *affordability* defines whether area residents can pay for the existing housing without sacrificing other essential goods or services.

## Availability

Two indicators are used to determine whether a housing market contains enough units to provide all households with dwellings and reasonable opportunities for mobility. The first is the net rental vacancy rate—the percentage of all rental units available for rent that meet minimum standards of habitability. The second is the median vacancy duration—the median length of time that available units remain on the market. These two indicators reveal whether a housing shortage exists.

New York City remains a city of renters, with 1,884,210 rental units (69.8 percent) and 817,476 owner units (30.2 percent) in 1987 (see Table 11.1). The proportion of owner-occupied dwelling units, however, has increased steadily since 1981, when 27.8 percent of the units were occupied by their owners. But the number of available habitable rental units in

**Table 11.1    Selected Characteristics**
**of New York City's Housing and Population: 1981 and 1987**

| Characteristic | 1981 | 1987 |
|---|---|---|
| Availability | | |
| Total number of occupied units | | |
|   Occupied rental units | 1,933,887 | 1,844,210 |
|   Occupied owner units | 746,112 | 817,416 |
|   Total vacant rental units | 42,157 | 47,486 |
| Net rental vacancy rate | 2.13% | 2.46% |
| Median vacancy duration | 1.9 mo. | 1.8 mo. |
| Vacancy rate for units | 1.78% | 0.96% |
|   < $300 rent | | |
| Median rent/mo. of vacant units | $240 | $450 |
| Adequacy | | |
| Percentage of dilapidated units | 4.2% | 2.1% |
| Percentage of units with > 3 | 20.6% | 14.4% |
|   maintenance deficiencies | | |
| Percentage of units with boarded-up | 27.4% | 19.9% |
|   units nearby | | |
| Percentage of units overcrowded | 6.5% | 7.1% |
| Affordability | | |
| Median income—all households | $12,800 | $20,000 |
| Median income—renters | $10,500 | $16,000 |
| Median income needed to afford | $9,600 | $18,000 |
|   median rent of vacant units | | |
| Percentage of renters with incomes | 34.4% | 31.4% |
|   < 125% of poverty | | |
| Percentage of renters with incomes | 25.4% | 24.2% |
|   below poverty | | |
| Median monthly rent | | |
|   Current dollars | $263 | $395 |
|   1987 constant dollars | $347 | $395 |
| Number of units with rents | 615,316 | 409,459 |
|   < $300/mo. | | |
| Median rent–income ratio | 27.0 | 29.0 |
| Percentage of renters with | 45.6% | 47.5% |
|   rent–income ratio > 30% | | |
| Percentage of renters with | 30.5% | 31.5% |
|   rent–income ratio > 40% | | |
| Housing Need | | |
|   Scale 1 | 57.1% | 55.3% |
|   Scale 2 | 47.6% | 44.2% |

*Source:* 1981 and 1987 Housing and Vacancy Surveys.

*Note:* In Scale 1, the rent–income ratio criterion is set at 30 percent; the criterion is set at 40 percent in Scale 2.

1987 (47,486) constituted only 2.46 percent of the rental stock. This represents a slight improvement over the 1981 vacancy rate of 2.13 percent, but it still falls far below the 5 percent vacancy rate which housing experts believe to be the minimum necessary for a smoothly functioning housing market. Not only are few units available for rent, but habitable vacant units remain on the market for only a short time, exacerbating the effects of the shortage. The median length of time that units remained unoccupied in 1987 was 1.8 months, down from 1.9 months in 1981.

These two indicators confirm that New York City suffers from a severe shortage of housing. This shortage persists despite a net gain of nearly 48,000 units of housing stock since 1981. Although this increase may not seem large in comparison to the size of the stock in 1981 (2,792,000 units), it represents a major change from past patterns. It is especially meaningful because it was the first time in 25 years that a net growth in housing occurred over a 6-year period.[6]

A low vacancy rate affects renters of all incomes. An examination of the characteristics of the vacant units, however, reveals that low-income renters face a particularly difficult time looking for housing. The vacancy rate for units renting below $300 per month was less than 0.96 percent in 1987. This represents a worsening of an already desperate situation, since the vacancy rate in 1981 for units renting below $300 per month already was a low 1.78 percent.

The severe shortage of housing is not the only problem facing low-income renters. Most of the available units are beyond the reach of the average renter household. Fifty percent of renter households earned less than $16,000 in 1987; this income enables households to afford a maximum rent of $400 per month. But the median rent of the vacant units in 1987 was $450 per month, which only households earning at least $18,000 per year, or $2,000 more than the renter median income, could afford.[7] In 1981, the median asking rent for vacant units was $240 per month, affordable to households earning $9,600 per year. Since the median income of renters in 1981 was $10,500, the average renter could afford this unit. Clearly, the available housing has grown further beyond the reach of the average renter since 1981.[8]

*Adequacy*

Concern over housing quality has historically driven the creation of housing codes and federal housing programs. Initially, attention was focused on the worst housing deficiencies, such as the absence of major systems and separate bathrooms, inadequate ventilation, and severe overcrowding. As these conditions have been nearly eliminated nationally and locally, concern has shifted to maintenance and upkeep. Unfortunately, no reliable measurement of building conditions for the entire city exists. The Housing and Vacancy Survey attempts to describe the quality of the occupied rental stock using four indicators of housing quality: dilapidation,[9] maintenance deficiencies,[10] presence of boarded-up buildings in the neighborhood,[11] and overcrowding.[12]

A comparison of the HVS results for 1981 and 1987 indicates a dramatic improvement in three of the four dimensions of housing quality in New York City during this time period. The number of dilapidated units has decreased from 79,000 in 1981 to 37,000 in 1987, a 53 percent improvement. Consequently, only 2.1 percent of all dwelling units posed a serious health threat to their occupants in 1987. A somewhat less precipitous, but equally important, drop occurred in the proportion of units with three or more maintenance deficiencies, from 20.6 percent in 1981 to 14.4 percent in 1987, a 30.1 percent decline. The HVS respondents' report of boarded-up structures nearby also declined between 1981 and 1987, from 27.4 percent to 19.9 percent, a shrinkage of 27.4 percent in 6 years. The only housing quality indicator that did not show marked improvement between 1981 and 1987 is overcrowding, which increased from 6.5 percent in 1981 to 7.1 percent in 1987. This comparison is misleading, however, since all of this increase occurred between 1981 and 1984 (from 6.5 percent to 7.7 percent), after which the percentage of overcrowded units decreased.

## Components of Affordability

Because housing is a market good, any consideration of housing problems must examine the ability of housing consumers to rent or purchase the existing stock. The issue is whether households can rent housing without sacrificing other necessary expenditures. Housing affordability is measured by examining the proportion of a household's income that is spent on housing. The generally accepted rule of thumb, codified in federal housing programs, was that households should pay no more than 25 percent of their income for rent. Despite serious criticisms that a uniform rent–income ratio was highly inappropriate because the proportion of income that households could afford to pay for housing without sacrificing other essentials varies greatly with household size and income, the 25 percent standard remained in effect until 1980, when the Reagan administration increased the proportion of household income that must be spent for housing in federal programs to 30 percent.[13] This figure has become the new norm for use in analyzing housing affordability: households paying more than 30 percent of their income for rent are considered to have a rent hardship or burden.

Analysis of housing affordability requires examination of trends in both renter income and rents, since changes in the rent–income ratio can result from changes in both the denominator (income) or the numerator (rent) of the ratio. Because this indicator measures both demand and supply aspects of housing, it has been criticized as an ambiguous, possibly even misleading, indicator of housing problems.[14] This criticism rests on the argument that increasing rent–income ratios reflect consumer preferences for better housing, even at higher rents, not lack of adequate housing at rents that do not impose burdens or hardships. The detailed knowledge of other changes in New York City's housing stock described earlier should help in ascertaining whether the observed trends in the rent–income ratio reflect increased problems facing renters.

## Trends in Household Income

The median income of all households in New York City increased 60 percent between 1980 ($12,500) and 1986 ($20,000).[15] This gain substantially exceeded inflation, resulting in a real growth in income of 16.9 percent over the 6-year period. All of the real growth in income occurred after 1983, since income grew more slowly than inflation between 1980 and 1983. This real gain in income between 1983 and 1986 is a positive sign, because it reverses a 6-year trend of real losses in household income between 1977 and 1983.

Trends in renter income paralleled those for all households. The median income of renter households in 1986 was $16,000, an increase of 52 percent since 1980. In real terms, the median renter income declined by 1.4 percent between 1980 and 1983, then rebounded during the next three years by 12.9 percent. The real growth in renter income for the 6-year period between 1980 and 1986 was 11.3 percent.

The 1987 HVS also shows that the rate of poverty declined between 1980 and 1986. Slightly more than 24 percent of all renter households had incomes below the poverty line in 1986, a drop of 10.7 percent since 1983 and 4.7 percent since 1980.[16] The poor and so-called near-poor renter population—households with incomes between 100 and 125 percent of poverty—also appeared to decline from 34.4 percent in 1980 to 31.4 percent in 1986. Again, all of this decline occurred after 1983, since the poor and near-poor population increased from 1977 to 1983.[17]

Despite these improvements, the gap between the poorest and richest households widened during these years. The average income of the poorest 20 percent of the households grew at a much slower pace than the average income for the rest of the population between 1977 and 1986, with the most marked difference occurring during the 1983 to 1986 period.[18] By 1986, the wealthiest households, on average, earned 20 times more than the lowest income households: that ratio had been only 14.5 in 1981.[19]

*Trends in Rent*

The median gross rent, or rent plus utilities, was $395 per month in New York City in 1987, a current dollar increase of 50.2 percent since 1981. After adjusting for inflation, rents jumped by 13.8 percent between 1981 and 1987. As with incomes, most of this increase (9.3 percent) came during the 3-year period between 1984 and 1987.[20] This represents the largest real growth in rents since 1978, a rate of growth more than double that (4.6 percent) experienced between 1981 and 1984.

This strong real growth in rents is an important sign of the overall improvement in the economic vitality of New York City's rental inventory. The overall strengthening of the investment climate for housing, though, poses problems for lower income renters who must rely on the low-rent segment of the inventory. The number of units renting below $300 per month in 1987 constant dollars, which households earning $12,000 in 1987 could afford, fell by 205,857 units (a 33 percent decrease) from 1981.[21] As a consequence, units renting at or below $300 per month (in constant 1987 dollars) comprised only 26 percent of the rental stock in 1987, down from 35.9 percent in 1981. This dwindling inventory of low-rent units probably has made a large contribution to the affordability problems discussed below.

*Affordability of Rental Housing*

Real income declined between 1980 and 1983 before jumping by more than 12 percent during the next 3 years. But real rents increased by 4.6 percent between 1981 and 1984 and then another 9.3 percent by 1987. It is not surprising, then, that the median rent–income ratio increased from 27 percent to 29 percent in the early period, since rents rose much faster than incomes. After 1984, incomes rose slightly faster than rents, but the median rent–income ratio remained constant at 29 percent.

The increase in the median rent–income ratio was accompanied by a growth in the percentage of renters suffering from a rent hardship. Approximately 47.5 percent of all renter households in 1987 paid more than 30 percent of their income for rent, compared to 45.6 percent in 1981. Even if a more stringent criterion, a 40 percent rent–income ratio, is used to measure rent burden, affordability worsened even more during these 6 years (30.5 percent in 1981 versus 32.9 percent in 1987). According to federal standards, then, nearly one-half of all New York City renter households paid too much of their income for rent in 1987. This problem is particularly acute for the lowest income renters. Over half the renters in the four lowest income deciles paid more than 40 percent of their income for rent in 1987; over half the households in the three lowest deciles paid more than 50 percent of their income for rent.[22] These results indicate graphically that a large percentage of New York City renters cannot afford their dwelling units and, therefore, sacrifice other essential goods and services.

### The Need for Housing Assistance in New York City

These trends indicate that the New York City housing market improved substantially since 1981. The demand for housing has noticeably strengthened, especially when compared with the trends of the previous years. Real rents rose substantially; this increased economic viability encouraged investment in the housing stock, and the quality of the housing improved considerably. Driven by declining interest rates, growing population, expanding employment opportunities, and rising real incomes, these trends stemmed the flood of housing losses that had devastated the city's neighborhoods between 1970 and 1984.[23]

Yet the strengthening of the housing market also placed pressure on a relatively fixed supply of housing, leading to increased overcrowding, loss of occupied and available affordable low-rent units, and increased rent burdens for many households. While housing quality and the overall investment climate improved, housing affordability worsened. Moreover, the recovery left many New Yorkers still living in substandard physical conditions.

The number and percentage of renter households needing assistance to remove poor physical conditions or to eliminate rent burdens can be estimated by forming a housing need scale from the variables used to measure housing quality and affordability.[24] This scale was constructed by combining three indicators of housing quality (dilapidation, three or more maintenance deficiencies, and overcrowding) with an indicator of rent hardship. If a dwelling unit met any one of the four criteria, the household was considered to have a housing need. Two different estimates of need were identified. The first used a rent–income ratio in excess of 30 percent to measure rent burden, while the second estimate used a ratio of 40 percent or more.[25]

The first estimate of need indicates that the percentage of city households needing housing assistance increased from 57.1 in 1981 to 59.2 in 1984, before declining to 55.3 in 1987. Most of this decline was due to the marked improvement in the physical condition of housing observed between 1984 and 1987. Even with the decline in need, the majority of renter households in the city require some form of intervention to eliminate either poor physical living conditions or the burden of paying too much of their income for rent.

Replacing the 30 percent rent–income ratio with the 40 percent ratio produces a lower estimate of housing problems in each of the three years: 47.6 percent in 1981, 49.6 percent in 1984, and 44.2 percent in 1987. The pattern of change, however, remains the same. Even with the more stringent rent–income ratio, a substantial percentage (44.2 percent) of renter households in New York City had serious housing problems in 1987.

## The Dynamics of Change In Housing Conditions

The previous section described aggregate changes in the New York City housing market based the 1981, 1984, and 1987 cross-sectional files of the Housing and Vacancy Survey. This section uses the longitudinal file of dwelling units included in each of these three Housing and Vacancy Surveys to analyze the underlying causes of these changes. It decomposes the variables measuring dwelling unit and resident characteristics into four categories: (1) improvement of the unit/household's situation between 1981 and 1987 so that it would no longer be considered a problem; (2) deterioration of its situation so that it would be considered a problem; (3) continued existence of a problem situation for all 6 years between 1981 and 1987; and (4) continued existence of a non-problematic condition during this period. This classification makes it possible to distinguish units or households with chronic problems that have persisted for 6 years from those whose situation appears to be more transitory, moving into or out of problematic conditions. Table 11.2 presents the results of this analysis.

Two patterns emerge. First, a substantial amount of change occurred in both directions between 1981 and 1987. The condition of a substantial number of units or of their occupants improved, while many others deteriorated during this period.[26] Thus, in the midst of an overall improvement in conditions, a substantial percentage of the units or their residents still suffered setbacks. Similarly, a significant percentage of units or residents experienced improvements even when the overall citywide trends ran in the other direction.

Four types of change experienced by many housing units that run counter to general trends are particularly relevant: decline in real income;

**Table 11.2    Change in Housing and Socioeconomic Characteristics:**
**1981–1987**

| Indicator<br>Type of Change, 1981–1987 | Cross-Sectional Totals | | | Composition of Change<br>1981–1987 |
| --- | --- | --- | --- | --- |
| | 1981<br>% | 1984<br>% | 1987<br>% | % |
| Tenure (% Renter) | 28.80 | 30.60 | 30.70 | |
| Own to rent | | | | 4.57 |
| Rent to own | | | | 6.45 |
| Remain own | | | | 24.26 |
| Remain rent | | | | 64.73 |
| Race (% Nonwhite) | 37.40 | 40.70 | 42.40 | |
| White to nonwhite | | | | 9.20 |
| Nonwhite to white | | | | 4.51 |
| Remain nonwhite | | | | 52.52 |
| Remain white | | | | 33.78 |
| ≥ 3 Maintenance Deficiencies | 20.00 | 20.80 | 14.70 | |
| Increased to > 3 | | | | 8.76 |
| Decreased to < 3 | | | | 14.52 |
| Remain > 3 | | | | 6.81 |
| Remain < 3 | | | | 69.91 |
| Overcrowding | 5.50 | 6.30 | 6.00 | |
| Became overcrowded | | | | 4.08 |
| No longer overcrowded | | | | 4.71 |
| Remain overcrowded | | | | 1.43 |
| Never overcrowded | | | | 89.78 |
| Boarded-up Buildings on Block | 26.20 | 23.20 | 18.50 | |
| None to some | | | | 7.85 |
| Some to none | | | | 15.98 |
| Remain some | | | | 11.69 |
| Remain none | | | | 64.48 |
| Change in Housing Quality Scale* | 19.50 | 19.70 | 13.70 | |
| Decline | | | | 8.30 |
| Improvement | | | | 14.15 |
| Remain poor | | | | 6.11 |
| Remain good | | | | 71.44 |
| Growth in Real Income | NA | NA | NA | |
| Real decline | | | | 46.33 |
| Real growth | | | | 53.65 |
| No change | | | | 0.01 |

**Table 11.2** (*continued*)

| Indicator<br>Type of Change, 1981–1987 | Cross-Sectional Totals | | | Composition<br>of Change |
|---|---|---|---|---|
| | 1981<br>% | 1984<br>% | 1987<br>% | 1981–1987<br>% |
| Public Assistance | 9.70 | 10.30 | 9.70 | |
| Off to on P.A. | | | | 5.40 |
| On to off P.A. | | | | 5.85 |
| Remain on P.A. | | | | 4.39 |
| Remain off P.A. | | | | 84.35 |
| | | | | |
| Income < 125% Poverty | 28.30 | 28.70 | 25.70 | |
| Went below 125% poverty | | | | 11.16 |
| Went above 125% poverty | | | | 14.33 |
| Remain below 125% poverty | | | | 15.06 |
| Remain above 125% poverty | | | | 59.45 |
| | | | | |
| Real Rent Growth | NA | NA | NA | |
| Real decline | | | | 36.92 |
| Real growth | | | | 62.62 |
| No change | | | | 0.45 |
| | | | | |
| % Units Renting < $300 | 36.30 | 32.50 | 26.00 | |
| (1987 Constant $) | | | | |
| Loss of low rent units | | | | 17.22 |
| Gain of low rent units | | | | 5.29 |
| Remain > $300 | | | | 55.25 |
| Remain < $300 | | | | 22.24 |
| | | | | |
| Afford Median Vacant Unit | 55.60 | 50.00 | 46.10 | |
| Decrease in affordability | | | | 21.16 |
| Increase in affordability | | | | 11.87 |
| Remain unaffordable | | | | 34.46 |
| Remain affordable | | | | 32.51 |
| | | | | |
| Rent–Income Ratio > 30% | 42.90 | 45.60 | 44.60 | |
| Increased > 30% | | | | 19.03 |
| Decreased < 30% | | | | 18.39 |
| Remain > 30% | | | | 25.11 |
| Remain below 30% | | | | 37.47 |
| | | | | |
| Rent–Income Ratio > 40% | 29.90 | 32.20 | 31.20 | |
| Became burdensome | | | | 16.71 |
| No longer burdensome | | | | 16.12 |
| Remain burdensome | | | | 14.43 |
| Remain affordable | | | | 52.74 |

277

Table 11.2 (continued)

| Indicator<br>Type of Change, 1981–1987 | Cross-Sectional Totals | | | Composition<br>of Change |
| | 1981<br>% | 1984<br>% | 1987<br>% | 1981–1987<br>% |
| --- | --- | --- | --- | --- |
| Change in Rent–Income Ratio | NA | NA | NA | |
| Decrease | | | | 47.09 |
| Increase | | | | 50.53 |
| No change | | | | 2.38 |
| | | | | |
| Housing Need Scale 1† | 56.40 | 59.40 | 54.90 | |
| Develop need | | | | 16.90 |
| No longer needy | | | | 19.80 |
| Remain needy | | | | 38.30 |
| Never needy | | | | 25.00 |
| | | | | |
| Housing Need Scale 2‡ | 47.00 | 49.70 | 44.10 | |
| Develop need | | | | 16.50 |
| No longer needy | | | | 20.70 |
| Remain needy | | | | 28.30 |
| Never needy | | | | 34.40 |

Source: 1981, 1984, and 1987 Housing and Vacancy Surveys.

* A unit is considered to have poor housing quality if it is dilapidated or has more than three maintenance deficiencies.
† Housing need exists if one of the following conditions is met: it is dilapidated, has more than three maintenance deficiencies, is overcrowded, or pays more than 30 percent of its income for rent.
‡ This scale is identical to Housing Need Scale 1, except that a ratio of 40 percent is used to measure rent hardship.

increase in units whose residents' incomes fell below 125 percent of poverty; decline in real rents; and increasing housing need. While the incomes of 53.7 percent of the occupants of units in the longitudinal HVS file increased in real terms during this period, 46.3 percent of the units' residents experienced a real decline in income. Almost one-half of the units thus had a net loss in the purchasing power of their occupants even though the buying power of the median New York household grew by 16.9 percent. Similarly, 11.1 percent of the units had households whose incomes fell below 125 percent of the poverty level between 1980 and 1986, compared to 14.3 percent of the units whose residents' incomes rose above this level.

Changes counter to overall city trends can also be observed on the supply side. While real rents increased in the median unit by 13.8 percent between 1981 and 1987, 36.9 percent of the units suffered a real loss in rents. In addition, a housing problem emerged in 16.9 percent of the rental units between 1981 and 1987, even though housing need declined by 3 percent on a citywide basis.

A similar pattern of changes also emerges where overall conditions are worsening. For example, the ability of the average renter household to afford the median vacant available unit declined during the 6-year study period, yet this unit became more affordable to 12 percent of the city's renter households. In addition, the rent–income ratios of 18.4 percent of the unit occupants declined during the 6 years studied, even though the overall rent–income ratio was increasing.

Table 11.2 also shows that many of the problem conditions identified in 1987 have existed continuously in a large number of units since 1981. That 50 percent of the units with these difficulties in 1987 had the same problems 6 years earlier suggests that these are chronic difficulties not easily changed or removed by market forces. Table 11.3 presents the percentage of dwelling units characterized by each problem in 1987 and the percentage of these units which also had the condition 6 years earlier.

Six problems appear to be chronic or persistent: boarded-up buildings in the neighborhood; incomes below 125 percent of poverty; absence of units renting for less than $300 per month; inability of the average household to afford the median rent of available units; rent–income ratios greater than 30 percent; and housing need. The percentage of units with these problems which also had them 6 years earlier ranges from 56.9 for rent burden to 76.2 for absence of low-rent units. Three of the problems (boarded-up buildings, 125 percent of poverty, housing need) declined citywide during the study period while the incidence of the other three problems increased. With the exception of overcrowding, more than 40 percent of the units with all of the other housing-related problems listed in Table 11.3 in 1987 also had them in 1981.

These findings suggest that many of the city's rental units have resisted the types of improvement likely to be generated by the private market. Some of their problems, such as overcrowding, poor housing quality, boarded-up structures nearby, resident incomes below 125 percent of poverty, and resident reliance on public assistance, are not widespread and have been declining, so that chronically needy units are a relatively small proportion of the citywide total. Other problems, however, such as high rent burden, inability to afford the median vacant unit, absence of low-cost units, and housing need, are widespread, and the percentage of units with chronic needs is quite sizeable. Furthermore, the prospect of improvement in these affordability problems appears bleak because of the

Table 11.3   Percentage of Units
with Problems in 1987 also Experiencing Problems in 1981

| Type of Problem | Percentage of Units with Problems in 1987 | Percentage of Problem Units with Problems in 1981 and 1987 |
|---|---|---|
| Adequacy | | |
| > 3 maintenance deficiencies | 14.4 | 43.7 |
| Boarded-up buildings nearby | 19.9 | 59.8 |
| Overcrowded units | 7.1 | 23.3 |
| Poor housing quality scale | 13.2 | 42.4 |
| Affordability | | |
| Trends in Income | | |
| Income < 125% poverty | 25.7 | 57.4 |
| Households receiving public assistance | 9.7 | 44.8 |
| Trends in Rents | | |
| Loss of units with rents < $300/mo. | 26.0 | 76.2 |
| Median vacant unit unaffordable | 46.1 | 62.0 |
| Affordability | | |
| Rent–income ratio > 30% | 47.5 | 56.9 |
| Rent–income ratio > 40% | 31.5 | 46.3 |
| Housing Need | | |
| Scale 1 | 55.3 | 69.4 |
| Scale 2 | 44.2 | 63.2 |

*Source:* 1981 and 1987 Housing and Vacancy Surveys.

persistence of these problems through a period of strong economic growth.

Three variables were used to analyze the factors associated with the different types of changes observed: whether the unit was occupied by the same household during the 6-year period; shifts in the race of the households occupying the unit; and growth or decline in the income of the unit residents (income below 125 percent of the poverty level). The first variable identifies how much of the observed change in the unit or household was caused by entry of new residents into the unit since 1981 rather than a shift in the status of the residents occupying the unit for the entire study period. The latter two examine whether the observed changes are associated with changes in the race or income of the occupants due either to existence of new occupants or changes in the characteristics of existing residents.

The results are presented in Tables 11.4 to 11.6. Three important findings emerge from examining these relationships. First, units with new residents generally experience the same types of changes as do units continuously occupied by the same household. Improvements in housing quality (maintenance deficiencies, prevalence of boarded-up buildings, housing quality scale), reduction in residents with incomes below 125 percent of poverty, real income growth, and increases in real rents did occur more often in units experiencing turnover between 1981 and 1987 than in units occupied by the same household, but the differences typically were not large. This suggests that improvements in housing quality are linked to unit turnover, possibly because the owner can charge higher rents.

Less positively, occupant turnover also appears to lead to increases in overcrowding and rent hardship. Thus, while rent increases may improve quality, some residents may have suffered hardships in exchange for this improvement. Persistent or chronic problems also appear to exist in units regardless of their pattern of occupancy. A change of occupants did not produce an improvement in housing or socioeconomic conditions in most units; instead, problems persisted even after the entry of new residents.

Second, changes in household income have a clear-cut impact on housing conditions. Table 11.5 indicates that units where the residents' income increased above 125 percent of the poverty level experienced big improvements in housing quality and affordability. For example, nearly 56 percent of the units whose occupants' income increased no longer paid more than 30 percent of their income for housing. Similarly, 21 percent of these households saw an improvement in the quality of their units, compared to 13 percent of the households whose income always exceeded 125 percent of poverty.

Just as increases in resident income led to improvements in housing conditions, decline in income created problems for tenants. Units whose occupants' incomes decreased below 125 percent of poverty during this period became less affordable to the tenants and more overcrowded as a result of this change. Surprisingly, the physical quality of these units did not decline; rather, 15 percent of the units whose households fell below this income level were improved, while only 11 percent suffered a decline in housing quality. Little change in housing conditions seemed to occur in the absence of changes in resident incomes, since units continuously occupied by households with incomes below 125 percent of the poverty level were characterized by chronic problems of housing quality and af-

**Table 11.4    Change in Housing and Socioeconomic Characteristics: 1981–1987, by Pattern of Occupancy**

|  |  |  |  | Type of Resident | |
|---|---|---|---|---|---|
| | | | | Inmover After | Same Resident |
| Indicator | 1981 | 1984 | 1987 | 1981 | 1981–1987 |
| Type of Change, 1981–1987 | % | % | % | % | % |
| Tenure (% renter) | 28.80 | 30.60 | 30.70 | | |
| Own to rent | | | | 6.50 | 3.50 |
| Rent to own | | | | 7.49 | 5.87 |
| Remain own | | | | 11.77 | 31.13 |
| Remain rent | | | | 74.24 | 59.49 |
| Race (% Nonwhite) | 37.40 | 40.70 | 42.40 | | |
| White to nonwhite | | | | 16.77 | 5.16 |
| Nonwhite to white | | | | 6.77 | 3.30 |
| Remain white | | | | 41.20 | 58.56 |
| Remain nonwhite | | | | 35.26 | 32.99 |
| $\geq$ 3 Maintenance Deficiencies | 20.00 | 20.80 | 14.70 | | |
| Increased to > 3 | | | | 9.60 | 8.19 |
| Decreased to < 3 | | | | 16.01 | 13.51 |
| Remain > 3 | | | | 7.10 | 6.61 |
| Remain < 3 | | | | 67.30 | 71.68 |
| Overcrowding | 5.50 | 6.30 | 6.00 | | |
| Became overcrowded | | | | 7.70 | 3.07 |
| No longer overcrowded | | | | 5.29 | 3.42 |
| Remain overcrowded | | | | 1.70 | 1.57 |
| Never overcrowded | | | | 85.84 | 91.93 |
| Boarded-up Buildings on Block | 26.20 | 23.20 | 18.50 | | |
| None to some | | | | 7.18 | 8.31 |
| Some to none | | | | 17.57 | 14.91 |
| Remain some | | | | 11.67 | 11.70 |
| Remain none | | | | 63.59 | 65.08 |
| Change in Housing Quality Scale* | 19.50 | 19.70 | 13.70 | | |
| Decline | | | | 9.09 | 7.76 |
| Improvement | | | | 15.67 | 13.11 |
| Remain poor | | | | 6.46 | 5.87 |
| Remain good | | | | 68.78 | 73.26 |

Table 11.4 (*continued*)

| | | | | Type of Resident | |
| | | | | Inmover After | Same Resident |
| Indicator<br>Type of Change, 1981–1987 | 1981<br>% | 1984<br>% | 1987<br>% | 1981<br>% | 1981–1987<br>% |
|---|---|---|---|---|---|
| Growth in Real Income | | | | | |
| Real decline | | | | 41.64 | 48.87 |
| Real growth | | | | 58.36 | 51.11 |
| No change | | | | 0.00 | 0.02 |
| | | | | | |
| Public Assistance | 9.70 | 10.30 | 9.70 | | |
| Off to on P.A. | | | | 8.45 | 3.78 |
| On to off P.A. | | | | 7.80 | 4.81 |
| Remain on P.A. | | | | 4.71 | 4.22 |
| Remain off P.A. | | | | 79.04 | 87.18 |
| | | | | | |
| Income < 125 % Poverty | 28.30 | 28.70 | 25.70 | | |
| Went below 125% poverty | | | | 12.49 | 10.45 |
| Went above 125% poverty | | | | 18.97 | 11.83 |
| Remain below 125% poverty | | | | 13.32 | 15.59 |
| Remain above 125% poverty | | | | 55.21 | 61.73 |
| | | | | | |
| Real Rent Growth | | | | | |
| Real decline | | | | 22.78 | 46.09 |
| Real growth | | | | 77.00 | 53.31 |
| No change | | | | 0.22 | 0.60 |
| | | | | | |
| % Units Renting < $300 (constant $) | 36.30 | 32.50 | 26.00 | | |
| Loss of low rent units | | | | 23.37 | 13.24 |
| Gain of low rent units | | | | 3.82 | 6.25 |
| Remain > $300 | | | | 60.02 | 52.16 |
| Remain < $300 | | | | 12.80 | 28.35 |
| | | | | | |
| Afford Median Vacant Unit | 55.60 | 50.00 | 46.10 | | |
| Decrease in affordability | | | | 21.29 | 21.07 |
| Increase in affordability | | | | 17.54 | 8.06 |
| Remain unaffordable | | | | 29.82 | 37.58 |
| Remain affordable | | | | 31.35 | 33.29 |

**Table 11.4** (*continued*)

| Indicator<br>Type of Change, 1981–1987 | 1981<br>% | 1984<br>% | 1987<br>% | Inmover<br>After<br>1981<br>% | Same<br>Resident<br>1981–1987<br>% |
|---|---|---|---|---|---|
| | | | | Type of Resident | |
| Rent–Income Ratio > 30% | 42.90 | 45.60 | 44.60 | | |
| Became burdensome | | | | 22.59 | 16.69 |
| No longer burdensome | | | | 22.01 | 16.02 |
| Remain burdensome | | | | 24.62 | 25.43 |
| Remain affordable | | | | 30.78 | 41.86 |
| | | | | | |
| Rent–Income Ratio > 40% | 29.90 | 32.20 | 31.20 | | |
| Became burdensome | | | | 19.73 | 14.72 |
| No longer burdensome | | | | 19.00 | 14.23 |
| Remain burdensome | | | | 14.17 | 14.61 |
| Remain affordable | | | | 47.10 | 56.44 |
| | | | | | |
| Change in Rent–Income Ratio | | | | | |
| Decrease | | | | 45.08 | 48.41 |
| Increase | | | | 52.96 | 48.94 |
| No change | | | | 1.96 | 2.66 |
| | | | | | |
| Housing Need Scale 1† | 56.04 | 59.40 | 54.90 | | |
| Develop need | | | | 18.23 | 16.05 |
| No longer needy | | | | 21.97 | 18.30 |
| Remain needy | | | | 39.94 | 37.24 |
| Never needy | | | | 19.86 | 28.41 |
| | | | | | |
| Housing Need Scale 2‡ | 47.00 | 49.70 | 44.10 | | |
| Develop need | | | | 18.36 | 15.34 |
| No longer needy | | | | 22.81 | 19.30 |
| Remain needy | | | | 29.62 | 27.51 |
| Never needy | | | | 29.21 | 37.86 |

*Source:* 1981, 1984, and 1987 Housing Vacancy Surveys.

\* A unit is considered to have poor housing quality if it is dilapidated or has more than three maintenance deficiencies.

† Housing need exists if one of the following conditions is met: it is dilapidated, has more than three maintenance deficiencies, is overcrowded, or pays more than 30 percent of its income for rent.

‡ This scale is identical to Housing Need Scale 1, except that a ratio of 40 percent is used to measure rent hardship.

**Table 11.5    Change in Housing and Socioeconomic Characteristics: 1981–1987, by Change in Income of Resident**

| Indicator<br>Type of Change, 1981–1987 | 1981<br>% | 1984<br>% | 1987<br>% | Income<br>Increased<br>> 125%<br>Poverty<br>% | Income<br>Decreased<br>< 125%<br>Poverty<br>% | Always<br>< 125%<br>Poverty<br>% | Always<br>> 125%<br>Poverty<br>% |
|---|---|---|---|---|---|---|---|
| Tenure | 28.80 | 30.60 | 30.70 | | | | |
| Own to rent | | | | 3.40 | 4.80 | 2.01 | 4.75 |
| Rent to own | | | | 8.00 | 5.02 | 1.55 | 6.43 |
| Remain own | | | | 14.55 | 15.99 | 6.66 | 33.55 |
| Remain rent | | | | 74.06 | 74.19 | 89.78 | 55.26 |
| | | | | | | | |
| Race (% Nonwhite) | 37.40 | 40.70 | 42.40 | | | | |
| White to nonwhite | | | | 14.82 | 11.12 | 7.30 | 8.08 |
| Nonwhite to white | | | | 4.94 | 4.08 | 5.20 | 4.18 |
| Remain white | | | | 38.07 | 40.12 | 24.68 | 62.64 |
| Remain nonwhite | | | | 42.17 | 44.68 | 62.83 | 25.10 |
| | | | | | | | |
| ≥ 3 Maintenance Deficiencies | 20.00 | 20.80 | 14.70 | | | | |
| Increased to > 3 | | | | 9.17 | 10.76 | 14.13 | 7.11 |
| Decreased to < 3 | | | | 21.43 | 17.13 | 19.44 | 12.24 |
| Remain > 3 | | | | 7.37 | 13.78 | 15.23 | 4.01 |
| Remain < 3 | | | | 62.04 | 58.34 | 51.20 | 76.64 |
| | | | | | | | |
| Overcrowding | 5.50 | 6.30 | 6.00 | | | | |
| Became overcrowded | | | | 3.94 | 8.61 | 7.77 | 2.94 |
| No longer overcrowded | | | | 7.28 | 6.54 | 7.03 | 2.79 |
| Remain overcrowded | | | | 2.10 | 3.21 | 6.79 | 1.43 |
| Never overcrowded | | | | 86.68 | 81.64 | 78.41 | 92.84 |
| | | | | | | | |
| Boarded-up Buildings on Block | 26.20 | 23.20 | 18.50 | | | | |
| None to some | | | | 7.72 | 9.51 | 10.27 | 6.69 |
| Some to none | | | | 19.16 | 20.73 | 19.86 | 15.33 |
| Remain some | | | | 13.47 | 14.00 | 26.31 | 7.04 |
| Remain none | | | | 59.65 | 55.76 | 43.56 | 70.94 |
| | | | | | | | |
| Change in Housing Quality<br>   Scale* | 19.50 | 19.70 | 13.70 | | | | |
| Decline | | | | 9.39 | 10.41 | 13.83 | 7.44 |
| Improvement | | | | 21.43 | 18.41 | 18.94 | 13.12 |
| Remain poor | | | | 7.95 | 13.48 | 15.64 | 3.93 |
| Remain good | | | | 61.23 | 57.70 | 51.59 | 75.51 |
| | | | | | | | |
| Growth in Real Income | NA | NA | NA | | | | |
| Real decline | | | | 2.81 | 98.48 | 57.09 | 44.31 |
| Real growth | | | | 97.19 | 1.52 | 42.91 | 55.66 |
| No change | | | | 0.00 | 0.00 | 0.00 | 0.02 |

285

# Table 11.5 (continued)

| Indicator / Type of Change, 1981–1987 | 1981 % | 1984 % | 1987 % | Income Increased > 125% Poverty % | Income Decreased < 125% Poverty % | Always < 125% Poverty % | Always > 125% Poverty % |
|---|---|---|---|---|---|---|---|
| Public Assistance | 9.70 | 10.30 | 9.70 | | | | |
| Off to on P.A. | | | | 2.59 | 21.96 | 12.13 | 1.70 |
| On to off P.A. | | | | 21.22 | 3.19 | 14.96 | 1.36 |
| Remain on P.A. | | | | 3.25 | 2.43 | 26.24 | 0.02 |
| Remain off P.A. | | | | 72.94 | 72.42 | 46.67 | 96.92 |
| | | | | | | | |
| Real Rent Growth | NA | NA | NA | | | | |
| Real decline | | | | 24.45 | 43.31 | 44.93 | 34.73 |
| Real growth | | | | 75.09 | 55.91 | 54.80 | 64.88 |
| No change | | | | 0.46 | 0.78 | 0.27 | 0.39 |
| | | | | | | | |
| % Units Renting < $300 (1987 constant $) | 36.30 | 32.50 | 26.00 | | | | |
| Loss of low rent units | | | | 31.88 | 18.57 | 15.05 | 14.64 |
| Gain of low rent units | | | | 3.74 | 11.20 | 6.04 | 4.05 |
| Remain > $300 | | | | 42.66 | 41.16 | 26.58 | 71.89 |
| Remain < $300 | | | | 21.72 | 29.07 | 52.33 | 9.42 |
| | | | | | | | |
| Afford Median Vacant Unit | 55.60 | 50.00 | 46.10 | | | | |
| Decrease in affordability | | | | 1.09 | 68.37 | 4.69 | 22.58 |
| Increase in affordability | | | | 48.44 | 0.00 | 0.31 | 7.48 |
| Remain unaffordable | | | | 44.56 | 31.44 | 94.74 | 7.48 |
| Remain affordable | | | | 5.90 | 0.19 | 0.26 | 62.46 |
| | | | | | | | |
| Rent–Income Ratio > 30% | 42.90 | 45.60 | 44.60 | | | | |
| Became burdensome | | | | 1.93 | 67.33 | 11.10 | 15.84 |
| No longer burdensome | | | | 55.73 | 1.17 | 8.44 | 14.94 |
| Remain burdensome | | | | 26.97 | 21.88 | 67.73 | 7.78 |
| Remain affordable | | | | 15.37 | 9.62 | 12.73 | 61.44 |
| | | | | | | | |
| Rent–Income Ratio > 40% | 29.90 | 32.20 | 31.20 | | | | |
| Became burdensome | | | | 1.73 | 71.59 | 13.24 | 9.39 |
| No longer burdensome | | | | 57.49 | 0.95 | 14.69 | 7.23 |
| Remain burdensome | | | | 12.07 | 7.60 | 50.62 | 2.07 |
| Remain affordable | | | | 28.71 | 19.86 | 21.45 | 81.32 |
| | | | | | | | |
| Change in Rent–Income Ratio | NA | NA | NA | | | | |
| Decrease | | | | 87.55 | 4.14 | 41.63 | 46.99 |
| Increase | | | | 10.95 | 95.49 | 57.08 | 49.46 |
| No change | | | | 1.51 | 0.37 | 1.30 | 3.55 |

**Table 11.5** (*continued*)

|  |  |  |  | Type of Income Change | | | |
|---|---|---|---|---|---|---|---|
|  |  |  |  | Income Increased > 125% Poverty | Income Decreased < 125% Poverty | Always < 125% Poverty | Always > 125% Poverty |
| Indicator Type of Change, 1981–1987 | 1981 % | 1984 % | 1987 % | % | % | % | % |
| Housing Need Scale 1† | 56.04 | 59.40 | 54.90 |  |  |  |  |
| Develop need |  |  |  | 3.02 | 43.42 | 8.19 | 18.37 |
| No longer needy |  |  |  | 46.37 | 1.74 | 6.76 | 21.10 |
| Remain needy |  |  |  | 42.78 | 50.13 | 77.22 | 18.12 |
| Never needy |  |  |  | 7.83 | 4.71 | 7.83 | 42.41 |
| Housing Need Scale 2‡ | 47.00 | 49.07 | 44.20 |  |  |  |  |
| Develop need |  |  |  | 3.74 | 47.69 | 8.63 | 16.14 |
| No longer needy |  |  |  | 50.88 | 3.29 | 12.20 | 18.75 |
| Remain needy |  |  |  | 30.23 | 38.63 | 65.90 | 10.05 |
| Never needy |  |  |  | 15.14 | 10.39 | 13.26 | 55.05 |

*Source:* 1981, 1984, and 1987 Housing and Vacancy Surveys.

* A unit is considered to have poor housing quality if it is dilapidated or has more than three maintenance deficiencies.

† Housing need exists if one of the following conditions is met: it is dilapidated, has more than three maintenance deficiencies, is overcrowded, or pays more than 30 percent of its income for rent.

‡ This scale is identical to Housing Need Scale 1, except that a ratio of 40 percent is used to measure rent hardship.

fordability. Clearly, changes in the incomes of renter households affected both the adequacy and affordability of the rental housing.

Finally, racial transition appears to have had a mixed impact on the status of the housing units.[27] Table 11.6 indicates that units continuously occupied by nonwhite households were more likely than other units to experience an increase in rent hardship and a persistence of affordability and quality problems. But a transition from white to nonwhite occupancy appears to be associated with declines in the percentage of households with incomes below 125 percent of poverty, rent–income ratios in excess of 30 percent, and increases in real income and real rent. Although a change in the method of measuring race requires caution in interpreting the data, this finding suggests that higher income nonwhites are replacing lower income whites in some areas of racial transition.

But transition from nonwhite to white occupancy seems to be associated with a reduction in the percentage of public assistance recipients, boarded-up buildings, overcrowding, maintenance deficiencies, residents with housing need, and poor housing conditions. This finding is consistent with the observation that transition from nonwhite to white occupan-

**Table 11.6** Change in Housing and Socioeconomic Characteristics in 1981–1987, by Change in Race of Occupants

| Indicator<br>Type of Change, 1981–1987 | 1981<br>% | 1984<br>% | 1987<br>% | White to<br>Nonwhite<br>% | Nonwhite<br>to White<br>% | Remain<br>White<br>% | Remain<br>Nonwhite<br>% |
|---|---|---|---|---|---|---|---|
| **Tenure (% renter)** | 28.80 | 30.60 | 30.70 | | | | |
| Own to rent | | | | 5.84 | 4.61 | 5.08 | 3.69 |
| Rent to own | | | | 7.13 | 8.08 | 6.48 | 4.70 |
| Remain own | | | | 18.21 | 12.14 | 33.73 | 16.48 |
| Remain rent | | | | 68.82 | 75.17 | 54.72 | 75.13 |
| | | | | | | | |
| **≥ 3 Maintenance Deficiencies** | 20.00 | 20.80 | 14.70 | | | | |
| Increased to > 3 | | | | 9.85 | 11.18 | 6.08 | 11.95 |
| Decreased to < 3 | | | | 16.04 | 19.08 | 9.39 | 20.72 |
| Remain > 3 | | | | 7.08 | 7.37 | 2.52 | 12.74 |
| Remain < 3 | | | | 67.03 | 62.37 | 82.00 | 54.58 |
| | | | | | | | |
| **Overcrowding** | 5.50 | 6.30 | 6.00 | | | | |
| Became overcrowded | | | | 9.51 | 7.22 | 2.06 | 7.73 |
| No longer overcrowded | | | | 4.87 | 7.62 | 2.07 | 7.57 |
| Remain overcrowded | | | | 1.81 | 2.64 | 0.75 | 2.84 |
| Never overcrowded | | | | 83.82 | 82.53 | 95.12 | 81.86 |
| | | | | | | | |
| **Boarded-up Buildings on Block** | 26.20 | 23.20 | 18.50 | | | | |
| None to some | | | | 8.29 | 8.20 | 5.55 | 11.05 |
| Some to none | | | | 16.03 | 19.31 | 11.54 | 22.09 |
| Remain some | | | | 7.78 | 9.94 | 3.12 | 23.51 |
| Remain none | | | | 67.90 | 62.54 | 79.80 | 43.35 |
| | | | | | | | |
| **Change in Housing Quality Scale*** | 19.50 | 19.70 | 13.70 | | | | |
| Decline | | | | 9.48 | 10.89 | 6.10 | 12.29 |
| Improvement | | | | 15.42 | 20.34 | 9.76 | 20.77 |
| Remain poor | | | | 8.08 | 7.77 | 2.64 | 12.22 |
| Remain good | | | | 67.03 | 61.00 | 81.50 | 54.72 |
| | | | | | | | |
| **Growth in Real Income** | NA | NA | NA | | | | |
| Real decline | | | | 39.92 | 47.09 | 45.97 | 47.83 |
| Real growth | | | | 60.08 | 52.91 | 54.00 | 52.17 |
| No change | | | | 0.00 | 0.00 | 0.03 | 0.00 |
| | | | | | | | |
| **Public Assistance** | 9.70 | 10.30 | 9.70 | | | | |
| Off to on P.A. | | | | 7.54 | 6.30 | 1.96 | 10.62 |
| On to off P.A. | | | | 7.69 | 13.94 | 1.47 | 11.60 |
| Remain on P.A. | | | | 2.89 | 5.15 | 0.68 | 11.26 |
| Remain off P.A. | | | | 81.88 | 74.61 | 95.90 | 66.51 |

*Table spanning header: Type of Racial Transition*

288

**Table 11.6** (*continued*)

| Indicator<br>Type of Change, 1981–1987 | 1981<br>% | 1984<br>% | 1987<br>% | White to<br>Nonwhite<br>% | Type of Racial Transition<br>Nonwhite<br>to White<br>% | Remain<br>White<br>% | Remain<br>Nonwhite<br>% |
|---|---|---|---|---|---|---|---|
| Income < 125% Poverty | 28.30 | 28.70 | 25.70 | | | | |
| Went below 125% poverty | | | | 13.28 | 10.19 | 8.72 | 13.98 |
| Went above 125% poverty | | | | 22.94 | 16.01 | 10.72 | 17.10 |
| Remain below 125% poverty | | | | 11.82 | 17.62 | 7.27 | 26.65 |
| Remain above 125% poverty | | | | 51.97 | 56.18 | 73.28 | 42.27 |
| | | | | | | | |
| Real Rent Growth | NA | NA | NA | | | | |
| Real decline | | | | 24.64 | 28.85 | 39.60 | 36.40 |
| Real growth | | | | 74.96 | 71.15 | 59.97 | 63.03 |
| No change | | | | 0.40 | 0.00 | 0.42 | 0.57 |
| | | | | | | | |
| % Units Renting < $300<br>(Constant $) | 36.30 | 32.50 | 26.00 | | | | |
| Loss of low rent units | | | | 24.52 | 19.36 | 13.14 | 20.51 |
| Gain of low rent units | | | | 4.78 | 5.54 | 4.72 | 5.91 |
| Remain > $300 | | | | 53.82 | 61.21 | 65.64 | 41.92 |
| Remain < $300 | | | | 16.89 | 13.89 | 16.50 | 31.65 |
| | | | | | | | |
| Afford Median Vacant Unit | 55.60 | 50.00 | 46.10 | | | | |
| Decrease in affordability | | | | 18.79 | 23.57 | 19.29 | 22.90 |
| Increase in affordability | | | | 20.39 | 16.69 | 10.87 | 10.55 |
| Remain unaffordable | | | | 33.80 | 30.37 | 24.30 | 45.60 |
| Remain affordable | | | | 27.01 | 29.37 | 45.53 | 20.95 |
| | | | | | | | |
| Rent–Income Ratio > 30% | 42.90 | 45.60 | 44.60 | | | | |
| Became burdensome | | | | 22.43 | 20.81 | 17.17 | 20.01 |
| No longer burdensome | | | | 24.98 | 21.40 | 17.81 | 17.17 |
| Remain burdensome | | | | 22.89 | 29.82 | 21.06 | 29.33 |
| Remain affordable | | | | 29.69 | 27.96 | 43.97 | 33.50 |
| | | | | | | | |
| Rent–Income Ratio > 40% | 29.90 | 32.20 | 31.20 | | | | |
| Became burdensome | | | | 22.00 | 18.61 | 14.37 | 17.62 |
| No longer burdensome | | | | 20.23 | 16.48 | 15.38 | 15.75 |
| Remain burdensome | | | | 13.08 | 19.61 | 10.84 | 18.09 |
| Remain affordable | | | | 44.68 | 45.30 | 59.42 | 48.55 |
| | | | | | | | |
| Change in Rent–Income Ratio | NA | NA | NA | | | | |
| Decrease | | | | 47.09 | 43.83 | 50.80 | 43.77 |
| Increase | | | | 49.93 | 52.36 | 47.09 | 53.90 |
| No change | | | | 2.98 | 3.81 | 2.12 | 2.33 |

**Table 11.6** (*continued*)

| Indicator<br>Type of Change, 1981–1987 | 1981<br>% | 1984<br>% | 1987<br>% | Type of Racial Transition | | | |
| | | | | White to<br>Nonwhite<br>% | Nonwhite<br>to White<br>% | Remain<br>White<br>% | Remain<br>Nonwhite<br>% |
|---|---|---|---|---|---|---|---|
| Housing Need Scale 1† | 56.04 | 59.40 | 54.90 | | | | |
| Develop need | | | | 20.22 | 17.35 | 17.93 | 15.08 |
| No longer needy | | | | 22.20 | 22.89 | 20.46 | 18.05 |
| Remain needy | | | | 39.76 | 45.74 | 28.05 | 47.94 |
| Never needy | | | | 17.81 | 14.01 | 33.56 | 18.93 |
| | | | | | | | |
| Housing Need Scale 2‡ | 47.00 | 49.70 | 44.20 | | | | |
| Develop need | | | | 21.76 | 17.05 | 17.19 | 14.53 |
| No longer needy | | | | 22.04 | 20.50 | 20.46 | 20.56 |
| Remain needy | | | | 30.96 | 36.34 | 17.47 | 38.39 |
| Never needy | | | | 25.24 | 26.11 | 44.88 | 26.52 |

*Source:* 1981, 1984, and 1987 Housing and Vacancy Surveys.

* A unit is considered to have poor housing quality if it is dilapidated or has more than three maintenance deficiencies.

† Housing need exists if one of the following conditions is met: it is dilapidated, has more than three maintenance deficiencies, is overcrowded, or pays more than 30 percent of its income for rent.

‡ This scale is identical to Housing Need Scale 1, except that a ratio of 40 percent is used to measure rent hardship.

cy typically occurs in the process of gentrification, since upgraded housing quality and rising incomes are two of its hallmarks. Examination of the spatial pattern of changes in the next section supports the conclusion that transition from nonwhite to white occupancy is, at least in part, associated with gentrification.

## Spatial Patterns in Race, Income, and Housing

Changes in housing conditions and the socioeconomic status of New York City households have been quite uneven. Many households benefited from the economic boom of the 1980s, but others experienced absolute and relative decline. This section investigates how these uneven results have been distributed across the city and examines whether some sub-areas improved between 1981 and 1987 while others stagnated or declined. Three types of change are examined: racial transition, income, and housing need.

Studies of spatial change along these dimensions over the last 15 years have typically tried to ascertain the relative prevalence of gentrification—the physical improvement of a neighborhood combined with the replacement of its lower income by a higher income population—and decline. These studies have usually examined changes in real estate activity and resident characteristics at the census tract or neighborhood level to identify the direction of neighborhood change.[28] But they are constrained by the unavailability of data since the 1980 census.

Using the Housing and Vacancy Survey (HVS), however, we can analyze geographic trends in housing and selected socioeconomic conditions in New York City since 1980. This source is limited in two respects. First, urban change is best studied at a low level of aggregation, such as a census tract, because the full complexity of spatial patterns often cannot be discerned at a larger scale. The HVS is aggregated, however, by subborough areas, 54 combinations of census tracts with populations ranging from a low of 78,395 to 214,048 in 1987.[29] The large scale of these areas makes it impossible to detect fine or detailed patterns of change. Trends occurring in a distinct section of a subborough may be masked by overall trends if households that have changed in opposite directions reside in different parts of the areas. But even at this large scale, a number of interesting and important patterns are evident.

Second, the HVS contains only a few demographic and socioeconomic variables, limiting the richness of the analysis. For example, it lacks education and occupation data, two of the most important indicators of gentrification. Despite these limitations, however, the HVS data permit us to identify important trends in the improvement and decline of different geographical areas in New York City.

*Racial Transition*

Analysis of the spatial distribution of the increase in New York City's nonwhite population reveals four patterns[30]: (1) the minority presence in previously overwhelmingly white outlying areas of Brooklyn, Queens, and Staten Island has increased; (2) the nonwhite population also has increased in areas that had moderately large nonwhite populations in 1981; (3) most of the heavily minority areas in 1981 experienced a net loss or deconcentration of nonwhite households, although a substantial concentration remains; and (4) 12 areas that, with two exceptions, had sizeable nonwhite populations in 1981 have become increasingly white.[31]

Because of the overall increase in the nonwhite population, it is not surprising that nonwhite households increased in 43 of the 54 subboroughs between 1981 and 1987; the average percentage increase was 23.67 percent.[32] Figure 11.1 shows that the greatest increases occurred in 4 areas of Queens (Astoria, Sunnyside/Woodside, Elmhurst/Corona, Middle Village/Ridgewood), 2 areas of Brooklyn (Bensonhurst and Sheepshead

**Figure 11.1    Percentage Increase in Nonwhite Households: 1981–1987**

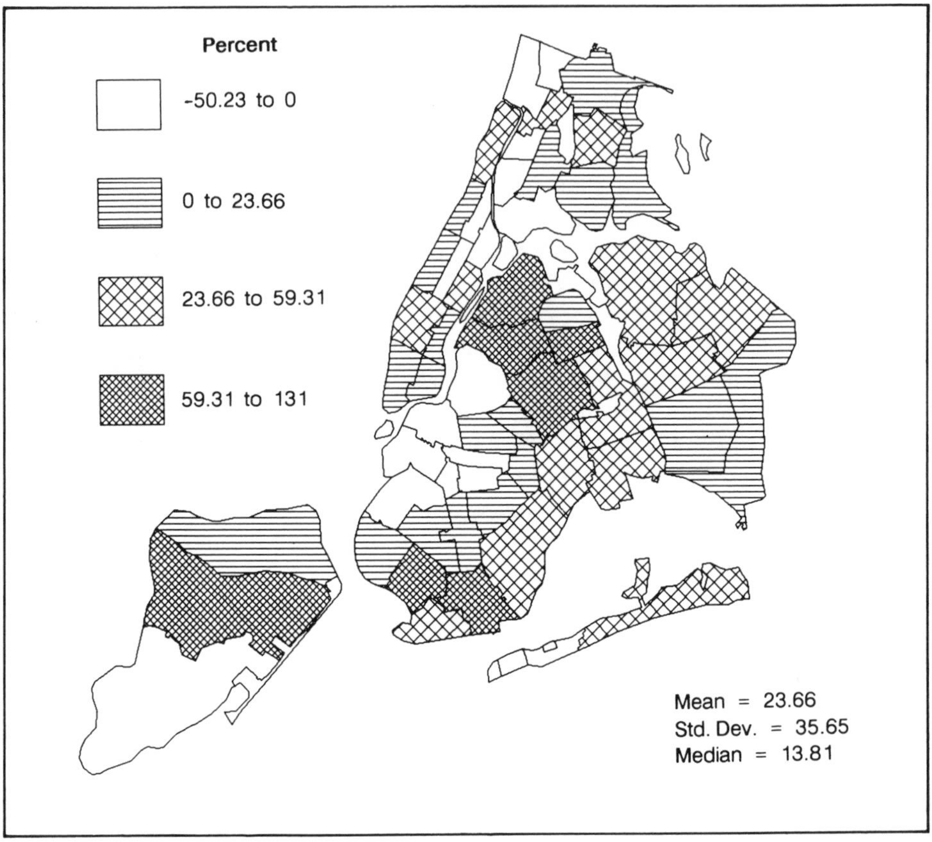

Source: New York City Housing and Vacancy Survey.

Bay/Gravesend), and the North Shore of Staten Island. In 6 of these 7 areas, less than 20 percent of the households were nonwhite in 1981. On average, their percentage approximately doubled. Whereas only 1 of these areas contained 20 percent or more nonwhite households in 1981, 3 did by 1987. Six areas also had greater-than-average increases in the absolute number of minority households.

Fourteen other areas also experienced greater-than-average increases during the 6-year study period; 6 were in Queens, 3 each in Brooklyn and Manhattan, and 2 in the Bronx. All but 2 of these areas also were predominantly white in 1981, with minority households comprising less than 20 percent of the total in 8 of the 14 subboroughs. The percentage of nonwhite households also increased in 6 areas where nonwhite households comprised between 21 percent and 63 percent of the population in 1981, indicating a growing concentration of nonwhites in some areas amid the larger trend of deconcentration. By 1987, 9 of these 14 areas had more than 20 percent minority households. The absolute increase in the number of minority households also exceeded the citywide average in 11 of these 14 subboroughs.

Nonwhite households clearly moved into white areas between 1981 and 1987. But unlike the 1960s and 1970s, this was not black succeeding white. In all but 3 of the 21 areas with above-average minority gains, the bulk of the increase appears to have occurred as the result of the inmigration of non-Puerto Rican Hispanic and Asian households. Where increases in black and Puerto Rican households occurred at all in these 21 areas, it was generally quite small relative to the increases in Asian and non-Puerto Rican Hispanic households. It also appears that much of the increase in the nonwhite population in these areas—and throughout the city—stems from foreign immigration, since 11 of these 21 subboroughs contained a greater-than-average proportion of foreign-born households in 1987.

While the minority presence grew in predominantly white areas, the subboroughs with the heaviest concentration of nonwhite households in 1981 (more than 74 percent nonwhite) appeared to experience an outflow of minority households between 1981 and 1987. Three areas in the Bronx (Mott Haven/Hunts Point, Highbridge/South Concourse, University Heights/Fordham), 2 in Manhattan (Central and East Harlem), and 2 in Brooklyn (North Crown Heights/Prospect Heights, South Crown Heights) experienced a net loss of minority households during these 6 years. Three others experienced below-average increases in nonwhite households, while only 1 gained more nonwhite households than the citywide average. Despite this deconcentration, however, Figure 11.2 shows that the most heavily minority areas in 1981 remained the greatest minority concentrations in 1987.

Finally, 12 areas appeared to experience an increase in white households between 1981 and 1987. With the exception of the Northwest Bronx and the South Shore of Staten Island, these areas all contained more than 40 percent nonwhite households in 1981. Although the absolute and percentage increase in white households in most of these areas is quite small, it is interesting that they run counter to the citywide trend.

The nonwhite to white racial transition appears to be linked to gentrification in at least 7 subboroughs: Brooklyn Heights/Fort Greene, Park Slope/Carroll Gardens, Sunset Park, North Crown Heights/Prospect Heights, South Crown Heights, and Williamsburgh/Greenpoint in Brook-

**Figure 11.2   Percentage of Units Occupied by Nonwhite Households:
1981 and 1987**

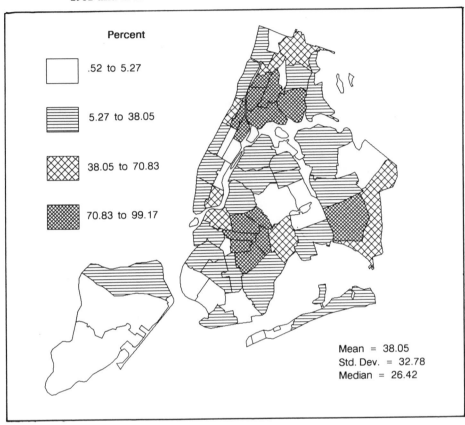

Percent

.52 to 5.27

5.27 to 38.05

38.05 to 70.83

70.83 to 99.17

Mean = 38.05
Std. Dev. = 32.78
Median = 26.42

*Source:* New York City Housing and Vacancy Survey.

lyn, and East Harlem in Manhattan. Some of the change in the 2 Bronx
areas may also be due to renewed interest in Bronx neighborhoods.

### Income

The majority of New York City households experienced a real growth in
income between 1980 and 1986. This gain was widely distributed: more
than one-half of the households had real income gains in 37 of the 54
areas. As Figure 11.3 shows, 27 areas had above-average (53.7 percent)
increases in the percentage of residents experiencing a net gain in pur-

**Figure 11.3 Percentage of Units with Residents
Experiencing a Real Gain in Income: 1980–1986**

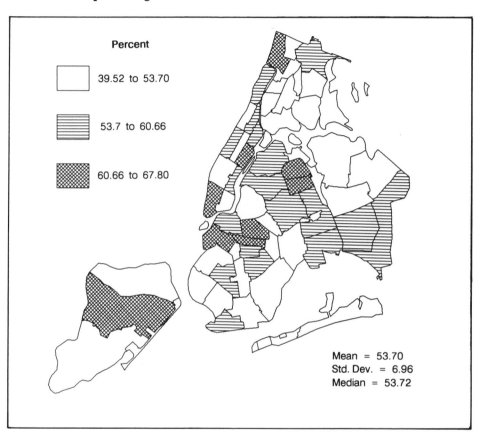

*Source:* New York City Housing and Vacancy Survey.

chasing power. These 27 areas are located throughout the 5 boroughs, although income gains are most prevalent in Queens (9 of 13 areas) and Manhattan (7 of 10 areas), while Brooklyn (8 of 18 subboroughs), Staten Island (1 of 3 areas), and the Bronx (2 of 10) had less widespread gains.

Where real income grew, the percentage of area residents with incomes below 125 percent of the poverty level declined.[33] Interestingly, some of these areas—among them Park Slope/Carroll Gardens, Bedford Stuyvesant, and North Crown Heights/Prospect Heights in Brooklyn—had relatively high concentrations of low income households in 1980, while other areas with widespread real gains in income; for example, Greenwich Vil-

**Figure 11.4    Percentage Increase in Units with Residents
Living at 125 Percent or Below the Poverty Level: 1980–1986**

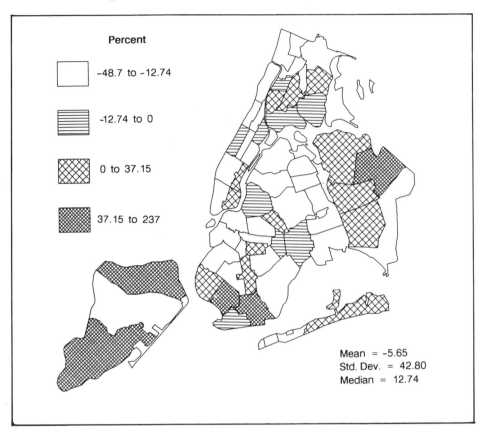

Percent

-48.7 to -12.74

-12.74 to 0

0 to 37.15

37.15 to 237

Mean = -5.65
Std. Dev. = 42.80
Median = 12.74

*Source:* New York City Housing and Vacancy Survey.

lage/Downtown and the Upper East Side in Manhattan, contained few
low income households in 1980.

Although many areas of the city benefited substantially from the economic growth, low income residents increased in one-third of the subboroughs, as Figure 11.4 shows. The changing location of the low income
population suggests that both deconcentration and concentration of low
income households may have occurred.

The percentage of households with low incomes declined in 18 of the
22 subboroughs where more than 30 percent of the households had low

incomes in 1981.[34] These areas were located in northern Manhattan, the Bronx, and Brooklyn. By 1987, 7 of these areas—2 in the Bronx and 5 in Brooklyn—had less than 30 percent of their households below 125 percent of the poverty level. In the 5 Brooklyn areas (Bedford Stuyvesant, Crown Heights/Prospect Heights, Park Slope, Sunset Park, and Borough Park), this apparent decline may reflect the inmigration of higher income households accompanying the strengthening of the housing markets, since each experienced upgrading or gentrification during this period.

At the same time that many areas with large concentrations of low income households in 1981 were losing this population, others with low concentrations were gaining them. The 5 areas with the lowest concentration (less than 15 percent) of low income households in 1981 (Stuyvesant Town/Turtle Bay in Manhattan, Flushing/Whitestone and Hillcrest/ Fresh Meadows in Queens, and the North and South Shores of Staten Island) all experienced above-average percentage gains in low income households between 1981 and 1987.[35] In addition, 5 more areas with low concentrations (between 14.5 percent and 23 percent) in 1981 (Jamaica and Bellerose in Queens and Bay Ridge, Bensonhurst, and Sheepshead Bay in Brooklyn) saw a greater-than-average gain in low income households by 1987.

Although deconcentration of low income households appears to be the dominant trend, some concentration of these households also appears to have occurred. Four of the 18 areas where the percentage of low income households grew (Bushwick in Brooklyn, the Lower East Side/Chinatown in Manhattan, and Morrisania/Belmont and Highbridge/South Concourse in the Bronx) already contained a high concentration (more than 30 percent) of low income households in 1981. In another 3 areas (South Crown Heights and Flatbush in Brooklyn and Rockaways in Queens), more than 26 percent of the households reported incomes below 125 percent of the poverty level in 1981. By 1987, the concentration of low income households exceeded 30 percent in 2 of these 3 areas.

Finally, despite 6 years of overall positive change in real incomes, New York City still contains 10 subboroughs (4 in Brooklyn, 4 in the Bronx, and 2 in Manhattan) with persistent concentrated poverty (see Figure 11.5). More than 28 percent of the households in these areas have had incomes below 125 percent of the poverty level since 1981; in 9, chronically low income households exceed 30 percent.[36] Although the percentage of households with low incomes declined slightly in 6 of these 9 areas, they remain areas where many of the residents are not participating in the city's economic growth.

**Figure 11.5  Percentage of Units Occupied by Households with Incomes Below 125 Percent of Poverty: 1980 and 1986**

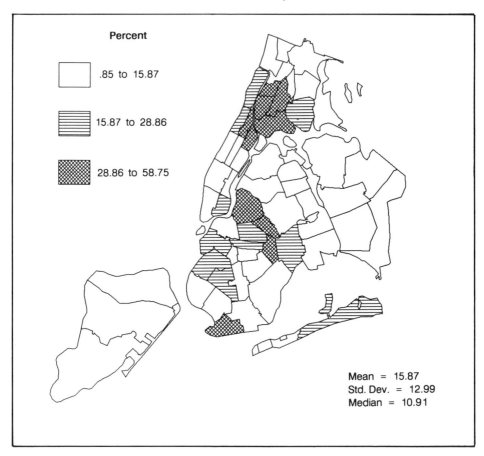

*Source:* New York City Housing and Vacancy Survey.

## Housing Need

Housing need was widespread in 1981; Figure 11.6 shows that the majority of households required some form of housing assistance in 24 of the 54 subboroughs.[37] The 28 subboroughs with greater-than-average need (more than 47.23 percent of the renter households with a housing need) were concentrated primarily in the Bronx (6 of 10), Brooklyn (13 of 18), and Manhattan (6 of 10).[38] Nineteen of these high need areas contained a

**Figure 11.6   Housing Units with Residents Demonstrating "Housing Need":
1981, Housing Need Scale 2**

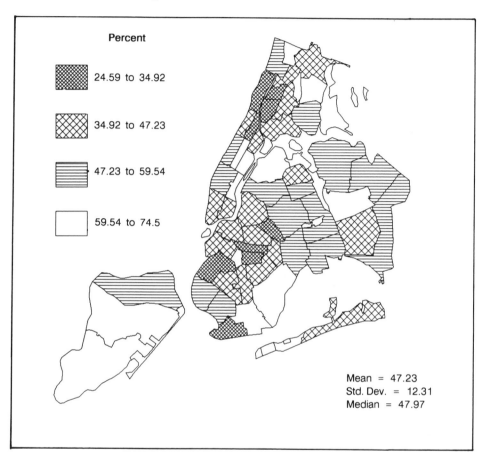

Percent

24.59 to 34.92

34.92 to 47.23

47.23 to 59.54

59.54 to 74.5

Mean = 47.23
Std. Dev. = 12.31
Median = 47.97

*Source:* New York City Housing and Vacancy Survey.

greater-than-average incidence of both substandard physical conditions
and unacceptably high rent burdens in 1981. With a few exceptions, the
location of these problem areas in 1981 is not surprising, since almost all
also had an above-average incidence of dwelling units occupied by low
income households.

Four major conclusions can be drawn from the pattern of changes in
housing need since 1981. First, housing need decreased in the majority
(37) of the subboroughs between 1981 and 1987; some of the largest declines occurred in subboroughs with high levels of need in 1981 (Mott

**Figure 11.7   Percentage Increase in Units with Residents Demonstrating "Housing Need": 1981–1987, Housing Need Scale 2**

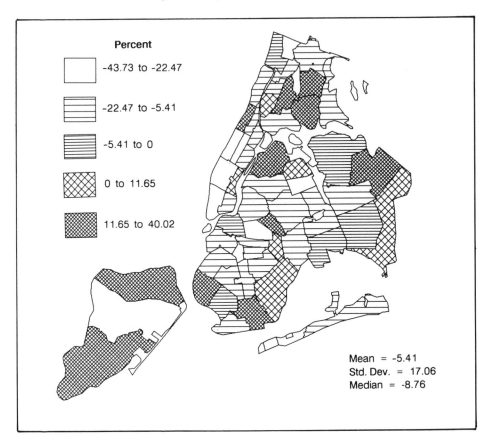

*Source:* New York City Housing and Vacancy Survey.

Haven in the Bronx, Washington Heights, Central Harlem, East Harlem, and Greenwich Village in Manhattan, and Williamsburgh/Greenpoint, Bedford Stuyvesant, Sunset Park, Borough Park, Flatbush, East Flatbush, and Coney Island in Brooklyn) (see Figure 11.7).

Second, housing need declined in most (22) of the so-called high problem areas in 1981, with most of the reduction resulting from an improvement in building conditions.[39] Although less prevalent, the incidence of rent hardship declined in 14 of the 28 areas with the greatest percentage of households suffering from rent burdens in 1981. Counter to the dominant trend, however, housing problems worsened in 6 areas already characterized by above-average needs in 1981 (Morrisania and Highbridge in the Bronx, Morningside Heights/Hamilton Heights in Manhattan, Bushwick and Brownsville in Brooklyn, and Jackson Heights in Queens).

Third, while many areas with the greatest housing need in 1981 improved during the 6-year study period, 8 of the least troubled areas in 1981 experienced increases in housing problems by 1987.[40] This stemmed both from declines in housing quality and increases in rent–income ratios. Two areas (Pelham Parkway in the Bronx and Bay Ridge in Brooklyn) experienced increases in both of these problems; housing conditions worsened in 1 (Astoria in Queens), while rent–income ratios alone worsened in the remaining 5 areas (Sheepshead Bay and Flatlands in Brooklyn, Bayside in Queens, the South Shore of Staten Island, and Stuyvesant Town/Turtle Bay in Manhattan).

Fourth, despite the improvements, housing need remains high in many areas; 29 subboroughs exhibited a greater-than-average (43.28 percent) level of housing need in 1981[41] (see Figure 11.8). Furthermore, this pattern of need was stable. Of the 28 worst areas in 1981, 23 still showed prevalent housing problems in 1987. Put the other way, of the 29 areas with the greatest incidence of housing need in 1987, 23 had the most pervasive housing problems in 1981. The link between poor physical conditions and excessive rent burdens also remains, although it has weakened somewhat since 1981 as overall housing quality has improved while affordability has worsened. Seventeen of the 29 areas with the greatest incidence of housing need in 1987 have above-average concentrations of both quality and affordability problems.

Not only has housing need remained high in many areas of New York City, it has persisted for 6 years in a substantial percentage of the city's dwelling units. More than 27 percent of the rental housing inventory provided continuously inadequate accommodations to its occupants because of poor physical conditions, overcrowding, or excessive rent burdens during the study period. Twenty-eight subareas had a greater-than-average (27.19 percent) level of persistent housing need in 1987 (see Figure 11.9). In 2 (Mott Haven and Highbridge in the Bronx), the majority of renter households had housing problems in both 1981 and 1987; in another 7, the percentage of renters with chronic housing problems ranged from 35.85 percent to 50 percent.[42]

The areas with the greatest overall and chronic housing need are concentrated in the Bronx and Brooklyn; these boroughs contain 19 of the 29 areas with greater-than-average housing need in 1987 and 21 of the 28 areas with relatively high levels of persistent housing problems. The majority of the subboroughs in the Bronx (8 of 10) and Brooklyn (12 of 18) have above-average housing need, while only one-half of Manhattan's

**Figure 11.8   Housing Units with Residents Demonstrating "Housing Need":
1987, Housing Need Scale 2**

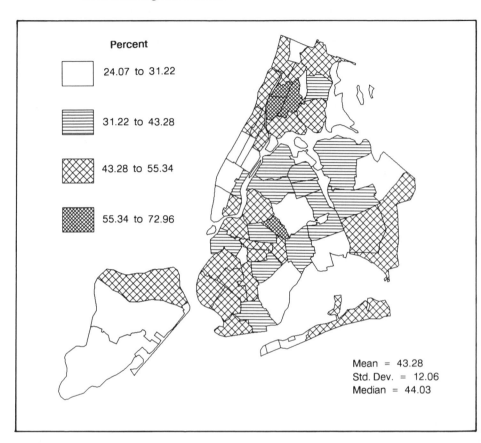

*Source:* New York City Housing and Vacancy Survey.

subboroughs and a fraction of those in Queens (3 of 13) and Staten Island
(1 of 3) had similar levels of need.

The housing need in all but 2 of the Bronx and Manhattan high need
areas involves both poor quality housing and excessive rent burdens.[43]
Poor quality housing does not dominate Brooklyn's housing problems,
although 6 of the 12 high need areas do contain relatively large amounts
of substandard housing. Four have both quality and affordability problems (Williamsburgh/Greenpoint, Bushwick, North Crown Heights, and
Brownsville), while 2 others (Brooklyn Heights/Fort Greene and South
Crown Heights) have only quality problems. All of these subboroughs,

**Figure 11.9    Percentage of Housing Units with "Housing Need":
1981 and 1987, Housing Need Scale 2**

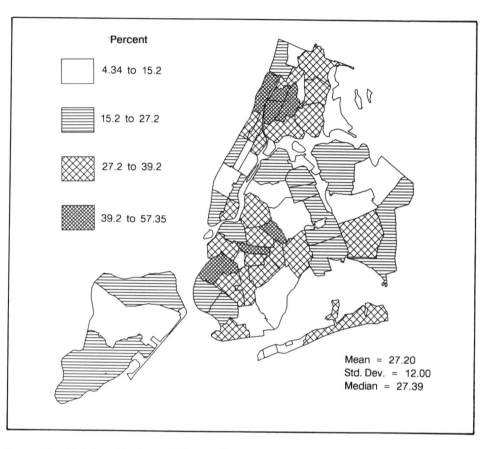

Percent

☐ 4.34 to 15.2

▤ 15.2 to 27.2

▨ 27.2 to 39.2

▥ 39.2 to 57.35

Mean = 27.20
Std. Dev. = 12.00
Median = 27.39

*Source:* New York City Housing and Vacancy Survey.

which also had high levels of poor quality housing and high rent burdens
in 1981, were predominantly minority areas with relatively large low income populations.[44]

Six of Brooklyn high need subboroughs appeared to have good quality
housing but above-average concentrations of households with excessive
rent burdens. These areas (Sunset Park, Bay Ridge, Bensonhurst, Borough
Park, Coney Island, and Flatbush) differed from those with quality problems in 1981 in that, for the most part, they had relatively good housing,
were predominantly white, and had relatively low concentrations of low
income households.[45] Spatially, subboroughs with only quality problems

tended to be older neighborhoods located closer to Manhattan, while the areas with only affordability problems were newer neighborhoods in the southern-most sections of Brooklyn. Finally, with one exception (Jamaica in Queens), the housing problems in the Queens and Staten Island high need subboroughs involved excessive rent burdens but not poor quality housing.[46]

## Conclusion

The economic resurgence of the 1980s sparked a major transformation of New York City's housing market, improving housing quality markedly, and reducing housing abandonment to a trickle. It added a growing but still inadequate number of new units to the housing stock, reduced housing need, and improved the economic viability of the rental inventory by increasing real rents substantially. These trends were certainly good news for owners of rental housing and public officials trying to stem the tide of abandonment and increase the supply of housing. Unfortunately, their good news was bad news for low income households, who experienced a worsening ability to afford either the occupied or the vacant habitable stock.

The underlying changes that drove these overall trends were felt unevenly across New York City. Many units and their occupants experienced an improvement in their situation, but many others saw their status deteriorate despite the direction of overall trends. Furthermore, despite this flux, chronic problems of rent burdens and housing need persisted in much of the rental inventory, especially those units continually occupied by low income households. Change in housing conditions, or the lack of it, appears inextricably linked to shifts in the income of unit occupants.

The uneven distribution of trends in housing and socioeconomic conditions has a clear spatial dimension. Shifts in the location of the low income population, nonwhite households, and housing need suggest that both deconcentration and concentration occurred during the 1980s. The predominant trend was one of deconcentration away from the areas that had the highest concentration of low income households in 1981, producing a higher incidence of these households by 1987 in areas that had relatively low concentrations in 1981.[47] Similarly, the nonwhite share of the population declined in the predominantly nonwhite areas in 1981, while it increased in outlying areas of the city containing relatively small nonwhite populations in 1981.

Deconcentration appears to have been the dominant trend, yet, low-income residents, nonwhites, and housing need appear to have become more concentrated in some areas of the city which already had had these characteristics in 1981. The share of nonwhites increased in a small number of areas with moderate to large concentrations of these households in 1981. Similarly, housing need increased in some subboroughs with high levels of housing need in 1981. Poverty became more concentrated in Bushwick, the Lower East Side, and the Central South Bronx, and it also worsened in South Crown Heights and Flatbush and the Rockaways.

Despite these patterns of overall improvement and the tendency towards diffusion of low income and nonwhite households, many areas of the city had chronic problems of low income and housing need. In 9 of the city's 54 subboroughs, more than 30 percent of the rental units were occupied by households with low incomes in both 1981 and 1987. Furthermore, high concentrations of income problems and housing need coexist in many areas, most of which also contained the highest percentage of nonwhite households in 1981 and 1987. These high need problem areas are concentrated in the Bronx, northern Manhattan, and central and southeast Brooklyn.

The wide extent of chronic housing and income problems suggests that private market forces are not likely to eliminate the city's housing problems, since they have persisted through a period of strong economic growth. It is unlikely that these conditions will be alleviated without massive levels of public intervention to improve the housing stock and to increase the income of the low income population. The city has embarked on a housing program of record proportions to create new housing and upgrade the existing stock. This, however, addresses only part of the housing problem now facing the city, namely, its quality. Moreover, this is the part most improved by market forces during the 1980s. But the city's policies and programs frequently are not tailored to address the unique situations of specific neighborhoods, especially the coexistence of chronic income and housing problems. Affordability now ranks alongside the persistence of concentrated housing and income problems in many of the city's neighborhoods as the major issues facing the city. Until those at the bottom of the worsening income distribution have more resources with which to seek housing, and the city government targets resources to break up the concentrations of chronic problems, these issues are not likely to be resolved.

# Notes

1. See Stegman, Michael A., *Housing and Vacancy Report, New York City, 1987* (New York: Department of Housing Preservation and Development, City of

New York, April 1988), p. 2. The preliminary census count for 1990 shows a slight decline but has been contested.

2. Bailey, Thomas, "Black Employment Opportunities," in Brecher, Charles, and Raymond D. Horton, eds., *Setting Municipal Priorities, 1990* (New York: New York University Press, 1989), p. 85.

3. See Bailey, "Black Employment Opportunities" and Chapter 2 in this book for a discussion of these trends.

4. See Marcuse, Peter, *The Dynamics of Rental Housing in New York City* (New York: Department of Housing Preservation and Development, City of New York, 1978), for a discussion of inventory changes between 1975 and 1978; Stegman, Michael A., *Housing in New York: Study of a City, 1984* (New York: Department of Housing Preservation and Development, City of New York, 1984); Stegman, *Housing and Vacancy Report*, for an analysis of trends in the housing inventory between 1978 and 1987.

5. See Stegman, *Housing in New York*, p. 221.

6. Stegman, *Housing and Vacancy Report*, p. 199.

7. This calculation assumes that households can afford to pay a maximum of 30 percent of their income for housing, the standard used in subsidized housing programs.

8. Weitzman, Philip, *Worlds Apart: Housing, Race/Ethnicity and Income in New York City, 1978–1987* (New York: Community Service Society, 1989), has developed an index of rental housing affordability patterned after the homeownership affordability index used by the National Association of Realtors. Weitzman's index indicates that the affordability of rental housing has declined 18.7 percent since 1981, with the biggest drop (11.1 percent) occurring since 1984.

9. A judgment made by HVS interviewers that the buildings "are in such poor physical condition as to pose a threat to the health and well-being of their occupants." Stegman, *Housing and Vacancy Report*, p. 124.

10. Households interviewed in the HVS were asked questions about six important dimensions of housing quality: use of additional heating sources to supplement the regular heating system; breakdown in the regular heating system; cracks or holes in walls or ceilings; holes in floors; broken plaster or peeling paint; and rodent infestation. Units with problems in three or more of these areas appear to be viewed as substandard by Stegman, although this is never stated explicitly. Three or more maintenance deficiencies will be used here as an indicator of poor housing quality.

11. HVS respondents were asked whether there were any boarded-up structures in their neighborhoods.

12. More than 1.01 persons per room.

13. See Stone, Michael E., "Housing and the Economic Crisis: An Analysis and Emergency Program," in Hartman, Chester, ed., *America's Housing Crisis*

(New York: Routledge & Kegan Paul, 1985), for a thorough critique of the use of a uniform rent–income ratio.

14. See Salins, Peter D., "America's Permanent Housing Problem," in Salins, Peter, ed., *Housing America's Poor* (Chapel Hill: The University of North Carolina Press, 1987); Weicher, John C., "Housing Quality: Measurement and Progress," in Rosenberry, Sara, and Chester Hartman, eds., *Housing Issues of the 1990s* (New York: Praeger, 1989); *Report of the President's Commission on Housing* (Washington, DC: Government Printing Office, 1982) for examples of these critiques.

15. The income data reported in the 1981 HVS are for the 1980 calendar year, while the income data contained in the 1987 HVS are for the 1986 calendar year.

16. The poverty line for a family of four in 1986 fell between $11,113 and $11,302, depending on the number of related children under 18 residing in the unit. See Stegman, *Housing and Vacancy Report*, p. 229, for a listing of poverty-level incomes.

17. The conclusion that the poor and near-poor population declined during this period should be viewed with some caution. The large number of doubled-up households (102,878) in 1987 reported by Stegman, *Housing and Vacancy Report*, p. 142, may have led to an underestimation of the amount of poverty and near-poverty, either because some unknown number of poverty households living with another household were not counted by the HVS or because the total income of the two households doubled-up in the unit may have exceeded 125 percent of the poverty level.

18. Stegman ranked all households by income and then divided the population into ten income deciles of approximately equal size. The poorest 20 percent thus are households in the lowest two income deciles. In current dollars, the average income of households in the lowest income decile increased by 10.8 percent between 1983 and 1986, and 55.9 percent between 1977 and 1986, while the average income of the households in the top six deciles grew by more than 24 percent and 95 percent during the same two periods.

19. See Stegman, *Housing and Vacancy Report*, p. 106, and Weitzman, *Worlds Apart*, p. 33, for analyses of the income disparities of households by income decile.

20. See Weitzman, *Worlds Apart*, p. 24.

21. The $12,000 income level is slightly above the poverty line ($11,113–$11,302); the $300 rent is slightly below the public assistance shelter allowance ($312) for a family of four. See Weitzman, *Worlds Apart*, p. 45.

22. See Stegman, *Housing and Vacancy Report*, p. 118.

23. Stegman also attributes the improvement to public sector activity, such as code enforcement, issuance of tax abatements and exemptions, provision of below-market financing and grants, and rehabilitation of tax-foreclosed buildings.

24. This estimate of housing need is more limited than others that have been constructed in that it does not consider how many units are required to create a reasonable vacancy rate, usually set at 5 percent. But, at the same time, it is more encompassing than other estimates of need because it includes households with rent burden as part of the need. Other estimates typically express only the number of new units required to adequately house the current and/or future population.

25. These indicators of housing need differ from one recently developed by Weitzman, *Worlds Apart*. In his formulation, housing need was indicated if any of these conditions were met: (1) a housing unit was dilapidated, overcrowded, or had three or more maintenance deficiencies; (2) a household's income was at or below 125 percent of the poverty level *and* the rent–income ratio was 30 percent or more; and (3) the rent–income ratio equaled or exceeded 40 percent.

26. The unit of analysis in the HVS longitudinal file is the dwelling unit. Changes in the characteristics of the unit occupants thus reflect either changes in the status of occupants who have resided there since 1981 or replacement of the occupant in 1981 with a new household sometime between 1981 and 1987.

27. The findings pertaining to race must be interpreted with caution because the HVS changed the way it measured race between 1981 and 1987. In 1981, race data were collected through interviewer observation. In 1987, respondents were asked to identify their race. Consequently, differences in the coding of race for the same household interviewed in 1981 and 1987 could exist.

28. See DeGiovanni, Frank, *Displacement Pressures on the Lower East Side* (New York: Community Service Society of New York, 1987), for an example of this type of study. See Chall, Daniel, "Neighborhood Changes in New York City during the 1970s. Are the Gentry Returning?" *Federal Reserve Bank of New York Quarterly Bulletin* (Winter 1983–84): 38–48; Marcuse, Peter, "Gentrification, Abandonment and Displacement: Connections, Causes and Policy Responses in New York City," *Journal of Urban and Contemporary Law* 28: (1985) 193–240, for divergent approaches to the issue of gentrification in New York City.

29. The subboroughs resemble the 59 community districts in New York City quite closely, although they are not identical because the latter split many census tract boundaries. The subborough designations of units in the 1987 survey can be traced back to 1984 and 1981 through the time series file of the HVS.

30. Nonwhites include all households who identified themselves as blacks, Puerto Ricans, Hispanics from countries other than Puerto Rico, Asians or Pacific Islanders, American Indians, Aleuts, Eskimos, and other races.

31. As stated in note 27, the analysis of the race data must be viewed with caution because of the change in the way the data were collected. It is possible that some of the racial transition observed reflects differences in how people of the same race were coded in the two years. Unfortunately, the size of this methods artifact cannot be estimated.

32. The percentage increase in nonwhite households was computed by dividing the net gain in nonwhite households (the absolute increase in nonwhite households minus the absolute gain in white households) between 1981 and 1987 by the number of nonwhite households in 1981. This procedure was used to calculate the percentage increase in all of the change variables discussed below.

33. The correlation between percentage of households with real income growth and percentage decline in households with incomes less than 125 percent of the poverty level (.502) is statistically significant.

34. The rate of increase in poor and near-poor households is negatively correlated with the incidence of low income households in 1981.

35. Overall, one-third (18) of the subboroughs experienced an increase in low income households between 1981 and 1987. These areas are nearly proportionally spread out over the five boroughs, with Queens and Staten Island containing a slight overrepresentation of these areas.

36. These areas are Mott Haven/Hunts Point, Morrisania/Belmont, Highbridge/South Concourse, and University Heights/Fordham in the Bronx; Williamsburgh/Greenpoint, Bushwick, and Coney Island in Brooklyn; and Central Harlem and East Harlem in Manhattan.

37. As described above, Housing Need Scale 2 uses a 40 percent rent–income ratio to measure affordability. This criterion was employed instead of 30 percent or more to identify the areas with the most severe housing needs. As Table 11.2 shows, the higher rent–income ratio yields somewhat smaller overall and subborough estimates of housing need.

38. The parentheses give the number of subboroughs in each borough that had a greater-than-average incidence of need in 1981. In addition to those listed, 3 of the 13 Queens subareas and none of the Staten Island areas also had a high level of housing need in 1981.

39. The physical quality of housing improved in 20 of the 23 subboroughs with the greatest incidence of poor-quality housing in 1981.

40. The 9 areas are Throgs Neck and Pelham Parkway in the Bronx; Bay Ridge, Bensonhurst, Sheepshead Bay, and Flatlands in Brooklyn; Astoria and Howard Beach in Queens; and South Shore in Staten Island.

41. The majority of renter households in 13 subboroughs, and more than 40 percent of the renters in 21 other areas, required some form of housing assistance. Using the 30 percent rent–income ratio standard, the majority of renter households in 28 subboroughs would have required housing assistance in 1987.

42. In the remaining 14 areas, the percentage of rental units characterized by housing needs in both 1981 and 1987 ranges between 27.19 percent (the citywide average) and 35.85 percent.

43. One Bronx subborough has below-average affordability and quality problems, yet still has above-average housing need, while one Manhattan area has poor quality housing but not excessive rent burdens.

44. The 4 areas with quality and affordability problems had above-average concentrations of low income households in 1981, while the other two areas had slightly below-average presence of low income households.

45. Two of the areas (Sunset Park and Flatbush) had above-average levels of poor quality housing in 1981, while 3 (Sunset Park, Borough Park, and Coney Island) had above-average concentrations of low income households in 1981.

46. The Jamaica area of Queens had both quality and affordability problems.

47. While these conclusions await further and more reliable analysis with the 1990 census, they appear to constitute an exception to William J. Wilson's argument that poverty has become increasingly concentrated, in *The Truly Disadvantaged: The Inner City, the Underclass, and Public Policy* (Chicago: University of Chicago Press, 1987).

# APPENDIX 11.1: Methodology and Data Sources

This study analyzes data drawn from the 1981, 1984, and 1987 Housing and Vacancy Surveys (HVS) conducted by the U.S. Census Bureau for the City of New York. Rent control laws require the city to periodically investigate the condition and supply of the housing stock to measure vacancy rates for the purpose of determining whether controls should be continued. The HVS serves this purpose. It contains a wealth of information on New York City's housing stock, especially the rental inventory. It also includes important, though less extensive and comprehensive, data on the occupants of the dwelling units. The Survey provides a unique means for tracking intercensal changes in New York City's housing and population.

The surveys are a cross-sectional sampling of housing units drawn from several sources, including the 1970 census records, New York City Certificates of Occupancy for units constructed between April 1970 and December 1986, and lists of units converted from nonresidential to residential use. Each unit included in the inventory is assigned a unique identification number. The same inventory of units is surveyed every 3 years, with minor additions and deletions made to account for new construction and units lost to demolition, abandonment, or neglect. The three cross-sectional files were used in the analysis presented in the first section of the chapter.

A longitudinal dataset for the 1981, 1984, and 1987 HVS files was constructed by eliminating units vacant in any one year of the survey and then linking the samples through the unique indentification number.

Match-merging the 1981 and 1984 samples reduced the 1981 file from 14,188 to 12,668 records (a loss of 1,520 records) and reduced the 1984 file from 13,865 to 12,668 records (a loss of 1,197 records). The 1981–84 file was then matched to the 1987 file, causing an additional 1,089 records to drop out of both the 1981 and 1984 files. The 1987 sample lost 2,589 records. The final dataset resulting from linking the 1981, 1984, and 1987 HVS files consists of 11,579 records for housing units surveyed and occupied in each of the three years (see Table 11A.1). The second and third sections analyze this dataset. The longitudinal dataset was used in the spatial analysis because the geographic identification codes were not included in the 1981 and 1984 surveys, thus precluding use of the cross-sectional files for this analysis.

The unmatched cases (dwelling units that were not surveyed in successive years) for 1981, 1984, and 1987 were compared to the matched cases of the longitudinal file to determine whether the match-merging procedure introduced any systematic biases into the longitudinal dataset. Although the values of ten selected indicators of housing adequacy and affordability in the unmatched samples appear to vary within 2–3 percentage points of the values of the same indicators in the longitudinal file, no consistent or systematic pattern in these differences is apparent. Thus, use of the longitudinal file built for the 1981, 1984, and 1987 datasets does not appear to have introduced systematic bias into the final sample analyzed.

**Table 11A.1   Construction of Study Analysis File**

|  | 1981 | 1984 | 1987 |
|---|---|---|---|
| Total Occupied Units | 14,922 | 14,597 | 14,996 |
| Linked records | 14,188 | 13,865 | 14,168 |
| Unlinked records | 734 | 732 | 828 |
| Matched Records 81–84 | 12,668 | 12,668 | — |
| Loss | 1,520 | 1,197 | — |
| Matched Records (81–84)–87 | 11,579 | 11,579 | 11,579 |
| Loss | 1,089 | 1,089 | 2,589 |
| Total Loss | 2,609 | 2,286 | 2,589 |

PART **V**

# Political Inequality

# 12

# The Changing Character of Community Politics in New York City: 1968–1988

## Susan S. Fainstein / Norman I. Fainstein

> My whole theory of urban change. . .is based precisely
> on what I call the productive fading away of social movements,
> which have been 'betrayed' and fulfilled at the same time.[1]

Nearly two decades have elapsed since urban activism reached its apogee in American cities. Both betrayed and fulfilled, community groups have become part of regular urban politics, routinely consulted but rarely pressing for large-scale transformation. Contemporary grass-roots activism is better captured by the term community politics than the term social movement, as urban groups have become more modest in their aims and less threatening to established power. Nevertheless, in many places they continue to articulate the interests of urban communities and bureaucratic clients. In that way, they affect the character of urban regimes and the quality of community life, albeit with great variation in effectiveness from city to city.

New York's recent history reflects the national trend. The city has a rich experience of civic activism.[2] Even before the protest movements of the 1960s, it evidenced community resistance to urban redevelopment and highway projects.[3] It harbored the country's most successful rent control movement,[4] and in the United Housing Foundation (UHF) it possessed a unique institution which, backed by organized labor, developed working-class housing on a large scale. By 1958 a reform movement within the Democratic party caused Mayor Wagner to break with the regular party organization and forced the leadership to become more concerned with community issues.

In the mid-1960s, as city spending for social programs was rapidly rising, minority groups in New York mobilized through a multifaceted political movement. The Ford Foundation and the Kennedy administration, responding to the political and economic demands of the national civil rights movement, established a number of antipoverty, community action agencies in the city.[5] These included HARYOU-ACT in Harlem, Mobilization for Youth on the Lower East Side of Manhattan, the citywide Council against Poverty, and the Model Cities program. They were involved in tumultuous contests for political control, becoming the targets of community mobilization as well as providing resources that could be used by popular movements. Mobilized community residents forced the city to abandon all highway schemes that would physically divide the city and to jettison some urban renewal plans aimed at transforming lower class neighborhoods; they obtained a civilian review board over the police (ultimately blocked in a referendum); and they mounted a welfare rights movement that added thousands of recipients to the rolls as well as increasing benefits.

The most significant mobilization in terms of its immediate impact developed around education. A series of school boycotts and other protest activities forced a commitment to integration by the Board of Education.[6] But the Board's failure to implement that commitment caused black communities to shift their objective from integration to control of their local schools. In 1968 the movement for community control of education precipitated a three-month teachers' strike and polarized the city along racial lines. In the end, white opposition resulted in "compromise" school decentralization legislation in Albany which restored power to school officials and the teachers union.[7]

A combination of national and local factors caused the ebbing of minority-based urban social movements in New York. The demise of the national civil rights movement and the reelection of Richard Nixon in 1972 isolated New York's activists. Locally, white ethnic reaction and fiscal problems caused John Lindsay to withdraw from his previous high level of support for minority aspirations. The recession of 1973–75 and the fiscal crisis of 1977–78 reinforced the new conservative balance of political forces.[8] Edward Koch was elected mayor in 1977 by a coalition of the city's Jewish and white Catholic voters. Watched over by business-dominated bodies entrusted with restoring the city's financial integrity, the Koch administration proved inhospitable to the formation of new progressive movements.

Despite a housing crisis and increasing income inequality, militancy has been at most sporadic.[9] Minority leadership has largely chosen to work within the regular political system, and community groups have received only limited concessions in response to their demands.[10] Community activists have lacked a broad economic program and appear baffled by the appropriate stance toward economic development policy. The city's present office-centered approach threatens low-income people with employment mismatch and residential displacement, but stagnation deprives them of jobs and tax base.

The issue for community groups is not simply coming out for or against growth but getting the right kind of growth. Community leaders, however, except for those working in neighborhood economic development corporations, have not sought to influence the composition of industry in the city. They have restricted themselves mainly to the traditional realms of collective consumption, turf defense, and crime control. And they have largely operated in isolation from the electoral arena. Consequently, their role in shaping the character of the city has been more limited than their capacity to mobilize participation would suggest.

Our 1976 analysis of community politics in New York concluded:

Decentralization and the creation of new linkage structures enlarge the number of groups participating in the policy-making process and increase the legitimacy and bargaining power of the relatively deprived. In other words, deprived minorities in many urban areas have now been absorbed into the pluralist bargaining system. Where once their impact on the political marketplace was no more substantial than that of the impoverished consumer on the economic one, they may now participate on a level analogous to the individual with some money to spend but little to invest. The predictable result is compromise, an occasional gain, but no major redistribution across social classes.[11]

At that time the city had not recovered from the effects of two recessions, was suffering from a major outflow of population, and was on the brink of fiscal collapse. Throughout most of the 1980s New York experienced a high level of economic growth, low unemployment, population increase, and a growing revenue base. As measured by economic indicators, its situation resembled that of the late 1960s when community militancy and influence were at their peak under the Lindsay administration. Also as in the Lindsay years, the city government launched many major redevelopment projects and expanded the city payroll. Similarly, the political atmosphere was racially charged owing to some widely publicized police shootings of blacks and to the Howard Beach case, where a white mob attacked three black men, resulting in the death of one. Nevertheless, in contrast to the 1960s, community politics in 1990 is no more militant than it was in our 1976 description.

## Dimensions of Contemporary Activism

The movements of the 1960s were potent in part because their social bases converged. In particular, the movement for community control of schools combined the dimensions of racial identity, client status, and geography.[12] Although these bases still give rise to mobilization, they now tend to be disaggregated.

### Race and Ethnicity

Militant civil rights organizations have largely faded as mobilizing forces in New York. During the 1960s the Congress on Racial Equality (CORE), the Black Muslims, the Black Panthers, and the National Association for the Advancement of Colored People (NAACP) organized many protests around such issues as education and police brutality. Although demonstrations reminiscent of earlier times have occurred in response to recent racially charged incidents, they have not been carried out under the auspices of established organizations and have not signalled the development of a coherent movement.

The most significant of the incidents was the death of a black man as he was fleeing the attack of a group of white youths in Howard Beach, Queens, in December 1986. More than a thousand marchers walked through Howard Beach to protest the fatal assault in an event echoing the civil rights marches.[13] Attorneys C. Vernon Mason and Alton Maddox, representing the survivors of the attack, refused to let their clients cooperate with investigators of the case until a special prosecutor was appointed; this strategy ultimately attained its objective. Maddox declared that his responsibility extended beyond "just practic[ing] law in order to serve my clients. I have to try to change the basic power equation of New York."[14]

Subsequently, the two attorneys and other black leaders sought to use the case as the basis for organizing a new movement to combat racism. On the day of the verdicts, in which three defendants were convicted of manslaughter, the two lawyers, along with the Reverends Al Sharpton and Herbert Daughtry, headed a "Day of Rage." By blocking subway and bridge links between Brooklyn and Manhattan, demonstrators disrupted rush hour traffic for hundreds of thousands of people.[15] The arrest of 69 protestors caused a further demonstration by hundreds of black supporters in the Brooklyn Criminal Courthouse.[16] In the following month Maddox, Mason, Sharpton, and Daughtry again led marches through Brooklyn against racism. In 1989 a similar racial attack in Bensonhurst provoked a new set of demonstrations.

The series of protests unquestionably heightened racial consciousness within the city and stimulated efforts by mainstream clergy and political leaders to promote interracial harmony. Even with the further impetus of the Jesse Jackson presidential primary campaign and the election of a black mayor, however, it did not spawn an identifiable social movement or a specific set of objectives. Although the leadership sought to imitate the style of Martin Luther King, it failed to win much sympathy within the liberal white community.

The involvement of Mason, Maddox, and Sharpton in the case of Tawana Brawley in 1988 seems to have discredited their leadership. Brawley was, they alleged, a victim of police abuse in Dutchess County. But after enormous publicity, the weight of evidence indicated that the civil rights leaders were probably involved in fabricating evidence. As of this writing, Mason and Maddox are defending themselves from civil suits and disbarment while Sharpton was acquitted of charges of fraud and larceny. The final outcome of the events associated with Brawley was a severe blow to the credibility of black activism for civil rights.[17]

*Client Status*

The citywide movements for community control of schools and health care and the welfare rights organization have long since vanished. The remaining significant mobilization based on client status operates at the neighborhood level to gain housing for low and moderate income people, although neighborhood groups occasionally form citywide fronts, most prominently in the Metropolitan Council on Housing, to lobby the city for additional resources and oppose various costly redevelopment schemes.

The most important, genuinely citywide group is the Coalition for the Homeless. This organization has been extraordinarily effective in forcing the city government to respond to the situation of the homeless. It is not, however, based in the constituency it serves but rather consists of care providers and their supporters. It was founded in 1982 by Robert Hayes, an attorney. While still an associate in a major Wall Street law firm, Hayes successfully sued the city in 1979, requiring it to provide clean, safe shelter to every man who sought it. Subsequent litigation extended the right to women and families. By 1985 the coalition consisted of a ten-person staff and active members in 40 cities around the country.[18] It brings lawsuits on behalf of its constituency and operates food and recreation programs for homeless people. Its efforts have been directed at obtaining improved services, banning the destruction of single-room-occupancy hotels, upgrading shelter programs, and developing permanent housing to replace temporary quarters. In 1987 the coalition, which relies on corporations, foundations, and government subsidies for its funding, had a $1.2

million yearly budget and pro bono assistance from major law firms which had brought more than a dozen suits.[19]

The Coalition for the Homeless resembles the National Welfare Rights Organization of the 1960s in being founded by a committed professional. But while the welfare rights group also pursued litigation, it focused mainly on organizing people. It sponsored numerous demonstrations to bring attention to grievances and demand improved benefit levels.[20] The participants in these demonstrations were primarily welfare recipients, in contrast to the marchers in a 1987 rally on behalf of the homeless who were mostly middle class, liberal supporters.[21]

In sum, the Coalition for the Homeless derives from New York City's long tradition of urban progressivism in which middle and upper class elements have worked for improved social services. It has as its constituency the most needy of the city's population, and it can demonstrate remarkable achievements in attaining its aims. But it remains an advocacy and service organization, not a mass movement.

### Neighborhood

The most visible active groups in New York continue to be neighborhood-based. Their issues are local—the improvement of neighborhood conditions. Virtually all neighborhood leaders identify drugs, crime, housing, and education as the major problems of their areas. They address these problems by pressuring established authority to take action and by seeking to raise funds from government, private donors, and investment institutions. Protest actions such as sit-ins and marches remain part of their repertoire, but they do not voice Alton Maddox's objective of changing the basic power equation of New York. Rather, they seek to gain a hearing and to attain the capacity to operate community programs.

Community boards are the most important multi-issue neighborhood organizations. Fifty-nine in number, they were established in their present form under the 1975 revision of the City Charter to encompass districts ranging from 100,000 to 200,000 in population. Their members are appointed by the borough presidents and city council. They have advisory power over planning decisions and are consulted on questions of service delivery and budgeting. Their formal powers are weak, and their mode of appointment guarantees that their members will not be the most militant elements in the community. Nevertheless, they do advocate community interests, usually defending small business and low-income households against the expansionary ambitions of real estate developers.[22]

Community board meetings offer a forum, attended by administrative and elected officials, in which other neighborhood organizations raise issues of concern on topics ranging from police to housing to sanitation. As a North Bronx community leader commented:

> The main link between the city and the district is the community board. It has become the mediator between politicians, city officials and local residents.

Nevertheless, community organizations—which include block associations, merchants groups, housing and economic development corporations, police precinct councils, etc.—also pursue their agendas through whatever additional political or bureaucratic path they can locate. These alternative routes include direct contacts with officials in the state legislature, borough president's office, city council, and the service bureaucracies. Consequently, neighborhood politics, while active, has a rather disjointed character and varies considerably from one community planning district to another. The effectiveness of neighborhood organizations depends on the entrepreneurial abilities and political connections of their leaders. It depends also on general community characteristics to the extent that a particular district has a population containing activists. But no district manifests a highly mobilized general constituency.

## The Case of the Crown Heights Neighborhood[23]

We have studied one central Brooklyn neighborhood in some depth in order to describe the quality of community activism in contemporary New York. Although it has not felt the major real estate development pressures that have stimulated strong counter-mobilizations in Manhattan, its housing market is tight. Despite having a predominantly poor black population, it appears to be at the high end in level of participation and ideological commitment to community improvement for the benefit of low-income people. Examination of the neighborhood therefore shows the possibilities for community activism by an impoverished population under ordinary circumstances in the present period.

Crown Heights has a long history of community participation, with many of the same individuals remaining active for decades.[24] When the city set up an experimental Office of Neighborhood Government (ONG) in Crown Heights (a precursor to the present community board-district manager system) in 1972, community organizations responded by joining together in the Crown Heights Board of Community Affairs (CHBOCA). This body, unique in the city, was composed of representatives of 35 organizations. Its chairperson, who is now the head of the community board, stated CHBOCA's goals:

> We see CHBOCA as the policy-making body for ONG. CHBOCA has as its goal sign-off power over programs and priorities of ONG; we want the goals of the office to be interpreted through CHBOCA; we want to have a veto over who is on staff. We also wish to have a working relationship with the agencies of the city government that allows us to have sign-off power over the programs, personnel and budgets of the decentralized agency offices.[25]

As the quotation indicates, leaders in the early 1970s were continuing to demand community control of neighborhood institutions. But CHBOCA also reflected a crucial shift toward the present system of regularized community input. In the words of CHBOCA's chair:

> We need an orderly interpretation of the feelings of the community. . . . We need to get away from street rhetoric and have a formal mechanism for community input.[26]

Crown Heights' present neighborhood groups concern themselves almost entirely with collective consumption issues. The only exception is the businessmen's association, which meets monthly to discuss common problems, and which helps members seeking financing or technical assistance. The community board, which has "drawn in new people as well as old warhorses," holds well-attended monthly meetings. Its committees, which include non-board members, focus on specialized areas like housing and economic development and do most of the board's work.

Housing is the major issue on which the community board has attempted to affect city policy. Despite the existence of many streets with handsome brownstones, Crown Heights has not yet experienced gentrification. It has, however, begun to feel the interest of real estate speculators; consequently, city-owned property, acquired through tax foreclosure, has risen in value and is sought by private developers. Until recently the city has auctioned such property to the highest bidder, thereby obtaining a lump-sum payment and returning it to the tax rolls. The new purchaser usually holds the property vacant, awaiting the propitious moment either to resell or develop.

Community housing advocates have objected through the board to the deleterious neighborhood effect of maintaining derelict buildings as well as to their being priced beyond the reach of not-for-profit developers. The city temporarily halted auctions but did not officially announce a change of policy. The community board has proposed an elaborate housing plan for the area, but it has received no indication as to whether the city will make use of it in implementing its $5 billion housing program. It also has pressed local banks to fulfill their obligations under the federal Community Reinvestment Act.

The most effective proponents of housing programs have been church-affiliated. One community leader noted:

If it wasn't for the churches, nothing would be happening. This is the only really hopeful group in terms of development. The rest are fragmented, kept quiet, coopted.

The Brooklyn Ecumenical Council (BEC), consisting of 25 churches throughout Brooklyn, sponsored a housing development corporation. It had a city commitment of 1,800 units of in rem[27] housing which it was rehabilitating. Financing came from a variety of public, private, and philanthropic sources, including the Roman Catholic Archdiocese and the Local Initiative Support Corporation (LISC).

BEC spent 5 years working to get approval and financing for its program. Since it had no track record in development, it experienced difficulty in attracting funds and political backing. Its tactics, developed in a program called "Denunciation and Annunciation," reflected a combination of protest actions against the city's housing auction system, conventional and unconventional uses of influence, and bureaucratic organization. Its staff worked through the Brooklyn church leadership to gain the support of Brooklyn Union Gas, the state AFL-CIO, the city's Public Development Corporation, and the New York City Partnership, a Rockefeller-led, business-sponsored group oriented toward social improvement. It took over the office of a prominent real estate developer to enlist his support; it obtained 10,000 names on a petition. Once it attained financing for its projects, it had to develop an organization capable of building them. The words of one of its officials summed up the kinds of calculations engaged in by this and many other community organizations: "We must say no and yes."

The district's elected officials have responded to demands from community groups by lobbying the mayor's office and state government. While Mayor Koch was regarded as abrasive and opposed to community interests, the borough president, the state senator, and one of the city council members were universally rated as helpful. But, as one respondent put it, "the elected officials aren't leaders. The community has to put pressure on them." Another declared:

Elected officials are ineffective except as allies to neighborhood people, and what they push for. But there's a feeling on the part of residents that politicians' promises are not kept.

A long-time activist explained:

The active civic organizations are not political. I used to be the district co-leader. But I got out of politics because it was too dishonest, there were too many elections to prepare for, it was too distracting. There is so much infighting among the Democratic leaders that it defuses community interest.

Thus, even though they have considerable access, community groups are not integrated into the governing coalition.

In Crown Heights, active, stable community organizations continue to play a customary role. One hears little rhetoric demanding community power, and the division between community and electoral politics is maintained. Groups restrict themselves to consumption issues, where they have been reasonably successful in achieving investments in housing and infrastructure and improved services.

## The Status of Neighborhood Groups in 1990

Although improved services and better housing are important in poor neighborhoods, they do not change the economic position of residents. Efforts at fostering community economic activity have been modest. The most significant such program in the city is Bedford-Stuyvesant Restoration. Its present situation reveals the limits on production-oriented community organizations in New York.

Founded in 1967 by Senator Robert Kennedy, Bed-Stuy Restoration, located in central Brooklyn, enlisted numerous corporate sponsors.[28] Using federal and city funds, it developed a shopping center, backed local, minority-owned businesses, attracted an IBM branch plant, constructed and rehabilitated housing, and provided health, employment placement, and other social services.

Since its peak, Restoration has lost two-thirds of its staff due to funding cuts. Yet it is still large relative to other such programs in the country, with a core staff of 38. It receives some revenues from its various commercial and residential projects, including a supermarket and a Burger King, but its continued dependence on shrinking public support prevents it from expanding its programs. Bed-Stuy Restoration is essentially a staff-run group; New York contains few if any grass-roots mobilizations aiming at industrial or commercial development or employee ownership.

The effect of the recent decade of large-scale immigration on community activism is not yet clear. Asian groups, especially Koreans, have formed strong commercial associations. As well as providing mutual assistance, these groups have been lobbying for commercial rent control. A *Newsday* poll of Brooklyn residents indicated that immigrants voted in city elections at a much lower rate than did either first generation or other respondents (35 percent versus 72 percent and 64 percent respectively). Surprisingly, however, they claimed to have participated in community board and school board meetings at a comparable level to the first generation born in the United States and only slightly less than the rest.[29] Different nationalities vary considerably according to their level of participation depending on their language abilities, their legal status, and their native culture.

Despite hostility from the mayor's office, declines in funding, ideological counterattacks, and population change, New York's community activists can point to visible achievements over many years: a few large projects, notably Westway and Columbus Circle, have been halted or revised;[30] a major portion of the city's capital budget has been committed to housing programs; and many neighborhoods have been stabilized and reinvigorated. Community activism has not, however, maintained its former influence nor taken some of the paths followed elsewhere.

## Comparisons with Progressive Regimes in Boston and Chicago

Like New York, Boston and Chicago experienced downtown booms and consequent displacement pressures as a result of their roles as financial and business centers. Active community groups in both have demanded that municipal governments direct a share of the proceeds from commercial expansion to neighborhood improvements and housing for the benefit of working-class people.

Boston (unlike Chicago) has adopted a linkage ordinance.[31] The success of neighborhood groups in achieving this objective occurred simultaneously with the election of Mayor Raymond Flynn, who backed the program. Flynn based his campaign on a neighborhood alliance which supported his populist, confrontational style; he portrayed his predecessor, Kevin White, as the creature of real estate interests.[32] A white man who played on the traditional antagonisms of Boston's working class toward Brahmin corporate elites, he was able to attract the white ethnic groups that in New York supported Edward Koch's very different orientation.

More surprising, perhaps, he has managed to incorporate blacks into his governing coalition, despite his earlier record of opposition to school desegregation and his defeat of a black candidate, Mel King, in the primary. Unlike their New York counterparts, Boston's community groups have not been reluctant to involve themselves in electoral politics. In part, they did so because they had a candidate who spoke to their cause. But conversely the neighborhood movement produced the candidate, as well as his opponent. New York has not so far had a mayoral candidate with roots in neighborhood politics. Moreover, New York's larger minority population makes it unlikely that a white candidate could put together a winning coalition based on neighborhood interests. Harold Washington's victory in Chicago as a progressive candidate presents a more probable model for New York, but his difficulties and the developments in the wake of his death indicate the problems that a minority mayor faces in seeking redistributive policies in a racially polarized city.

Washington's 1983 platform resembled Flynn's; his electoral base, however, differed. While black voters provided most of his support, Washington needed to attract white allegiance if he was to govern effectively. Rather than simply seeking the support of business elites, as other black mayors often had, he also tried to attract backing from white neighborhood organizations. Many of these groups had come together in a coalition called Save Our Neighborhoods/Save Our City (SON/SOC). SON/SOC derived its modus operandi from the Alinsky tradition of community mobilization but placed a greater emphasis on coalition building than did Alinsky. It sought a linkage program that would tax development and turn the proceeds over to neighborhoods to allocate as they saw fit. Harold Washington generally supported the principle of linkage but was never able to reach a satisfactory accommodation with SON/SOC on the components of the policy. Moreover, he could not overcome the tensions around race and generalized mistrust of government that separated his administration from his mobilized white constituents.[33]

At the time of this writing, it is unclear what effect the election of David Dinkins, an African-American, will have on development policy in New York. He did not run for office on a neighborhood program, and as Manhattan borough president he used his vote on the Board of Estimate to support such large Manhattan projects as the redevelopment of 42nd Street. Nevertheless, upon becoming mayor, he did appoint a number of individuals associated with progressive causes to high positions. Even if he should wish to oppose development interests, however, it is questionable whether he has the political backing to do so. Because New York's minority population is divided about equally between blacks and Hispanics, Dinkins lacks the solid constituency to which Harold Washing-

ton could turn. Nor does New York have any citywide grouping comparable to SON/SOC proposing a general program that would redistribute
some of the benefits from downtown development to lower-income
neighborhoods.[34]

The separation of New York's neighborhood groups from the political
arena led them to focus on specific issues rather than on a citywide program. Hence, although no stable, broad coalition has pressed for linkage
programs, community interests have attained dedicated expenditures derived from new development in certain instances. New York has, in fact,
raised far more money from new development than has Boston, where
linkage is estimated to generate $37 to $52 million over a 10-year period.[35]
For example, when residents of Clinton, the working-class neighborhood
adjacent to the 42nd Street Project Area, failed to halt redevelopment,
they asked for mitigation payments from the developer. The city instead
pledged $25 million of its own funds over 10 years for neighborhood use,
primarily for housing improvements, as mitigation for the project impacts.[36] The city and state have also pledged over $1 billion in proceeds
from the development of Battery Park City in the lower-Manhattan financial district to subsidize low- and moderate-income housing throughout
New York. The contribution does not come from private developers but
from the Battery Park City Authority, which owns the land underlying
the project and participates in the profits.[37] The funds are part of an announced $5.2 billion housing program. At the same time, however, Mayor
Koch continued to reject the concept of a linkage policy for all new developments, and community organizations failed to form a coalition to press
for such a policy. At the time of this writing, the Dinkins administration
had not taken a position on linkage.

## The Future of Community Politics

Our discussion implies that New York's community activists would be
more effective if they could unite to back electoral candidates of their
persuasion and thereby have a greater impact on citywide programs.
Some would object that such a course would merely lead to cooptation.[38]
Indeed, by definition, a social movement cannot fit within the boundaries
of institutionalized party politics. Yet, movements cannot achieve their
goals by working only on the outside. Body-Gendrot describes a successful grass-roots mobilization in Paris where "both approaches were combined: grass-roots involvement and the use of political channels of action."[39] As Andre Gorz contends, politics always involves contradictions.
Social movements cannot succeed through normal politics, but neither

POLITICAL INEQUALITY

can they achieve their aims autonomously.[40] They must therefore work both inside and outside institutionalized politics. At the moment, community groups in New York belong neither to a social movement nor to electoral politics; they are interest groups that buffer the regime from unmediated citizen discontent while also stimulating its responses to community demands. Despite severe economic upheaval, their character and influence have remained largely stable since 1974.

We can only speculate why this may be so. The city's sheer size and division into five boroughs make it extremely difficult for any community leader to develop a citywide constituency without backing from a political party. Until 1990 the subordination of the City Council to the Board of Estimate afforded little opportunity to community-based progressives to use the Council to make a name.[41] Finally, the community board system may well deflect activists from more politicized modes of interest articulation.

Whether community groups become more powerful forces within the New York scene depends on both national and local factors. The community movements of the late 1960s operated within a national context of racial self-consciousness and delegitimation of bureaucracy. A national government that sought to combat poverty was also conducive to community action.[42] Lacking such a broader impetus, New York's community groups will most likely remain pragmatic actors seeking neighborhood improvement. Their effectiveness in determining city policy will depend on the existence of a progressive regime with broad political support.[43] The lack of integration between community and electoral politics, however, makes such a regime less likely than in some other cities.

# Notes

1. Castells, Manuel, "Commentary on C.G. Pickvance's 'The Rise and Fall of Urban Movements,'" *Environment and Planning D: Space and Society* 3 (1985): 55–61.

2. For a more detailed discussion, see Fainstein, Susan S., and Norman I. Fainstein, "Economic Restructuring and the Rise of Urban Social Movements," *Urban Affairs Quarterly* 21 (1985): 187–206.

3. See Davies, James Clarence, III, *Neighborhood Groups and Urban Renewal* (New York: Columbia University Press, 1966); Lowe, Jean, *Cities in a Race with Time* (New York: Random House, 1967).

4. Schwartz, Joel, "Tenant Power in the Liberal City, 1953–1971," in Lawson, Ronald, ed., *The Tenant Movement in New York City, 1904–1984* (New Brunswick, NJ: Rutgers University Press, 1986).

5. Clark, Kenneth, *Dark Ghetto* (New York: Harper & Row, 1965); Marris, Peter, and Martin Rein, *Dilemmas of Social Reform* (New York: Atherton, 1967); David, Steven, "Welfare: The Community Action Controversy," in Bellush, Jewell, and Steven David, *Race and Politics in New York City* (New York: Praeger, 1971), pp. 25–58; Fainstein, Norman, and Susan Fainstein, *Urban Political Movements* (Englewood Cliffs, NJ: Prentice-Hall, 1974).

6. Rogers, David, *110 Livingston Street* (New York: Random House, 1968).

7. Fantini, Mario, Marilyn Gittell, and R. Magat, *Community Control and the Urban School* (New York: Praeger, 1970); Fainstein and Fainstein, *Urban Political Movements* , Chap. 2.

8. Morris, Charles R., *The Cost of Good Intentions* (New York: W. W. Norton, 1980).

9. See Katz, Steven, and Margit Mayer, "Gimme Shelter: Self-Help Housing Struggles within and against the State in New York City and West Berlin," *International Journal of Urban and Regional Research* 9 (March 1985): 15–46.

10. As in other cities, community-based organizations have, to be sure, taken on a major role as third-party payees delivering services. But this function puts further constraints on their ability to oppose the city government or its private-sector allies.

11. Fainstein, Norman I., and Susan S. Fainstein, "The Future of Community Control," *American Political Science Review* 70 (September 1976): 922.

12. Fainstein and Fainstein, *Urban Political Movements*, Chap. 1.

13. *New York Times*, December 28, 1986.

14. *New York Times*, January 12, 1987.

15. *New York Times*, December 22, 1987.

16. *New York Times*, December 23, 1987.

17. *New York Times*, June 22, 28, 1988.

18. *New York Times*, November 3, 1985, Sec. 4.

19. *New York Times*, October 7, 1987.

20. Cloward, Richard A., and Frances Fox Piven, *The Politics of Turmoil* (New York: Pantheon, 1974), pp. 127–131.

21. *New York Times*, December 21, 1987.

22. Marcuse, Peter, "Neighborhood Policy and the Distribution of Power: New York City's Community Boards," *Policy Studies Journal* 16 (Winter 1987–1988): 277–289.

23. This discussion concentrates on the part of Crown Heights north of Eastern Parkway represented by Community Board 8. Although the district south of Eastern Parkway also has a mainly black population, its community board is dominated by Hasidic Jews. Formerly, the two parts of Crown Heights were treated as a single district. When the present district boundaries were established after the 1975 Charter revision, however, the city deliberately segmented off the politically influential Hasidim so as to allow them control of

their district. In 1980 District 8 was 85 percent black, 9 percent Hispanic, and 6 percent white. Seventy-eight percent of its housing units were renter-occupied (City of New York, Department of City Planning, *Demographic Profile: A Portrait of New York City from the 1980 Census* (New York: City of New York, Department of City Planning, 1983), pp. 60–61). The 1979 median household income of the district was $9,010 as compared to the citywide median of $13,855 and the Brooklyn median of $11,919 (City of New York, Department of City Planning, *1980 Census Data, Part 1—Income, New York City Boroughs Community Districts,* (New York: City of New York, Department of City Planning, 1983), pp. 2, 80). By 1986, the city's housing and vacancy survey showed a 90 percent black population and a median household income of $14,000 compared to a citywide median of $20,000 for all households and $16,939 for black households (Stegman, Michael A., *Housing and Vacancy Report, New York City, 1987* (New York: City of New York, Department of Housing Preservation and Development, 1988), pp. xvii, 155, 157). There has been a heavy influx of Caribbean blacks into the area.

24. The authors originally studied Crown Heights in 1972 as part of the New York Neighborhood Study at the Bureau of Applied Social Research, Columbia University. Recent material, including interviews with Crown Heights community leaders, was collected by Susan Fainstein with the assistance of Susana Fried in 1988.

25. Fainstein, Susan S., et al., *Community Leadership and the Office of Neighborhood Government in Bushwick, Crown Heights, and Wakefield-Edenwald* (1973), p. 47. Interim Report, New York City Neighborhood Project, Bureau of Applied Social Research, Columbia University, mimeo.

26. Ibid., p. 60.

27. Housing acquired by the municipal government for default in payment of property taxes.

28. Powledge, Fred, "New York's Bedford-Stuyvesant; A Rare Urban Success Story," *AIA Journal* 65 (May 1976): 45–59.

29. *New York Newsday*, "Brooklyn: The Politicians" (November 5, 1987), p. 29.

30. Westway was to be an expressway built on landfill in the Hudson River; the Columbus Circle project was to be an enormous office building that would cast a large shadow over Central Park.

31. Linkage programs require a commitment from developers that they will contribute housing or public services in return for permission to build a commercial project. Typically, a builder will put money in a housing trust fund based on the number of square feet in the building. Boston's program was modeled on San Francisco's; the latter was the first large city to adopt such an ordinance. At the time it did so, neighborhood organizations had captured, then lost, the mayor's office but had retained considerable clout within the Board of Supervisors. The program applied to all developers of office projects adding at least 50,000 square feet of space. Developers could satisfy their obligation by either building the housing themselves or providing a financial contri-

bution. In Seattle, which adopted a linkage program in 1984, developers were required to contribute to housing development only if they received a density bonus (Pickman, James, and Benson F. Roberts, "Tapping Real Estate Markets to Address Housing Needs," *New York Affairs* (1985): 3–17). A slate of council candidates in Hartford won election in 1985 on a platform supporting linkage. In 1986, however, they disavowed their earlier support for the policy (Neubeck, Kenneth J., and Richard E. Ratcliff, "Urban Democracy and the Power of Corporate Capital: Struggles over Downtown Growth and Neighborhood Stagnation in Hartford, Connecticut," in Cummings, Scott, ed., *Business Elites and Urban Development* (Albany: SUNY Press, 1988), pp. 299–332).

32. Swanstrom, Todd, "Urban Populism, Uneven Development, and the Space for Reform," in Cummings, *Business Elites and Urban Development*, pp. 135–142.

33. Bennett, Larry, "The Dilemmas of Building a Progressive Urban Coalition: The Linked Development Debate in Chicago," *Journal of Urban Affairs* 9,3 (1987): 263–276.

34. See Pickman and Roberts, "Tapping Real Estate Markets."

35. Swanstrom, "Urban Populism," p. 141.

36. Fainstein, Susan S., "The Politics of Criteria: Planning for the Redevelopment of Times Square," in Fischer, Frank, and John Forester, eds., *Confronting Values in Policy Analysis* (Beverly Hills: Sage, 1987), pp. 232–247. The money was to come from general city and state revenues rather than a tax on the project itself, and therefore the concession did not satisfy those who wanted the two linked so as to set a precedent. Ironically, while the neighborhood started receiving the funds committed to it, the project, four years after its approval by the Board of Estimate, had not yet begun. If the money had in fact been linked to the project, no return would yet have been realized.

37. Schmalz, Jeffrey, "New York Reaches Accord on Housing," *New York Times* (December 27, 1987). In another project on city-owned land on the Lower East Side, the developer has agreed to a cross-subsidy program whereby part of the profit from market-rate condominiums will provide an estimated subsidy of $32 million for the development of rental housing (Oser, Alan, "Using Condo Sales to Assist New Rentals," *New York Times* (April 10, 1988), R9). The developer of a luxury development in Clinton agreed to rehabilitate ten buildings, to be occupied by various lower-income groups and to be operated by a not-for-profit organization, in return for a special zoning permit (Oser, Alan, "Shaping Four Acres in Mid-Manhattan," *New York Times* (May 22, 1988), R9).

38. See Clarke, Susan E., and Margit Mayer, "Responding to Grassroots Discontent: Germany and the United States," *International Journal of Urban and Regional Research* 10 (September 1986): 401.

39. Body-Gendrot, Sophie N., "Grass-roots Mobilization in the Thirteenth Arrondissement of Paris: A Cross-national View," in Stone, Clarence N., and Hey-

wood T. Sanders, eds., *The Politics of Urban Development* (Lawrence: University of Kansas Press, 1987), pp. 125–143.

40. Gorz, Andre, *Farewell to the Working Class* (Boston: South End Press, 1982), p. 12.

41. Councilwoman Ruth Messinger provided the only counter example. Subsequently she became the Manhattan borough president.

    The Board of Estimate was declared to constitute a denial of the principle of one-person, one-vote by the U.S. Supreme Court and went out of existence in mid-1990.

42. See Pickvance, C.G., "The Rise and Fall of Urban Movements and the Role of Comparative Analysis," *Environment and Planning D: Society and Space* 3 (1984), pp. 31–53, for a discussion of the importance of context in determining the success of urban movements.

43. See Swanstrom, "Urban Populism," p. 144.

# 13

# Political Inequality

## John Hull Mollenkopf

## Introduction

Although the changes described in earlier chapters have had a profound impact on New York City's class structure, racial and ethnic composition, and geography, they have had much less impact than might be expected on its electoral politics, at least until the mayoral elections of September and November 1989. In particular, New York City resisted the political succession of ethnic whites by native-born blacks that has taken place in most of the nation's other largest cities. Nor, for reasons that will be explored below, is the city likely to experience such a racial succession, despite the election of the city's first black mayor, David N. Dinkins, in November 1989. To the contrary, despite the fact that non-Hispanic whites are a minority of the city's population and despite the city's liberal tradition, New York was characterized during the administration of Mayor Edward I. Koch by a conservative, primarily white, dominant electoral coalition, by systematic underrepresentation of blacks and Latinos, and by disarray among potential challengers to the mayor.

The election of Mayor Dinkins reverses some of these conditions. But given his narrow margin of victory, a mere 43,000 out of 1,780,000 ballots cast, it is instructive to ask what factors led to the political exclusion characteristic of the 1970s and 1980s, how those conditions changed or were overcome in order to elect Mayor Dinkins, and what the implications are for the durability of Dinkins' electoral coalition.

As late as the 1950s, New York was an overwhelmingly white, ethnic city where blacks and Latinos constituted only a small minority. While it has always had a concentration of banks and corporate headquarters, the New York of the 1950s retained extensive port activities and manufacturing employment. Only 40 years later, the economic and demographic contrast is nearly complete. The production and distribution of goods has dwindled, and advanced corporate services (especially finance), nonprofit services like hospitals and universities, and public service production now drive the city's economy. Non-Hispanic whites constitute about 46 percent of the population, while blacks, Latinos, and Asians make up the majority. Native-born whites are an even smaller minority; the city's most rapidly growing population groups are immigrants from the Caribbean and Asia.[1] Movies like "On the Waterfront" could rightly depict the 1950s New York as a white, male, ethnic, blue collar city where unions, political machines, and corruption flourished. Today, this social stratum and the institutions built on it have almost vanished; black, Latino, Asian, and women service sector workers now predominate.

Historically, shifts of this magnitude have led growing but unrepresented constituencies to challenge the prevailing political order and, after a period of conflict, led that order to incorporate these groups into varying degrees of dominance and subordination. As shifting economic and demographic tides eroded the foundation of the prevailing political order, growing but excluded groups sought ways to gain a greater share of power. Moments of crisis often triggered their entry, as when the Depression of the 1930s enabled a maturing urban, industrial, immigrant working class to emerge as a factor in national party realignment. This perspective suggests that the arrival of nonwhite majorities in large central cities over the last two decades should also lead to the reorganization of dominant coalitions in urban politics. And so it happened in most of the other old, large, northern central cities—but not, until 1989, in New York.[2]

The established political order in New York successfully resisted full representation of the city's new majority of minority groups. A definitive count must await release of the 1990 census, yet a 1987 census study indicates that the city was about 46 percent non-Hispanic white, 24 percent non-Hispanic black, 23 percent Hispanic, 4 percent non-Hispanic Asian, and 2 percent other.[3] By contrast, all citywide officeholders were white until Dinkins' election in 1989. Dinkins had been Manhattan borough president since 1985, and a Latino, Fernando Ferrer, became Bronx borough president in 1986 upon the conviction of his predecessor, thus giving blacks and Latinos each one vote out of eleven on the powerful Board of Estimate (abolished in 1989 pursuant to a successful legal challenge). These gains, however, only restored the influence that Percy Sutton and Herman Badillo had ceased exercising 20 years ago when they gave up the Manhattan and Bronx borough presidencies. The blacks and

Latinos who made up approximately 47 percent of the city's population thus held no citywide influence and only 18 percent of the votes on the Board of Estimate. On the previously inconsequential City Council, blacks and Latinos held nine of the thirty-five seats (26 percent) in 1989. Minority legislative voting power has thus been under half their proportion of the population. Most crucially, in contrast to the Lindsay era, Mayor Koch did not need to rely on strong support from blacks and Latinos to forge his electoral majority.[4]

New York thus presents a paradox: until the Dinkins victories of 1989, its electoral politics had not realigned to reflect the great changes that have taken place in the social and cultural terrain on which it rests.[5] This produced a political and electoral inequality parallel to, the social and economic inequalities described in other chapters. This chapter explores why that inequality arose and how the Dinkins candidacy overcame it, at least for the time being, in the primary and general elections of 1989. Although political inequality operates on many other important dimensions, this chapter focuses on the electoral inequality on which the others are predicated.

Group succession is an old issue in New York City politics. The political establishment has confronted the problem of incorporating potentially destabilizing groups for a century and a half. Beginning in the 1850s, an Irish and German working class sought to displace the English-stock and native-born commercial elite, succeeding by the 1870s. As their numbers mounted after the turn of the century, Italian and Jewish immigrants began to challenge the Irish-dominated political machine in the 1930s and gained hegemony by the 1950s. After World War II, blacks and Puerto Ricans in turn began to challenge the dominant Italian and Jewish establishment in Harlem, Brooklyn, and later Southeastern Queens.[6] Violence attended the bid each of these groups made for power, and all generated radical alternatives to the prevailing establishment. Urban social movements have been the handmaidens of political reform.

Until recently, New York's political system absorbed these conflicts through a process of reform and realignment that simultaneously "tamed" the challengers while reconstituting the dominant coalition.[7] Reformers mobilized disgruntled outsiders to challenge the establishment. They sometimes won mayoral elections, but sooner or later the regulars, or the "machine," regained office, but on the basis of a broader coalition that included elements of the previously insurgent groups.

Scholars have differed on how the dialectic between regulars and reformers enabled the political system to absorb excluded groups while denying the radical implications of their challenge. Katznelson has argued that the separation of work and residence in the nineteenth century attenuated the class basis of electoral politics, a condition that later deflected black protest in northern Manhattan in the late 1960s.[8] Bridges contends that the existence of mass franchise before the formation of the working class led New Yorkers to invent the political machine which, after the mid-nineteenth century, then shaped and contained class interests.[9] Along related lines, Shefter shows how New York's political leaders required Jews and Italians to repudiate radicalism as a condition for a place in the establishment.[10] And Piven and Cloward have stressed the role of welfare and poverty programs in absorbing and deflecting black urban protest.[11]

Whatever the mechanism of containment, three things are clear about the process of political succession in New York City. First, it takes decades. The Irish arrived in substantial numbers in 1848, but did not elect an Irish mayor until the 1880s, although Tammany was in Irish hands earlier. Jews and Italians arrived between 1890 and 1910, but did not fully displace Irish leaders from the Democratic party until the 1950s. (La Guardia, a Republican, was elected in 1933, but an Italian Democratic mayor was not elected until 1950, and a Jewish Democratic mayor not until 1973.) Blacks and Puerto Ricans arrived during and after World War II, but a black mayor was elected only in 1989.

Second, the process of incorporation is selective. It extracts a high price from contending groups, providing symbolic gains to the many while reserving substantive rewards for a relatively few leaders. Cooptation transforms the radical rhetoric of the excluded into the pragmatic dialogue of the insider. This tempering of the radicalism of insurgent groups has occurred notwithstanding the failure of incorporation to improve the group's relative socioeconomic position quickly or substantially.

Finally, race has introduced a qualitatively different element into the politics of group succession. The reform process that forced earlier dominant coalitions to incorporate growing but underrepresented groups has stalled or failed for blacks and Hispanics. New York's black and Puerto Rican populations began to grow rapidly around 1940, and their first officeholders were elected shortly thereafter. In 1969, the Lindsay administration relied on black and Puerto Rican votes for victory and promised to institutionalize a multiracial dominant political coalition.[12] City government certainly used public funds to coopt minority leaders and cool protest among the growing black and Latino constituencies.[13] But subsequent trends reversed these developments. Not only was black and Latino participation in the dominant coalition not institutionalized, subsequent administrations reversed some of the gains of the late 1960s under the goad of the fiscal crisis and conservative Republican administrations in Washington.

Some would argue that the city's fiscal crisis accounts for the failure of the political system to consolidate black and Latino representation.[14] The 1975 fiscal crisis constrained city spending on social services and prompted city government to emphasize private investment. From 1978 onward, federal spending on urban programs, particularly manpower and housing, also declined. Moreover, the city's recovery took place under the purview of fiscal monitors seeking to please investment constituencies. On the surface, it might be plausible to conclude that these trends demobilized black and Latino political participation. But this would be a non sequitur. Why did New York move away from incorporating blacks and Latinos when other large cities with fiscal difficulties did not? And did exclusion from the dominant coalition persist despite an economic boom after 1977 that allowed the city to finance rapidly increasing expenditures from its own tax base, including greater spending on social programs?[15] Austerity cannot explain political inequality when the former has been abating while the latter has increased. What then does?

## Explaining Political Inequality in New York City

Three conceptually distinct explanations may account for the large gap between population and elected representation during the 1970s and 1980s: first, that the relatively low income, educational attainment, and political efficacy of minority individuals lead to lower participation, and therefore lower representation; second, that the structural organization of the political system discriminates against minorities; and third, that leaders of potential members of an insurgent coalition are so disorganized or fragmented that they cannot mount a credible challenge. Although there is some evidence for each of these perspectives, this chapter argues that the second and third, and the interaction between them, are most persuasive.

One approach holds that individual attributes like income, education, occupation, religion, ethnicity, and family background interact with party identification, issues, and candidate personality to influence whether individuals vote and for whom. Such seminal studies as *The Changing American Voter* and the Michigan national election studies adopt this view.[16] They would explain the absence of minority political incorporation by the relatively low income and education of blacks and Puerto Ricans and that their greater political alienation produced low voter turnout and thus less representation. In this view, racial and economic inequalities may be mapped directly onto political inequalities. The belief among New York

City's political practitioners that minority communities do not vote corresponds to this view.

Alternative explanations focus instead on how the political system patterns political participation, promoting some forms and dampening others. One variant, associated with radical analysts but also characteristic of the work of V. O. Key and W. D. Burnham, locates the source of political exclusion and underrepresentation in the rules of the political game (eligibility, control over ballot access), the candidate selection process, how districts are apportioned or reapportioned, the character of party competition (or lack of it), the composition of the dominant coalition, and the propensities of various possible sources of political mobilization (regular party organizations, public unions, churches, etc.).[17] This approach would explain the weakness of minority political incorporation in terms of deliberate exclusion, the continued importance of regular Democratic organizations, and the lack of political competition in a weakly organized one-party system.

An alternative structural explanation grounds minority political exclusion in weak political organization and leadership within black and Latino constituencies, the decay of urban social movements that formerly propelled them, and a consequent susceptibility to cooptation.[18] This view would explain the dominant political coalition's failure to include blacks and Latinos in more than a marginal or subordinate way neither in terms of individual attributes nor of racial bias in the rules of the game, but as a failure of political leadership and political mobilization among blacks and Latinos, themselves.[19] These two alternatives to individualistic explanations are of course not mutually exclusive. The biases built into a political structure and the strategic choices made by those operating within it strongly influence each other.

These competing explanations of electoral inequality in New York City can be evaluated by examining a data base consisting of registration, turnout, and candidate vote totals for all citywide elections since 1982 for the 60 New York State assembly districts (ADs) in the city, together with demographic information from the 1980 census grouped by AD.[20] Unlike survey data, which are prone to reporting error on such questions as whether the respondent is registered or cast votes, this data set thus allows us to examine the impact of a wide range of individual and structural factors on the basis of actual political behavior in New York.[21] Before turning to this analysis, however, we must first consider the nature of New York City's electoral arena.

*The City's Electorates*

New York City has a varied political geography. The growing but relatively poor black and Latino populations are concentrated in and around ghetto centers like Central and East Harlem, the Lower East Side, the South Bronx, and Bedford-Stuyvesant in Brooklyn. Whites, who tend to be much better off, have held onto their East and West Side enclaves in Manhattan. During the 1980s, they invaded some minority areas, such as the Lower East Side, and transformed loft factory districts like SoHo and Tribeca. Middle class Italians and Jews have also formed enclaves on the city's periphery, from Riverdale in the Bronx to Bayside in Queens around to Canarsie and Bensonhurst and Bay Ridge in Brooklyn. Areas of immigrant influx punctuate this pattern, most notably the Chinese settlements in Chinatown, Flushing and Elmhurst in Queens, and Sunset Park, Brooklyn; the West Indian communities of Crown Heights and Flatbush in Brooklyn and Cambria Heights, Queens; the Dominicans in Washington Heights; and the Latin American zone of Jackson Heights, Queens.

Democratic party leaders have drawn 60 assembly districts upon this terrain, which serve the function of wards for the five county party organizations.[22] After initially resisting black and Latino representation in the 1940s and 1950s, party leaders began to create ADs that would concentrate these populations and ensure black and Latino seats.[23] With an average 1980 population of 118,000, all ADs contain a variety of racial and ethnic components, but the high degree of geographic segregation means that most ADs have a predominant racial/ethnic character. The 1982 redistricting produced 13 majority-black, 3 majority-Latino ADs, and 8 other districts where blacks and Latinos combined outnumber whites. The 36 majority-white ADs also generally contain a preponderant ethnoreligious group, either Jews or white Catholics, of whom Italian-Americans are most numerous. Ten ADs have a minority population of over 30 percent; 16 ADs are 70–85 percent white, and 10 are over 85 percent non-Hispanic white.[24] In other words, despite the fact that non-Hispanic whites were only a bare majority of the city's population in 1980, there were 36 white ADs and 24 minority ADs in 1980 because the minority ADs were constructed to concentrate minority constituencies.[25] Class and income are strongly related to race, with Puerto Ricans and Dominicans at the bottom, non-Hispanic whites on top, and blacks about halfway in between. Asians have moved close to the white median income.[26] As the individualist explanations would have it, political participation varies across ADs. In the 1984 Reagan landslide, for example, Latino ADs contributed only 4 percent of the total New York City vote, black ADs 18 percent, and white ADs the remaining 78 percent.

These ADs contain two different kinds of electorates. From the national perspective, the two million or more who vote in presidential general elections are most important. (Over 2.3 million voted in the 1984 presidential election and 1.9 million in 1988, a steady decline from the 3 million votes cast in 1960.) Gubernatorial general elections draw the next largest number of voters, about 1.7 million, while mayoral general elections have drawn about 1.3 million. In the broadest electorates, Republicans draw more support than registration numbers alone might suggest. (Ronald Reagan won almost 40 percent of the votes in 1984, even though Republicans made up only 15 percent of registered voters.) These elections are also dominated by white voters who are older and better off than minority residents.

A second, far smaller electorate is crucial for power in New York City and Albany, however: the seven hundred thousand or so voters who regularly cast ballots in Democratic primaries. Since the Democratic nominee usually wins office, those seeking to capture City Hall must first win a majority, or at least a 40 percent plurality, of the votes in this constituency.[27] Since the city casts 60 percent of the state Democratic primary vote, the city also has a large influence on the gubernatorial primary outcome. These primary electorates are only a third the size of the presidential general electorate. Only 688,000 votes were cast in the 1985 mayoral primary in which Edward Koch overwhelmingly defeated his black and white liberal challengers, and only 749,000 votes in the hotly contested 1982 gubernatorial primary that Koch lost to Mario Cuomo. In contrast to the general electorate, blacks and Latinos are much better represented in the Democratic primary electorate, both because they are much more likely than whites to be registered Democrats and are also more likely to be able to vote for black or Latino candidates in the primary.

Of approximately 5.2 million voting age residents, about 3 million are currently registered. Democrats comprise about two-thirds of this number. The next largest group, 15 percent, declined to state a party, while Republicans enrolled only 14 percent. (The tiny Liberal and Conservative parties attracted less than 1 percent each.) The Democratic turnout was only 37 percent in the 1985 mayoral primary. Put another way, less than 13 percent of the voting age population voted in the election that determined who would be mayor.

## The Democratic Primary Electorate

The Democratic primary electorate was remarkably stable from 1960 to the mid-1970s at about 750,000 voters. The hotly contested 1977 primary in which Mayor Koch emerged against Jewish, Italian, black, and Puerto

**Table 13.1    Votes Cast and Turnout, by AD Race,**
**1984 Presidential General and 1985 Mayoral Primary Elections**

| AD Race | 1984 General | | 1985 Primary | |
| (Number) | Vote | Turnout % | Vote | Turnout % |
|---|---|---|---|---|
| Black (13) | 422,990 | 70.4 | 129,464 | 26.8 |
| (Percentage of total) | 18.1 | | 18.8 | |
| Latino (3) | 93,054 | 68.2 | 35,521 | 31.2 |
| | 4.0 | | 5.2 | |
| Minority (8) | 264,708 | 71.8 | 91,392 | 32.0 |
| | 11.3 | | 13.3 | |
| White (10) | 374,275 | 78.6 | 112,260 | 34.5 |
| | 16.0 | | 16.3 | |
| Whiter (16) | 722,433 | 82.1 | 208,400 | 36.2 |
| | 30.9 | | 30.3 | |
| Whitest (10) | 460,431 | 83.4 | 111,209 | 33.5 |
| | 19.7 | | 16.2 | |
| Total (60) | 2,335,470 | 76.9 | 688,553 | 33.4 |

Source: NYC Board of Elections. Turnout based on total and Democratic registration as of May 1985.

Rican candidates drew an exceptionally large 916,000 votes, while the 1981 and 1985 races in which he was reelected drew below-average numbers: 581,000 in 1981 and 675,000 in 1985. Except for 1977, turnout has hovered at around one-third of the registered voters.

A simple tabulation of votes cast by ADs of different predominant racial characteristics appears to bear out the received wisdom that minority groups do not vote. Table 13.1 presents votes data for the 1984 general election and the 1985 mayoral primary: predominantly minority ADs cast only a third of the votes in the 1984 presidential election and only slightly more in the 1985 Democratic primary. Clearly, any candidate would have to get substantial support from white areas to win under these conditions. Even if a minority candidate could attract every minority voter, he or she would still need a quarter of the white votes, a level of white support that only Thomas Bradley of Los Angeles (and more recently David Dinkins in New York) had ever attracted in a first-time race against a white opponent.

It is possible that lower incomes, less education, and less political efficacy account for lower registration and turnout in minority ADs. Table 13.2 shows, however, that this is not the case for registration. Controlling for the fraction of the population who are of voting age and report to the

Table 13.2   Population, Eligibility, Registration, and Turnout,
by AD Racial Composition in New York City
(AD averages in thousands)

| AD Race (Number) | Total 1980 Population | Voting Age Population % | Citizen Rate % | Adjusted Voting Age Population | 9/85 Total Registered | Registration Adjusted Voting Age Population |
|---|---|---|---|---|---|---|
| Hispanic (3) | 116,000 | 64.5 | 93.3 | 69,800 | 45,800 | 65.6 |
| Minority (8) | 121,000 | 70.1 | 85.7 | 72,700 | 46,000 | 63.3 |
| Black (13) | 118,000 | 69.2 | 86.1 | 70,300 | 46,400 | 66.0 |
| White (10) | 118,000 | 75.9 | 86.2 | 77,200 | 47,700 | 61.8 |
| Whiter (16) | 120,000 | 80.3 | 90.2 | 86,900 | 54,800 | 63.1 |
| Whitest (10) | 119,000 | 80.3 | 93.0 | 88,900 | 55,300 | 62.2 |

Source: 1980 Census STF4(A) grouped by AD and New York City Board of Elections.

census that they are citizens (adjusted VPOP), it turns out that black and Latino ADs actually had slightly *higher* rates of registration than the white ADs despite their lower socioeconomic status. This finding goes squarely against the stereotype that minorities do not register. This stereotype is an artifact of the relative youth and lack of citizenship among New York's black and Latino residents. In fact, the voter registration campaigns designed to promote Jesse Jackson's candidacy in the 1984 presidential primary produced substantial registration gains in black and Latino ADs, to the extent that registration rates of the *eligible* residents slightly exceeded that of white areas.[28]

While all ADs started out with the same total 1980 population, the minority ADs had about one-sixth fewer *eligible* residents. The second and third columns of Table 13.2 indicate that blacks and Latinos are both younger and less likely to be citizens than the white population. Roughly 80 percent of the population of the 26 whitest ADs was 18 years of age or older in 1980, while only 69 percent of the black population and 64 percent of the Hispanic population had attained that age. This is a function both of racial succession—the selective migration of younger whites out of the city and younger minority families into it—and higher fertility among blacks and Latinos than among whites. This difference is particularly obvious among youth: over 80 percent of those entering the public school system are black, Hispanic, or Asian.

The minority population also contains many more foreign-born people who are not naturalized. While one of eight persons in the black ADs admitted to the 1980 census that they were not citizens, only one of sixteen did so in the whitest ADs. The Latino AD citizenship figure in Table 13.2 is probably high, although Puerto Ricans, who make up roughly 55 percent of the Latino population, are citizens. The other 45 percent, however, are foreign-born, post-1965 immigrants from such places as the Dominican Republic, Cuba, and Columbia, who tend not to be citizens. Many more foreign-born claimed to be citizens than actually were in the 1980 census.[29] A recent study by the Commonwealth of Puerto Rico in New York City cited census sources as estimating that 26 percent of voting age Latinos were not citizens.[30] About 20 percent of the Latinos in black and mixed minority ADs said they were not citizens. Thus, Table 13.2 clearly overestimates Latino citizenship and underestimates the ratio of registration to eligible population. Even so, it shows that noncitizenship substantially diminishes black and Latino eligibility.

But registration does not always translate into votes. The strong differences in turnout between the 1988 Democratic presidential primary and the 1988 presidential election shown in Table 13.3 make this quite clear. In the primary, black and Latino ADs, which average about 80 percent Democratic registration, contributed several thousand more votes on average than did the white ADs. While Latino turnout lagged behind the turnout in white areas, minority ADs matched white ADs and black ADs substantially exceeded them, pulling up the overall city average. Clearly, the presence of a charismatic black candidate had a strong impact on black political mobilization. This contrasts strongly with the 1985 mayoral primary in which a weak black candidate elicited the city's lowest average number of votes and the lowest turnout rate in black ADs. (Latino AD turnout exceeded black and minority AD turnout in 1985 because three Puerto Ricans were running for city council president.)

In sum, the nostrum that "minority groups don't vote" is a half truth. While fewer of New York City's black and Latino residents register or cast votes than is true of whites, this does not seem to be explained by their relative poverty or lack of education. Despite these conditions, black and Latino registration as a proportion of *the potentially eligible population* exceeded that of whites. Their youth and the high proportion of immigrant noncitizens do explain the low ratio of voters to population. Moreover, the political system did not nominate black or Latino candidates for citywide or higher offices, thus failing to give blacks and Latinos a special reason to vote in general elections. When strong black and Latino candi-

**Table 13.3   Average Votes Cast and Turnout, by AD Racial Composition (AD averages in thousands)**

| AD Race (Number) | 1988 Primary | Turnout % | Jackson % | 1988 General | Turnout % | Dukakis % |
|---|---|---|---|---|---|---|
| Latino (3) | 14.3 | 44.3 | 70 | 30.0 | 62.1 | 85.3 |
| Minority (8) | 14.7 | 49.1 | 63 | 28.5 | 64.2 | 82.6 |
| Black (13) | 17.5 | 57.4 | 88 | 28.7 | 63.4 | 88.5 |
| White (10) | 13.7 | 50.2 | 31 | 33.6 | 71.6 | 62.3 |
| Whiter (16) | 11.5 | 52.9 | 22 | 41.9 | 74.8 | 61.2 |
| Whitest (10) | 11.8 | 48.3 | 11 | 42.1 | 75.9 | 51.5 |
| Total (60) | 15.4 | 51.7 | 44 | 34.0 | 69.9 | 66.7 |

*Source:* New York City Board of Elections.

dates did run in a Democratic primary, as in the case of Jesse Jackson's 1988 presidential campaign, black turnout *exceeded* that of whites.

At this point, we may tentatively reject the argument that individual socioeconomic characteristics drive electoral inequality in New York City. Blacks and Latinos wield less electoral power than their numbers warrant not because they are poorer and less educated, but rather because they are more likely to be ineligible and have been presented with electoral choices that do not strongly appeal to them. Once these factors are taken into account, minority groups are in some instances *slightly more* politically mobilized than the white population. Moreover, this differential is magnified because blacks and Latinos are much more likely than whites to register as Democrats and to participate in the Democratic primary, the normal route to power in City Hall. This counterbalances the lack of eligibility.

The basic causes of political inequality cannot be found in individual characteristics or even in the requirements that reduce minority eligibility (though these are obviously important). Rather, we must find them in the dynamics *within* the local political system and the Democratic primary electorate that shape the formation of dominant coalitions. For twelve years, Mayor Edward I. Koch succeeded in forging a dominant electoral coalition that could win majorities without black or Latino votes, thus benefiting by the underlying racial tensions in the city. He also took advantage of divisions between and within the black and Hispanic electorates. For their part, until the 1988 Jackson victory and the 1989 Dinkins victories, black and Latino political leaders were not able to forge a common cause with liberal whites to challenge the dominant Koch coalition. The inner dynamics of a weakly organized one-party system reinforced these tendencies.

## The Forging of a Conservative Dominant Coalition

### White Support for the Koch Coalition

It is well known that whites strongly supported Mayor Koch in the 1985 Democratic mayoral primary. Multiple regression analysis of the 1985 results shows, however, that white ethnic groups varied in their support: white Protestants were least supportive, the Irish and Italians were moderately supportive, but the Jewish population was wildly supportive. The Russian and Polish ancestry data from the 1980 census may be used as a rough proxy for the Jewish population. This variable is far and away the strongest predictor of votes for the mayor in 1985. Unlike white Catholics, Jews are heavily Democratic and like other ethnic groups favor candidates of their own group. Moreover, Mayor Koch brilliantly articulated the *zeitgeist* of New York's traditionally liberal Jews as they moved toward the right.[31]

As might be expected, controlling for the size of the white population, ADs where the white population has higher rates of graduate training, professional occupations, and non-family households were slightly less likely to have supported the mayor in 1985. The mayor thus started his quest for an electoral majority with strong support from an ethnic group, Jews, which constitutes about 15 percent of the city's population and 25–30 percent of the Democratic primary electorate. He also drew strong support from white, non-Hispanic Catholics.

### Divisions Within: Minority Support for the Koch Coalition

Certain black spokesmen accused Mayor Koch of polarizing race relations in New York, and he often behaved in ways that give credence to their charges. Given strong white ethnic support for him, one might infer that his large electoral majority in 1985 rested on racial polarization. In fact, it did not. According to exit polls, Mayor Koch drew 37 percent of the black vote and 70 percent of the Hispanic vote against black and white liberal challengers.[32] What is the basis for this minority support?

Blacks most consistently opposed the mayor. Blacks are the most segregated ethnic group in New York; while the black and Hispanic populations often border on each other, they overlap only along a few borders, such as between Harlem and East Harlem or Bushwick and Bedford-Stuyvesant. Assembly districts are large enough, and have been so drawn, however, that even the most solidly black districts have some Hispanics, and a good number of ADs are quite mixed. If we control for the proportion Hispanic across minority ADs, the black voting age population is consistently and strongly negatively related to support for the mayor.

Even in overwhelmingly black ADs, however, Mayor Koch still won 35 percent of the vote in 1985. Interestingly, both the prevalence of black welfare families and the incidence of highly educated blacks had a statistically significant negative impact over and above that of race on support for Koch. ADs with more black local government employees also were more likely to oppose Koch, while ADs with many West Indians were a bit more likely to support him, though neither was statistically significant. We may hypothesize, then, that the mayor's black support was more likely to be found within the blue collar, immigrant "middle" of the black community.

Latinos are economically worse off than any other group in New York City and believe they are discriminated against and should work together politically with blacks, yet they overwhelmingly supported the mayor and declined to vote for his black opponent in the 1985 primary.[33] Nor did they support Jesse Jackson in 1984. There are several reasons why this may be so. There has been black/Latino political competition for many years. Although Latinos were almost as numerous as blacks at the beginning of the decade and probably now outnumber blacks, Latinos have only a third as many elected officials, a fact they resent.[34] When asked to choose a racial identity, Latinos clearly prefer white to black. In the 1980 census, 50 percent of Hispanics said they were "white" and 40 percent "other," with only 10 percent saying "black." In addition, Latinos are consistently more likely than any other group, including white non-Hispanic Catholics, to identify themselves as conservatives (about a third of Latinos do so).

There are also important ethnic differences *among* Latinos. Of the 20 ADs that are at least one-fifth Latino, five are primarily non-Puerto Rican. They are better off, much less likely to be citizens (and hence to vote), a bit more likely to support the mayor, and less inclined to have voted for one of the Puerto Rican city council president candidates in 1985. They were also less likely than the Puerto Rican ADs to support Jesse Jackson in

1988. A 1984 presidential election exit poll confirmed these aggregate patterns. It found that 73 percent of Latino voters were Puerto Rican, 14 percent Dominican, 5 percent Cuban, and 8 percent other Latin American. While 42 percent of Puerto Ricans preferred Mayor Koch to Herman Badillo, a Puerto Rican former borough president, 61 percent of the Cubans and 52 percent of the Dominicans preferred Koch.[35] Thus the mayor did better with foreign-born Latinos as well as with black immigrants.

Mayor Koch targeted his 1985 campaign effort to improve his support among Latinos and blacks. His campaign manager reported that he invested fully half of his $7 million war chest in field operations, the great bulk of them in minority neighborhoods. Further, the mayor assiduously developed a network of minority supporters through contracts granted to community-based social service operations. Many recipients of these contracts were associated with the regular Democratic party organizations in the outer boroughs; none took an overt stand against his reelection. Finally, the regular Democratic political culture nourished through such contracts had a considerable base in minority neighborhoods. Both survey data and aggregate analysis suggest that the presence of strong regular Democratic political clubs increased minority support for the mayor in 1985.[36]

### Divisions Between the Potential Challengers

While Mayor Koch capitalized on the cleavages that have emerged in postindustrial New York, they divided his would-be challengers during most of the 1980s. The feminization of the labor force, the rise of new service occupations, the subtle revolution in household formation, and immigration from the Caribbean and Asia have produced a cultural and political fragmentation that simple race and class dichotomies do not capture. These emerging differences did not prevent Mayor Koch from organizing the conservative dominant coalition—indeed they aided its formation—but they severely fragmented the potential opposition to this coalition.

The failed effort to find a consensus challenger to Mayor Koch in 1985 provides an example of how emerging cleavages undermined potential challengers. Manhattan black leaders forced the selection of a weak black candidate rather than turn to a Puerto Rican or a white woman; this candidate came in a poor third in the primary. The debacle deepened divisions between blacks and Hispanics, male and female black leaders, Manhattan and Brooklyn black leaders, and black regulars and black reformers.[37]

The weakly organized, one-party nature of New York City's political system has reinforced this fragmentation of potential challengers. As Martin Shefter has written,

> Although factionalism saps the political strength of New York's racial minorities, it is more a symptom than the ultimate cause of their weakness. Such factionalism characterizes politics under conditions of low electoral mobilization: politicians who do not undertake to outmobilize their opponents seek to prevail by outmaneuvering them.[38]

New forces are crosscutting the old distinctions of race and class. Native-born blacks and Puerto Ricans are declining, while West Indian, Dominican, and Asian immigration is on the rise. Male-dominated occupations are growing slowly or contracting, while female-dominated occupations are expanding. These differences not only divide potential insurgents, they have provided fertile ground for the dominant coalition to divide and conquer.[39] A multivariate analysis of the relationship between an AD's white, black, and Latino populations with their propensity to vote for white, black, and Latino candidates in 1985 made clear how deep they can be. White ADs voted strongly for whites but not for black or Hispanic candidates; black ADs voted against white candidates, strongly for black ones, and were indifferent to Hispanic candidates; meanwhile, Latino ADs voted against white candidates, for Hispanic candidates, and were indifferent to blacks.

In most of the 1980s, therefore, political inequality in New York did *not* take the form of simple exclusion or demobilization. Three planes of division within the electorate reinforced the conservative dominant political coalition in 1985 and deterred challengers to it: (1) Mayor Koch's strong racial and ethnic appeal to white voters, bolstered by the overall pattern of racially polarized voting; (2) ethnic, class, and nativity differences, as well as between black regulars and black insurgents, fostered divisions within the black and Latino constituencies that enabled the mayor to build significant support; and (3) divisions between white liberals, blacks, and Latinos, and the fragmented leadership of these constituencies deterred the formation of a challenging coalition.

## The Decay of the Koch Coalition

On November 7th, 1989, the voters of New York City elected David N. Dinkins mayor over Rudolph Giuliani by a 43,000 vote margin out of some 1.78 million ballots cast. This stunning victory could not have been more different than four years earlier, when Mayor Koch humiliated his

**Table 13.4    The Liberal Coalition in New York City: 1969 and 1989
Mayoral General Elections**

|  | 1969 | | 1989 | |
|---|---|---|---|---|
|  | Voters % | JVL % | Voters % | DND % |
| Non-Hispanic Whites | 79 | 42 | 56 | 27 |
| Catholic | 43 | 21 | 24 | 18 |
| Jewish | 30 | 44 | 18 | 35 |
| Non-Hispanic Blacks | 15 | 83 | 28 | 91 |
| Latinos | 6 | 67 | 13 | 65 |
| Other | — | — | 3 | 33 |
| Total | — | 44 | — | 50 |

*Sources:* 1969 Louis Harris Associates Exit Poll; 1989 *New York Times*/WCBS Exit Poll.

*Notes:* JVL = John V. Lindsay-L (against Mario Proccacino-D and John Marchi-R). DND = David N. Dinkins-D (against Rudolph Giuliani-R, L).

black challenger, beating him in ten out of the thirteen black ADs. Dinkins attracted about 27 percent of the non-Hispanic white vote, as well as 91 percent of the black vote and 65 percent of the Latino vote. His support mirrored the last time, two decades previously, that a biracial, liberal coalition had been formed in a mayoral general election in New York (see Table 13.4). This was all the more remarkable given that only 40 percent of the likely voters knew enough about Dinkins to form an opinion a year earlier, though they were largely positive.

For Dinkins to have come from this relative obscurity to topple a highly skilled and well-regarded mayor and then to defeat a highly regarded prosecutor in a campaign notable for Giuliani's aggressive attack was truly unprecedented. Only Tom Bradley's ascent to office in Los Angeles provides a comparable case, and he had run a vigorous previous race for the office with strong backing from liberal whites, especially Jews, for whom he was a route to power, in contrast to the situation in New York. How, given all the barriers, did he achieve such a stunning result? How had structural conditions changed since 1985 to make it possible?

First, Dinkins overcame the deeply embedded barriers to the formation of a multiracial, liberal insurgent coalition within the Democratic party. These include the divisions within the black political leadership, the tensions between blacks and Latinos, racial polarization among whites, and the hold of county party regular organizations over black and Latino political mobilization in the Bronx and Queens. The decay of support for Koch within the Democratic electorate was a precondition to Dinkins's victory. The corruption scandal, the white liberals' mounting dismay over the state of race relations, and the 1988 Jackson campaigns all fostered this result.

Mayor Koch and two of the county party leaders with whom he was closely allied (Stanley Friedman of the Bronx and Donald Manes of Queens) gave Koch's potential opponents considerable help. Starting with Manes's suicide in early 1986, it was revealed that Friedman and Manes had used the influence Koch had granted them to skim money from city contracts with private parking ticket collection agencies, get kickbacks on the granting of cable television franchises, and award the contract for purchase of hand-held computers to a company in which Friedman and Manes held a secret stake. This cascaded into many more revelations, a number of which involved the mayor's personal circle.[40] These events not only undermined the mayor's approval rating among the general public, but they severely weakened the Bronx and Queens regular Democratic organizations on which Koch had counted to help hold a substantial portion of the black and Latino vote in line. Many black and Latino district leaders allied with the regular county organizations endorsed Dinkins over Koch. Four years earlier, they could not have done so.

Simultaneously, the Howard Beach stampede of a black man to his death on a busy highway, the Central Park "wilding" attack by black youths on a white woman investment banker, and the Bensonhurst murder of a black by a gang of Italian kids (and an assault on Latino kids in the same area only a few days later) persuaded most New Yorkers that race relations were on a downward curve. Although Mayor Koch took a forthright stand against the perpetrators of the Howard Beach and Bensonhurst attacks, many whites felt that his criticisms of blacks (whether the "poverty pimps" of his first term or Jesse Jackson in his last) and his stalwart defense of the white middle class were simply not consistent with improving racial harmony. In the final analysis, a significant portion of white public opinion joined blacks and Latinos in turning against Mayor Koch because of race relations as well as the corruption scandal.

But even this was not sufficient to determine Dinkins' victory, since whites constituted a majority of the likely electorate even in the Democratic primary. Were non-Hispanic whites to be polarized racially, Koch would win. Furthermore, an alliance—of blacks, who might make up 33 percent of the Democratic primary electorate if highly mobilized, with Latinos, who might make up 15 percent, and liberal whites, who might make up another 15 percent—could not be assumed.

Two campaigns enabled Dinkins to build the necessary coalition for the primary. The first was the Jesse Jackson's New York City presidential primary campaign in early 1988. The second was Dinkins's own. In contrast with 1984, virtually all of New York's black politicians and most of its Latino politicians supported Jackson in 1988. They were joined by District Council 37 (the rank-and-file city employees union) and Local 1199 (the hospital workers' union). In contrast with the 1985 primary, when Mayor Koch won 60 percent of the Latino vote, Jackson won 70 percent. The cooperation of black and Latino leaders and the support of black and Latino electoral constituencies in the Jackson campaign proved the core elements for Dinkins' campaign.

Jackson had won only 43 percent of the primary vote in New York City, giving him a bare plurality against Dukakis and Gore. As other Democratic primary candidates faded, it became increasingly clear that Dinkins would have to win a larger plurality against Koch. The Dinkins campaign could not simply reproduce the Jackson campaign: it needed support from many more white voters, and especially from the relatively liberal Jewish vote. (White Protestants, though liberal, constitute only about 5 percent of New York's voters.)

Having consistently supported pro-Israeli foreign policy positions and liberal Jewish causes and rejected Louis Farrakhan, Dinkins was well positioned to make this appeal. In doing so, Dinkins also had to risk and deflect criticism from nationalist elements of the black community. Dinkins undertook a vigorous effort to win support from white voters, gaining strong support from Ruth Messinger, a liberal Manhattanite who ran a well-organized campaign to become Manhattan borough president, as well as from State Attorney General Robert Abrams and others. Coming shortly before the primary, the Bensonhurst killing crystallized feelings among white liberals that a basic moral choice had to be made in favor of Dinkins. Finally, since Koch would need black and Latino votes to win a general election, he did not vigorously attack Dinkins. Table 13.5 shows the strength of the Dinkins effort and the decay of support for Koch across the board.

Dinkins won 51 percent of the primary vote against Koch's 43 percent. While the Koch campaign put all of its funds into media, the Dinkins campaign mounted a large get-out-the-vote force and did a good job of targeting these resources on favorable areas.[41] Dinkins came out of the primary with a twenty-point polling lead over Giuliani, who had been heavily pounded by a $12 million negative campaign by Ron Lauder in the Republican primary.

Winning the general election promised to be more difficult than defeating Koch. Rudolph Giuliani was no Bernard Epton: he had jailed corrupt Democrats like Stanley Friedman alongside Wall Street insiders and Mafia dons. Since voters perceived crime and drugs as the city's key problems, who better to fight them than a prosecutor? Moreover, half of New York's

**Table 13.5  Democratic Mayoral Primary Votes: 1985 and 1989
(averages by AD racial makeup)**

| AD Racial Makeup | 1985 Turnout % | 1985 Koch % | 1989 Turnout % | 1989 Koch % |
|---|---|---|---|---|
| Black (13) | 26.8 | 41.8 | 56.0 | 10.8 |
| Latino (3) | 31.1 | 60.9 | 45.2 | 30.6 |
| Minority (8) | 31.9 | 57.7 | 48.0 | 28.4 |
| White (10) | 34.7 | 69.6 | 49.1 | 53.7 |
| Whiter (16) | 36.2 | 71.4 | 51.4 | 59.6 |
| Whitest (10) | 33.5 | 78.0 | 50.3 | 71.3 |
| Total (60) | 33.4 | 63.4 | 51.2 | 44.4 |

*Source:* New York City Board of Elections.

*Note:* Turnout expressed as percentage of registered Democrats as of May 1985 and April 1989.

voting aged citizens are Catholics; Giuliani could count not only on the normal 35 percent Republican fraction of the general electorate, but could also exhort middle class white Koch constituencies to defect on the basis of issues, race, and ideology. While Dinkins could also count on a 35–38 percent core of black, Latino, and white liberal support, that still left 25–30 percent of the vote up for grabs. This swing vote was overwhelmingly white and middle class.

From Dinkins' perspective, the most winnable part of this swing vote were middle and lower-middle class Jewish residents of the city's periphery. Jesse Jackson was thus respectfully disinvited from further campaigning. The Giuliani forces, guided by the acerbic Roger Ailes, mounted what can only be called a brutal attack on David Dinkins in an attempt to swing white constituencies toward Giuliani. They used Dinkins's previous failure to file timely income tax returns and his poorly documented transfer of Inner City Broadcasting stock to his son to try to associate Dinkins with the corrupt Democrats Giuliani had prosecuted. While this unrelenting negativism undoubtedly firmed up black support for Dinkins and drove some whites and Latinos into Dinkins's arms, it also cost Dinkins a great deal of white swing support. Major Democratic figures, led by the newly statesmanlike Mayor Koch and Governor Cuomo, rallied to Dinkins's defense. The county party organizations, which certainly did not like the idea of a Giuliani mayoralty, endorsed Dinkins.

In the final event, record numbers of white Democrats defected to Giuliani, particularly Jews living in areas like Marine Park and Canarsie in

Brooklyn and Kew Gardens and Fresh Meadows in Queens. These voters
had given Michael Dukakis his victory over George Bush in New York.
Although white non-Hispanic Catholics were less likely to vote Democratic, those who were normally so inclined also defected in record numbers. Given that Giuliani got votes from five out of six white Catholics
and one out of four Latinos, the support that over six out of ten Jewish
voters gave him was almost enough to make Rudolph Giuliani New
York's next mayor.

But not quite. Dinkins' capacity to organize a substantial field operation, the loyalty of a core of white liberals, and an increase in Latino
support for Dinkins as compared to the primary made the difference.
Spurred by Giuliani's attacks and the field operations, blacks turned out
in record numbers for a general election, particularly in the central Brooklyn areas of Bedford-Stuyvesant and Crown Heights. (Blacks normally
turn out better in primaries than in generals.) White Protestants and more
secular liberal Manhattan Jews stood by Dinkins. Gentrified areas like
Chelsea, the Village, SoHo, and Park Slope in Brooklyn all gave Dinkins
two-thirds of their votes. Finally, despite their Catholicism and conservatism, Latinos gave Dinkins over seven out of ten votes, though their turnout was low and they constituted only 13 percent of the total vote. Gender was also important. Women voters outnumber men in each
demographic group. Dinkins was clearly identified not only as pro-choice,
but as pro-children, pro-parenting, and pro-education compared to Giuliani. In each ethnic group, women were somewhat more likely than men
to support Dinkins.

## Conclusion

Does the inauguration of David Dinkins on January 1, 1990, mark a fundamental change in the patterns of political inequality that characterized
New York City during most of the 1970s and 1980s? In one sense, the
answer to this question must be affirmative. Blacks, Latinos, and liberal
whites, who were at best peripheral to the previous dominant electoral
coalition, became central components in the new one. Mayor Dinkins's
appointments have reflected these constituencies, which will in turn have
channels of access and participation that were previously closed. In terms
of the theoretical framework offered by Browning, Marshall, and Tabb,
minority and liberal political incorporation has clearly taken place in New
York City. This will certainly attenuate previous patterns of political
inequality.

On the other hand, Mayor Dinkins must govern now that he has been elected. He must not only maintain his electoral coalition, he must forge working relationships with the major institutional powers of the city. The narrowness of his election victory, the persistence of the divisions that previously made it difficult to organize an insurgent coalition, and the vast economic, social, and cultural distance between Dinkins's electoral base and major power-holders will make it difficult for him to attack the patterns of political inequality in any frontal way. If he falters in managing the tension between them, a job made all the more difficult by an impending recession, his opponents are sure to mobilize against him. In the balance hangs the fate of equalizing political power on a more permanent basis.

# Notes

An earlier version of this chapter benefited from criticism from the SSRC working group members, executive committee members of the CUNY Center for Social Research, and Asher Arian, Art Goldberg, Angelo Falcon, and Phil Thompson.

1. Mollenkopf, John, "The Postindustrial Transformation of the Political Order in New York City," in Mollenkopf, J., ed., *Power, Culture, and Place: Essays on New York City* (New York: Russell Sage Foundation, 1988), describes these economic and demographic changes and assesses their impact on various social groupings. See also the chapter by Bailey and Waldinger; Waldinger, Roger, "Changing Ladders and Musical Chairs: Ethnicity and Opportunity in Post-industrial New York," *Politics and Society* 15,4 (1986–1987): 369–402; and Waldinger, Roger, "Immigration and Urban Change," *Annual Review of Sociology* 15 (1989):211–232.

2. Of the twenty largest central cities in 1980, ten (New York, Chicago, Philadelphia, Baltimore, Washington, Indianapolis, Milwaukee, Columbus, Boston, and Cleveland) were outside the South and West. Four had non-Hispanic white populations of 70 percent or more—Indianapolis, Milwaukee, Columbus, and Boston. Of the remaining six, only New York had not elected a black mayor by 1989, although Baltimore did not elect its first black mayor, Kurt Schmoke, until 1987.

3. Stegman, Michael, *Housing and Vacancy Report, New York City 1987* (New York: Department of Housing Preservation and Development, April 1988), Table 2.3, p. 4, based on a sample of 22,000 households. A 1988 CUNY survey with a sample of 2,000 households produced comparable results. The March 1988 *Current Population Survey* annual demographic supplement, also with a sample of 2,000 households, found 47 percent non-Hispanic white,

22.4 percent non-Hispanic black, 24.5 percent Hispanic, and 6 percent non-Hispanic other.

4. Mollenkopf, John, "New York: The Great Anomaly," in Browning, Rufus, Dale Marshall, and David Tabb, eds., *Race and Politics in American Cities* (New York: Longman, 1990); Mollenkopf, John, *The Wagner Atlas: New York City Politics, 1989* (New York: The Wagner Institute, CUNY, 1989). Though he did not need their votes to get re-elected in 1985, exit polls suggest he won about 37 percent of the black vote and 70 percent of the Latino vote.

5. For an extended analysis of minority political incorporation, see Browning, Rufus, Dale Marshall, and David Tabb, *Protest Is Not Enough: The Struggle of Blacks and Hispanics for Equality in Urban Politics* (Berkeley: University of California Press, 1984). They define it operationally as formal representation among elected officials (mayor, city council) and participation in the dominant political coalition.

6. For an excellent overview of black political development in the five boroughs, see Thompson, J. Phillip, "The Impact of the Jackson Campaigns on Black Politics in New York, Atlanta, and Oakland" (Ph.D. dissertation, Political Science Program, CUNY Graduate Center, 1990). See also Green, Charles, and Basil Wilson, *The Struggle for Black Empowerment in New York City: Beyond the Politics of Pigmentation* (New York: Praeger, 1989), Chapters 4–6, and Lewinson, Edwin, *Black Politics in New York City* (New York: Twayne Publishers, 1974). No recent comprehensive discussion is available for Latinos, but see Jennings, James, *Puerto Rican Politics in New York* (Washington, DC: University Press of America, 1977); Georges, Eugenia, "New Immigrants and the Political Process: Dominicans in New York" (Center for Latin American and Caribbean Studies, New York University, Occasional Paper 45, April 1984); and Falcon, Angelo, "Black and Latino Politics in New York City: Race and Ethnicity in a Changing Urban Context," *New Community* 14,3 (Spring 1988): 370–384.

7. Lowi, Theodore, *At the Pleasure of the Mayor* (New York: Free Press, 1964), p. 200. See also Shefter, Martin, "Political Incorporation and the Extrusion of the Left: Party Politics and Social Forces in New York City," *Studies in American Political Development* 1 (1986), pp. 50–90; and Gerson, Jeffrey, "Building the Brooklyn Machine: Jewish and Black Succession in the Brooklyn Democratic Party Organization, 1919–1964" (Ph.D. dissertation, Political Science Program, CUNY Graduate Center, 1990).

8. Katznelson, Ira, *City Trenches* (New York: Pantheon, 1981).

9. Bridges, Amy, *A City in the Republic: Ante-Bellum New York and the Origins of Machine Politics* (New York: Cambridge University Press, 1984).

10. Shefter, "Political Incorporation and the Extrusion of the Left."

11. Piven, Frances Fox, and Richard Cloward, *Regulating the Poor* (New York: Pantheon, 1971).

12. Kimball, Penn, *The Disconnected* (New York: Columbia University Press, 1972), Chapter 9, "Mobilizing Minority Voters in New York City." See Table

5. Black and Puerto Rican votes provided 16.5 percentage points of Lindsay's plurality of 42.4 percent in 1969.

13. Morris, Charles, *The Cost of Good Intentions* (New York: Norton, 1980); Shefter, Martin, "New York City's Fiscal Crisis: The Politics of Inflation and Retrenchment," *The Public Interest* 48 (Summer 1977): 98–127; Katznelson, Ira, *City Trenches*.

14. See for example, Tabb, William K., *The Long Default: New York City and the Urban Fiscal Crisis* (New York: Monthly Review Press, 1982) and Lichten, Eric, *Class, Power & Austerity: The New York City Fiscal Crisis* (South Hadley, MA: Bergin and Garvey, 1986).

15. See Chapter 4 in this book.

16. Nie, Norman, Sidney Verba, and John R. Petrocik, *The Changing American Voter* (Cambridge: Harvard University Press, 1976). See also Goldberg, Arthur S., and Asher Arian, "The American Urban Electorate in the 1988 Presidential Election." Paper presented to the 1989 Annual Meeting of the American Political Science Association, Atlanta.

17. Key, V. O., Jr., *Southern Politics in State and Nation* (New York: Vintage, 1949); Burnham, W. D., *Critical Elections and the Mainsprings of American Politics* (New York: Norton, 1966). See also Piven, Frances Fox, and Richard Cloward, *Why Americans Don't Vote* (New York: Pantheon, 1988). This theme is developed in Mollenkopf, "New York: The Great Anomaly," in Browning et al., eds., *Race and Politics*, and Mollenkopf, "The Decay of Liberalism: One Party Politics New York Style," *Dissent* special issue on New York (Fall 1987): 492–495.

18. On the general problems of organizing, see Olson, Mancur, *The Logic of Collective Action* (New York: Schocken Books, 1969). Frances Piven and Richard Cloward offer a critique of minority political mobilization in *Poor People's Movements: Why They Succeed, How They Fail* (New York: Pantheon, 1977).

19. For example, Walters, Ronald, *Black Presidential Politics in America* (Albany: State University of New York Press, 1988) criticizes black political leaders for committing themselves to the Democratic party rather than trying to exercise the balance of power between the two parties. Green and Wilson, *Struggle for Black Political Empowerment*, and Falcon, "Black and Latino Politics," focus on the weakness and fragmentation of political leadership and the shortcomings of their strategic choices.

20. Census data are drawn from STF4 tract-level data, which provide detailed information on ancestry for non-European immigrants as well as occupation, industry of employment, and household income by race and Spanish origin. Tracts that are split by AD boundaries were allocated to the various ADs on the basis of the percentage of blocks that fell into each.

21. For a presentation of these data, see Mollenkopf, John, *The Wagner Atlas: New York City Politics, 1989*. These data have their own limits, of course, particularly the unmeasured demographic change that has taken place since 1980.

22. Each of New York City's five counties has a legally distinct county party organization with a county party leader elected by the male and female district leaders of the ADs in that county.

23. Gerson, "Building the Brooklyn Machine," describes this process in Bedford-Stuyvesant in the late 1940s and 1950s. New York's ADs were not redistricted between 1917 and 1943; they were redistricted again in 1953, when the 6th AD was created for Bertram Baker, Brooklyn's first black assemblyman, who finally won election in 1958. This and the abutting 17th AD concentrated the black population and ensured that blacks were not a major factor in other, white ADs. Both black and white legislators have favored concentration of the black population, because ADs must be at least roughly 75 percent black and Latino before election of a minority legislator becomes highly likely.

24. This classification sorts the population into three mutually exclusive groups, non-Hispanic whites, non-Hispanic blacks, and Latinos. Asians represent a substantial proportion of only two ADs.

25. While ADs must generally have more than 75 percent black and Latino population before electing a minority assemblyman, whites represented two ADs with more than 70 percent minority populations, AD 32 in Queens, the area around Kennedy Airport, and AD 42 in Brooklyn, East Flatbush during the 1980s.

26. Stegman, *Housing and Vacancy Report*, Tables 5.1a, 5.1b.

27. If no candidate wins a plurality of at least 40 percent in the September Democratic primary, the two highest vote-getters hold a run-off one month later. The Democratic nominee faces those of other parties in November. Given the large margin of Democratic registration, its nominee generally wins. Only when large numbers of Democrats defected to an independent or fusion candidacy, as in the cases of Fiorello La Guardia and John Lindsay, does this rule not hold true. Thus so-called prime voters, those who regularly vote in Democratic primaries, are a much-targeted group by political campaigns.

28. Demographic changes since 1980 might affect these results, but the available evidence points toward a *decline* of the native-born black and Puerto Rican population during the 1980s as well as a considerable slowing of the decline of the white native-born population to perhaps 5 percent. Thus the conclusion drawn remains valid. See Stegman, *Housing and Vacancy Report*, Table 2.1.

29. Evelyn Mann, head of the Population unit at the Department of City Planning, estimates that 200,000 foreign-born people falsely claimed to be citizens in the 1980 census.

30. Velazques, Nydia, et al., "Puerto Rican Voter Registration in New York City: A Comparison of Attitudes Between Registered and Non-Registered Puerto Ricans" (Migration Division, Department of Labor and Human Resources, Commonwealth of Puerto Rico, January, 1988), p. 2.

31. Rieder, Jonathan, *Canarsie: The Jews and Italians of Brooklyn Against Liberalism* (Cambridge: Harvard University Press, 1985). See also Harris, Louis, and Bert Swanson, *Black–Jewish Relations in New York City* (New York: Praeger, 1970).

32. CBS/*New York Times* exit poll, September 1985.

33. Velazquez, "Puerto Rican Voter Registration," p. 9, finds that 56 percent of registered Puerto Ricans do not believe Puerto Ricans get their fair share from New York City; 62 percent felt discriminated against; 63 percent felt blacks and Puerto Ricans should work together.

34. Falcon, Angelo, "Race and Ethnicity in New York City Politics: Racial Dualism Versus Ethnic Pluralism." Paper prepared for the SSRC Committee on New York City (November 1988), p. 9. The Latino population is also much less segregated and concentrated than the black population, making it more difficult to win assembly, senate, or council seats.

35. HACER/National Hispanic Women's Center, "New York City Hispanics: Who Votes and How?" (1985).

36. A 1988 CUNY survey revealed that one out of eight black registered Democrats was a member of a political club. Black club members were more than twice as likely to support Mayor Koch (31 percent) as those who are not in clubs (13 percent).

37. For accounts of this episode, see Thompson, "The Impact of the Jackson Campaigns," and Green and Wilson, *Struggle for Black Empowerment*, pp. 105–108.

38. Shefter, Martin, *Political Crisis/Fiscal Crisis* (New York: Basic Books, 1987), p. xv.

39. New York provides an interesting analogy to the one-party politics of the South in the 1950s described by Key, V. O. Jr., *Southern Politics in State and Nation*, Chapter 14.

40. Newfield, Jack, and Wayne Barrett, *City for Sale: Ed Koch and the Betrayal of New York* (New York: Harper & Row, 1988) details these events.

41. A public campaign finance reform limited Mayor Koch to spending less than half the funds he had raised against much weaker challengers in 1985.

PART **VI**

# The Dual City in Comparative Perspective

# 14

# Poles Apart: Urban Restructuring in New York and Los Angeles

## Edward W. Soja

A new round of urbanization is reshaping the forms and functions of the world's cities. Its specific contours and meaning are still being debated, as are its intensity and permanence as they relate to earlier periods of rapid urban change. It is clear, however, that the contemporary city is significantly different from the city of just 20 years ago. In response to these changes, current research has focused on analysis of *urban restructuring*, a term that has come to summarize the distinctive dynamics of urbanization in the late twentieth century.[1]

Drawing from the growing literature on urban restructuring, this chapter examines the recent experiences of perhaps the two most symptomatic centers of the new urbanization in the United States, New York City and Los Angeles. This comparative view of the peak points of the U.S. urban hierarchy provides a broad panorama of the restructuring processes affecting other cities and regions in different combinations and intensities.

## Urban Restructuring in Historical Perspective

Urban restructuring is associated with a major redirection of secular trends induced by severe shocks to preexisting conditions of urban growth and development. Its contemporary dynamics thus need to be evaluated against the backdrop of the larger economic and political crises that marked the end of the long postwar boom and, more specifically, the series of urban explosions within virtually all the advanced industrial countries in the late 1960s. These events vividly announced both the imminent decline of an older urban era and the beginning of a new urbanization. This new urbanization arises from the public and private search for strategies that adapt better to the "urban crisis" and restore the conditions for social stability and economic growth.

This politically charged urban restructuring process is still in progress and continues to be filled with competitive conflicts between the old and the new, between an inherited and a projected order, between continuity and change. It is an intrinsically open-ended process, unpredetermined in its ultimate outcome, tentative and experimental in its sustaining strategies. The impact and intensity of urban restructuring thus differs from city to city, confounding most attempts at easy generalization. Nevertheless, there are some broad patterns and trends emerging from this contemporary restructuring. But before turning to the similarities and differences in the urban restructuring of Los Angeles and New York, we must set the current scene in the context of earlier periods of rapid urban change.[2]

The new urbanization is the fourth of a series of innovative urban restructurings that have reshaped the capitalist city over the past two centuries. The first occurred between 1830 and 1850, capping what Hobsbawm called the Age of Revolution.[3] It transformed the mercantile capitalist city into the classical forms of the competitive, entrepreneurial, and extraordinarily centralized industrial capitalist city of the mid-nineteenth century, best exemplified in the United States by New York, Philadelphia, and Chicago.

Beginning in the 1870s and lasting for more than two decades, a second round of restructuring decentralized industrial production and employment while concentrating commercial and financial capital in the skyscraping citadels of an expanded central business district. Again, New York and Chicago were the paradigmatic centers of this "new" urbanization, which overlaid the urban landscape with the characteristic features of the corporate capitalist city, still highly centralized but now increasingly stretched through suburban expansion to a truly metropolitan scale.

Through the Great Depression and World War II, a third restructuring magnified many of the trends that had shaped the corporate capitalist city: industrial decentralization, increasing oligopoly in financial control and corporate organization; growing suburbanization and metropolitanization (now including significant portions of blue collar workers); the further packing of the inner city rings with racial and ethnic minorities (as the white middle class filtered outward to the suburbs); and above all, the powerful expansion of the role of the state in every sector of the economy, subsidizing and choreographing this complex reconfiguration. An even more sprawling, polycentric, politically fragmented, and bureaucratically planned urban mosaic emerged from this restructuring to become rather tensely consolidated in the postwar years.

This different capitalist city is now increasingly being described as Fordist, after its most expansive system of industrial production; or alternatively as Keynesian, signifying its state-managed "social contract" and welfare systems. Its metropolitan frame was the locus of mass production and mass consumption, of assembly lines and tract-house suburbs, of productivity deals and welfare doles, all impelled by the driving demands of that quintessentially Fordist of products, the automobile. Appropriately enough, the most paradigmatic cities were no longer New York and Chicago but Detroit and Los Angeles, the two fastest growing and most autocentric metropoles of the mid-twentieth century.

That the earliest and most explosive sparks signaling the crisis and restructuring of the Fordist City were struck in the streets of Los Angeles and Detroit should not be surprising. The deep worldwide recession of 1973–75 generalized the disintegrative malaise set off by the earlier urban uprisings and contributed to the proliferation of urban crises in virtually every advanced industrial capitalist city, including the New York City fiscal crisis. As had happened several times before, the existing urban structure and political economy seemed unable to sustain continued growth and social stability at the same time. Patchwork reforms and welfare payoffs were no longer enough. A much deeper social, economic, and political reconfiguration appeared necessary.

The preceding chapters in this volume provide detailed glimpses of a post-Fordist, post-Keynesian, and perhaps even postindustrial and postmodern New York. They trace a complex path that is both unique and generalizable to many other major metropolitan regions.

## Income Polarization and the Dual City

One of the most characteristic features of the new urbanization in Los Angeles and New York has been a dramatically widening divide between the rich and the poor. An increasingly polarized city both socially and spatially has been taking shape in the economic recovery of the New York metropolitan region and in the almost continuously booming economy of Greater Los Angeles. Between 1969 and 1987, the proportion of male year-round, full-time workers (YRFT) earning $20,000–$40,000 decreased significantly in Los Angeles County while those earning less than $20,000 and more than $40,000 increased. By the end of this period, the lowest wage bracket (under $10,000 in 1986 dollars) had doubled in size from 7 to 14 percent of all YRFT workers, a percentage that is now higher than that of the United States as a whole.[4]

Low-wage workers (defined in conjunction with the poverty level) increased in total numbers from 114,000 in 1969 to 467,000 in 1987, a rate of growth 16 times that of the total population of Los Angeles County. There was also a major ethnic recomposition of this segment of the labor market. The percentage Anglo dropped from 62 to 25, while the Latino proportion (excluding Chicanos) rose fivefold from 11 to 55 percent. Poverty statistics for Los Angeles County portray a similar picture: overall rates growing to higher than the national average (15.6 versus 13.5 in 1987), with a dramatically increasing Latinization of the poor and with a significant proportion of the poor employed in low-wage jobs. New York City has experienced a similar growth of the poverty population, but a much greater percentage of this growth is attributable to job loss (especially in manufacturing) rather than to the proliferation of low-wage jobs (including in manufacturing) that has characterized the economic polarization of Los Angeles.

Reference to manufacturing employment highlights another contrast between New York and Los Angeles. Greater Los Angeles (five counties) has become the largest manufacturing region in North America, and Los Angeles County, despite a recent slowdown in employment growth, now contains almost as many industrial workers as the New York and Chicago SMSAs combined. But whereas only about 6 percent of manufacturing jobs in 1969 were classified as low-wage, over 20 percent were, in 1987.[5] In other words, income polarization appears to have been intensified by the continued expansion of manufacturing.

Income polarization in the United States has often been explained in terms of deindustrialization and the structural shift to low-paying jobs in the service sectors, usually connected to some form of the postindustrial hypothesis. This is an inadequate explanation for Los Angeles. The service sectors have grown rapidly to surpass manufacturing in the total employment picture in Los Angeles, and there has been extensive deindustrialization, primarily within what was the largest Fordist industrial complex in the western United States. But there has also been a significant reindustrialization in Los Angeles, with expansive growth in both high technology (aerospace, electronics) and low technology (apparel, furniture) industrial sectors. Rather than reducing poverty and income inequalities, however, reindustrialization appears to have aggravated both.

The black population of Los Angeles probably comes closest to fitting the conventional "underclass" model. As in New York, many blacks have dropped out of the formal labor force entirely, and both unemployment and poverty rates remain extremely high. High-wage employment (more than $40,000) has increased steadily over the past two decades but still remains a small proportion of all YRFT jobs (less than 5 percent, about the same as for Chicanos). The proportion of low-wage jobs, however, has dropped significantly to a level comparable to the Anglo population and less than half that for Chicanos.

Blacks have apparently refused to accept (or have been excluded from) low-wage employment, and thus they form a relatively small proportion of the working poor. Nevertheless, they have probably suffered most from the decline of Fordist blue collar industries and gained least from the region's robust reindustrialization. Public sector employment has helped to buffer the now slowly decreasing black population against much greater downward mobility, swelling the middle-wage stratum to a higher proportion (over 86 percent in 1987) than for any other ethnic group.[6] Amongst the homeless and in what some have called the growing permanent underclass, however, blacks are disproportionately represented.

The growing polarization of the urban political economy is thus a complex phenomenon. It has been accelerated by the general decline in real wages that has distinctively characterized the restructuring of the U.S. economy over the past two decades and, with little historical precedent, persisted even through the prolonged growth cycle in the 1980s. It has been associated with deindustrialization and job loss, but it also occurs in conjunction with industrial expansion and job growth. In New York and Los Angeles, in particular, it has been intensified by a massive inflow of migrants from Third World countries bulging out the bottom ranks of the urban labor market and with a booming expansion of certain specialized sectors generating extraordinary wealth at the upper end of the income ladder.

Brint estimates that the professionals of New York make up close to one-third of the labor force, a figure that is probably roughly the same for Greater Los Angeles (with more scientists and engineers and fewer stockbrokers and securities analysts). Taken together, the executive-professional-managerial "overseers" and the predominantly minority and immigrant "underclass" may now be the majority of both cities' populations, a far cry from the old dual city of the proletariat and the industrial bourgeoisie.

## Regional Polarization and World City Formation

To understand more clearly the causes and consequences of this complex polarization process, it is necessary to view New York and Los Angeles from a more macro-analytical perspective. Looking first at the national scale, New York and Los Angeles have become centrally involved in another kind of polarization that is linked to the processes of urban restructuring. For the first time since the Great Depression and only the second time since the Civil War, regional income inequalities in the United States appear to be increasing. Moreover, rapid economic expansion seems to be highly concentrated in two megalopolitan zones, christened several decades ago as Boswash and Sansan, the urbanized regions stretching from Boston to Washington D.C. and from San Francisco to San Diego.

The megacities of New York and Los Angeles, with a population of over thirty million and a gross economic product greater than all but a half dozen countries, are today the propulsive heartlands of Boswash and Sansan and the primary growth poles of an increasingly bicoastal economy. Between 1981 and 1985, for example, the Atlantic coastal states plus California (containing 42 percent of the U.S. population) accounted for 69 percent of real income growth and 58 percent of all new jobs.[7]

This growing regional polarity confounds the simple Sunbelt-Frostbelt or North-South dichotomy that appeared so relevant in the early stages of the current period of restructuring. There are many growth centers outside this bicoastal concentration, but the evidence of the 1980s suggests that the patterns of urban restructuring that have taken shape in the megacities of Boswash and Sansan have become particularly advantageous for continued economic expansion in the late twentieth century. New York and Los Angeles are not the only growth regions within these two megalopolitan zones, and any further analysis of regional polarization would have to examine more closely the new urbanization in such centers as San Diego, the Bay Area and Silicon Valley, Boston, and Baltimore and Washington. But there is another dimension to the bicoastal economy that refocuses our attention on the NY-LA comparison: the consolidation of New York and Los Angeles as "World Cities," specialized metropolises serving an increasingly globalized economy.

Restructuring has affected not only the urban political economy. Since the 1960s, there has also been a deep restructuring of the longstanding international division of labor between First, Second, and Third Worlds, based largely upon an unprecedented internationalization of the production of goods and services. This global decentralization and the attendant rise of transnational corporate management systems created increasing burdens on existing financial and transactional arrangements. A global network of specialized World Cities quickly took shape to service and sustain this expansive internationalization. In the deindustrializing North Atlantic Basin, domestic deregulation allowed New York and London to retain (and even expand) their preeminence as global financial centers. In the Pacific Basin, Tokyo and more recently Los Angeles (superseding San

Francisco) also became dominant nodes in the premier circuit of World Cities. Today, these four financial panopticons, the capitals of global capitalism, span and scan the globe in a 24-hour sequence of shifts, assisted by a constellation of regional command centers and amazing new technologies of information and monetary exchange.

Within this quadrumvirate of leading World Cities, New York is more comparable to London than to Tokyo or Los Angeles. Both London and New York contain highly specialized concentrations of transactional expertise organized to service global capital markets. This orientation restricts somewhat the multiplier effects of the booming FIRE (finance, insurance, real estate) sector on the local metropolitan economy. When growth in the FIRE and related sectors is excluded, the residual urban economies of London and New York are characterized by massive job loss and deindustrialization (except perhaps for the sprawling outer reaches of the metropolitan region).

Whereas the immediate connections between the financial and the industrial economy in New York and London have been stretched to the breaking point, in Tokyo and Los Angeles they remain productively combined and interactive. As World Cities, Tokyo and Los Angeles are major centers of industrial production as well as financial services. Moreover, their growing financial services, in comparison to Lower Manhattan and The City, are less geographically concentrated (and less insular) within the metropolitan landscape.

There are other major differences between New York and Los Angeles as World Cities. Los Angeles still has a long way to go to catch up with New York in total office space, major corporate headquarters, and in the overall size and scope of its FIRE sector. But it has been moving fast in each of these areas, especially in the 1980s. In 1985, for example, a peak year for both New York and Los Angeles in building construction, the total value of new office space added was $252.4 million in New York to $384.6 million in Los Angeles. The U.S. Department of Commerce figures for new industrial building were $10.8–$135.2 million; and for additions and alterations to existing stock, $60.6–$285.5 million.[8] Between 1980 and 1985, total deposits in Los Angeles banks and S&Ls increased by more than 60 percent, while those in New York declined. Although their number is dwindling, New York City has many more headquarters of Fortune 500 companies (66 to 7 in Los Angeles in 1986); but for *Inc.* magazine's list of the 500 fastest growing small and middle-sized companies in 1988, Los Angeles County leads by 24 to 6.

In all of these comparisons, a key factor is again the robust industrial growth of the Los Angeles region, fostered significantly by massive inputs of defense expenditures during most of the 1980s. The federal government, especially through the military-focused Keynesianism of the Reagan administration, has contributed greatly to the growth of Los Angeles. These contributions are not only confined to industrial production, for they have made Los Angeles a primary node in another insidious circuit of global (if not interplanetary) transactions and high technology telecommunication based on managing military rather than financial information. This too is part of its role as a leading World City.

Even after noting these contrasts between New York and Los Angeles, it is important to emphasize some similarities. World City formation has condensed in both what is probably the largest and most diverse representation of global cultures that has ever existed anywhere. Although their outreach as World Cities is based on a different mix of sectoral specializations, they have both also become increasingly polarized, with expanding extremes of wealth and poverty. Marking these two extremes are perhaps the largest concentrations in the industrial world of the characteristic social groupings that have multiplied in the wake of the new urbanization: the homeless and the native-born underclass, the working poor and the super-rich, the "dinks" (double income-no kids) and the "yuppies" (hyperconsuming urban professionals).

To push the Los Angeles–New York comparison still further, it is necessary to move to a more micro-analytical scale and explore the intraurban geography of restructuring and polarization, the changing urban landscapes being produced by the new urbanization. Here too there are significant differences and similiarities.

# The Urban Geographies
# of Post-Fordism and Postmodernity

Over the past 10 years the Los Angeles urban region has been an active research laboratory for examining and conceptualizing what have been termed as post-Fordist and postmodern urbanization processes.[9] This has focused attention on the organizational and transactional structures of firms, branches, and sectors within the local economy; on the changing composition of territorial labor markets and the urban social and spatial division of labor; and on the modes of political and ideological practice that have helped to legitimize and regulate the emergent post-Fordist "regime of flexible accumulation," a transactions-intensive production system based on diverse forms of flexibility in technology, corporate organizational structures, and the use of labor. Reduced to its basic arguments, this approach to contemporary urban restructuring highlights many of the same processes of change and development that have been described thus far in most of the earlier chapters of this volume and in the present comparison of New York and Los Angeles. In addition, however, it attempts to connect the various manifestations of contemporary urban restructuring into a comprehensive and cohesive thesis on the historical and geographical distinctiveness of contemporary urbanization and industrialization processes, using the Los Angeles region as a paradigmatic case.

The post-Fordist geography of Los Angeles—and with some modifications, of New York as well—is being socially created from the crisis-induced dynamics of restructuring, from what has been described earlier as the search for restored social stability and increased productivity and profits. Integral to this search at the national scale has been a disciplining or "rationalization" of the labor force, especially the middle ranks of highly unionized and relatively well-paid manufacturing workers employed in the large Fordist industries that were central to the postwar economic boom. Plant closures and "runaway" relocations, union-busting and labor givebacks, deregulation and dismantlement of many welfare benefits, stagflation and the general decline in average real wages, as well as overall manufacturing employment—all have contributed to the trend-reversing deindustrialization of America. In Los Angeles and New York, restructuring and rationalization shrank the once bulging middle-wage stratum and created new, post-Fordist landscapes of despair and abandonment in many of the old black and white working class neighborhoods that made Fordism work. In its wake, South Central Los Angeles (site of the Watts riots in 1965) and the South Bronx became the twin symbols of the most disastrous effects of this highly selective deindustrialization.

As noted earlier, the black population has probably suffered most from the new urbanization. In much of South Central Los Angeles, the rates of poverty, unemployment, and infant mortality are even higher than at the time of the riots. Much the same can be said for parts of Harlem, Brooklyn, and the Bronx, a cruel reflection of the effectively punitive discipline imposed on the population that most radically threatened the Fordist order in the 1960s. Even more cruelly perhaps, these most devastated landscapes are becoming increasingly attractive to ambitious developers, dreaming of the profitable possibilities of "post-disaster" reconstruction for a very different population.

Some of the refugees from these landscapes of despair, mainly white, have succeeded in being upwardly and outwardly mobile, filtering into the wealthier pole of the dual city labor market. A much greater proportion have added to another characteristic and growing feature of the post-Fordist city: the multijob household. Economic restructuring in the United

States, as opposed to that of Europe and Japan, has been associated with significant new job generation and with a much more rapid decline in the number of "traditional" one-breadwinner families. This largely accounts for the continued national increase in average household income at the same time as real wages per job have been falling.

Permutations upon the multijob household (the aforementioned dinks, the rapid increase in part-time and contingent labor, in moonlighting, in the number of employed women with young children, in low-wage jobs, and the working poor) are found at every level of the income ladder. These household types existed prior to the current period of restructuring, but they have proliferated to an unprecedented degree over the past two decades and they have had a growing effect on the changing urban-built environment. The booming fast-food industry is perhaps the most obvious manifestation of this lengthening of paid work-hours per household, but its influence pervades more deeply into the entire urban economy. It both contributes to and complicates income polarization, increasingly affects urban planning priorities and the design of housing, shapes the form and content of the media and advertising, stresses the transit system of the city, and aggravates environmental degradation. Were it not for this income-expanding strategy, the American economy might now be in the depths of the greatest economic depression since the 1930s. Because of it, we are faced with a different set of costs and crises.

The post-Fordist geographies of Los Angeles and New York are filled with the impacts of deindustrialization, income polarization, labor market fragmentation, and the lengthening of "residential" working hours. But we must add to these geographies the impacts of several related features of the new urbanization: the formation of technologically innovative and growth-inducing industrial and specialized service districts, the increasing internationalization of the local economy, and the massive influx not only of global capital but of an extraordinary global labor force. We now have the much fuller menu of the restructuring processes transforming the post-Fordist urban landscape.

The new industrial districts that have taken shape in Los Angeles have received particularly intensive investigation and have become models for similar research throughout the industrial and industrializing world.[10] This has given the literature on Los Angeles a much stronger industrial emphasis than has the recent research on New York City. In the works of Scott on the "technopoles" of Southern California, of Morales on the automobile industry, of Storper and Christopherson on the entertainment industry, a detailed picture emerges of the dynamics of post-Fordist economic restructuring, the rise of flexible production systems for both goods and services, and the changing relations between production-work-territory in shaping urban development.[11]

The focal points in this picture are the various territorial production complexes in the inner and "outer" cities of the Los Angeles urban region. The Orange County complex has received the greatest attention, deservedly so for it is the quintessential post-Fordist technopole and the generative source for a remarkably new kind of urban-suburban landscape. Another industrial complex stretches along the Pacific shores of Los Angeles County, specialized in aerospace and national defense-related activities, while a third is growing rapidly just to the north, in the west San Fernando Valley and eastern Ventura County. With the San Diego Freeway as its backbone, this long swathe of high technology industry sustains the largest urban population of scientists, mathematicians, engineers, computer specialists, and weapons experts in the world—Los Angeles' fulsome new technocracy.

But there are other production complexes and urban districts characterized by the flexible specializations of post-Fordism. A multinodal financial, banking, and legal services complex is based in the new skyscrapers of downtown Los Angeles, which stretches nearly twenty miles along Wilshire Boulevard, with a significant outlier growing in the heart of Orange County at Irvine and Newport Beach. Downtown Los Angeles is also the center of a still growing garment district highly adaptive to the most changeable of fashions and styles and able, much like the most advanced high technology industries, to deliver its goods "just-in-time." And then there is what the locals call "The Industry," producing more popular entertainment commodities than anyplace on earth in an axis linking Studio City and Universal City to the north to Century City and Culver City in the south.

Again, all these activities existed prior to the current restructuring, but they have grown rapidly in recent years and, more importantly, they have increasingly agglomerated in expanding clusters of flexibly organized small and middle-sized companies hiving off to subcontract to large (and formerly more vertically integrated) firms. This process, whether high or low technology-based, whether involving the production of goods or the provision of specialized services, has contributed significantly to the formation of the dual city in Los Angeles, for its labor demands fall primarily at the two extremes of the income ladder and much less on the more likely to be unionized middle ranks.

At first glance, one might argue that New York does not fit this picture of Los Angeles, that it is more conventionally postindustrial rather than decidedly reflective of a new post-Fordist regime of flexible accumulation that continues to revolve around industrial production. Nonetheless, within a sixty-mile radius around Lower Manhattan (a similar range to one definition of the Greater Los Angeles region) there still remains the country's second-largest manufacturing region. While the five-borough core has lost over 600,000 manufacturing jobs since 1960, the outer rings have actually gained slightly in manufacturing employment. Even more rapid expansion in wholesaling and commercial office development has occurred in the growing outer cities of New York—the Trans-Hudson City and Princeton corridor of northern New Jersey, Westchester-White Plains, Fairfield-Stamford-Greenwich—and they appear much more like service and/or research hubs than industrial districts. But in or around them are nearly as many manufacturing workers as in Los Angeles County and it is very likely that this still sizeable industrial base is experiencing many of the same changes in production technology, corporate organization, and labor-management systems as have been occurring in Los Angeles. To some extent, a fixation upon the dramatic developments in the deindustrialized core of New York City—what might be described (pace Tom Wolfe) as the "vanity of the bonFIREs"—may be blocking recognition of the more characteristically post-Fordist dynamics of peripheral urbanization and industrialization in the larger metropolitan region.

If we include producer services within a broadened definition of "industry" and consider transactional information as a commodity, then even the Manhattan corporate service complex appear much less postindustrial and more post-Fordist. Producer services account for more than half of what Drennan calls the "export industry" jobs in New York City; and the massive financial services node in Lower Manhattan has many of the characteristics of the flexibly specialized, post-Fordist technopoles of Southern California. Instead of a new technocracy to symbolize its most propulsive economic sector, however, New York City has its bankers, stockbrokers, securities analysts, corporate lawyers, and advertising executives.

In both New York and Los Angeles, the dynamics of post-Fordist urban restructuring (albeit through somewhat different sectoral mixes) have been associated not only with the rapid growth of export industries but also with the importation of massive quantities of foreign capital and labor—almost surely more than any other two cities in the world. This immigrant capital and labor has been as vital to the recovery of New York City and the continued growth of the Los Angeles economy as any domestic restructuring, whether of corporate management systems, of household employment strategies, or of the technology of producing goods and services. And they have equally intensely reshaped the urban geographies of Los Angeles and New York.

Prime properties in downtown Los Angeles and most new high-rise developments are now predominantly owned by foreign capital (a much higher percentage than in Lower Manhattan), with Japanese investment having risen to the lead in recent years just ahead of Canadian, British, and Dutch capital. As in New York City, the inner residential ring of Los Angeles has become the primary homeland of a largely Third World labor force, as most of the Anglo working class and the professional-managerial strata have fled to higher ground. The pattern is neater in Los Angeles, for there has been relatively little gentrification around the city center (despite the encouragements of powerful public and private interests). Instead, the city center is rimmed by an almost continuous girdle of ethnic neighborhoods: Little Tokyo, Koreatown, Little Manila, the great barrios of East Los Angeles and Echo Park-Alvarado (home to most of the 400,000 Salvadorans who have moved in since 1980), a downtown as well as suburban Chinatown, and an increasingly pinched salient of predominantly black Los Angeles. Except for skid row, still mainly black, the inner city is overwhelmingly Latino and Asian, drawn mostly from countries rimming the Pacific Ocean.

Embedded most densely in the inner ring but existing throughout the region is a contemporary American version of the vast squatter settlements and bustling underground economies of Third World cities. One of the industrial world's largest concentrations of the homeless is just the most visible manifestation of an endemic housing crisis that pervades the dual city of post-Fordism and has induced new strategies of "flexible" residential adaptation. A recent *Los Angeles Times* survey discovered that perhaps as many as 250,000 people were living in backyard buildings of various sorts, bartering their labor and paying rent for what is often just a taped-up garage without kitchen or toilet facilities. Measures of residential overcrowding have reached peak levels, while small hotels and motels are being increasingly filled with hotbedding families, sleeping in sequence as they attempt to save enough money to rent a place of their own. There are no extensive *favelas* or *bidonvilles*, but there is a more hidden and dispersed equivalent that in Los Angeles may contain upwards of a half million residents.

This population also practices a form of flexible specialization to survive in the post-Fordist and post-Keynesian world, taking advantage of any opportunity available for food, shelter, and the protection of life. The growing drug trade has been invaded by these subsistence strategists, some of whom have become international entrepreneurs and local benefactors, funding community development efforts after years of neglect by city governments and planning authorities. With crime and gang activity increasing and well over a million people living below the poverty level, more public effort is being given to patrol and control the boundaries of the urban poor, keeping these survival strategies in their place, than to housing and community development. In today's Los Angeles, "Trespassers Will Be Shot" is not only a sign that one frequently sees in the rich suburbs, it is an implicit message posted, graffitoed, or otherwise signaled throughout the landscape, from gang turfs to freeway lanes, from the residential strongholds of the shrinking middle class to the "smart" office buildings of the new downtowns.

The upper professionals are also among the most aggressive territorial in-fighters struggling to establish and maintain their living and leisure spaces in the restructured terrain. They tend to be younger and more nouveau riche than their Fordist predecessors, who typically moved quietly to the suburbs in privatized strongholds far from the male breadwinner's workplace. The present generation demands much more and has the public and private power to make its demands fit into the crowded, edgy, and fragmented built environment. As Boyer notes for New York City, "Luxury neighborhoods, food shops, boutiques, entertainment zones, and television and information nodes are commanding more and more territory and displacing many of the city's former residents, functions, and services."[12]

The post-Fordist dual city is thus becoming increasingly filled with violent edges, colliding turfs, and interpenetrating spaces as the much clearer, hierarchical lines and territorialities of an earlier urban era seemingly melt into air. Instead of the older, simpler "tale of two cities," one rich and one poor, there is what Eric Lampard calls "a compendious and unwieldy narrative of many 'cities' and a multitude of interests, almost all of them suffused with nostalgia for times and places that never really were."[13] Ironically perhaps, it has been this compendious, pluralistic, and nostalgic narrative that has helped to sustain and legitimize the most expansive growth strategies of urban restructuring in New York and Los Angeles, and to prevent the fragmented post-Fordist metropolises from exploding under the impact of their evisceration.

At this point, we are at the edge of another important dimension of the urban restructuring of New York and Los Angeles, one more finely attuned to the changing cultural logic, political discourse, and ideological practices of the late twentieth century city. For reasons of space and time, however, this exploration of the postmodern geographies of the city cannot be accomplished here. It must await another round of interpreting the new urbanization of New York and Los Angeles.

# Notes

1. For some of the most recent studies of urban restructuring in the United States, see Fainstein, Susan S., et al., *Restructuring the City* (New York: Longman 1986); Smith, Michael P., and Joe R. Feagin, eds., *The Capitalist City: Global Restructuring and Community Politics* (Oxford: Basil Blackwell, 1987); Harvey, David, "Flexible Accumulation Through Urbanisation: Reflections on 'Post-modernism' in the American City," *Antipode* 90 (1987): 260–286; Beauregard, Robert A., ed., *Economic Restructuring and Political Response* (Newbury Park, CA: Sage Publications, 1988); Feagin, Joe R., *Free Enterprise City: Houston in Political-Economic Perspective* (New Brunswick, NJ: Rutgers University Press, 1983); Scott, Allen J., *Metropolis: From the Division of Labor to Urban Form* (Berkeley and Los Angeles: University of California Press, 1988); Beauregard, Robert A., ed., *Atop the Urban Hierarchy* (Totowa, NJ: Rowman & Littlefield, 1989); and Soja, Edward W., *Postmodern Geographies: The Reassertion of Space in Critical Social Theory* (London: Verso, 1989).

2. A more detailed discussion of the material in this section can be found in "The Historical Geography of Urban and Regional Restructuring," Chapter 7 in Soja, *Postmodern Geographies.*

3. Hobsbawm, Eric J., *The Age of Revolution 1789–1848* (New York: New American Library, 1962).

4. Schimek, Paul, "Earnings Polarization and the Proliferation of Low-wage Work," *The Widening Divide: Income Inequality and Poverty in Los Angeles* (Los Angeles: Graduate School of Architecture and Urban Planning, UCLA, 1989).

5. Schimek, "Earnings Polarization."

6. Ibid.

7. Joint Economic Committee Report on The Bicoastal Economy, 1986.

8. Beauregard, ed., *Atop the Urban Hierarchy.*

9. Soja, *Postmodern Geographies*; Scott, "Technopoles."

10. Scott, Allen J., *Metropolis.*

11. Scott, "Technopoles of Southern California" (Los Angeles: UCLA Research Papers in Economic and Urban Geography, 1989) No. 1; Morales, Rebecca, "The Los Angeles Automobile Industry in Historical Perspective," *Environment and Planning D: Society and Space* 4 (1986): 289–303; Storper, Michael, and Susan Christopherson, "Flexible Specialization and Regional Industrial Agglomerations," *Annals of the Association of American Geographers* 77 (1987): 194–217; Scott, Allen J., and Michael Storper, eds., *Production, Work, Territory: The Geographical Anatomy of Industrial Capitalism* (Boston: Allen & Unwin, 1986).

12. Boyer, M. Christine, "The Return of Aesthetics to City Planning," *Society* (1988): 49–56.

13. Lampard, Eric. E., "The New York Metropolis in Transformation: History and Prospect. A Study in Historical Particularity," in Ewers, W., et al., eds., *The Future of the Metropolis* (New York: De Gruyter, 1986), p. 92.

# 15

# A Dual to New York?
# London in the 1980s

## Ian Gordon / Michael Harloe

## Introduction

In the 1980s, after a long period of decline during which time British influence in the world shrank and its own region outgrew it, London regained star billing in the world urban system alongside New York and Tokyo as one of three global financial centers. This new role is owed less to political authority over scattered territories, as in the past, than to a central place system of markets in which it is the highest status center within the Greenwich Mean Time zone. It is the most internationalized of the three centers and the only one in which the trading day can be made to overlap with those in both of its counterparts.

The rapid redevelopment of Docklands in inner east London, as an adjunct to the financial core in the City of London and a desirable residential area for affluent young financial and business service sector workers, symbolizes the manner in which this change has come about, as well as the "go for it" aspirations of those currently guiding the city's development. Social indicators also show change and revival. Since the early 1980s, greater London's population and employment levels appear to have stabilized or even exhibited modest growth, after decades of shrinkage.[1] On the employment side, this clearly reflects the growth in financial and business services which are now the dominant employment sector and the only source of significant expansion. The substantial deregulation of the City in 1986 opened up the financial markets to direct participation by foreign finance houses and clearly contributed to this trend.

London in the 1980s had, in fact, shifted away from regulation and public sector activity towards a more fragmented and explicitly market-directed approach in almost all aspects of urban life. Central government initiatives, such as the creation and underwriting of the London Dockland Development Corporation in 1982, removed planning powers from local authorities. More fundamental still has been the abolition, after a century of London-wide local government, of the Greater London Council (GLC) and now the Inner London Education Authority, leaving all powers in the hands of either central government or 32 small boroughs (and the still independent City Corporation). There have also been important moves to cut back the overall level of public sector activity in London.

In various respects, apart from this fracturing of its political authority, London seems to have paralleled New York developments in recent years, coming to resemble it more closely under the common influence of world economic and financial developments. In each case, massive loss of industrial employment provides a backdrop to the revival of the 1980s. Casual street level empiricism also suggests a shared experience of poverty and destitution, with growing numbers of homeless people and beggars in these two economically "successful" cities.

Important differences in their situations must be recognized, however, if London's experience is to be compared with that of New York. London is the only really large city in a small but quite densely populated nation, and the United Kingdom is more centralized than the United States. Urban politics has largely reflected national politics and, until the last days of the GLC, there has been nothing remotely resembling New York machine politics. It is also significant that London has been at the heart of the U.K.'s most economically dynamic region for the last century, and during the first half of this period the city itself was the leading center of technological innovation. The relative failure of the British national economy since 1945 has been an important influence on the development of consumer demand, on the resources available for investment and public expenditure, and because of labor market linkages, on the experience of unemployment in London. To some extent, however, because of its role in managing overseas investment and shorter term capital flows, the London economy may actually have done rather better than elsewhere out of the decline of the U.K.'s industrial economy. A final point of contrast is the much more limited salience of immigration, ethnicity, and race in a city where the black and Asian minorities still represent less than a fifth of the population.

The remainder of this chapter examines the evidence for the city's economic revival and increasing social polarization and then analyzes the changed character of urban politics, discussing the broad processes involved so as to facilitate comparison with the New York experience.

## Has There Really Been An Economic Revival in London?

Between 1961 and 1984, employment in Greater London fell by some 800,000 jobs (18 percent). The decline was heavily concentrated in manufacturing, which lost 55 percent of its employment. Over the same period the city's population fell from 8 to 6.5 million. Since 1983 employment appears to have stabilized, with a net gain of 150,000 jobs up to Spring 1988, and is currently forecast to grow by a further 50,000 or so in the period up to the end of the century.[2] Population levels have also risen since 1983–4, and trend-based official forecasts envisage a continuation of this growth for the foreseeable future.

This recent turning point appears to coincide with a period of growth in the national economy led by the expansion of financial and business services. However, the turning point relative to the national economy was earlier, at the onset of the recession at the end of the 1970s, when there was a halt to the downward trend in London's share of national employment for the first time since the early 1950s. Two different elements also need to be distinguished in population changes. The cessation of population decline in 1984 resulted from an upturn in international migration, in which London has always shared disproportionately. But the rate of decline had already been heavily cut back by reduced levels of outmigration to other parts of southern England since the recessions of the 1970s.

The one obvious factor linking the reversal of decline in employment with that in population is the upsurge in City employment associated with financial market deregulation in 1986, which contributed to increased immigration as foreign financial establishments brought in staff. This event has no bearing on the quantitatively larger changes in the pattern of domestic migration, and its short-term effects on employment were superimposed on an already strong upward trend in financial and business services dating from the late 1950s.

Indeed, recent forecasts of continuing growth in London employment are based on the combined effects of the ending of regional dispersal policies and the shift in the industrial structure toward sectors of long-term growth.[3] Significantly, 1985 seems to be the point in time at which net employment gains replaced net losses and when financial and business service employment overtook that in the manufacturing sector. The two events also appear to have occurred together in New York in 1978; its experience of economic recovery was longer and better documented.[4]

However, the main difference is that London's population and employment decline had been much longer established. For London, decline came to be seen as the natural trend for a mature, fully built-up city, with shrinking numbers resulting from the persistent and general demand for lower densities of occupation. In New York, by contrast, net employment decline seems to have been limited to the period between 1969 and 1977, while falling absolute population is recorded only during the 1960s and 1970s. One possible view of this contrast is that full development of the available space (to density standards which clearly differ between the two cases) was achieved later in New York. This might be partly attributable to New York's ethnic and racial mix since the early 1960s, on the assumption that the black and Latino population cannot afford to match the space standards being demanded by the departing white population. In London, where the growth of ethnic minority population has been far more limited, no such radical shift in the composition of the population has interfered with the dispersion of the central city population.

A further contrast is that the crisis of the 1970s in New York had no direct parallel in London. In New York the fiscal crisis, the subsequent deep cuts in public employment, and the loss of *Fortune* 500 head offices both reflected and contributed to physical and social deterioration. These factors plus high taxes contributed to an impaired image of the city, while residential abandonment exacerbated the population loss.[5] None of these elements have so far played a major role in London. Public sector employment continued to grow strongly through the 1970s and has not yet gone into reverse despite the imposition of much tighter resource constraints by the Thatcher government. Only now are the continuing control of local property tax (rate) levels by central government and the recent replacement of rates by a regressive poll tax threatening to cause significant cuts in local authority employment. However, corporate mergers in the 1960s and 1970s boosted the number of companies run from London and, while back-office activities have been dispersed and regional offices reinforced, London has largely retained and strengthened its hold on control functions in the industrial and commercial sectors.

In terms of image and quality of life, inner east London in particular has clearly suffered from dereliction and other problems in the aftermath of dock closures in the early 1970s (although its status had never been high), and there is citywide concern over crime and racial conflict. But there is no evidence that these have ever played a large role in causing population and employment change at a London-wide level. Indeed, the upgrading of many inner city residential areas through gentrification, which has been a continuing trend since the 1960s, may have contributed more to population decline by reducing residential densities. Nor has employment decline caused population decline; faster or slower growth in London jobs is reflected instead in the buildup of population in the commuting field beyond the metropolitan Green Belt. Rather, this suburbanization has substantially reduced the demand for many consumer services which are important sources of employment in London. This had also been an important factor in the downturn in retail employment in New York during the 1969–77 period. In London it has played a more continuous role, being checked only by the late 1970s recession in the national and regional housing market, which slowed the rate of migrational loss to other parts of the south from about 110,000 per year between the mid 1960s and the mid 1970s, to about 35,000 per year. Growth of financial and business services, however, has continued through the 1960s, 1970s, and 1980s, apparently unaffected either by local demand factors or, with the acceptance of higher rise offices, by space constraints.

Such a banal interpretation of the switch from net decline to net growth in London employment is encouraged by the relative stability of past trends, particularly in the manufacturing sector. Manufacturing contraction in London has been chronic regardless of national economic fluctuations, rather than being concentrated in particular crisis periods. Despite an acceleration of decline in New York in the early 1970s—and a quite different industrial structure in which the garment industry is much more important and engineering much less so—a similarly inexorable trend appears to have been operating there too.

In the London case the sharp fall in manufacturing employment has not been accompanied by any great reduction in the area of land occupied by industry.[6] The average amount of industrial land per manufacturing worker has been rising by about 3 percent per year, as labor productivity and the land requirements of output increase. In fact, the competitive pressure across much of London was to convert industrial land to warehouse or office use, rather than to expand its area as would have been necessary to support existing employment levels. As Fothergill and Gudgin rather baldly argued, manufacturing employment decline in London may reflect obstacles to the output growth which would have been required to retain job levels.[7]

A complementary explanation of manufacturing decline in London emphasizes the changing spatial division of labor within the U.K. As multiplant firms grew and located plants more strategically, particularly in the 1960s,[8] manufacturers decentralized their more routine production activity from London to more peripheral regions offering reserves of labor. Such moves also enabled them to introduce new investment and/or change work practices that might have been prevented by a well-organized existing work force. Since the recession of the late 1970s, however, this strategy seems to have become less appropriate to their needs. Certainly, the slack labor market of this period has allowed firms to accomplish major changes in technology, labor relations, and pay rates without the need for a geographical move, or, as in the case of the former Fleet

Street newspapers moving to Docklands, with only short distance moves. Also, insofar as there was a new emphasis on flexibility in production and a tendency to vertical disintegration in the 1980s, both of these developments encouraged a reconcentration of activities rather than an extrapolation of the previous dispersion that took place during the 1960s and early 1970s. It would probably be wrong, however, to expect that much of this reconcentration of production would occur within London itself.

Whether London's recent revival is durable must be open to some question. The period of actual growth has so far been very short. The initial relative improvement in population and employment trends in the late 1970s was the product of recession conditions whose relevance may now be passing. The recent shift into actual growth was also caused by essentially short-term factors, including Big Bang and an influx of international migrants, linked with a period of unusually rapid economic growth over which there the shadows of Black Monday and sharp rises in U.K. interest rates have already passed. However, so far the stock market crash appears to have had less effect on City employment, actual and expected, than is being suggested for the New York case, perhaps because London is much less involved in or dependent on the stock dealings of large numbers of direct private investors. Likely levels of job losses in financial services from the post–Big Bang peak have been put at around 20,000, much of which is probably a reflection of initial over-capacity in the period when many institutions sought to compete across a much wider range of markets and services than they had previously done. Even discounting the recent boom, the long-term upward trend in financial and business service employment in London, involving growth to near saturation in a succession of subsectors and markets, shows no signs of having come to its end. The real question is whether, like previous growth sectors in the city, it will not find rising rents and wages caused by its own expansion a sufficient incentive to slough off larger proportions of its activities to lower-cost locations.

The prospects for continued population growth are even more uncertain. It is more realistic to expect that revival in the housing industry and lower energy costs will again stimulate substantial net outmigration to other parts of the South East—with some consequent effect on the level of consumer service employment in London.

## Is London Becoming a Dual City?

When the issue of social polarization in London last came to the fore in the early 1970s, there was substantial confusion over precisely what polarization implied, and the thesis that it had been increasing over the previous decade remained not proven.[9] The question was then posed almost entirely in terms of a crude social class composition of the resident population, particularly of the inner areas, whereas the current debate is more broadly conceived. The scope for ambiguity and confusion is thus greater.

To rehearse some of the obvious possibilities, inequality may be framed in terms of the levels of real income enjoyed by individuals, with greater polarization taking the form of a change in the "shape" of the income distribution.[10] Alternatively, it may be conceived in terms of social or occupational mobility, with the creation of new barriers to movement between statuses and labor market segments, or the disappearance of old paths to security and social advancement. Or it may involve a focus on specific dimensions of welfare, relating, for example, to degrees of success in the housing and labor markets and the short- or long-run chances of becoming and remaining homeless, inadequately housed, unemployed, or underemployed. On the political front, the issue may be formulated as a real or perceived breakdown in the institutions of pluralism, with an increasing proportion of the population being or feeling effectively excluded. Finally, increasing polarization may relate essentially to increasing residential segregation with the focus on the performance of areas, rather than of individuals.

Household income inequality has increased since the late 1970s in an even more marked way in London than in the rest of the country. The interquartile income ratio, standing at 2.85 for Greater London and 2.82 nationally in 1978/9, had risen to 3.54 and 3.34, respectively, by 1985/6.[11] This repeated the pattern of the early 1970s economic upswing, although in the intervening period of stagflation, income inequality in London seems to have grown more slowly, against the national trend. On this measure the degree of income inequality does not yet appear to have reached that observed in New York, where in 1986 the interquartile ratio stood at about 3.81;[12] but although increasing inequality was evident in both cities, particularly in the early 1980s, the gap between the New York and London has halved over the past decade. In real terms the incomes of the lowest quartile actually fell by about 8 percent between 1979/80 and 1985/6.

The level of unemployment was a significant influence on these changes. As in other parts of the country, the London unemployment rate rose sharply in the wake of the two oil price crises of the 1970s, from under 2 percent in 1974[13] to 10.5 percent in 1983. Subsequently, despite growing employment, and against the national trend, it continued to drift upwards until late 1986; by 1988 on the current official definition it stood at 9 percent, corresponding to about 8 percent on the ILO/OECD conventions. In Inner London as a whole it was about half as high again, while some areas in the inner East End had unemployment rates about twice as high. During the recent upswing of the London economy, these disparities increased markedly. Only in the commuter ring outside London has unemployment been substantially reduced. Underlying this increasing spatial concentration of unemployment there appears to be a concentration among those groups in the weakest position within the labor market, who are becoming increasingly marginalized as high unemployment persists. Recent forecasts produced for London planners envisage a continuation of unemployment at about its current level up to the end of the century, both for London as a whole and particularly in the inner areas.[14]

While the overall level of unemployment in London is much higher than in New York, overall participation rates are significantly lower in New York, which may imply a substantial element of concealed unemployment. In fact, participation rates in New York have been steadily falling behind U.S. levels over the past 20 years, whereas in London there has been a slow increase, as compared with the national average.[15] This simply reflects a mature labor market.

Homelessness has also increased dramatically in recent years. The number of officially recognized "homeless households" doubled from 15,000 to 30,000 between 1979 and 1986, although the real number of homeless, including those not accepted as such by local authorities, is clearly much greater. By 1986, over half the new allocations of council (public) housing went to such households. Even so, the legal duty on councils to provide for the official "homeless" could be met in many cases only by recourse to bed and breakfast accommodation in poor quality "hotels." Such accommodation cost London councils £62.8 million in 1986/7 against £4.0 million only 5 years earlier.

Geographic polarization also seems to be increasing, with the "worst" parts of London exhibiting a deterioration relative to other localities within the city on such indicators as overcrowding, unemployment, female economic activity, and the distribution of single-parent and ethnic minority households.[16] (These shifts reflect actual polarization at the individual and household level, as well as new patterns of residential segregation in the London housing market.) In addition, metropolitan level polarization is occuring since outmigration to the commuter areas beyond the Green Belt has been socially and demographically selective. Moving depends on being able to buy a house. Even in 1980/1, when house prices were lower in relation to income, this ruled out the lower 40 percent of households from outward movement, imparting a downward bias to the social composition of the London population. At the other end of the spectrum, gentrification has been locally important, although at least up until 1981

scarcely evident in the overall profile of the GLC or Inner London populations. We cannot yet tell what role accelerated gentrification may have
played in the particularly rapid growth of professional and technical
workers among the London population since 1979. In any case, given the
generally slower rate of movement out to the commuter areas over this
period, selective migration within the London labor market area cannot
explain much of the income polarization in London evident during the
1980s.

At a more local level, the worst deprivation is found in the areas of
inner east London where the higher density public housing estates have
been concentrated. Ethnic segregation is much less marked in London
than in New York, and secondary in significance to class segregation.
Thus, whereas in the 1981 census there were only 3 wards in London (of
754) with over 60 percent black and/or Asian population, Stegman shows
that 8 (of 54) subborough areas in New York have over 90 percent of their
population from "minority groups."[17] Nevertheless, particular ethnic
groups are concentrated in various parts of Inner London and some of its
bordering areas, both in lower-priced, owner-occupied districts and in
public housing estates. These areas, as well as the areas of general long-
term deprivation, have shown particularly strong increases in unemployment and other problems in the 1980s. In the inner city council estates,
poor maintenance and physical deterioration have gone hand-in-hand
with changing socioeconomic composition, creating what are euphemisti-
cally called "hard to let" estates. The population in these may typically
include both older white working class households and younger households from a mix of disadvantaged groups, including unskilled singles
and couples, single-parent families, and many from ethnic minorities. The
combination of disadvantages on these estates can be compounded by
racial tensions among people who have no real option of moving, with
the possibility of severe social conflicts.

## How Are These Polarizing Tendencies to Be Explained?

Several of these tendencies are by no means peculiar to London but may
be found in many other parts of Britain, including still depressed northern
industrial cities, and even semirural areas within the growth regions of
Southern England. Even where the phenomena are more marked or evident in London, urban processes may have played little if any role in their
genesis. Let us consider then five broad types of explanation of increasing
dualism in London.

## Declining Employment

In the latter part of the 1970s, inner city poverty and deprivation were blamed on the cities' economic decline. Loss of employment opportunities in London was seen as the prime cause. Reflection on the fact that the rapid expansion of the late nineteenth century produced "the bitter cry of outcast London" ought to have led to scepticism about this attribution. However, it displaced earlier individualistic diagnoses of the "pathology" of inequality and became the rationale for the job creation initiatives of Labour-controlled boroughs and the Greater London Council, and for central government's promotion of urban economic development through incentives to private investment.

A decade later, the connection looks a lot more tenuous, or possibly more complex. First, in the case of unemployment, which ought to be more directly linked to employment change than any other aspect of deprivation, it is striking that even in its worst decade of decline in the 1970s, London unemployment was on a par with that in the growth areas of the mid 1980s and significantly below the then prevailing national levels of unemployment. Employment declines were evidently matched by a quite independent process of labor supply dispersal as workers sought larger, cheaper, or better housing outside the city, and subsequently found more accessible workplaces out there. Second, strong migrational and commuting responses to shifting patterns of opportunities rapidly absorbed the residual effects of poorer employment performance in London.[18] Neither of these equilibriating factors has been operating as strongly on the high unemployment of the 1980s, but over this period London's employment performance was not especially bad, even in manufacturing. In other words, unemployment in London seems only weakly related to job losses. Levels of unemployment in excess of those elsewhere in Southern England primarily reflect the weak competitive position of many groups of the Inner London population in the regional labor market.

The indirect impact of manufacturing job loss on the structure of employment opportunities available to those without formal qualifications (some 40 percent of the London labor force) may be more important. The majority of the manufacturing employment loss eliminated relatively secure or stable work, as did closure of the upstream docks in the 1970s. Public sector employment growth partly compensated for the loss of stable jobs for unqualified Londoners, but this ended in the 1980s. Jobs in growing sectors have thus become polarized between the financial and business service sectors, which traditionally offer secure jobs to workers with some form of qualification, and the private consumer services, including the burgeoning hotels and catering sector, where jobs are highly unstable and opportunities for training or advancement limited, but which do take largely unqualified workers.

## National Recession and Unemployment

The sharp 1979–1982 recession affected London employment rather lightly. This reflected the high proportion of service employment and weak representation of the heavier industries which suffered most elsewhere. In fact, the most notable casualties of the 1980s recession in London were to be found among the outer London engineering firms which had grown up during the interwar recession, when the city had escaped even more lightly. However, in the early 1980s London also benefited from a virtual halt to employment decentralization (and some recentralization) as investment dried up, while physical constraints on growth ceased to be a problem.

And yet, as we have seen, London unemployment increased sharply over this period. For an explanation of this we have to look to labor market linkages between the city, other parts of Southern England, and the regions of the Midlands and North, which were the main victims of deindustrialization. At least two-thirds of the additional unemployment in London was the consequence of shifts in the balance of labor migration (and to a lesser extent of commuting) induced by job losses elsewhere.[19] The most visible element was an influx of young single people looking for jobs in the high turnover labor markets of Inner London. The continued availability of furnished rented accommodation in inner west London has also attracted young job seekers, but in the 1980s their numbers were added to the homeless population, if not to those officially recognized as such. Much of the migrational effect of job losses elsewhere, however, would have taken the form of fewer emigrants out of the London labor market (including its commuter hinterland), leading to increased competition for the stock of jobs available.

In this slacker labor market the young and the traditionally disadvantaged groups, such as black and Asian workers, the unskilled or unqualified, and public sector tenants, have borne the brunt of higher levels of unemployment. These groups are for the most part similarly disadvantaged in other British labor markets, but some, like black workers and public sector tenants, are disproportionately represented in Inner London.[20] The persistently high levels of unemployment resulting from decline in the industrial economy have interacted with long-established patterns of inequality in London to produce widening disparities in the experience of particular areas and social or ethnic groups.

## Tax Benefits and Service Changes

The earlier income comparisons included social security benefits but not tax deductions. Overall receipts of cash benefits have increased greatly since 1979, because of the much greater extent of unemployment, but their real per capita value did not keep pace with average earnings growth. Tax reforms have also added significantly to disposable income inequality. These national changes have had substantial effects on Londoners' welfare, without being directly connected to the restructuring of the city's economic and social base. Other aspects of the government's fiscal and monetary policy have, however, had more specific effects on conditions of life in the city.

The redistribution of central government's Rate Support Grant away from inner city authorities (via a reworking of the formula) in the early 1980s severely hit many of the poorer London authorities. Government-imposed rate caps and the replacement of rates by a poll tax and a centrally set uniform business rate have also led to cutbacks in services to some of the most deprived groups and have further weakened the capacity of authorities to deliver organized and effective services.

National policies have also sharply reduced the availability of public housing in London. The decline of private rental housing, now mainly available only on short-term contracts and at high rents, has left mainstream housing provision to private ownership, on one hand, and council housing, on the other, with very different conditions of access to the two. Prevailing London house prices put the former beyond most of the working class, who have become increasingly reliant on the public sector. However, the advent of the Thatcher government in 1979 slashed council housing starts in London from 20,000 in 1975 to a mere 1,200 dwellings in 1985/6. In addition, since 1980, public housing tenants have had a right to buy their accommodation, thus reducing the stock available for reletting. Generally, tenants have been more interested in buying single-family housing than apartments. Since the former are more likely to be located in the outer areas, their privatization has accentuated the spatial polarization of housing opportunities in London and reduced the opportunities for Inner London tenants to move out to better housing and better access to new jobs.

## Growth, Displacement, and Polarization

Employment growth concentrated in high-paying occupations may also create polarization by adding to the variance in income levels. Whether this has any really negative effects for those at the lower end of the income distribution must, however, depend largely on what if anything is displaced by this growth. Thus, if purchasing power at the top end of the housing market is increased in an area of inelastic supply, individuals farther down the housing market may suffer.

Property prices in London have soared since the early 1980s, leading the house price inflation which has now spread across the greater part of the country. From 1983–8 the London house price index rose by 160 percent, against about 130 percent nationally. The London boom partially reflected the growth of highly paid jobs, especially for relatively young workers in the financial and business service sectors. The extended working hours for some of these jobs, plus the demands of Yuppie lifestyles and the improved image of parts of Inner London, have all encouraged a growing demand for London housing, which can only be partially satisfied by expensive new developments, notably in Docklands. The house price explosion multiplied the number of concealed or "potential" households, estimated at 250,000 in a 1986/7 survey, who could not afford the £57,000 then being paid by the average first-time buyer in London. It has also discouraged recruitment to a range of public sector jobs, from nursing to senior posts in local government, for which the "London allowance" now clearly fails to cover higher living costs in the city. The resulting vacancies or appointments of inferior staff are reported to be seriously affecting the quality of service delivery in many areas.

The property boom is having other negative effects. Small business developments in some inner areas are being priced out of the property market, as craft industries were a century ago when banking and insurance expanded.[21] Even the expenditure of the increasingly affluent minority has some negative effects, biasing the employment structure towards unstable private consumer services, such as catering.

*Flexible Labor*

The London labor market has been characterized by high rates of job turnover because these are facilitated by dense concentrations of workers and employers and also because for much of its history small firms with unstable markets have played a large role in its economy. The casual labor market and the "residuum" working in it were a central factor in the problems of inner city poverty and social conflict up to the end of the nineteenth century.[22] Thereafter, larger scale manufacturing enterprises, unionization/decasualization of the docks, and the development of major public sector employers stabilized employment opportunities and social life. As already noted, these changes have now been substantially reversed. The slackening labor market has encouraged London employers to emphasize numerical flexibility in their employment strategies. For example, the privatization of such public services as cleaning in schools and hospitals encouraged private contractors to undercut in-house tenders, and each other. The Inner London labor market thus appears to be moving towards a recasualization, increasing the proportion of the labor force at risk of recurrent unemployment and reducing incentives to acquire human capital.

## The Politics of Dualism

The conflict between radicals, seeking to respond to these social and economic issues at a metropolitan level, and localist conservatives, concerned to avoid substantial redistribution and protect their own environments, has been a long-running theme in London politics. In the late 1880s, another time of acute social polarization, the issue was resolved institutionally by creating a London County Council with a territory encompassing the then built-up area of the city. Within years a Conservative prime minister was complaining, in a now familiar way, about the "megalomania" of LCC's Progressive administration.[23] He reacted not by abolishing the LCC but by creating a lower tier of boroughs to share in the functions of government. Continuing geographical expansion of the city in the first half of this century took many of the key issues of London development, and much of the conservative resistance, outside the purview of the LCC, which came under Labour control from the 1930s on. Only in the mid 1960s was there belated recognition of these changes, with the creation of the Greater London Council incorporating the whole area within the Green Belt; although by then the city's main growth was occurring in freestanding towns and villages beyond the Belt, in the Outer Metropolitan Area. One motive for this change was to break Labour control of the city by incorporating Conservative voting homeowners from the suburbs. However, what resulted was an oscillation of control between the two parties which weakened policy-making on key issues such as housing, planning, and transportation. The enhanced powers given to boroughs and the drawing of borough boundaries in a way that highlighted the division between Labour Inner London boroughs and the surrounding ring of mainly Conservative outer boroughs enabled the latter to escape many of the costs of dealing with urban deprivation and decay. The weak powers and unstable political majority of the GLC put it in a much weaker position than the City of New York to respond to economic and social change in the metropolis.

In the course of time, with continuing decentralization of potential owner-occupiers, it might have been expected that the Labour Party would again have come to firmly control local government across the Greater London area. During the past decade, however, two new factors intervened to upset this prospect.

Economic and social change diminished the Labour Party's traditional electoral base in the organized manual working class. Their numbers declined especially fast in London, as a result of manual job losses and of the outward movement of more affluent workers to owner-occupation in areas of affordable housing outside the GLC area. The male manual-labor white working class and its trade unions dominated traditional Labour politics. It supported redistributory welfare programs, such as council housing, but it was also deeply conservative in its attitudes to women and ethnic minorities. In areas such as Inner London this working class was increasingly being replaced by a new and far more fragmented series of groupings, including lower-paid workers in service industries—many of them women, ethnic minorities, the unemployed, and single-parent families. And new issues and demands emerged.

From this disintegration of London's traditional Labour politics a new urban left emerged during the 1970s, led in part by public sector white collar workers, women, and blacks. They sought to build a new electoral base out of the now fragmented urban working class and use it to advance socialism both nationally and locally. Their platform extended traditional left programs, including public housing, cheap transport, and social and community services, to new concerns, such as racism, sexism ecology, participation, and policing. Also, through the Greater London Enterprise Board, they sought strategic intervention in industrial restructuring.

The other new element has been the New Right policies vigorously pursued by the Thatcher government since 1979. Their policies sought to reduce the Public Sector Borrowing Requirement but more fundamentally to downgrade public expectations of welfare and promote a more market-oriented ideology. Local authorities have been a prime target in this campaign, since this diverted responsibility for the implementation of cuts away from Whitehall, and an escalating series of reforms sought to limit spending, increase the private sector role in providing public services, and sensitize local electors to the costs of collective consumption. Inner urban areas in London and elsewhere have come to be a central ground for this campaign. In part this was because of local authority resistance to central government directives. But it also reflects an increasingly explicit assertion by government that these areas' problems (particularly unemployment) are caused by a "culture of dependency," and a lack of "enterprise." Intentionally echoing "Victorian values," the need is then seen for external authorities to ensure greater discipline and retraining of the work force and to demonstrate, through projects such as the Docklands development, what can be achieved through enterprise and a market approach (albeit with heavy public investment as a trigger).

Thus, two emergent political and ideological strategies, reflecting the respective concerns of the gainers and losers in the restructuring of opportunities in the city, were in confrontation in London. This conflict displaced the interest-based contest between more and less affluent members of the "middle mass" from the center of the political stage in London. The media, especially the Conservative-dominated popular press, which went out of its way to find examples of "loony left" local council policies, amplified the new left challenge to central government, often pandering to the worst racist and sexist prejudices of their readership. Most attention was given to the London case with boroughs such as Brent, with a left, black leadership, and the GLC leader Ken Livingstone (now a Brent MP) coming to national prominence.

This dualization of London politics has proceeded a good deal faster than real changes in the social and economic structure of the city, being a belated response to some of these and an anticipation of others. It has had a quite disastrous effect, however, on the city's capacity to respond in an orderly and humane way to the issues posed by revival and polarization. At the instigation of the prime minister and a number of other prominent members of the New Right, the GLC was stripped of powers and then abolished (along with other metropolitan counties). Later, the Inner London Education Authority was also abolished. Their powers have been divided between the boroughs and central government. In the case of planning, for example, all that remains of a strategic role is a joint committee of the boroughs, with a small technical staff, to advise the secretary of state for the environment on the strategic guidance which he will issue to boroughs as planning authorities.

Severe financial constraint and the growing impossibility of delivering on their policy commitments have placed new left boroughs in a situation of conflict, confusion, and retreat. Financial cuts, mismanagement, internal political conflict, and the demoralization of officials have put local services in a state of disorganization or near-collapse in some areas. In 1988 even Ken Livingstone protested at the mishandling of his poorer constituents by Brent officials. This conflict and disorganization result largely from the external pressure that the powerful central government has exerted on newly emergent political coalitions that lack the sociocultural coherence and organizational experience of the old Labour movement. Its effects can then be used by government supporters to legitimate the attack on the new urban left in particular, and more generally on the role and scope of local government.

## Conclusion

London in the 1980s appears to have experienced an economic revival similar in a number of respects to the slightly earlier revival in New York, although against a background of longer-term decline. The basis of this revival, however, appears to lie less in recent developments in the world economy than in long-term shifts in the relative importance of industrial and financial or business service employment. The evidence suggests that, analogous to some trends in New York, household incomes and access to secure housing and employment are becoming more polarized. In London, such polarization derives not only from the restructuring of the city economy but from persistently high levels of national unemployment and central government policies. The strongest manifestations of dualism, however, are to be found in the political sphere where, for both historical and institutional reasons, conditions in the two cities are probably most different. London government escaped the fiscal crisis that hit New York City following its period of economic decline in the 1970s. In the face of a strong central government, however, issues of revival and polarization in the 1980s have brought London politics and government to an intensifying state of crisis for which there seems no obvious or impending solution.

## Notes

This chapter derives from a project on "Economic Change, Urban Revival and Social Polarisation: London compared to New York," supported by the Economic and Social Research Council and the Research Fund of the University of Kent. We are grateful to our colleague Nick Buck for his contributions to this chapter, although the usual disclaimers apply.

1. Greater London is the continuously built-up area within the metropolitan Green Belt established in 1938, which separates the city from the ring of postwar growth farther out in the Outer Metropolitan Area. Greater London, administered from its creation in 1965 to 1985 by an elected Greater London Council, remains independent of the "shire" counties which form the first tier of local government in the surrounding region. Its population of six and one half million is closely comparable with New York City, but its area is twice as large and is more self-contained in labor market terms, with 83 percent of its

workers being resident within the city, against about 75 percent in New York. The "City of London" consists of a tiny area of inner London where the financial district is located and with a special form of local government. In 1985 its resident population was only about 5,000.

2. Buck, Nicholas, and Ian Gordon, *Employment Forecasts for Greater London.* Final Report to the London Planning Advisory Committee (1986); CBI, 1988.

3. Tyler, 1986; Buck, Nicholas; Ian Gordon; and K. Young, *The London Employment Problem* (London: Oxford University Press, 1986).

4. Ehrenhalt, Samuel M., "New York City in the New Economic Environment: New Risks and a Changing Outlook" (New York: Bureau of Labor Statistics, June 1988).

5. Lampard, Eric E., "The New York Metropolis in Transformation: History and Prospect. A Study in Historical Particularity," in W. Ewers et al., eds., *The Future of the Metropolis* (New York: De Gruyter, 1986).

6. In the 1972–1981 period the rate of land release from industrial use was about one-fifth of the rate of employment decline.

7. Fothergill, S., and G. Gudgin, *Unequal Growth; Urban and Regional Employment Change in the UK* (London: Heinemann, 1982).

8. Massey, Doreen, *Spatial Divisions of Labor* (London: MacMillan, 1984).

9. Donnison, D., and D. C. Eversley, eds., *London: Urban Patterns, Problems, and Policies* (London: Heinemann, 1973).

10. Pahl, Ray E., "Some Research on Informal Work, Social Polarisation and Social Structure," *International Journal of Urban and Regional Research* 12 (1988): 247–267.

11. Biennial average figures from the Family Expenditure Survey.

12. Stegman, Michael A., *Housing and Vacancy Report, New York City, 1987* (New York: Department of Housing Preservation and Development, City of New York, April 1988).

13. On a residential basis, the overall rate amongst people normally working in London, including commuters, would be somewhat lower.

14. P. A. Cambridge Economic Consultants and Urban and Regional Studies Unit, University of Kent, *Economic Strategic Advice: Economic and Employment Change in London.* Final Report to the London Planning Advisory Committee (1988).

15. Ehrenhalt, "New York City in the New Economic Environment."

16. Townsend, P., P. Corrigan, and U. Kowarzik, "Poverty and Labour in London," *Survey of Londoners' Living Standards* 1 (London: Low Pay Unit, 1987).

17. Stegman, *Housing and Vacancy Report.*

18. Buck, Gordon, and Young, *The London Employment Problem;* Gordon, Ian, "Evaluating the Impact of Employment Changes on Local Unemployment," *Regional Studies* 22 (1988): 135–147.

19. Buck, et al., *The London Employment Problem.*

20. Buck and Gordon, *Employment Forecasts for Greater London.*
21. Stedman Jones, Gareth, *Outcast London* (London: Oxford University Press, 1971).
22. Stedman Jones, *Outcast London.*
23. Young, K., and P. L. Garside, *Metropolitan London: Politics and Urban Change 1837–1981* (London: Edward Arnold, 1982).

# PART VII

# Conclusion

# Conclusion:
# Is New York a Dual City?

## Manuel Castells / John Mollenkopf

> Any city, however small, is in fact divided into two,
> one the city of the poor, the other of the rich, these are
> at war with one another, and in either there are many
> smaller divisions, and you would be altogether beside
> the mark if you treated them all as a single State.
>
> Plato, *Republic*, IV, 422B

## The Transformation of New York's Social Structure During the 1980s

The analyses presented in this volume show a complex social dynamic that differs from the journalistic images of New York City. After the fiscal crisis of 1975, New York underwent an economic, social, and political restructuring. This restructuring was strongly influenced by the financial elite and guided by a new political coalition in the context of an increasingly interdependent world economy and the rise of neoconservatism in American national politics.

Helped by the growing importance of new information technologies, New York has emerged from this period holding a dominant economic position in the international system. It joins Tokyo and London as the nerve centers of the new world economy. The consolidation of New York as the main global city in North America triggered an economic boom during the 1980s, expressed in the high standards of living of a substantial proportion of the population, the dramatic rise of Manhattan real estate, and the rapid transformation of the city's spatial structure.

This economic growth has been extremely uneven across sectors, trans-

**399**

forming New York's productive basis. Producer services, particularly finance and corporate services, have spearheaded the growth of the metropolitan economy both in job creation and in value generation, while manufacturing decline has accelerated. In this sense, the restructuring of New York must be seen in the broader context of the process of postindustrial transformation of our society.

But the shift from manufacturing to producer services does not exhaust the reality of New York's economy. Consumer services also play an important role in the economy, as do social services like education and health. In spite of the fiscal retrenchment of the late 1970s, the public sector recovered its role in generating jobs during the 1980s at levels similar to those of the late 1960s. Some observers have also emphasized the rise of the "informal economy"—activities as diverse as sweatshop manufacturing, gypsy cabs, residential renovation, and "off-the-books" childcare. Together with criminal activities, New York's underground economy seems to have grown as rapidly as the city's role as a world financial center.

Between 1977 and the stock market crash of October 1987, New York sustained an unprecedented economic boom, with median household income rising about 20 percent in real terms as a result of the prosperity. The city's population is still poorer than in the 1960s, however, relative to the region, state, and nation, partly because of the losses in income during the 1970s and partly because of growing inequality and the characteristics of new immigrants to the city.

The population decline of the 1970s (about 800,000 people) was stabilized during the 1980s, largely due to a dramatic wave of new immigration from the Caribbean, Latin America, and Asia. As a result, in spite of a slowdown of the white families' flight to the suburbs, New York has become a city where the minorities are the majority in 1990 and where more than a quarter of the population is foreign-born. Thus, the metropolis is increasingly a world city, not only in terms of its linkages to the global economy but also in the multiethnic, multicultural composition of its population.

The city's growing prosperity during the 1980s coincided with the increasing inequality among its residents. As the Introduction has shown, income inequality increased substantially between 1977 and 1986. The higher the income of a stratum, the faster its income grew during that period. Thus, the ratio of the income earned by the top 10 percent to that earned by the bottom 20 percent has increased from 5.7 in 1977 to 7.6 in 1986. Furthermore, the real income of the bottom 10 percent actually decreased by 10.9 percent, while the real income of the next lowest decile declined by 6.6 percent. As a result, poverty rates have increased during the decade, from about 19 percent to about 23 percent of New York's population. Indeed, there is a process of social polarization, not just inequality: the rich are becoming richer and the poor are becoming poorer in absolute terms.

Nevertheless, the complexity of New York's social structure cannot be reduced to a dichotomy between the two extremes of the scale of income distribution. The transformation of the economy, and therefore of the occupational structure, has resulted in the differential evolution of various social groups, whose interests, values, and collective attributes shape the dynamics of the local society. Looking at New Yorkers from the perspective of the occupational system, the following occupational strata appear to be most distinctive:

a. Executives, managers, and professionals, whose share of total labor force in New York is now close to 30 percent, represent the upper middle class (or lower upper class) who most directly benefit from economic prosperity, in spite of the threatening downturns linked to financial volatility. Although the top of this group, the upper professionals, do not constitute a dominant social class, in the analysis of Steven Brint, they do form a well-defined social group with specific cultural trends and largely common economic interests. This group, in all its diversity, represents the social basis for the policies of economic growth and social restructuring which characterized the 1980s, and it comprises the people who benefit most from these policies.

b. An army of clerical workers, predominantly women, constitute the new working class of the service economy, as studied by Cynthia Epstein. They hold lower-paid jobs, strongly influenced by the rapid technological changes that generally improve productivity while sometimes sacrificing the quality of work life.

c. Low-skilled workers, both salaried and self-employed, most often immigrants, who provide miscellaneous consumer services and whose working conditions and social situations are increasingly heterogeneous, contributing to the growing fragmentation of the social structure.

d. Immigrant manual workers, particularly Dominicans and Chinese, who toil in the remaining manufacturing activities that seek to confront foreign competition by downgrading their wages and working conditions.

e. A growing middle class based in the public sector that assures employment opportunities for native minorities, particularly native blacks, along with traditional white ethnic groups from working class origins (Italians, Irish). Municipal services and the expansion of health and education provide the occupational basis for the persistence of organized labor and for the revival of labor unions' culture as an important, and too often neglected, segment of New York's society. This is, in fact, a pivotal social grouping whose organizational capability influences the directions of politics and policies in New York far beyond their quantitative weight in the occupational structure or their strategic importance in the dynamics of the metropolitan economy.

f. The substantial proportion of adult New Yorkers who remain outside the formal labor force, partly as a consequence of a dropout rate of about 37 percent in the city's high schools. (In 1987, the ratio of employed to total population among people 16 and older was 71.5 percent for men and 40.6 percent for women, ten points below the national averages. Female-headed households, partly those living on welfare, are among this economically deteriorating segment of the population.) Given the diversity of living conditions in this group, it is difficult to provide a quantitative estimate of its importance.[1]

The social structure of New York is determined by the interaction among these six segments and others not included in this schematic presentation. However, the analyses presented in this volume suggest that, in spite of their diversity, the relationships among these groups, and therefore the overall evolution of the local society, are dominated by two opposing forces:

a. The upper professionals of the corporate sector form an organizational nucleus for the wider social stratum of managers and professionals. They constitute a coherent social network whose interests are directly linked to the development of New York City's corporate economy.

b. The remaining social strata occupy increasingly diverse positions and have plural interests and values. Neighborhood life thus becomes increasingly diverse and fragmented, hindering alliances among these groups.

As a result, the tendency toward cultural, economic, and political polarization in New York takes the form of a contrast between a comparatively cohesive core of professionals in the advanced corporate services and a disorganized periphery fragmented by race, ethnicity, gender, occupational and industrial location, and the spaces they occupy.

The gender and ethnic specificity of the distinctive occupational groupings reinforces this opposition between an articulate core and a disarticulated plurality of peripheries. The core is predominantly male and white, while the peripheries are made up of diverse ethnic minorities, often differentiated by gender, as among black women clerical workers. It might help us to understand the social dynamics of New York to think of local society as made up of a predominantly male and white professional-managerial group; a female clerical working class, characterized by ethnic diversity; a miscellaneous services sector formed by a disproportionately immigrant labor force, both salaried and self-employed; a public sector divided between white ethnic and native black New Yorkers, with an internal hierarchy in terms of gender; a downgraded manufacturing sector concentrating a high proportion of male and female Latino workers; and a marginal sector, outside the formal labor force, with a strong proportion of minority youth (particularly native blacks and Puerto Ricans) and female-headed households.

This social puzzle is even more complex because the convenient dichotomies actually hide major cleavages within each category. For instance, we know now that the opposition between majority and minority does not begin to exhaust the extraordinary cultural, economic, and political differences among blacks, Latinos, and Asians. Furthermore, Bailey and Waldinger have shown that different immigrant groups have varied in terms of job mobility. Thus, while most immigrants lack the franchise and many have a vulnerable legal status, their economic trajectories vary according to educational background, economic assets, group strategy, and how the larger society has responded to them.

What those outside the core economic strata have in common is precisely their diversity, their heterogeneity, their externality to the well-structured social core directly connected to the strategic command centers of the corporate economy. The dichotomy that provides an actual basis for the "dual city" is that between the organized center and the disorganized peripheries of New York's local society. This differential capacity for social organization is expressed and reinforced, as this volume shows, in the cultural, spatial, and political structure of New York.

Culturally, the analysis by Moss and Ludwig of the mass media shows that some media are central and common, generally reflecting the native middle class culture, while an increasing diverse set of other community and ethnic newspapers, radio, and television programming are busy digging the city's trenches, to use Ira Katznelson's classic term.

Spatially, Harris (for the metropolitan area) and DeGiovanni and Minnite (for the city's neighborhoods) show how New York has become an increasingly segregated city. The rapidly increasing land values in sections of the city have halted residential abandonment and stepped up gentrification, reinforcing the social and ethnic boundaries of each neighborhood. As in the latter part of the nineteenth century, immigrant enclaves have spatially crystallized cultures and social networks which have made the city more vital and diverse, yet have fragmented its social patterning. The fear of displacement by real estate speculation reinforces defensive, territorial reactions. And the estrangement or ethnic succession among social groups creates additional barriers to the weaving of the social fabric of the new, emerging city. Street crime and territorially based gangs sanction, materially and symbolically, the social and ethnic cleavages that divide the city, as Mercer Sullivan has shown. At the limit, homelessness throws people out of their social networks, transforming their dereliction into wandering flows that inhabit the interstices of public space, making hallways, parks, and subway stations into visible images of the invisible social logic. The juxtaposition of conspicuous consumption and social degradation in the same space, often in the streets of the urban core of the world's capital, triggers the social fears and the public discourse about the "dual city."

The absence of corrective measures from the public sector has made these developments all the more pronounced. Brecher and Horton show the decline of public spending, measured as the share of the city's economic product, during most of the 1980s. They also present evidence that public spending was shifted from redistribution to development. Housing programs in particular were scaled down, particularly at the federal level. Thus, while market tendencies became more unequal, although undoubtedly dynamic, the public sector did not play a redistributive and corrective role, but amplified the trends towards income inequality, spatial segregation, and lack of adequate services for a large segment of the population.

This public stance was linked to the absence of significant social movements and political challenges during the 1980s. Susan and Norman Fainstein show how community organizations were coopted during the 1960s, reduced to a series of specific interest groups that could be diffused one by one in their interaction with the local political establishment. Mollenkopf's chapter explores the barriers to forming an alternative to the Koch coalition and discusses how, with the election of David Dinkins in late 1989, the barriers were overcome, at least for a time. Whether his administration can, or will, challenge the local political system's capacity to disorganize the variety of dominated constituencies while articulating the interests of the economically dominant core of white, male upper professionals remains to be seen. The capacity of the core to organize while the peripheries are fragmented and disorganized has fundamentally shaped social dynamics in the new New York.

But any social construction develops its own contradictions. The visible social brutality (expressed in the image of the dual city) and the cynicism with which political leaders sanctioned it, often provocatively led by former Mayor Edward I. Koch, undermined the mechanisms of social control and led to a crisis of political legitimacy. In social terms, the increase of street crime, public misgivings about social degradation, the surge of interethnic and interclass violence, and the corruption of an unchecked political machine reached a breaking point in 1989.

In political terms, the collapse of Mayor Koch's electoral coalition in the 1989 Democratic primary and the narrow failure of Republican Rudolph Giuliani to regroup the socially dominant interests around a message of conservative reform mark the limits of one-dimensional politics as a viable instrument for managing the social tensions of such a dynamic and complex city.

## The Dual City and Social Theory

What, then, do the studies presented in this volume have to say regarding the potential rise of a dual city as a new type of urban social structure, of which New York is a forerunner? How can the results of these studies be reorganized to respond to the questions raised by different traditions of social theory that analyze the issue of urban dualism?

The dual city is a useful ideological notion because it aims to denounce inequality, exploitation, and oppression in cities, breaking with the organicist and technocratic views of cities as integrated social communities. But its underlying assumptions are rarely made explicit, because those who employ it tend to favor social critique over social theory. The political and emotional charge of a dualist approach and the failure to spell out its assumptions means that it cannot comprehend the complexity of urban social reality, which is certainly not reducible to a simple dichotomy.

Yet this ideological notion can be useful because it introduces differentiation, stratification, and potential contradiction and conflict in the realm of analytic categories which otherwise tend to see the city in a functionalist framework. The introduction of the polemical notion of dualism forces the analysis to account for inequality and contradiction, opening the way for a richer and more dynamic understanding of cities in the best tradition of theories of social change.

We must, however, distinguish between the ability to raise important issues and the capacity to analyze them. To do the latter, we must identify the different causal frameworks underlying the themes of urban dualism. We can then make explicit the hypotheses implicit in the dual city approach and relate them to broader perspectives on social structure.

The opposition between affluence and poverty in a shared urban space is a classical theme of urban sociology, particularly of the Chicago School, as developed in Zorbaugh's fascinating book *The Gold Coast and the Slum*.[2] Social stratification theory enables us to understand that space, and particularly the space of the large metropolis, is socially differentiated in

terms of residence and amenities, following a hierarchy of income, education, and occupation, symbolically translated into social prestige.
Three models of sociospatial differentiation can be distinguished:

a.  The pre-industrial pattern of social strata mixing in the same space, as in the case of the nobility and its servants in the European cities of the Modern Age. Although social distance was clear enough and decisively enforced, spatial segregation was not necessary to maintain social distinction and to reproduce the relative position of each status.

b.  The urban-industrial pattern of spatial differentiation of social groups across specific neighborhoods within the city. Social distance was maintained through the logic of the real estate market and by economic and cultural barriers, as exemplified in the emergence of the large industrial city observed by the Chicago School.

c.  The pattern of metropolitan segregation, linked to the post–World War II city of mass production and consumption, in which social strata occupy spatially and legally distinct segments of the metropolitan space. Increased distances among social strata are institutionalized in the autonomy of suburban governments and their ability to exclude lower-income groups. This pattern has been exemplified by the twin processes of middle class suburbanization and the social and physical deterioration of the central city in the United States.

It is important to understand when, how, and why a postindustrial city reproduces, modifies, or combines these different patterns of sociospatial differentiation. Two distinctions must be kept in mind when addressing this matter: (1) the fundamental distinction between spatial differentiation and spatial segregation, with only the latter entailing physical distance between the residential location of social groups; and (2) the historical possibility of reversing the patterns of social occupation of a given space through urban restructuring, as expressed in the gentrification of central city areas which become exclusive spaces occupied by the new urban elites. The interplay between differentiation and segregation, shaped by the evolution of culture and technology, can translate into different spatial forms that crystallize up and down the ladder of social stratification.

From the perspective of social stratification theory, the dual city notion cannot capture the diversity of urban social strata and their differentiation in residential space. But this notion usefully emphasizes one trend—both the upper and the lower strata of a given society grow at disproportionate rates. Under such conditions, it could be argued that the extremes tend to occupy quite specific spaces (the exclusive space of the elite, the rundown city of the destitute social groups), while the rest of the city is characterized by a gradual social differentiation that follows the variations of the hierarchical social structure. This model presents us with not two cities but three: two specific spaces, metropolitan heaven and inner city hell, and elsewhere the stratified differentiation of urban and suburban space. And in New York, the trip from heaven to hell can sometimes be traversed in a few short blocks. The dual city could then refer either to the contrast between the top and the bottom, or to the opposition between the logic of segregation (as manifested at the extremes of the scale) and the logic of differentiation, underlying the broad middle of urban social stratification. In both cases, however, it is important to emphasize that the polarization thesis, in spite of its thundering overtones of class analysis, is but a specific version of social stratification theory: it reasons in terms of upper and lower levels in the scale of social prestige and economic wealth, without much reference to the actual role of the social groups to which it refers in the process of production or in the city's power relationships. Thus, in the perspective of the polarization thesis, the dual city becomes a simple matter of empirical testing of two basic questions:

a. Are the top and the bottom of the social scale in a given city growing faster than the middle (with the key methodological issue being how to construct the scale to measure the social distribution)?

b. How does such polarization, if it exists, translate into spatial distribution of the top and the bottom of the local society, and how does such specific residential location affect overall sociospatial dynamics?

### Cultures, Cities, and Dualism

A second major analytical current underlying the dual city theme refers to cultural duality. There is a dialectic between social discrimination and spatial segregation on the one hand, and the spatial clustering in patterns of symbolic identity and cultural affinity on the other. Culturally defined groups (remember, ethnicity and race are a matter of culture) select their spaces defensively or are confined to given spaces by discrimination. Urban space then becomes a vehicle for expressing and reproducing ethnically based cultures. Territoriality—national, regional, ethnic, and communal—is a fundamental factor in cultural identity. For ethnically oppressed groups, the territory of their confinement tends to coincide with economically depressed areas, since social stratification overlaps with racial discrimination.

However, it is essential to differentiate between the two processes in order to understand their interaction (e.g., to understand the specific space of the black middle class and the extent to which it has moved out of the ghetto or rather moved to its periphery). In this analytical context, the dual city notion could be simultaneously extremely relevant and dangerously misleading. It misleads by reducing the variety of subcultures (particularly in ethnically diverse societies) to a simple dichotomy. But it accurately highlights the process of racial discrimination according to which dominant cultures put dominated cultures in their place. Given the role played by space in enforcing racial and ethnic discrimination, and indeed reinforcing the material basis for in-group identity and out-group hostility, urban dualism could capture the more pronounced manifestations of racism in the organization of society.

However, as the relationship between ethnicity, culture, and territory becomes more fluid, the dual city notion becomes more misleading. The ethnic-cultural dimension of urban dualism helps us understand the old pattern of ghetto formation in the United States, which is still a major factor, but it can get in the way of understanding how the new immigrants have created a new spatial dynamic by diversifying nonwhite areas, and how the white middle class has made incursions into the borders of inner city depressed neighborhoods. In other words, while the ethnic-cultural characterization of the dual city points at basic elements of urban social dynamics, it must be integrated into a broader comprehension of the new cultures and the new spatial relationships among them.

For example, the gender division of labor at work and at home specifies how men and women relate to the city in their use of space and urban services, and indeed the making of the urban social structure. One might argue, for example, that suburbanization without mass transit could happen only when women provided "free" and flexible transportation services to their husbands and children. Thus, the massive entry of suburban white women into the labor force helped generate the current transportation problem (with middle class households using two cars at peak hours) and may also have increased the attraction of central city living for the new professional couples. Along the same lines, dual career families' need for childcare has influenced residential choices, revived the market for immigrant women as baby-sitters, and paced the movement of people in time and space around the city, adding a new commuting activity to the traditional journeys to work. We could consider a differential reading of the city in terms of gender, thus introducing a new meaning of urban dualism on the basis of the expression of a fundamental cleavage of the social structure in spatial processes.

## Unbalanced Development, Marginality, and the Urban Underclass

A different intellectual tradition in the social sciences has associated urban dualism with a model of urban development that excludes a large segment of the population from the jobs and income generated by economic growth. The strongest analytical current in this perspective originated in Latin America. It aimed to understand why and how increased industrialization and GNP growth, concentrated in the largest metropolitan areas, went hand in hand with accrued urban poverty and an ever-growing proportion of people excluded from the formal labor market and formal housing and urban services.

The basic proposition of this theory focused on the increasing disparity between the characteristics of capital and the characteristics of labor. Modern manufacturing and high level service activities tend to be capital-intensive and require a limited amount of skilled labor, while most of the would-be workers lack education and skills and tend to be redundant in strictly economic terms. The classical debate between Fernando Henrique Cardoso and Jose Nun turned on the notion of an "excessive reserve army of labor" which, in Nun's formulation, had become dysfunctional for the capitalist system.[3] While this pattern achieved GNP growth, it polarized the social structure not only in terms of rich and poor, or between professionals and manual laborers, but more fundamentally between those included in the generation of jobs and income and those excluded from it. The result, in some Latin American formulations, was the emergence of urban marginality. This view postulated a social and ecological situation where the mainstream economic, social, and spatial structure stood in opposition to "the margins," who jeopardized the social equilibrium but whose existence could be denied because they were irrelevant to the economy.

This notion of marginality received devastating and convincing criticism, summarized and elaborated by Janice Perlman.[4] Squatter settlements or unemployed people are not "outside the society"; instead, they occupy a specific position and perform specific services in the urban social structure. But if the notion of marginality is an ideological myth, as Alain Touraine argued, like the dual city notion, it points at a specific, new characteristic of the social structure and introduces the idea that a simple social system contains a dual logic.[5] Research on Latin American cities shows that this dual logic is expressed not through a different relationship between labor and capital, but through state actions toward different segments of the population and labor force. In the Latin American model of urban development, the state perpetuates and reinforces the segmentation of the society. In contrast to the U.S. view that labor market segmentation generates social dualism, Latin American research shows that politics channels different sectors and excludes strata from the formal labor market.

In this perspective the dual city refers to the spatial expression of different connections between the marketplace, different social strata, and political representation. This leads to specific urban forms located in specific places as well as to ad hoc urban services, such as housing, schools, health, social welfare, and public jobs. An American variant of this argument may be found in the argument that a jobs–skills mismatch or cultural and institutional biases against minorities and displaced workers have created an urban underclass.

Here again, dualism does not refer to a position in the social hierarchy but to the ability of groups and individuals to enter the avenues of the new sources of wealth, however conditioned by the hierarchy of the system. Residential segregation and the deterioration of urban public services give this social dualism a persistent spatial form. Since the new informational economy (in both high technology and advanced services) provides the best occupational opportunities to those with high educational levels and cultural-technical skills, family background and the quality of schooling largely determine the ability of labor to enter the dynamic positions of the new occupational structure, as John Kasarda has argued. The dual city then results from two internally stratified systems, one related to the dynamic pole of growth and income generation, the other concentrating labor working in declining industries in spaces and institutions that offer no ladder for upward mobility, inducing the formation of subcultures of survival and helplessness.

### The Dual City and the Formation of Social Class

The dual city has a more fundamental meaning: it refers to the role of cities and urban social movements in forming social classes. We use the concept of social class in the Weberian sense to designate the social actors who, through the confrontation between their projects and interests, produce social values and political institutions. They may be defined according to place in the social relationships of production, but they exist only when they constitute themselves as social actors—in opposition to another social class that is their antagonist—by political and ideological means, including what Erik O. Wright calls their "organizational capacity."[6] Along the lines suggested by Gramsci, we propose that social classes never achieve social domination through sheer oppression of the subordinate classes, but that their power lies in their capacity to establish their social hegemony by constructing a dominant alliance with other classes and segments of classes.[7] Social movements are collective actions undertaken by subjects of social change whether or not they express class struggle.

To understand social change as it relates to cities, regions, and the spatial dimension of society, the most fundamental theoretical question is the relationship of social classes and social movements to spatial forms and processes. Two possible, equally important, readings on this question lead to quite different research questions. In one view, class struggle and social movements shape cities and regions. In the other, the characteristics of cities and regions and of spatial processes in general contribute to the formation of social classes and social movements.

The first view, that conflicting social actors form cities and regions, is not compatible with the notion of dualism. And yet, we often read about the opposition between "the bourgeois city" and "the working class city" as the spatial expression of class relationships. In fact, this formulation typically refers to social stratification theory, not class analysis. The exclusive neighborhoods or the working class wards are the spatial configuration of social inequality, itself the product of a class society, but not the direct work of a given social class. Social change in cities takes place under the combined pressure of the struggles between dominant and subordinate classes, social movements (which include at least gender-based, ethnic-based, national liberation, and citizen movements), and the relatively autonomous role of the state. This formulation cannot be reduced to a simple dualism.

The meaning of the dual city is much more relevant to the role of cities in class formation. This is a highly important, but poorly explored theme in urban sociology; its development could enable social research to break clearly with the economistic conceptualization that reduces social classes to agents in the production process.

If we consider that social classes result from the constant interplay between the structure of production and social organization and the historical development of collective actors aiming at social change, then the material conditions for collective action (of which space is a fundamental dimension) become crucial to understanding social classes and social movements both in the fulfillment of their historical role and in the frustration of their potential as hegemonic actors. In a clear departure from his original structuralist position, Nicos Poulantzas tentatively explored the role of territoriality in social class formation in his last book.[8] With the important exceptions of Anthony Giddens, Richard Sennet, and Edward Soja, however, most social class theorists have ignored this opening.

Several theoretical precedents demonstrate the fruitfulness of introducing the characteristics of cities into the analysis of social class formation. For example, Max Weber's *The City* (published in English as a single book but, in fact, a chapter of his *Economy and Society*) argued that the medieval city (that is, the free city enjoying local political autonomy, a free market, and some level of democracy in its institutions) provided the space in which the bourgeoisie could appear as a political actor able to fight for the institutional foundations of the new economic structure, especially free commerce.[9] Although functionalist sociology has emphasized Weber's analysis of the Protestant ethic as the cultural foundation of capitalism, this was by no means Weber's main argument about the rise of capitalism. In his fundamental work, *Economy and Society*, Weber insisted on the bourgeoisie's essential role as a sociopolitical actor; he emphasized that autonomous cities provided not just marketplaces but the political breathing space where new social values could be nurtured and a close interaction between political projects and economic institutions could be fostered.[10]

In a similar vein, although in a different intellectual and social context, Ira Katznelson's *City Trenches* sought to show how the spatial structure of American cities patterned social classes, and particularly the working class, in the United States.[11] The cultural self-containment of local communities, seeking to control their immediate territory through the tight solidarity of territorially based social networks and to defend it against a brutal and largely unknown host society, amplified the segmentation of American immigrant workers by the different ethnic backgrounds. The system of ward politics and patronage reinforced these spatial-ethnic cleavages and made it difficult to organize different social groups as workers. The existence of white male universal suffrage before the emergence of the working class also removed the need, in contrast to most of Europe, to politicize workers against the political system in order to win the franchise. This may well have been a fundamental element in the formation of the working class, the development of the union movement, and thus in the overall dynamics of social classes and class struggle in the United States.

These theoretical considerations lead us to suggest that the most important contemporary meaning of the dual city notion concerns the impact of urban form on the current process of class formation, as new collective actors struggle to emerge.

## The Meaning of Social Dualism in New York

Although this volume has not begun to exhaust the possible answers to questions about the rise of a dual city model of urban social structure in New York, we can now suggest several substantive arguments that might better illuminate the ongoing debate than did the impressionistic statements we found at the onset of our research program. Taking the various possible meanings of urban dualism in the order they were presented in the different traditions of social theory, we arrive at notably different conclusions about their usefulness to understanding the dynamics of New York and, beyond it, the transformation of the postindustrial city.

From the perspective of social stratification theory, we observe a pattern of growing income inequality as well as an increasing polarization of the occupational structure. These trends seem to be linked to the emerging occupational structure in the dominant global cities of the new information-based economy. However, the reproduction of such inequality in the spheres of collective consumption and public policy is not structurally determined. Occupational polarization and income inequality become translated into widespread urban dualism (that is, the simultaneous increase of affluence and misery among significant proportions of the population) only when public policy mirrors the naked logic of the market.

Nevertheless, a more rigorous analysis of social stratification would lead us to conclude that New York is not a dual city. The occupational system cannot be reduced to the top and the bottom of the urban social structure. It is characterized by a hierarchical diversity of social groups which are quantitatively and qualitatively as important as the upper professionals and the marginal poor. A dichotomous view of social stratification in New York is empirically and theoretically misleading; it misses the complexity and heterogeneity of social groupings that characterize postindustrial cities.

If we turn to the cultural meaning of urban dualism, New York's reality provides a mixed answer. New York's extraordinary cultural mosaic certainly cannot be reduced to two cultures. Ethnic minorities and different immigrant groups are not the only ones to have preserved, or even recreated, their own cultural background in this unmelted pot. The professional middle class is itself culturally heterogeneous, as Brint's analysis forcefully argues. However, a bipolarity does emerge between the mass media as purveyors of a dominant culture (but not the culture of the dominant elite, which is, in fact, another subculture in New York) and the diversity of specific ethnic-national subcultures typically organized along territorial boundaries. In this sense, New York offers an extreme expression of the distance between the "universalism" of the dominant media (which affects most people) and the "particularism" of how territorial and ethnic communities define their patterns of identity and communication, as Moss and Ludwig show. Thus, widespread cultural diversity (not dualism) dwells alongside, and in tension with, the common communication code of the mass media.

We may also say that New York and many other world cities are characterized by a dual social structure in another fundamental sense: a differential access to the formal labor market, leading to what William J. Wilson has termed an urban underclass.[12] While granting that the local labor market is complex, we must also acknowledge the reality of inclusion and exclusion, rooted in racial and social discrimination, channeled by the school system, and expressed in employer hiring practices.[13] Thus, although we know that urban marginality does not create a social stratum outside the social system and the norms of society, real barriers nevertheless block those with certain attributes from access to the jobs that convey privilege, influence, and wealth in our society. In this sense, New York is a dual city, in which much of its working-age population (and particularly its minority youth) is outside the formal labor market, creating the conditions for entry into the criminal economy, the informal economy, and the assisted economy, all of which are stigmatized and unregulated segments of the local society.

From a spatial perspective, New York is simultaneously increasingly dual and increasingly plural. On the one hand, real estate development and gentrification are pushing the poor and ethnic out of certain residential areas, especially in Manhattan, so that the city is becoming increasingly segregated in terms of class, race, and national origin. Dualism refers here to the opposition between white middle class areas (characterized by more non-family households and less child rearing, with their corollary of demand for personal services and the predilection for conspicuous consumption) and areas with a strong presence of ethnic minorities and/or immigrant cultures.

On the other hand, the predominantly minority areas are increasingly diverse. To consider the cultural mosaic of New York space as purely the expression of dualism is, in fact, to accept a white middle class prejudice that makes all minorities the same. Furthermore, the interpenetration of cultures and classes in the active street life of New York constitutes the epitome of urban diversity. It is precisely the breakdown of the mechanisms of social welfare and social control that evokes this strange mixture of homeless people and limousine-driven executives in the same urban space. But this spatial interaction must be observed at a closer and deeper level: subtle and sometimes obvious spatial boundaries protect many microspaces from excessive social promiscuity, as when public and private police forces drive the homeless from Grand Central, Penn Station, or certain public plazas. In sum, spatial practice in New York is characterized by the relentless but only intermittently successful effort to impose the logic of a dual society on a culturally plural city with an intense and socially mixed street life.

The dual city concept may also refer to the impact of a given urban structure on class formation, which is the process by which social groups become political-cultural actors who shape the evolution of societies. Our empirical analyses have a more indirect bearing on this theme. For example, this volume lacks a study directly addressing the characteristics, composition, and goals of New York's ruling elite, and particularly its financial elite. However, we have observed that the upper professionals exert a strong economic, cultural, spatial, and political impact on the city, while the constellation of subordinate or marginal groups is fragmented and disorganized.

The formation of a unified world economy organized around the ability to communicate and process information has generated both the global city and the informational city, expressed in its ability to centralize and control the information flows on which multinational corporations rely.[14] We hypothesize that the dual city is the social expression of the emerging spatial form of postindustrial society, while the global city is its economic expression, and the informational city its technological expression.

The postindustrial era is no exception to the proposition that any epoch is characterized by the emergence of a dominant class (in this case, the managerial technocracy allied to the global financial elite) which has a distinct spatial logic. The interests and organizational powers of the new dominant class arise within a space of flows; that is, networks that transmit and facilitate the analysis of economically and politically relevant information. All social strata have communications networks with access to certain kinds of information. But the new dominant class dominates the space of flows by having exclusive access to the most important information and by deploying power-holding organizations in these networks, which enable them, in theory, to execute unilateral decisions regarding the commitment of resources from any location.

But those who populate such power-holding organizations do need to operate from specific places. The space of flows therefore tends to be organized around specific nodes. The new professional-managerial class, in London as in New York, colonizes exclusive spatial segments which connect to each other in the city, across the country, and across the world, while isolating themselves from the fragments of local societies that are destroyed as patterns of work and residence are selectively reorganized. The new international economy creates a variable geometry of production and consumption, labor and capital, management and information, which voids the productive meaning of any specific place outside its position in a network whose shape changes relentlessly following the messages of unseen signals and unknown codes.

New York's corporate world closely fits this logic. A fundamental goal of the restructuring that the city underwent during the 1970s and 1980s was to supersede places with a network of information flows. This process symbolized the restructuring of the capitalist system as a whole. Power-holding organizations have avoided historically established mechanisms of social control, whether economic or political, because these mechanisms depend upon territorially based institutions. To achieve a space of flows connected only to other power-holders who share the values coded into the architecture of global information systems, power holders had to escape the social logics embedded in any particular locale.

The emergence of the space of flows has been conditioned on separating the organizations of power and production from the hierarchies of place-based societies. People live in places, power rules through flows. The Koch coalition's main achievement will probably have been to make the city's productive basis, and ultimately its prosperity, dependent on preserving the spaces and functions that the global elite and its army of professionals require. The Koch regime constructed an environment in which the new global elite can express its values and lifestyles with little interference from the life pulse of the majority of the city's residents.

The spatial forms and processes characterizing New York during the 1980s nurtured the rise of the new dominant class in its international dimension while fragmenting subordinate classes and fixing them in specific locales, ignorant of the macroprocesses at work beyond the control of local communities. Although communities are increasingly local in their concerns, organization, and political targets, the dominant class, including New York's elite, has developed an increasingly global perspective. The nodal points in their space of flows provide both managerial platforms for the global system and culturally protected spaces where members of the new dominant categories establish their lifestyles, define their values, and reproduce their networks.

These strategically important spaces, of which New York's are probably the most important, do not embrace the entire city. Rather, specific business centers and residential neighborhoods are connected to similar spaces throughout the world, both materially (transportation, telecommunications, international hotels, business services centers) and symbolically (consumption patterns, formal design, architectural styles). Local community spaces, by contrast, are extremely specific to their dwellers, to their culture, to their history, and to their social and political forms of organization.

The meaning of the dual city that best fits the reality of New York is thus the dichotomy we observe between the nodal segments of the space of globally interconnected flows and the fragmented and powerless locales of social communities. An international-informational dominant class, supported by the upper professionals, has been formed, while the subordinate classes have been disorganized and their isolation reinforced. New York is a dual city most fundamentally because its spatial restructuring has included some distinct segments of society in the making of history while excluding others.

Urban dualism is thus not a social attribute but a social process of class formation. It is an evolving reality. But New York's trajectory during the 1980s triggered contradictions and conflicts which may undermine the political actors who fostered urban dualism. Even though the Dinkins administration will doubtless respond to the interests of the corporate elite, it cannot survive if it follows the one-dimensional logic of its predecessor. It may thus seek to attenuate the trend towards the exclusion of large segments of the local society in the service of global corporate interests. Preserving social stability may require it to set up new mechanisms of social integration.

The fundamental trends giving rise to the postindustrial city as exemplified by New York will continue, however, to foster an exclusion that can be countervailed only by a mobilized, organized, and self-conscious local society. This book hopes to contribute modestly to such a fundamental debate by showing how the social conflicts and social innovations of tomorrow's world are being invented and experienced in New York today.

# Notes

1. Samuel M. Ehrenhalt, New York regional director of the U.S. Bureau of Labor Statistics, has estimated that it would take half a million more employed New Yorkers for the city to have the same labor force participation rate as the nation. This figure approximates the size of the social segment generally unaccounted for in the statistics of the occupational structure. As Ida Susser argues, children (and particularly minority children) are overrepresented among the dependents of this marginal sector of the population.

2. Zorbaugh, Harvey W., *The Gold Coast and the Slum* (Chicago: University of Chicago Press, 1929).

3. Cardoso, Fernando Henrique, and Enzo Faletto, *Dependencia y Desarrolla en America Latina* (Mexico: Siglo XXI, 1969); Nun, Jose, "Superpoblacion Relativa, Ejercito Industrial de Reserva y Masa Marginal," *Revista Latinoamerica de Socioligia* 69:2 (1969).

4. Perlman, Janice E., *The Myth of Marginality* (Berkeley: University of California Press, 1976).

5. Touraine, Alain, *La Parole et le Sang: Politique et Société en Amerique Latine* (Paris: Odile Jacob, 1988).

6. Wright, Erik, *Classes* (London: New Left, 1985).

7. Gramsci, Antonio, *Selections from the Prison Notebooks* (London: Lawrence Wisheart, 1971); one of the earliest studies of the formation of such coalitions was Poulantzas, Nicos, *L'Etat, le Pouvoir, le Socialisme* (Paris: Presses Universitaires Françaises, 1978).

8. Poulantzas, *L'Etat*.

9. Weber, Max, *The City* (Glencoe, IL: The Free Press, 1959).

10. Weber, Max, *Economy and Society* (Berkeley: University of California Press, 1978).

11. Katznelson, Ira, *City Trenches* (New York: Pantheon, 1981).

12. Wilson, William J., *The Truly Disadvantaged: The Inner City, the Underclass, and Public Policy* (Chicago: University of Chicago Press, 1987).

13. For evidence of continued discrimination, see Bailey, Thomas, "Black Employment Opportunities," in Brecher, Charles, and Raymond D. Horton, eds., *Setting Municipal Priorities, 1990* (New York: New York University Press, 1989), pp. 80–109.

14. Castells, Manuel, *The Informational City* (Cambridge, MA: Basil Blackwell, 1989).

# References

Abeles, Schwartz, Hackel, and Silverblatt, Inc., *The Chinatown Garment Industry Study* (New York: Report to ILGWU Locals 23-25 and the New York Sportswear Association, 1983).

Abramowitz, Mimi, *Regulating the Lives of Women: Social Welfare Policy from Colonial Times to the Present* (Boston: South End Press, 1988).

Armstrong, Regina, and David Milder, "Employment in the Manhattan CBD and Back-Office Location Decisions," *City Almanac* 18 (1984): 1-2, 4-18.

Auletta, Ken, *The Underclass* (New York: Random House, 1982).

Bagdikian, Ben, "The U.S. Media: Supermarket or Assembly Line?" *Journal of Communication* (Summer 1985).

———, *Media Monopoly* (Boston: Beacon Press, 1987).

Bailey, Thomas, *Immigrant and Native Workers: Contrasts and Competition* (Boulder, CO: Westview Press, 1987).

———, "Black Employment Opportunities," in Brecher, Charles, and Raymond D. Horton, eds., *Setting Municipal Priorities, 1990* (New York: New York University Press, 1989), pp. 80-109.

Bailey, Thomas, and Roger Waldinger, "A Skills Mismatch in New York's Labor Market?" *New York Affairs* 8, 3 (1984): 3-19.

Balmori, D. "Hispanic Immigrants in the Construction Industry: New York City, 1960-1982" (New York University Center for Latin American and Caribbean Studies Occasional Paper No. 38, 1983).

Baran, Barbara, "The Technological Transformation of White-Collar Work: A Case Study of the Insurance Industry," in Hartmann, Heidi, ed., *Computer Chips and Paper Clips: Technology and Women's Employment, Vol.II* (Washington, DC: National Academy Press, 1987).

Baxter, E., and Kim Hopper, *Public Places, Private Spaces* (New York: Community Service Society, 1981).

Beauregard, Robert A., "Capital Restructuring and the New Built Environment of Global Cities: New York and Los Angeles" (1989). Unpublished manuscript.

———, ed., *Economic Restructuring and Political Response* (Newbury Park, CA: Sage Publications, 1988).

———, ed., *Atop the Urban Hierarchy* (Totowa, NJ: Rowman & Littlefield, 1989).

Bell, Daniel, *The Coming of Post-Industrial Society* (New York: Basic Books, 1973).

**419**

Bell, Linda, and Richard Freeman, "The Facts About Rising Industrial Wage Dispersion in the US," Industrial Relations Research Association, *Proceedings* (May 1986).

Bellush, Jewel, and Steven David, eds., *Race and Politics in New York City* (New York: Praeger, 1971).

Beneria, Lourdes, "Subcontracting and Employment Dynamics in Mexico City," in Portes, A., M. Castells, and L. Benton, eds., *The Informal Economy* (Baltimore and London: Johns Hopkins University Press, 1989).

Bennett, Larry, "The Dilemmas of Building a Progressive Urban Coalition: The Linked Development Debate in Chicago," *Journal of Urban Affairs*, 9, 3 (1987): 263–276.

Berger, Suzanne, and M. J. Piore, *Dualism and Discontinuity in Industrial Societies* (Cambridge: Cambridge University Press, 1980).

Berne, Robert, and Emanuel Tobier, "The Setting for School Policy," in Brecher, Charles, and Raymond D. Horton, eds., *Setting Municipal Priorities, 1988* (New York: New York University Press, 1987).

Blumberg, Paul, *Inequality in an Age of Decline* (New York: Oxford University Press, 1980).

Body-Gendrot, Sophie N., "Grass-roots Mobilization in the Thirteenth Arrondissement of Paris: A Cross-national View," in Stone, Clarence N., and Heywood T. Sanders, eds., *The Politics of Urban Development* (Lawrence: University of Kansas Press, 1987), pp. 125–143.

Borjas, George J., and Marta Tienda, "The Economic Consequences of Immigration," *Science* 235 (February 6, 1987): 613–620.

Boswell, T. D., "Residential Patterns of Puerto Ricans in New York City," *Geographical Review* 66:1 (1976): 92–94.

Bourdieu, Pierre, *Distinction* (Cambridge: Harvard University Press, 1984).

Boyer, M. Christine, "The Return of Aesthetics to City Planning," *Society* (1988): 49–56.

Bradbury, Katherine L., "The Shrinking Middle Class," *New England Economic Review* (September-October 1986).

Braverman, Harry, *Labor and Monopoly Capital* (New York: Monthly Review Press, 1974).

Brazelton, T. Berry, *Infants and Mothers*, Rev. Ed. (New York: Dell, 1983).

Brecher, Charles, and Raymond D. Horton, "Community Power and Municipal Budgets," in Lurie, Irene, ed., *New Directions in Budget Theory* (Albany: State University of New York Press, 1988).

————, eds., *Setting Muncipal Priorities, 1988* (New York: New York University Press, 1987).

————, eds., *Setting Municipal Priorities, 1990* (New York: New York University Press, 1989).

Bridges, Amy, *A City in the Republic: Ante-Bellum New York and the Origins of Machine Politics* (New York: Cambridge University Press, 1984).

*Broadcasting/Cablecasting Yearbook 1988* (Washington: Broadcasting Publications, 1988).

Browning, Rufus, Dale Marshall, and David Tabb, *Protest Is Not Enough: The Struggle of Blacks and Hispanics for Equality in Urban Politics* (Berkeley: University of California Press, 1984).

Buck, Nicholas, and Ian Gordon, *Employment Forecasts for Greater London*. Final Report to the London Planning Advisory Committee (1986).

———, "The Beneficiaries of Employment Growth: The Experience of Disadvantaged Groups in Expanding Labour Markets," in Hausner, V., ed., *Critical Issues in Urban Economic Development Vol. II* (London: Oxford University Press, 1987).

Buck, Nicholas, Ian Gordon, and K. Young, *The London Employment Problem* (London: Oxford University Press, 1986).

Buckley, Peter G., "Culture, Class, and Place in Antebellum New York," in Mollenkopf, J., ed., *Power, Culture, and Place: Essays on New York City* (New York: Russell Sage Foundation, 1988).

Burnham, W. D., *Critical Elections and the Mainsprings of American Politics* (New York: W. W. Norton, 1966).

Byrne, J. M., and R. J. Sampson, *The Social Ecology of Crime* (New York: Springer-Verlag, 1986).

Capecchi, Vittorio, "The Informal Economy and the Development of Flexible Specialization in Emilia-Romagna," in Portes, A., M. Castells, and L. Benton, eds., *The Informal Economy* (Baltimore and London: Johns Hopkins University Press, 1989).

Cardoso, Fernando Henrique, and Enzo Faletto, *Dependencia y Desarrolla en America Latina* (Mexico: Siglo XXI, 1969).

Castells, Manuel, "Commentary on C. G. Pickvance's 'The Rise and Fall of Urban Movements,'" *Environment and Planning D: Space and Society* 3 (1985): 55–61.

———, *The Informational City* (Cambridge, MA: Basil Blackwell, 1989).

Castells, Manuel, and Alejandro Portes, "World Underneath: The Origins, Dynamics, and Effects of the Informal Economy," in Portes, A., M. Castells, and L. Benton, eds., *The Informal Economy* (Baltimore and London: Johns Hopkins University Press, 1989).

Caves, R. E., "Industrial Organizations, Corporate Strategy, and Structure," *Journal of Economic Literature* 18 (1980): 64–92.

Center on Budget and Policies Priorities, *Smaller Slices of the Pie: The Growing Economic Vulnerability of Poor and Moderate Income Americans* (Washington, DC: Center on Budget Policies Priorities, November 1985).

Chall, Daniel, "Neighborhood Changes in New York City during the 1970s. Are the Gentry Returning?" *Federal Reserve Bank of New York Quarterly Bulletin* (Winter 1983–1984): 38–48.

Chaney, Elsa M., and Mary Garcia Castro, *Muchachas No More: Household Workers in Latin America and the Caribbean* (Philadelphia: Temple University Press, 1989).

Child Care Inc., *Basic Facts About Child Care in New York City* (New York, July 1987).

Chinitz, Benjamin, *Freight and the Metropolis* (Cambridge: Harvard University Press, 1960).

City of New York, Department of City Planning, *Demographic Profile: A Portrait of New York City from the 1980 Census* (1983).

———, *1980 Census Data, Part 1—Income, New York City Boroughs Community Districts* (1983).

———, *Atlas of the Census* (1985).

City of New York, Human Resources Administration, Office of Policy and Program Development, *Dependency* (June 1988).

———, *Dependency: Economic and Social Data for New York City, June 1988,* Vol. 5 (1989).

City of New York, Office of Economic Development, "Garment Center Study" (1987).

City of New York, Office of Management and Budget, *Report of Economic Conditions in New York City, July–December 1986* (1987).

City of New York, Office of the Mayor, Executive Budget, Fiscal Year 1989, *Message of the Mayor* (May 9, 1988).

City of New York, Police Department, Crime Analysis Section, *Arrests and Complaints, 1960–1982* (published each year).

Clark, Kenneth, *Dark Ghetto* (New York: Harper & Row, 1965).

Clarke, Susan E., and Margit Mayer, "Responding to Grassroots Discontent: Germany and the United States," *International Journal of Urban and Regional Research* 10 (September 1986): 401.

Cloward, Richard A., and Frances Fox Piven, *The Politics of Turmoil* (New York: Pantheon, 1974).

Cohen, Stephen S., and John Zysman, *Manufacturing Matters: The Myth of the Post-industrial Economy* (New York: Basic Books, 1987).

Colen, S., "Just a Little Respect: West Indian Domestic Workers in New York City," in Chaney, Elsa M., and Mary Garcia Castro, *Muchachas No More: Household Workers in Latin America and the Caribbean* (Philadelphia: Temple University Press, 1989).

Columbia University, "Immigration Research Project" (Program in Urban Planning, 1989).

———, "The Informal Economy in Low-Income Communities in New York City" (Program in Urban Planning, 1987).

Community Service Society of New York, "Displacement Pressures in the Lower East Side." Working Paper (1987).

Compaine, Benjamin, "The Expanding Base of Media Competition," *Journal of Communication* (Summer 1985).

Connelly, Harold X., *A Ghetto Grows in Brooklyn: Bedford Stuyvesant* (New York: New York University Press, 1977).

Conservation of Human Resources, *The Corporate Headquarters Complex in New York City* (Montclair, NJ: Allanheld Osmun, 1977).

Council of Economic Advisors, *Economic Report of the President 1988* (Washington, DC: U.S. Government Printing Office, 1988).

David, Steven, "Welfare: The Community Action Controversy," in Bellush, Jewel, and Steven David, eds., *Race and Politics in New York City* (New York: Praeger, 1971), pp. 25–58.

Davies, James Clarence, III, *Neighborhood Groups and Urban Renewal* (New York: Columbia University Press, 1966).

Dehavenon, A., *Toward a Policy for the Amelioration and Prevention of Family Homelessness and Dissolution: New York City's After-hours Emergency Assistance Units in 1986–1987*, The East Harlem Interfaith Welfare Committee (May 1987).

Deutermann, W. V., Jr., and S. C. Brown, "Voluntary Part-time Workers: A Growing Part of the Labor Force," *Monthly Labor Review* 101 (June 1978).

Diamond, Edwin, and Piera Pine, "The Media in the Game of Politics," in Bellush, Jewel, and Dick Netzer, eds., *Urban Politics, New York Style* (Armonk, NY: M. E. Sharpe, 1990), pp. 339–358.

DiMaggio, Paul, "Classification in Art," *American Sociological Review* 52 (1987): 440–455.

DiMaggio, Paul, and Michael Useem, "Social Class and Arts Consumption," *Theory and Society* 5 (1978): 141–162.

Donnison, D., and D. C. Eversley, eds., *London: Urban Patterns, Problems, and Policies* (London: Heinemann, 1973).

Drennan, Matthew, *Modeling Metropolitan Economies for Forecasting and Policy Analysis* (New York: New York University Press, 1985).

———, "Local Economy and Local Revenues," in Brecher, Charles, and Raymond D. Horton, eds., *Setting Municipal Priorities, 1988* (New York: New York University Press, 1987).

———, "An Econometric Model of New York City and Region: What It Is and What It Can Do," *Economic Development Quarterly* 3, 4 (November 1989).

———, "Information Intensive Industries in Metropolitan Areas of the United States," *Environment and Planning A* 21 (1989).

Edholm, F., O. Harris, and K. Young, "Conceptualizing Women," *Critique of Anthropology* 3, Issues 9, 10 (1977).

*Editor & Publisher International Yearbook, 1987* (New York: Editor & Publisher Co., 1987).

Ehrenhalt, Samuel, "The Outlook for the New York City Labor Market." Speech delivered to the Fifteenth Annual Institute on the Challenges of the Changing Economy of New York City (April 28, 1982).

———, "The New York Experience as a Service Economy" (New York: Bureau of Labor Statistics, U.S. Dept. of Labor, 1986).

———, "The Service Economy and Job Quality: The New York Experience" (New York: Bureau of Labor Statistics, U.S. Dept. of Labor, September 1986).

———, "New York City in the New Economic Environment: New Risks and a Changing Outlook" (New York: Bureau of Labor Statistics, June 1988).

———, "After the Crash: New York Prospects" (New York: Bureau of Labor Statistics, U.S. Dept. of Labor, July 1988).

Elliot, D. S., S. S. Ageton, S. S. Huizinga, B. A. Knowles, and R. Canter, *The Prevalence and Incidence of Delinquent Behavior: 1976–1980* (Boulder, CO: Behavioral Research Institute, 1983).

Epstein, Cynthia Fuchs, *Women in Law* (New York: Basic Books, 1981).

———, *Deceptive Distinctions: Sex, Gender, and the Social Order* (New Haven: Yale University Press, and New York: Russell Sage Foundation, 1988).

Fagan, Jeffrey, Elizabeth S. Piper, and Yu-Teh Cheng, "Contributions of Victimization to Delinquency in Inner Cities," *Journal of Criminal Law and Criminology* 78, 13 (1987): 408–428.

Fainstein, Norman I., "The Underclass/Mismatch Hypothesis as an Explanation for Black Economic Deprivation," *Politics & Society* 15, 4 (1986–1987): 403–451.

Fainstein, Norman I., and Susan S. Fainstein, *Urban Political Movements* (Englewood Cliffs, NJ: Prentice-Hall, 1974).

———, "The Future of Community Control," *American Political Science Review* 70 (September 1976): 922.

Fainstein, Susan S., "The Politics of Criteria: Planning for the Redevelopment of Times Square," in Fischer, Frank, and John Forester, eds., *Confronting Values in Policy Analysis* (Beverly Hills, CA: Sage, 1987), pp. 232–247.

Fainstein, Susan S., and Norman I. Fainstein, "Economic Restructuring and the Rise of Urban Social Movements," *Urban Affairs Quarterly* 21 (1985): 187–206.

Fainstein, Susan S., et al., *Community Leadership and the Office of Neighborhood Government in Bushwick, Crown Heights, and Wakefield-Edenwald*. Interim Report, New York City Neighborhood Project, Bureau of Applied Social Research, Columbia University, mimeo (1973), p. 47.

Fainstein, Susan S., et al., eds., *Restructuring the City* (New York: Longman, 1986).

Falcon, Angelo, "Black and Latino Politics in New York City: Race and Ethnicity in a Changing Urban Context," *New Community* 14, 3 (Spring 1988): 370–384.

———, "Race and Ethnicity in New York City Politics: Racial Dualism Versus Ethnic Pluralism." Paper prepared for the SSRC Committee on New York City, November 1988.

Fantini, Mario, Marilyn Gittell, and R. Magat, *Community Control and the Urban School* (New York: Praeger, 1970).

Farley, Reynolds, and Walter Allen, *The Color Line and the Quality of Life in America* (New York: Russell Sage Foundation, 1987).

Feagin, Joe R., *Free Enterprise City: Houston in Political-Economic Perspective* (New Brunswick, NJ: Rutgers University Press 1983).

Fernández-Kelly, M. Patricia, and Anna M. García, "Informalization at the Core: Hispanic Women, Homework, and the Advanced Capitalist State," in Portes, A., M. Castells, and L. Benton, eds., *The Informal Economy* (Baltimore and London: Johns Hopkins University Press, 1989).

Fernández-Kelly, M. Patricia, and Saskia Sassen, "Collaborative Study on Hispanic Women in the Garment and Electronic Industries in New York and California." Final Report to be submitted to the Revson, Ford, and Tinker foundations (in preparation).

Foner, Nancy, ed., *New Immigrants in New York* (New York: Columbia University Press, 1987).

Fothergill, S., and G. Gudgin, *Unequal Growth; Urban and Regional Employment Change in the UK* (London: Heinemann, 1982).

Foundation for Child Development, *Public Expenditures for Children, 1980–1983: The Impact of Federal Changes* (New York: Foundation for Child Development, 1985).

Freeman, Richard B., and Harry Holzer, eds., *The Black Youth Employment Crisis* (Chicago: University of Chicago Press, 1986).

———, "The Black Youth Employment Crisis: Summary of Findings," in Freeman, R., and H. Holzer, eds., *The Black Youth Employment Crisis* (Chicago: University of Chicago Press, 1986).

Gallo, Carmenta, "The Construction Industry in New York City: Immigrant and Black Entrepreneurs" (New York: Conservation of Human Resources Research Project on Newcomers to New York City, January 1983).

Garson, Barbara, *The Electronic Sweatshop: How Computers Are Transforming the Office of the Future into the Factory of the Past* (New York: Simon & Schuster, 1988).

Gelb, Joyce, *Feminism and Politics* (Berkeley: University of California Press, 1989).

Georges, Eugenia, "New Immigrants and the Political Process: Dominicans in New York" (Center for Latin American and Caribbean Studies, New York University, Occasional Paper 45, April 1984).

Gerson, Jeffrey, "Building the Brooklyn Machine: Jewish and Black Succession in the Brooklyn Democratic Party Organization, 1919–1964." Ph.D. Diss., Political Science Program, CUNY Graduate Center, 1990.

Gerson, K., *Hard Choices: How Women Choose Between Work, Career, and Motherhood* (Berkeley: University of California Press, 1985).

Ginzberg, Eli, "Technology, Women, and Work: Policy Perspectives," in Hartmann, Heidi, ed., *Computer Chips and Paper Clips: Technology and Women's Employment, Vol. II* (Washington, DC: National Academy Press, 1987).

Gitlin, Todd, "New Video Technology: Pluralism or Banality," *Democracy* (October 1981).

Glickman, Norman, "International Trade, Capital Mobility, and Economic Growth: Some Implications for American Cities and Regions in the 1980s," in Hicks, Donald, and Norman Glickman, eds., *Transition to the 21st Century* (Greenwich, CT: JAI Press, 1983), pp. 205–240.

Goldberg, Arthur S., and Asher Arian, "The American Urban Electorate in the 1988 Presidential Election." Paper presented to the Annual Meeting of the American Political Science Association, Atlanta, GA (1989).

Gordon, David M., Richard Edwards, and Michael Reich, *Segmented Work, Divided Workers: The Historical Transformation of Labor in the United States* (Cambridge: Cambridge University Press, 1982).

Gordon, Ian, "Evaluating the Impact of Employment Changes on Local Unemployment," *Regional Studies* 22 (1988): 135–147.

Gorz, Andre, *Farewell to the Working Class* (Boston: South End Press, 1982), p. 12.

Gramsci, Antonio, *Selections from the Prison Notebooks* (London: Lawrence Wisheart, 1971).

Green, Charles, and Basil Wilson, *The Struggle for Black Empowerment in New York City: Beyond the Politics of Pigmentation* (New York: Praeger, 1989).

Greenberg, David F., "Delinquency and the Age Structure of Society," *Contemporary Crises* (April 1977): 189–223.

———, "Age, Crime, and Social Explanation," *American Journal of Sociology* 91, 1 (1985): 121–132.

Grossman, David A., Lester M. Salamon, and David M. Altschuler, *The New York Nonprofit Sector in a Time of Government Retrenchment* (Washington, DC: Urban Institute Press, 1986).

HACER/National Hispanic Women's Center, "New York City Hispanics: Who Votes and How?" (1985).

Hacker, Andrew, *The New Yorkers: Profile of an American Metropolis* (New York: Mason-Charter, 1975).

Hammond, John L., "Yuppies," *Public Opinion Quarterly* 50 (1986): 457–501.

Hanier, Peter, Catherine Hines, Elizabeth Martin, and Gary Shapiro, "Research on Improving Coverage in Household Surveys." Paper presented to Bureau of the Census, Fourth Annual Research Conference, Arlington, VA, March 20–23, 1988.

Harris, Louis, and Bert Swanson, *Black-Jewish Relations in New York City* (New York: Praeger, 1970).

Harrison, Bennett, "Rationalization, Restructuring, and Industrial Reorganization in Older Regions: The Economic Transformation of New England Since World War II." Working Paper No. 72 (Cambridge: Joint Center for Urban Studies of MIT and Harvard University, 1982).

Harrison, Bennett, and Barry Bluestone, *The Great U-Turn: Corporate Restructuring and the Polarizing of America* (New York: Basic Books, 1988).

Harrison, Bennett, Barry Bluestone, and Chris Tilly, "The Great U-Turn: Increasing Inequality in Wage and Salary Income in the United States." Paper presented to the Fortieth Anniversary Symposium of the U.S. Congressional Joint Economic Committee, Washington, DC, January 16 and 17, 1986.

Hartmann, Heidi, ed., *Computer Chips and Paper Clips: Technology and Women's Employment, Vol. II* (Washington, DC: National Academy Press, 1987).

Hartmann, Heidi, Robert E. Kraut, and Louise A. Tilly, eds., *Computer Chips and Paper Clips: Technology and Women's Employment, Vol. I* (Washington, DC: National Academy Press, 1986).

Harvey, David, "Flexible Accumulation Through Urbanization: Reflections on 'Post-modernism' in the American City," *Antipode* 90 (1987): 260–286.

Hewlett, Sylvia, *A Lesser Life* (New York: Morrow, 1986).

Hicks, Donald A., *Advanced Industrial Development* (Boston: Oelgeschlager, Gunn, & Hain, 1985).

Hill, Richard Child, "Comparing Traditional Production Systems: The Case of the Automobile Industry in the United States and Japan," *International Journal of Urban and Regional Research* 13, 3 (September 1989): 462–480.

Hirschi, Travis, and Michael Gottfredson, "Age and the Explanation of Crime," *American Journal of Sociology* 89, 3 (1983): 552–584.

Hobsbawm, Eric J., *The Age of Revolution 1789–1848* (New York: New American Library, 1962).

Holmes, John, "The Organization and Locational Structure of Production Subcontracting," in Scott, Allen J., and Michael Storper, eds., *Production, Work, Territory: The Geographical Anatomy of Industrial Capitalism* (Boston: Allen & Unwin, 1986), pp. 80–106.

Hoover, Edgar, and Raymond Vernon, *Anatomy of a Metropolis* (Cambridge: Harvard University Press, 1959).

Hopper, Kim, Ida Susser, and S. Conover, "Economics of Makeshift: Deindustrialization and Homelessness in New York City," *Urban Anthropology* 14, 1–3 (1986): 183–236.

Horton, Raymond D., "Fiscal Stress and Labor Power." Paper presented to the Industrial Relations Research Association Annual Meeting, New York, December 28–30, 1985.

Hughes, Michael, and Richard A. Peterson, "Isolating Patterns of Cultural Choice," *American Behavioral Scientist* 26 (1983): 459–479.

Hunt, Allen H., and Timothy L. Hunt, "Recent Trends in Clerical Employment: The Impact of Technological Change," in Hartmann, Heidi, ed., *Computer Chips and Paper Clips: Technology and Women's Employment, Vol.II* (Washington, DC: National Academy Press, 1987).

———, "Clerical Employment and Technological Change: A Review of Recent Trends and Projections." Paper prepared for The Panel on Technology and Women's Employment and Related Social Issues (Washington, DC: National Research Council, 1985).

Hymer, Stephen, "The Multinational Corporation and the Law of Uneven Development," in Bhagwati, J., ed., *Economics and World Order from the 1970s to the 1990s* (New York: Macmillan, 1972).

Jennings, James, *Puerto Rican Politics in New York* (Washington, DC: University Press of America, 1977).

Johnson, Bruce D., et al., *Taking Care of Business: The Economics of Crime by Heroin Abusers* (Lexington, MA: Lexington Books, D. C. Heath, 1985).

Johnson, L. C., and R. E. Johnson, *The Seam Allowance: Industrial Home Sewing in Canada* (Toronto: Women's Press, 1983).

Kammerman, S., and C. Hayes, eds., *Families that Work: Children in a Changing World* (Washington, DC: National Academy Press, 1982).

Kasarda, John D., "Entry-level Jobs, Mobility, and Urban Minority Employment," *Urban Affairs Quarterly* 19, 1 (1983): 21–40.

———, "Hispanics and City Change," *American Demographics* (November 1984).

———, "Urban Change and Minority Opportunities," in Peterson, Paul E., ed., *The New Urban Reality* (Washington, DC: The Brookings Institution, 1985).

———, "Urban Industrial Transition and the Underclass," *The Annals of the American Academy of Political and Social Science* 501 (January 1989): 26–47.

Katz, Steven, and Margit Mayer, "Gimme Shelter: Self-Help Housing Struggles Within and Against the State in New York City and West Berlin," *International Journal of Urban and Regional Research* 9 (March 1985): 15–46.

Katznelson, Ira, *City Trenches* (New York: Pantheon, 1981).

Key, V. O., Jr., *Southern Politics in State and Nation* (New York: Vintage, 1949).

Kim, Ilsoo, "The Koreans: Small Business in an Urban Frontier," in Foner, N., ed., *New Immigrants in New York* (New York: Columbia University Press, 1987).

Kimball, Penn, *The Disconnected* (New York: Columbia University Press, 1972).

Kornblum, William, and James Beshers, "White Ethnicity: Ecological Dimensions," in Mollenkopf, J., ed., *Power, Culture, and Place: Essays on New York City* (New York: Russell Sage Foundation, 1988), pp. 201–221.

Kozol, J., *Rachel and Her Children* (New York: Crown, 1988).

Lampard, Eric. E., "The New York Metropolis in Transformation: History and Prospect. A Study in Historical Particularity," in Ewers, W., et al., eds., *The Future of the Metropolis* (New York: De Gruyter, 1986).

Lamphere, Louise, *From Working Daughters to Working Mothers: Immigrant Women in a New England Industrial Community* (Ithaca: Cornell University Press, 1987).

Landes, David S., *The Unbound Prometheus* (Cambridge: Cambridge University Press, 1969).

Lawrence, Robert Z., "Sectoral Shifts and the Size of the Middle Class," *Brookings Review* (Fall 1984).

Lawson, Ronald, ed., *The Tenant Movement in New York City, 1904–1984* (New Brunswick, NJ: Rutgers University Press, 1986).

Leichter, Franz, "Return of the Sweatshop: A Call for State Action" (New York: Office of State Senator Leichter, 1979).

———, "Return of the Sweatshop: Part II of an Investigation" (New York: Office of State Senator Leichter, 1981).

Levy, Frank, *Dollars and Dreams: The Changing American Income Distribution* (New York: Russell Sage Foundation, 1987).

Lewinson, Edwin, *Black Politics in New York City* (New York: Twayne, 1974).

Lichten, Eric, *Class, Power & Austerity: The New York City Fiscal Crisis* (South Hadley, MA: Bergin & Garvey, 1986).

Lieberson, Stanley, *A Piece of the Pie* (Berkeley: University of California Press, 1980).

Lindstrom, Diane, "Economic Structure, Demographic Change, and Income Inequality in Antebellum New York," in Mollenkopf, J., ed., *Power, Culture, and Place* (New York: Russell Sage Foundation, 1988).

Lowe, Jean, *Cities in a Race with Time* (New York: Random House, 1967).

Lowi, Theodore, *At the Pleasure of the Mayor* (New York: Free Press, 1964).

McGahey, Richard, "Economic Development and the Perception of Crime," *New York Affairs* 8, 1 (1983).

Mahler, Sarah J., "Dominican Migration to the United States and United States Immigration Policy: A Changing History," *Forum* (Santo Domingo, forthcoming).

Mann, Evelyn S., and Joseph J. Salvo, "Characteristics of New Hispanic Immigrants to New York City: A Comparison of Puerto Rican and Non-Puerto Rican Hispanics." Paper presented at the Annual Meeting of the Population Association of America (Minneapolis, MN: May 3, 1984).

Marcuse, Peter, *The Dynamics of Rental Housing in New York City* (New York: Department of Housing Preservation and Development, City of New York, 1978).

———, "Gentrification, Abandonment and Displacement: Connections, Causes and Policy Responses in New York City," *Journal of Urban and Contemporary Law* 28 (1985):193–240.

——, "Abandonment, Gentrification, and Displacement: Linkage in New York City," in Smith, N., and P. Williams, eds., *Gentrification of the City* (Boston: Allen & Unwin, 1986).

——, "Neighborhood Policy and the Distribution of Power: New York City's Community Boards," *Policy Studies Journal* 16 (Winter 1987–1988): 277–289.

——, "'Dual City': A Muddy Metaphor for a Quartered City," *International Journal of Urban and Regional Research* 13, 4 (December 1989): 697–708.

Marris, Peter, and Martin Rein, *Dilemmas of Social Reform* (New York: Atherton, 1967).

Massey, Doreen, *Spatial Divisions of Labor* (London: Macmillan, 1984).

Mieszkowski, Peter, "Recent Trends in Urban and Regional Development," in Mieszkowski, Peter, and Mahlon Straszheim, eds., *Current Issues in Urban Economics* (Baltimore: Johns Hopkins University Press, 1979).

Mollenkopf, John, "The Corporate Legal Services Industry," *New York Affairs* 9, 2 (1985): 34–49.

——, "The Decay of Liberalism: One Party Politics New York Style," *Dissent* (special issue on New York) (Fall 1987): 492–495.

——, "The Postindustrial Transformation of the Political Order in New York City," in Mollenkopf, J. ed., *Power, Culture, and Place: Essays on New York City* (New York: Russell Sage Foundation, 1988).

——, *The Wagner Atlas: New York City Politics, 1989* (New York: The Robert F. Wagner, Sr. Institute of Urban Public Policy, City University of New York, 1989).

——, "New York: The Great Anomaly," in Browning, Rufus, Dale Marshall, and David Tabb, eds., *Racial Politics in American Cities* (New York: Longman, 1990).

Morales, Rebecca, "The Los Angeles Automobile Industry in Historical Perspective," *Environment and Planning D: Society and Space* 4 (1986): 289–303.

Morales, Rebecca, and R. Mines, "San Diego's Full-Service Restaurants: A View from the Back of the House." Report, Center for U.S.-Mexican Studies, University of California-San Diego, 1985.

Morgen, Sandra, ed., *Gender in the Anthropology Curriculum* (Washington, DC: American Anthropological Association, 1989).

Morris, Charles R., *The Cost of Good Intentions* (New York: Norton, 1980).

Moss, Mitchell L., and Andrew Dunau, "Will the Cities Lose Their Back Offices?" *Real Estate Review* 17, 1 (1987): 62–68.

Mullings, Leith, "Gender in Applied Anthropology of the U.S.," in Morgen, Sandra, ed., *Gender in the Anthropology Curriculum* (Washington, DC: American Anthropological Association, 1989).

——, ed., *Cities of the United States* (New York: Columbia University Press, 1987).

Murphree, Mary C., "Rationalization and Satisfaction in Clerical Work: A Case Study of Wall Street Legal Secretaries." Ph.D. Diss., Department of Sociology, Columbia University, 1981.

Neubeck, Kenneth J., and Richard E. Ratcliff, "Urban Democracy and the Power of Corporate Capital: Struggles over Downtown Growth and Neighborhood

Stagnation in Hartford, Connecticut," in Cummings, Scott, ed., *Business Elites and Urban Development* (Albany: SUNY Press, 1988), pp. 299–332.

Newfield, Jack, and Wayne Barrett, *City for Sale: Ed Koch and the Betrayal of New York* (New York: Harper & Row, 1988).

New Jersey Department of Labor, "Study of Industrial Homework" (Trenton, NJ: Office of Wage and Hour Compliance, Division of Workplace Standards, 1982).

Newman, Katherine, *Falling from Grace: The Experience of Downward Mobility in the American Middle Class* (New York: Free Press, 1988).

New York Civil Liberties Union Foundation, "Homelessness, Poverty, Race and Displacement" (New York, March 1986).

New York Metropolitan Transportation Council, "Transit Ridership Effects of Journey to Work Changes," (New York: NYMTC, 1984).

———, "A Regional Review of Social, Economic and Travel Trends," *Metromonitor 1986* (New York: NYMTC, 1986).

New York State Council on Children and Families, *State of the Child in New York State* (Albany, 1988).

New York State Department of Labor, New York City Office, "A Quarter Century of Changes in Employment Levels and Industrial Mix" (Bureau of Labor Market Information, 1984).

———, *Annual Labor Area Report*, Fiscal Year 1985.

———, *Annual Labor Area Report*, Fiscal Year 1989.

New York State Department of Social Services, *Annual Report to the Government and the Legislature. Homeless Housing and Assistance Program.* (Albany, 1988).

New York State Inter-Agency Task Force on Immigration Affairs, "Statistics Related to the New York State Unemployment Insurance Fund," *Labor Research Report* 3 (1982).

———, *Report to the Governor and the Legislature on the Garment Manufacturing Industry and Industrial Homework* (Albany: State of New York, 1982).

New York State Inter-Agency Task Force on Immigration Affairs, Department of Labor, "Study of State-Federal Employment Standards for Industrial Homeworkers in New York City" (Albany: Division of Labor Standards, 1982).

———, "Workplace Discrimination Under the Immigration Reform and Control Act of 1986: A Study of Impacts on New Yorkers" (1988).

New York State Inter-Agency Task Force on Immigration Affairs, Department of Taxation and Finance, *The Task Force on the Underground Economy: Preliminary Report* (Albany: State of New York, 1982).

New York State Inter-Agency Task Force on Immigration Affairs, Office of the 28th State Senate District, "Banking on the Rich: Commercial Bank Branch Closings and Openings in the New York Metropolitan Area, 1979–1988" (Albany, 1989).

Nie, Norman, Sidney Verba, and John R. Petrocik, *The Changing American Voter* (Cambridge: Harvard University Press, 1976).

Noyelle, Thierry, "The New Technology and the New Economy: Some Implications for Equal Employment Opportunity," in Hartmann, Heidi, ed., *Computer Chips and Paper Clips: Technology and Women's Employment, Vol. II* (Washington, DC: National Academy Press, 1987).

————, "The Future of New York as a Financial Center." Paper prepared for conference on future shocks to New York, Citizen's Budget Commission, January 24, 1989.

————, *New York's Financial Markets* (Boulder: Westview, 1989).

Noyelle, Thierry, and Anna Dutka, *International Trade in Business Services: Accounting, Advertising, Law and Management Consulting* (Cambridge: Ballinger, 1988).

Noyelle, Thierry, and Penny Peace, "Information Industries." Paper prepared for conference on future shocks to New York, Citizen's Budget Commission, January 24, 1989.

Noyelle, Thierry, and Thomas M. Stanback, Jr., *The Economic Transformation of American Cities* (Totowa, NJ: Rowman & Allanheld, 1984).

Nun, Jose, "Superpoblacion Relativa, Ejercito Industrial de Reserva y Masa Marginal," *Revista Latinoamerica de Socioligia* 69, 2 (1969).

*OECD Employment Outlook* (Paris: OECD, September 1985).

Olson, Mancur, *The Logic of Collective Action* (New York: Schocken, 1969).

P.A. Cambridge Economic Consultants and Urban and Regional Studies Unit, University of Kent, *Economic Strategic Advice: Economic and Employment Change in London.* Final Report to the London Planning Advisory Committee (1988).

Pahl, Ray E., "Some Research on Informal Work, Social Polarization and Social Structure," *International Journal of Urban and Regional Research* 12 (1988): 247–267.

Papademetriou, Demetrios G., and Nicholas DiMarzio, *Undocumented Aliens in the New York Metropolitan Area* (New York: Center for Migration Studies, 1986).

Perlman, Janice E., *The Myth of Marginality* (Berkeley: University of California Press, 1976).

Pessar, P., "The Dominicans: Women in the Household and the Garment Industry," in Foner, N., ed., *New Immigrants in New York* (New York: Columbia University Press, 1987), pp. 103–130.

————, "The Linkage Between the Household and Workplace of Dominican Women in the U.S.," in Sutton, C., and E. M. Chaney, eds., *Caribbean Life in New York City* (New York: Center for Migration Studies, 1987).

Peterson, George, "Finance," in Gorham, W., and N. Glazer, eds., *The Urban Predicament* (Washington, DC: Urban Institute, 1976), pp. 35–119.

Peterson, Paul, *City Limits* (Chicago: University of Chicago Press, 1981).

————, ed., *The New Urban Reality* (Washington, DC: The Brookings Institution, 1985).

Pickman, James, and Benson F. Roberts, "Tapping Real Estate Markets to Address Housing Needs," *New York Affairs* (1985): 3–17.

Pickvance, C. G., "The Rise and Fall of Urban Movements and the Role of Comparative Analysis," *Environment and Planning D: Society and Space* 3 (1984): 31–53.

Piore, Michael, *Birds of Passage: Migrant Labor and Industrial Societies* (Cambridge: Cambridge University Press, 1979).

Piore, Michael, and Charles Sabel, *The Second Industrial Divide* (New York: Basic Books, 1984).

Piven, Frances Fox, and Richard Cloward, *Regulating the Poor* (New York: Pantheon, 1971).

———, *Poor People's Movements: Why They Succeed, How They Fail* (New York: Pantheon, 1977).

———, *Why Americans Don't Vote* (New York: Pantheon, 1988).

Portes, Alejandro, Manuel Castells, and L. Benton, eds., *The Informal Economy* (Baltimore and London: Johns Hopkins University Press, 1989).

Portes, Alejandro, and Saskia Sassen, "Making It Underground: Comparative Material on the Informal Sector in Western Market Economies," *American Journal of Sociology* 93 (1987): 30–61.

Poulantzas, Nicos, *L'Etat, le Pouvoir, le Socialisme* (Paris: Presses Universitaires Françaises, 1978).

Powledge, Fred, "New York's Bedford-Stuyvesant; A Rare Urban Success Story," *AIA Journal* 65 (May 1976): 45–59.

Preble, Edward, and John J. Casey, "Taking Care of Business—The Heroin User's Life on the Street," *International Journal of the Additions* 4 (1969): 1–24.

Pred, Allan, *City Systems in Advanced Economies* (New York: Wiley, 1977).

Pullman, Cydney, and Sharon Szymanski, "The Impact of Office Technology on Clerical Worker Skills in the Banking, Insurance and Legal Industries in New York City: Implications for Training." A Study for the Private Industry Council of New York City (New York: The Labor Institute, August 1986).

Quante, Wolfgang, *The Exodus of Corporate Headquarters from New York City* (New York: Praeger, 1976).

Rapp, Rayna, "Urban Kinship in Contemporary America: Families, Classes and Ideology," in Mullings, Leith, ed., *Cities of the United States* (New York: Columbia University Press, 1987).

Real Estate Board of New York, *Fact Book 1985* (March 1985).

———, "Rebuilding Manhattan: A Study of New Office Construction" (October 1985).

Regional Plan Association of New York, "The Effects of Headquarters Office Locations on Travel," *Technical Report No. 2* (New York: Regional Plan Association, 1983).

———, "New York in the Global Economy: Studying the Facts and the Issues." Presented to World Association of Major Metropolises meeting, Mexico City, April 1987.

Reiss, Albert J., and Michael Tonry, eds., *Crime and Justice, A Review of Research, Volume 8: Communities and Crime* (Chicago: University of Chicago Press, 1986).

Renooy, P. H., *Twilight Economy: A Survey of the Informal Economy in the Netherlands* (Amsterdam: Faculty of Economic Science, University of Amsterdam, 1984).

Ricketts, Erol, and Ronald Mincy, "Growth of the Underclass 1970–1980." Unpublished paper, The Urban Institute, February 1988.

Ricketts, Erol, and Isabel Sawhill, "Defining and Measuring the Underclass," *Journal of Policy Analysis and Management* 7, 2 (1988): 316–325.

Rieder, Jonathan, *Canarsie: The Jews and Italians of Brooklyn Against Liberalism* (Cambridge: Harvard University Press, 1985).

Riis, Jacob, *How the Other Half Lives* (New York: Dover, 1971 [1890]).

Rogers, David, *110 Livingston Street* (New York: Random House, 1968).

Rollins, J., *Between Women* (Philadelphia, PA: Temple University Press, 1984).

Rose, Damaris, "Rethinking Gentrification: Beyond the Uneven Development of Marxist Theory," *Environment and Planning D. Society and Space* 2, 1 (1984): 47–74.

Rosenberg, Terry J., *Poverty in New York 1980–1985* (New York: Community Services Society, 1987).

———, *Poverty in New York 1985–1988: The Crisis Continues* (New York: Community Services Society, 1989).

Rosenthal, A. M., *Thirty-Eight Witnesses* (New York: The New York Times, 1964).

Rosenwaike, Ira, *A Population History of New York* (Syracuse: Syracuse University Press, 1972).

Ross, Robert, and Kent Trachte, "Global Cities and Global Classes: The Peripheralization of Labor in New York City," *Review* 6, 3 (1983): 393–431.

Rubin, Marilyn, Ilene Weber, and Pearl Kamer, "Industrial Migration: A Case Study of Destination by City-Suburban Origin Within the New York Metropolitan Area," *Journal of the American Real Estate and Urban Economics Association* 6 (1978): 417–437.

Sacks, K., *My Troubles Are Going to Have Trouble with Me* (New Brunswick, NJ: Rutgers University Press, 1984).

———, "Toward a Unified Theory of Class, Race and Gender," *American Ethnologist* 16, 3 (1989): 534–551.

Salamon, Lester, "Rethinking Public Management: Third-Party Government and the Changing Forms of Government Action," *Public Policy* 29 (Summer 1981): 255–276.

Salins, Peter D., "America's Permanent Housing Problem," in Salins, Peter, ed., *Housing America's Poor* (Chapel Hill: University of North Carolina Press, 1987).

Sassen, Saskia, *The Mobility of Labor and Capital* (Cambridge: Cambridge University Press, 1988).

———, "Immigrant Women in the Garment and Electronics Industries in New York." Third Research Report Presented to the Revson Foundation, New York City, May 1989.

———, "New York City's Informal Economy," in Portes, A., M. Castells, and L. Benton, eds., *The Informal Sector: Theoretical and Methodological Issues* (Baltimore, MD: Johns Hopkins University Press, 1989).

———, *The Global City: New York, London, Tokyo* (Princeton, NJ: Princeton University Press, forthcoming).

Sassen, Saskia, and Wendy Grover, "Unregistered Work in the New York Metropolitan Area" (New York: Columbia University, Program in Urban Planning, Papers in Planning, 1986).

Sassen-Koob, Saskia, "The New Labor Demand in World Cities," in Smith, Michael P., ed., *Cities in Transformation: Capital, Class, and Urban Structure* (Beverly Hills, CA: Sage, 1984).

Sayre, Wallace, and Herbert Kaufman, *Governing New York City: Politics in the Metropolis* (New York: Russell Sage Foundation, 1960).

Schaffer, Robert, and Neil Smith, "The Gentrification of Harlem?" *Annals of the Association of American Geographers* 76, 3 (1987): 347–365.

Schimek, Paul, "Earnings Polarization and the Proliferation of Low-wage Work," *The Widening Divide: Income Inequality and Poverty in Los Angeles* (Los Angeles: UCLA, Graduate School of Architecture and Urban Planning, 1989).

Schwartz, Joel, "Tenant Power in the Liberal City, 1953–1971," in Lawson, Ronald, ed., *The Tenant Movement in New York City, 1904–1984* (New Brunswick, NJ: Rutgers University Press, 1986).

Scott, Allen J., *Metropolis: From the Division of Labor to Urban Form* (Berkeley and Los Angeles: University of California Press, 1988).

———, "The Technopoles of Southern California" (Los Angeles: UCLA Research Papers in Economic and Urban Geography, 1989), Number 1.

Scott, Allen J., and Michael Storper, eds., *Production, Work, Territory: The Geographical Anatomy of Industrial Capitalism* (Boston: Allen & Unwin, 1986).

Shannon, Lyle W., "Ecological Evidence of the Hardening of the Inner City," in Figlio, Robert M., Simon Hakim, and George F. Rengert, eds., *Metropolitan Crime Patterns* (Monsey, NY: Criminal Justice Press, 1986), pp. 27–53.

Sharff, J., "Families with Dead Sons," *Amsterdams Sociologish Tijdschrift* (December 1979).

———, "Free Enterprise and the Ghetto Family," *Psychology Today* (March 1981).

———, "The Underground Economy of a Poor Neighborhood," in Mullings, Leith, ed., *Cities of the United States* (New York: Columbia University Press, 1987), pp. 19–51.

Sharpe, William, and Leonard Wallock, "Tales of Two Cities: Gentrification and Displacement in Contemporary New York," in Campbell, Mary B., and Mark Rollins, eds., *Begetting Images: Studies in the Art and Science of Symbol Production* (New York: Peter Lang, 1989), pp. 169–199.

Sheets, Robert G., Stephen Nord, and John J. Phelps, *The Impact of Service Industries on Underemployment in Metropolitan Economies* (Lexington, MA: Heath, 1987).

Shefter, Martin, "New York City's Fiscal Crisis: The Politics of Inflation and Retrenchment," *The Public Interest* 48 (Summer 1977): 98–127.

———, "Political Incorporation and the Extrusion of the Left: Party Politics and Social Forces in New York City," *Studies in American Political Development* 1 (1986): 50–90.

———, *Political Crisis/Fiscal Crisis* (New York: Basic Books, 1987).

Sidel, R., *Women and Children Last* (New York: Viking, 1986).

Simon, R. J. and N. Sharma, "Women and Crime: Does the U.S. Experience Generalize?" in Simon, R. J., and N. Sharma, eds., *Criminology of Deviant Women* (Boston: Houghton Mifflin, 1979), p. 394.

Smith, Michael P., ed., *Cities in Transformation: Capital, Class, and Urban Structure* (Beverly Hills, CA: Sage, 1984).

Smith, Michael P., and Joe R. Feagin, eds., *The Capitalist City: Global Restructuring and Community Politics* (Oxford: Basil Blackwell, 1987).

Smith, Neil, "Of Yuppies and Housing: Gentrification, Social Restructuring, and the Urban Dream," *Environment and Planning D: Society and Space* 5 (1987): 151–172.

Smith, Neil, and Peter Williams, eds., *Gentrification of the City* (Boston: Allen & Unwin, 1986).

Smith, Robert C., "Migration, Development and the Effects of IRCA: A Study of Two Mexican Sending Communities and their U.S. Receiving Communities." Working Paper, Institute for Latin American and Iberian Studies, Columbia University, forthcoming.

Smolenski, Carol, "Informal Housing in New York City." Unpublished paper presented at the Division of Urban Planning, Columbia University, 1989.

Soja, Edward W., *Postmodern Geographies: The Reassertion of Space in Critical Social Theory* (London: Verso, 1989).

Soref, Michael J., "The Structure of Illegal Drug Markets: An Organizational Approach," *Urban Life* 10, 3 (October 1981): 329–352.

Sparks, Patricia, "The Impact of Office Automation on Working Women." Testimony before the Committee on Women, The Council of the City of New York, May 20, 1986.

Spinola, Steven, "Promoting Back Office Development in New York City," *City Almanac* 18, 1–2 (1984): 23–28.

Spitznas, T., "Estimating the Size of the Underground Economy in New York City," *The Regional Economic Digest* 1 (1981).

Stack, Carol, *All Our Kin* (New York: Harper & Row, 1974).

Stafford, Susan Buchanan, "The Haitians: The Cultural Meaning of Race and Ethnicity," in Foner, N., ed., *New Immigrants in New York* (New York: Columbia University Press, 1987).

Stafford, Walter, *Closed Labor Markets: Underrepresentation of Blacks, Hispanics, and Women in New York City's Core Industries* (New York: Community Service Society, 1985).

Stafford, Walter W., with Edwin Dei, *Employment Segmentation in New York City Municipal Agencies* (New York: Community Service Society, 1989).

Stamm, Keith R., *Newspaper Use and Community Ties: Toward a Dynamic Theory* (Norwood, NJ: Ablex, 1985).

Stanback, Thomas M., Jr., *Computerization and the Transformation of Employment: Government, Hospitals, and Universities* (Boulder, CO: Westview, 1987).

Stanback, Thomas M., Jr., and T. J. Noyelle, *Cities in Transition: Changing Job Structures in Atlanta, Denver, Buffalo, Phoenix, Columbus (Ohio), Nashville, Charlotte* (Totowa, NJ: Allanheld, Osmun, 1982).

Stanback, Thomas M., Jr., Peter J. Bearse, Thierry J. Noyelle, and Robert A. Karasek, *Services: The New Economy* (Totowa, NJ: Allanheld, 1984).

Stedman Jones, Gareth, *Outcast London* (London: Oxford University Press, 1971).

Stegman, Michael A., *The Dynamics of Rental Housing in New York City* (New York: Department of Housing Preservation and Development, City of New York, 1982).

———, *Housing in New York: Study of a City, 1984* (New York: Department of Housing Preservation and Development, City of New York, 1984).

————, *Housing and Vacancy Report, New York City, 1987* (New York: Department of Housing Preservation and Development, City of New York, April 1988).

Steinberg, Stephen, "The Underclass: A Case of Color Blindness," *New Politics* (Fall 1989).

Stepick, Alex, "Miami's Two Informal Sectors," in Portes, A., M. Castells, and L. Benton, eds., *The Informal Economy* (Baltimore and London: Johns Hopkins University Press, 1989).

Stone, Michael, "What Really Happened in Central Park: The Night of the Jogger and the Crisis of New York," *New York* (August 14, 1989): 30–43.

Stone, Michael E., "Housing and the Economic Crisis: An Analysis and Emergency Program," in Hartman, Chester, ed., *America's Housing Crisis* (New York: Routledge & Kegan Paul, 1985).

Storper, Michael, and Susan Christopherson, "Flexible Specialization and Regional Industrial Agglomerations," *Annals of the Association of American Geographers* 77 (1987): 194–217.

Sullivan, Mercer L., "Youth Crime: New York's Two Varieties," *New York Affairs* 8, 1 (Fall 1983).

————, "Teen Fathers," *Exploratory Ethnographic Study*. A Report to the Ford Foundation (New York: Vera Institute of Justice, mimeo, April 1985).

————, *Getting Paid: Youth Crime and Work in the Inner City* (New York: Cornell University Press, 1989).

————, "Absent Fathers in the Inner City," *The Annals of the Academy* (special issue on the underclass, Wilson, William Julius, ed.) 501 (January 1989): 48–58.

Susser, Ida, *Norman Street: Poverty and Politics in an Urban Neighborhood* (New York: Oxford University Press, 1982).

————, "Gender in the Anthropology of the U.S.," in Morgen, Sandra, ed., *Gender in the Anthropology Curriculum* (Washington, DC: American Anthropological Association, 1989).

Susser, Ida, W. Watson, and Kim Hopper, *Sociology in Medicine* (New York: Oxford University Press, 1985).

Susser, Ida, and J. Kreniske, "The Welfare Trap: A Public Policy for Deprivation," in Mullings, Leith, ed., *Cities of the United States* (New York: Columbia University Press, 1987), pp. 51–71.

Sutton, Constance, and E. M. Chaney, eds., *Caribbean Life in New York City* (New York: Center for Migration Studies, 1987).

Sviridoff, Michele, with Jerome E. McElroy, *Employment and Crime: A Summary Report*. A Report to the National Institute of Justice (New York: Vera Institute of Justice, mimeo, 1984).

Swanstrom, Todd, "Urban Populism, Uneven Development, and the Space for Reform," in Cummings, Scott, ed., *Business Elites and Urban Development* (New York: State University of New York Press, 1987), pp. 135–142.

Tabb, William K., *The Long Default: New York City and the Urban Fiscal Crisis* (New York: Monthly Review Press, 1982).

Tanzi, V., *The Underground Economy in the United States and Abroad* (Lexington, MA.: Heath, 1982).

Taylor, M. J., and N. J. Thrift, "Industrial Linkage and the Economy: I. Some Theoretical Proposals," *Environment and Planning* A 14, 12 (1982): 1601–1613.

Thompson, J. Phillip, "The Impact of the Jackson Campaigns on Black Politics in New York, Atlanta, and Oakland." Ph.D. Diss., Political Science Program, CUNY Graduate Center, 1990.

Tienda, Marta, "Puerto Ricans and the Underclass Debate," *Annals of the American Academy of Political and Social Sciences* 501 (January 1989).

Tobier, Emanuel, *The Changing Face of Poverty: Trends in New York City's Population in Poverty 1960–1990* (New York: Community Service Society of New York, 1984).

———, "The 'New' Immigration in the New York Metropolitan Region: Characteristics and Consequences." Unpublished paper presented at New York University, Graduate School of Public Administration, 1988.

Touraine, Alain, *La Parole et le Sang: Politique et Societé en Amérique Latine* (Paris: Odile Jacob, 1988).

Townsend, P., P. Corrigan, and U. Kowarzik, "Poverty and Labour in London," *Survey of Londoners' Living Standards* 1 (London: Low Pay Unit, 1987).

Tucker, M. B., "U.S. Ethnic Minorities and Drug Abuse: An Assessment of the Science and Practice," *International Journal of the Addictions* 20 (1985): 1021–47.

U.S. Department of Commerce, Bureau of the Census, "General Social and Economic Characteristics," *1980 Census of Population* (Washington, DC: U.S. Government Printing Office, 1983).

———, "Journey to Work," *1980 Census of Population* (Washington, DC: U.S. Government Printing Office, 1984).

———, "Place of Work," *1980 Census of Population* (Washington, DC: U.S. Government Printing Office, 1984).

———, "Detailed Population Characteristics, Census of the Population, New York State Volume" (Washington, DC: U.S. Government Printing Office, 1984).

———, *Statistical Abstract of the United States: 1987* 107 (Washington, DC: U.S. Government Printing Office, 1986).

———, *Statistical Abstract of the United States: 1988* 108 (Washington, DC: U.S. Government Printing Office, 1987).

———, *County Business Patterns* (Washington, DC: U.S. Government Printing Office, 1978, 1986).

———, "Money Income of Households, Families, and Persons in the United States," *Current Population Reports* P-60 No. 162 (1989), No. 129 (1981), and No. 75 (1970).

———, "Poverty in the United States 1987," *Current Population Reports* P-60, No. 163 (1989).

U.S. Department of Commerce, Bureau of Economic Analysis, "County and Metropolitan Area Personal Income," *Survey of Current Business* (April 1989).

U.S. Department of Labor, *Workforce 2000: Work and Workers for the 21st Century.* Study by the Hudson Institute for the U.S. Department of Labor (Washington, DC: U.S. Government Printing Office, 1987).

U.S. Department of Labor, Bureau of Labor Statistics, *Employment, Hours, and Earnings, States and Areas, 1939–82* (Washington, DC: U.S. Government Printing Office, 1984).

U.S. Department of Labor, Bureau of Labor Statistics, New York Regional Office, "The Current Population Survey as an Economic Indicator for New York City" (November 1989).

U.S. Department of Labor, Women's Bureau, *Women and Office Automation: Issues for the Decade Ahead* (Washington, DC: U.S. Government Printing Office, 1985).

U.S. House of Representatives, Committee on Ways and Means, "Background Material and Data on Programs Within the Jurisdiction of the Committee on Ways and Means," 1988 edition (Washington, DC: U.S. Government Printing Office, March 24, 1988), pp. 740–744.

U.S. House of Representatives, Subcommittee on Census and Population, "Central American Refugees" (Washington, DC: U.S. Government Printing Office, 1985), 54–176–0. Hearing before the Subcommittee, June 27.

Urban Research Center, New York University, "Wage Discrimination and Occupational Discrimination in New York City's Municipal Workforce: Time for a Change" (August 1987).

Valentine, B., *Hustling and Other Hard Work* (New York: Free Press, 1978).

Vallas, Steven Peter, "Computers, Managers and Control at Work," *Sociological Forum* 4, 2 (June 1989): 291–303.

———, "White Collar Proletarians? Changes in the Structure of Clerical Work and Levels of Class Consciousness," *The Sociological Quarterly* 28, 4 (1987): 523–541.

Velazquez, Nydia, et al., "Puerto Rican Voter Registration in New York City: A Comparison of Attitudes Between Registered and Non-Registered Puerto Ricans" (Migration Division, Department of Labor and Human Resources, Commonwealth of Puerto Rico, January 1988).

Vernon, Raymond, *Metropolis 1985* (Cambridge, MA: Harvard University Press, 1960).

Vogel, David, "New York, London, and Tokyo: The Future of New York as a Global and National Financial Center," in Shefter, Martin, ed., *Capital of the American Century?* (forthcoming).

Wacquant, L. J., and W. J. Wilson, "The Cost of Racial and Class Exclusion in the Inner City," *The Annals of the American Academy of Political and Social Science* (January 1988).

———, "Beyond Welfare Reform: Poverty, Joblessness, and the Social Transformation of the Inner City." Paper presented at the Rockefeller Foundation Conference on Welfare Reform (February 1988).

Wagner, Robert F., Jr., *New York Ascendant: The Report of the Commission on the Year 2000* (New York: Harper & Row, 1988).

Waldinger, Roger, *Through the Eye of the Needle: Immigrants and Enterprise in New York's Garment Trades* (New York: New York University Press, 1986).

———, "Changing Ladders and Musical Chairs: Ethnicity and Opportunity in Post-Industrial New York," *Politics & Society* 15, 4 (1986–1987): 369–402.

————, "The Problems and Prospects of Manufacturing Workers in the New York City Labor Market." Report prepared for the CUNY Worker Literacy Project (February 1988).

————, "Immigration and Urban Change," *Annual Review of Sociology* 15 (1989): 211–232.

————, "Race and Ethnicity," in Brecher, Charles, and Raymond D. Horton, eds., *Setting Municipal Priorities, 1990* (New York: New York University Press, 1989), pp. 50–79.

Waldinger, Roger, Howard Aldrich, and Robin Ward, eds., *Immigrants and Enterprise: Ethnic Business in Europe and the United States* (Beverly Hills, CA: Sage, forthcoming).

Waldinger, Roger, and Thomas Bailey, "The Youth Employment Problem in the World City," *Social Policy* 16, 1 (1985): 55–59.

Walters, Ronald, *Black Presidential Politics in America* (Albany: State University of New York Press, 1988).

Weber, Max, *The City* (Glencoe, IL: Free Press, 1959).

————, *Economy and Society* (Berkeley: University of California Press, 1978).

Weicher, John C., "Housing Quality: Measurement and Progress," in Rosenberry, Sara, and Chester Hartman, eds., *Housing Issues of the 1990s* (New York: Praeger, 1989).

Weitzman, Philip, *Worlds Apart: Housing, Race/Ethnicity and Income in New York City, 1978–1987* (New York: Community Service Society, 1989).

White, Stephen, "Toward a Modest Experiment in Cable Television," *The Public Interest* (Spring 1967).

Wilson, Clint, II, and Felix Gutierrez, *Minorities and Media: The End of Mass Communication* (Beverly Hills, CA: Sage, 1985).

Wilson, James Q., and Richard Herrnstein, *Crime and Human Nature* (New York: Simon & Schuster, 1985).

Wilson, William J., "The Urban Underclass in Advanced Industrial Societies," in Peterson, Paul E., ed., *The New Urban Reality* (Washington, DC: The Brookings Institution, 1985).

————, *The Truly Disadvantaged: The Inner City, the Underclass, and Public Policy* (Chicago: University of Chicago Press, 1987).

*Working Press of the Nation, Vol. 1: Newspaper Directory, 1988 Edition* (Chicago: The National Research Bureau, 1987).

Wright, Erik, *Classes* (London: New Left, 1985).

Young, K., and P. L. Garside, *Metropolitan London: Politics and Urban Change 1837–1981* (London: Edward Arnold, 1982).

Zorbaugh, Harvey W., *The Gold Coast and the Slum* (Chicago: University of Chicago Press, 1929).

Zuboff, Shoshana, *In the Age of the Smart Machine: The Future of Work and Power* (New York: Basic Books, 1988).

Zukin, Sharon, *Loft Living: Culture and Capital in Urban Change* (Baltimore: Johns Hopkins University Press, 1982).

# Name Index

Boldface numbers refer to figures and tables.

Susser, Ida, 15, 87, 207, 220*n*, 221*n*, 222*n*, 223*n*, 417*n*
Sutton, Percy, 334
Sviridoff, Michele, 242*n*
Swanson, Bert, 358*n*
Swanstrom, Todd, 331*n*, 332*n*
Szymanski, Sharon, 186, 194, 196, 198, 200*n*, 201*n*, 202*n*, 203*n*

Tabb, David, 353, 355*n*
Tabb, William K., 356*n*
Taylor, M. J., 95*n*
Thatcher government, 380, 388, 391
Thompson, J. Phillip, 354, 355*n*, 358*n*
Tienda, Marta, 97*n*
Tilly, Louise A., 201*n*, 202*n*
Times-Mirror Corporation, 248, **253**
Tobier, Emanuel, 20*n*, 126*n*, 152*n*, 221*n*, 244*n*, 250
Tolchin, M., 222*n*
Tonry, Michael, 243*n*
Touraine, Alain, 409, 418*n*
Townsend, P., 394*n*
Trachte, Kent, 151*n*
Tribune Company, 248
Trillin, Calvin, 151*n*
Trump, Donald, 38, 129, 160
Tucker, M. B., 244*n*

Unger, Craig, 152*n*
Union of Construction Contractors, 88
United Housing Foundation (UHF), 315
University of Kent: Research Fund of, 393; Urban and Regional Studies Unit of, 394*n*
Urban Research Center. *See* New York University
U. S. Bureau of the Census, 40*n*, 41*n*, 51, 98*n*, **133, 135, 137, 149,** 155, 156, 175*n*, 221*n*, 242*n*, 310; Current Population Reports, **30**
U. S. Department of Commerce, 367; Bureau of Economic Analysis, **28,** 40*n*
Useem, Michael, 176*n*

U. S. House of Representatives, Committee on Ways and Means, 20*n*
U. S. Supreme Court, 332*n*

Valentine, B., 222*n*
Vallas, Steven Peter, 195, 203*n*
Velazques, Nydia, 357*n*, 358*n*
Verba, Sidney, 356*n*
Vernon, Raymond, 40*n*, 129, 130, **131,** 131, **132, 133, 135,** 136, **137, 139, 144–148,** 151*n*, 152*n*
Vogel, David, 19*n*

Wacquant, L. J., 76*n*
Wagner, Robert, 315
Waldinger, Roger, 13, 15, 16, 19*n*, 20*n*, 21*n*, 43, 77*n*, 78*n*, 111, 152*n*, 178, 200*n*, 201*n*, 202*n*, 221*n*, 354*n*, 403
Wallock, Leonard, 13, 18*n*, 21*n*
Walters, Ronald, 356*n*
Ward, Robin, 77*n*
Washington, Harold, 326
Watson, W., 223*n*
Weber, Ilene, 151*n*
Weber, Max, 410, 412, 418*n*
Weicher, John C., 307*n*
Weitzman, Philip, 20*n*, 306*n*, 307*n*, 308*n*
White, Kevin, 325
White, Stephen, 266*n*
Williams, Peter, 151*n*
Wilson, Basil, 355*n*, 356*n*, 358*n*
Wilson, Eliot, 254, 266*n*
Wilson, James Q., 242*n*
Wilson, William Julius, 21*n*, 45, 76*n*, 97*n*, 222*n*, 244*n*, 310*n*, 414, 418*n*
Wolfe, Tom, 3, 372
Wright, Erik O., 411, 418*n*

Young, K., 220*n*, 394*n*, 395*n*

Zorbaugh, Harvey W., 405, 417*n*
Zuboff, Shoshana, 178, 197, 201*n*, 203*n*
Zukin, Sharon, 152*n*
Zysman, John, 18*n*

# Subject Index

of, 72; employment of foreign-born,
55–56, 67–68, **69, 70,** 74–75; gains
by, 68, 70; income distribution of,
**72;** inmigration of, 293; in London,
378, 385; in Los Angeles, 373; in
New York City, 27, 55, 334;
occupational distribution of, 68, **71;**
trends for, 44; underrepresentation
of, 162; young, 343. *See also*
immigrants; immigration; specific
issues
assembly districts (ADs), 170, **171,** 338,
339–345, 349, 356*n*, 357*n*; minority,
339, 341–343, 346; racial
composition of, 341–344, **341, 342,
344,** 346, **352;** relationship between,
348
assets, 7, 36
assistance: changes in housing, **277,
283, 286, 288;** housing, 279, 280,
287; need for housing, 274–275,
298, 309*n*; supplemental, 210. *See
also* public assistance
Astoria, Queens, 291, 301, 309*n*
Athens, 26
Atlantic coastal states, 366
auctions, 322
automobile, 363, 370; repair, 91, 92


baby sitters, 217–219, 408
Baltimore, 35, 354*n*, 366
banking, 7, 33, 34, **35;** employment,
38, **39,** 194, 200*n*; female workers in,
186; growth of international, 36;
salaries in, 196
banks, 9, 33; deposits in Los Angeles,
367; foreign, 6–7, 37; foreign
deposits in U.S., 6, 37
*Battery News,* 260, **261**
Battery Park City District, 120, 140,
260, 327
Bay Area, California, 366
*Bay News,* **261**
Bay Ridge, Brooklyn, 297, 301, 303,
309*n*; enclaves in, 339
*Bay Ridge Courier,* **261**
Bayside, Queens, 301, 339
*Bayside Times,* **262**

Bedford-Stuyvesant, Brooklyn, 143,
295, 297, 300; residents, 339, 346,
353
Bellerose, Queens, 297
Bensonhurst, Brooklyn, 291, 297, 303,
309*n*; attack, 4, 18*n*, 318, 350, 351;
enclaves in, 339
*Bensonhurst News,* **261**
Bergen County, New Jersey, **31, 131,**
144
biases: against minorities, 410; spatial,
36
Big Bang, 382
Birmingham, 35–36
black families: in large metropolitan
areas, 27–29, **28;** median income of,
**30**
black men, 44–45; employment of, 56;
incomes of, 46, 60, **61,** 61
Black Monday, 382
Black Muslims, 318
black population, 369; educational
attainments of, 16; growth of, 9,
336; in London, 385; of Los
Angeles, 364; space standards for,
380
black professionals, 162, 170, **171,** 173
blacks, 5, 13, 55, 101*n*, 142, 186, 357*n*,
358*n*; differences among, 403;
economic distress among, 47;
employment of, 47, **57, 59,** 365;
exclusion of, 8, 61, 337; foreign-
born, 15, 21*n*; gains made by, 111;
labor force participation rates for,
12; in London, 378, 391; in Los
Angeles, 373; media aimed at, 246,
265; median household income for,
13, **14,** 15, 330*n*; neighborhoods for,
143; in New York, 44, 334;
occupational status of, 16;
opposition to Koch coalition by, 346;
political participation of, 326, 338;
political views of, 170, 173;
programming for, 255, 258, 264;
representation of, 336–337, 338,
340; seats held by, 335; spending on
improving condition of, **168;** support
for Dinkins by, 4, 349–350,
352–353; underrepresentation of,
58, 162, 333; voting patterns of, **171,**

programs, 270, 271, 323, 404; public, 210, 384, 385, 388; redevelopment, 140; socioeconomic characteristics of, 268, **276, 278, 282–290,** 304; spatial distribution of, 268, 290–291; stock in New York City, 267–268, 270, 272, 305; structure shifts in, 220; trends in, 268, 304; for workers, 386. *See also* affordability; occupancy; renovations

housing conditions, 210, 268, 287; change in, 275, **276–278,** 278–281, **282–290,** 290; physical, 275, 299, 301, 306*n*

housing market, 270, 274; collapse of, 8; indicators used for, 268, 270, 272; in London, 389; in New York City, 123, 267, 274, 304, 321

housing need, **278,** 278–279, **280,** 298–305, 309*n*; changes in, **284, 287,** 287, **290;** estimates of, 274–275, 308*n*

housing quality, 270–271, **278,** 279, 304–305, 306*n*; changes in, **276, 282, 285, 288,** 301, 309*n*; indicators of, 271, 274; problems of, **280,** 281, 287, 301–303, 310*n*

housing units, 121–122, 142, 270; changes in, 275–290; deterioration of, 275; dilapidated, **269,** 271, 274, 308*n*; experiencing real gain in income, **295;** with housing need, **298, 299, 300, 302, 303;** inventory of, 310; low-rent, 274, 279, **283, 286, 288;** occupied, **269,** 271, 274, 280; occupied by nonwhites, **294;** with problems, 279, **280,** 280–281; with residents living below poverty level, **296,** 297; turnover, 281; vacant, **269,** 270, **283, 286, 288.** *See also* maintenance deficiencies; owner units; rental units

Housing and Vacancy Survey (HVS), 268, **269, 278, 280, 284, 287, 290, 294–296, 298, 299–300, 302–303,** 306*n*, 307*n* , 308*n*; files, 275, 278, 310–311; limitations, 291; purpose of, 271, 272

Howard Beach, Queens, 309*n*; attack, 4, 18*n*, 317–318, 350; neighborhood conflicts in, 143

Hudson County, New Jersey, **31,** 130, **131, 132,** 134, 142

human capital services (HCS), 157, 158, **159, 165;** ethnicity in, 162; professionals in, 161–162, 163, 170

Hunterdon County, New Jersey, **31**

hustling, 210

HVS. *See* Housing and Vacancy Survey

ILO/OECD conventions, 383

immigrant communities, 93, 101*n*

immigrants, 48, 75, 250, 343, 401, 413–414; Asian, 53, 67–68, 143, 334; black, 347; economic changes for, 44; employment opportunities for, 45, 46–47, 55, 77*n*, 91; Italian and Jewish, 335; job mobility of, 403; Latino, 10, 62, 89, 143, 334; low-skilled, 74; new, in New York City, 53, 400, 408; newspapers for, 251; programming for, 258, **259;** Third World, 82; turn-of-the century, 7; undocumented, 81, 88. *See also* foreign-born; minorities; specific groups and issues

immigration, 77*n*, 179, 190, 293, 378; from Asia, 9, 15, 179, 347, 348, 400; consequences of, 347; to England, 379; law, 1986 reform of, 73; new, 8, 9, 15; policy, 208

*Inc.* Magazine, 367

income, 52, 83, 339; average, 272–273; below 125% of poverty level, **277,** 278–281, **283,** 287, **289,** 295, **296,** 297, **298;** cutoff for upper professionals, 156–157; decline, 28, 273, 275, 278, 281; differences, 268; diffusion of low, 305; effect of gender and, 147; family, 20*n*, 28, 29, **30,** 98*n*; of New York firms, 38; per capita, 27–28, **28;** problems, 305; for professionals, 161–162, 164, 176*n*; ratio, interquartile, 383; real, changes in, 297, 400; received by New York families, 20*n*; spatial patterns in, 290, 294–298; trends for

increases, 122–124, 212, 273, 274, 278, 281, 304; median, 270, 273; monthly, **269;** regulations, 105, 122–124, 126; stabilization, 123–124; tax, commercial, 114, **116–117,** 118; trends in, 273, **280**
rental, housing, 126, 140, 216, 301; affordability of, 273–274; private, in London, 388
rental units, 287, 309*n;* available, 268, **269;** conversion of, to cooperatives, 100*n,* 141; low-cost, 273, **277,** 305; problems in, 279; quality of, 271; vacancy rate, 268
renters, incomes of, **269,** 270, 272–274, 304; changes in, 281, 287; low, 270, 273; lowest, 274; median, 270, 272. *See also* residents
representation, elected, 337
reproduction, 207; social, 208, 215–216, 218, 220
Republicans, 340, 351, 352
researchers, 156
residence: geography of, 129–130; influence of employment location on, 143, 145, 147; spatial patterns of, 5. *See also* commuting
residential areas, 120, 140; upgrading of, in London, 380. *See also* development
residents, **282–284,** 308*n;* change in income of, **285–287;** foreign-born, 143; housing needs of, **299, 300, 302;** low-income, 296–297; of Manhattan, 136–137; new, 280–281
restructuring, 6, 17, 368, 370; economic, 5, 16–17, 80, 142, 369, 393; goal of, 416; industrial, 45, 134; of New York, 399–400, 401; post-Fordist, 370, 372; urban, in historical perspective, 361–363; urban, in New York and Los Angeles, 361, 366, 368–369, 374
retail, 83, 84, 87, **165;** Asians in, 67–68, **69, 70,** 70, 74; blacks in, 56, **57, 60;** employment in, **50, 51,** 55, 83, 381; Hispanics in, 62, **63, 64;** jobs, 209; outlets, 86; trade sector, 163. *See also* sales

retailing in New York Metropolitan Region, **133**
revenue: options, 112; policies, 124; providers, 125, 126; sources, 112, **114,** 114, **116–117,** 118; system, 105
revenues, 39, 124; foreign, 36–38, **37;** local, 112, 113, 115, 127*n. See also* taxes
rich, 5, 363, 368, 401
Richmond County, **131**
Ridgewood, Queens, 291
*Ridgewood Times,* **262**
Riverdale, Bronx, 339
*The Riverdale Press,* **261**
RMA. *See* Regional Metropolitan Area
*Rockaway Press,* **262**
Rockaways, Queens, 297, 305
Rockland County, **28, 31,** 148
Russians, **166,** 345

*Sae Gai Times,* **252**
St. Louis, 35
salaries, 196. *See also* pay; wages
sales, **52,** 52, **53,** 91; Asians in, 68, **71;** blacks in, 58, **59;** Hispanics in, **65;** representatives, 163
sales taxes, 112–115, **116–117,** 118
sales workers: gender composition of, **149;** in Manhattan, 137; in New York Metropolitan Region, **135, 136,** 137, 141; voting patterns of, **171**
Salvadorans, 373
San Diego, 366; Freeway, 371
San Fernando Valley, 371
San Francisco, 34, 330*n,* 366–367
Sansan, 366
scheduling workers, **182, 184,** 184, **188;** jobs for, 185; minority women, **190, 191, 192**
schools, 108, 211–212; control of local, 316, 318, 319; nursery, 211, 218, 220
seats, 335, 339
Seattle, 331*n*
Secaucus, New Jersey, 250
Secaucus Meadowlands, 134
Second World, 366
secretaries, 6, **182,** 182, **183,** 187–188, 202*n;* classification of, 180; earnings of, 99, 196; education of, **194;** legal,

Standard Metropolitan Statistical Area (SMSA), 130, 148

*Star Reporter,* 262

*State of the Child in New York State* (M. Cuomo), 211

Staten Island, **28;** housing needs in, 301, 302, 304, 309*n;* housing supply in, 121; incomes in, 295, 297; newspapers published in, **253,** 260, **262;** North Shore, 292, 297; racial transition in, 291–293; reelection of Mayor Koch in, 4; South Shore, 293, 297, 301, 309*n;* weekly earnings in business services in, 85

*Staten Island Advance,* **252,** 260

*Staten Island Eagle,* **262**

*Staten Island Register,* **262**

status tensions, 172–173

stenographers, 181, **182,** 182, **183,** 183, 202*n;* education of women, **194;** minority women, **190, 191, 192;** white women, **188, 189;** women, **184,** 184, **185,** 185

stock market crash, 6, 7, 38, 382

stocks, 382

stratification, 156, 405, 407–408, 413

stratum, 160, 174, 402. *See also* business, strata of; professional strata; specific issues

Studio City, Los Angeles, 371

Stuyvesant Town/Turtle Bay, Manhattan, 297, 301

subboroughs, 291, 308*n,* 309*n;* housing need in, 298, 299–305; low-income households in, 296–297; minority households in, 292–293, 385

subcontracting, 80, 86, 90–92; arrangements, 101*n;* growth of, 88; promotion of, 83

subcontractors, 100*n*

subsidiary communications carrier (SCA), 257

suburbanization, 158, 362, 408; in London, 380; middle class, 406; pattern of, 140

suburbs, 136, 138, 139, 143, 400; contrast between Manhattan and, 150; employment trends in, 31; headquarters in, 36–37, **37;**

immigrants settling in, 143; incomes in, 27–28, **28, 30;** industries in, 132–134; inner ring, 137. *See also* manufacturing; specific groups and issues

subway, 119

succession: group, 335–336; political, 333, 336

Suffolk County, Long Island, **28, 31**

Sunbelt, 34, 36, 227

Sunset Park, Brooklyn, 293, 297, 300, 303, 310*n,* 339

supervision, 178

supervisors, **183,** 183, 193, 202*n;* black, 191; women, **185,** 186–188, **189, 194**

Supplementary Security Income program, 108

support: for Dinkins, 349, 352, 353; for Giuliani, 353; for Koch, 345–347; for Koch, decay of, 349, 351

survival strategies, 374, 410

Sussex County, New Jersey, **31**

sweatshops, 76*n,* 80, 86–89, 97*n,* 400; electronic, 183; growth of, 83, 87, 92

tabloids, 248

Taiwan, 33, 258

tax: benefits, 388; burden, 104, 118, 124, 126; evasion, 81; policy, 104, 114

taxes, 39, 112–118, 125–126; exported, 104, 113, 115, 118. *See also* income taxes; property; sales taxes; specific taxes

Taylorism, 199

TCU (transportation, communications, and utilities), 49, **50, 51;** Asians in, **69, 70;** blacks in, **57, 60;** Hispanics in, **63, 64**

teachers, 156, 158, 164, 170; union, 316

technical professionals, 170, **171**

technicians, 181, **182, 184, 188;** minority women, **190, 191, 192**

technocracy, 371, 372

technology, 33, 198, 200, 202*n;* advances in, 178, 183; automation, 197; in clerical work, 179, 181, 195; communications, 133; flexibility in, 368; high, 364, 371, 410;

shifts in, 202*n;* study of New York
City municipal, 190
working class, 391, 403, 411, 412
workplace, 145, 147–149; alienation
in, 197; American, 177; clerical, 178,
198, 199–200; geography of, 129;
opportunity, 193. *See also*
commuting
*World,* 246
World City formation, 365–368
*World Journal,* **252**
World War II, 130, 134, 335, 336;
changes in work force after, 193;
economic growth following, 82; rent
price controls established during,

104, 122; restructuring through, 362;
white flight after, 179
writers, 158, 164, 170
WXTV, 258, **259**

young, 45, 387. *See also* teenagers;
workers
youth, 343: attacks by, 350; economic
distress among, 47; minority, 403,
414
Yuppies, 156, 368; in London, 389

zoning, 104, 118, 121; laws, 119, 120;
ordinance, 119; regulations,
119–122; restrictions, 125